WHATEVER HAPPENED TO BRITISH JEWISH STUDIES?

Whatever Happened to British Jewish Studies?

Editors

Hannah Ewence
and Tony Kushner

VALLENTINE MITCHELL
LONDON • PORTLAND, OR

Parkes-Wiener Series on Jewish Studies
Series Editors: David Cesarani and Tony Kushner
ISSN 1368-5449

The field of Jewish Studies is one of the youngest, but fastest growing and most exciting areas of scholarship in the academic world today. Named after James Parkes and Alfred Wiener, this series aims to publish new research in the field and student materials for use in the seminar room, to disseminate the latest work of established scholars and to re-issue classic studies which are currently out of print.

The selection of publications reflects the international character and diversity of Jewish Studies; it ranges over Jewish history from Abraham to modern Zionism, and Jewish culture from Moses to post-modernism. The series also reflects the inter-disciplinary approach inherent in Jewish Studies and at the cutting edge of contemporary scholarship, and provides an outlet for innovative work on the interface between Judaism and ethnicity, popular culture, gender, class, space and memory.

First published in 2012 by Vallentine Mitchell

Middlesex House,	920 NE 58th Avenue, Suite 300
29/45 High Street, Edgware,	Portland, Oregon,
Middlesex HA8 7UU, UK	97213-3786, USA

www.vmbooks.com

British Library Cataloguing in Publication Data

Whatever happened to British Jewish studies?.
  1. Jews—Study and teaching—Great Britain—History—
20th century.
  I. Kushner, Tony (Antony Robin Jeremy) II. Ewence, Hannah.
  305.8'924'0071'041-dc22

ISBN 978 0 85303 954 9 (cloth)

Library of Congress Cataloging-in-Publication Data:

A catalog record has been applied for

This group of studies first appeared in a special issue of *Jewish Culture
and History*,
Vol. 12 No. 1-2 [ISSN 1462-169X]
published by Vallentine Mitchell & Co. Ltd.

Printed and Bound by CPI Group (UK) Ltd, Croydon, CR0 4YY

To the memory of Frank Cass
(1930 to 2007), publisher of Anglo-Jewry
and Lloyd Gartner
(1927 to 2011), its pioneer historian

Contents

INTRODUCTION

Whatever Happened to British Jewish Studies? In Search of Contexts

TONY KUSHNER AND HANNAH EWENCE

I

On 11 November 1893 in an address to the first meeting of the Jewish Historical Society of England (JHSE), Lucien Wolf made 'A Plea for Anglo-Jewish History'. Wolf explained how the society had come into being and the resistance that had been overcome: 'We were told that Anglo-Jewish history was a very small affair, that it was not likely to add much to the general history of our race, and that it would throw no light on the annals of our country.'[1] He added that such criticisms had 'not been sufficiently answered' – hence the vindicatory title of his lecture.[2] Wolf's greatest attention was given to what he called 'the local study of Jewish history', by which he meant the specific national context in which Jews had settled. 'In every country they have assimilated something of the national spirit' and then through migration 'local peculiarities have been periodically gathered up and redistributed until the whole racial character has been more or less affected by them'.[3]

The chronological focus of Wolf's address was on the post-expulsion period – first when Jews were officially excluded from England and, second, the early years of readmission. In the years that followed, if somewhat slowly, the JHSE found sufficient place for itself within Anglo-Jewry to promote the history of the community, especially in its most 'ancient' form (that is from the medieval to the early years of re-admission) at a local and national level. It is largely true to say that it was local rather than national historians who recognised the worth and interest of studying the country's Jewish minority.[4] When scholars such as Edward Freeman and Goldwin Smith *did* approach the Jews at a national level, it was more often than not to present them in a negative light as subversive and inherently alien. Not surprisingly, as David Cesarani has emphasised, early Anglo-

Jewish historiography had a defensive and even apologetic tone.[5]

Yet for all their internal and external tensions, the battles to create first the Anglo-Jewish Exhibition in 1887 and the JHSE six years later did produce a heightened historiographical sense of awareness and purpose. Presidential addresses of the JHSE before the First World War were often driven to justify Anglo-Jewish history as both historically and socially important – it would help bolster the confidence of the community and strengthen identity as well as presenting it positively to the outside world as long-standing, rooted and loyal. Here was a Jewish community that had made and would continue to make a positive contribution if it was treated with tolerance and respect.

What this initial burst of energy did not create, beyond the JHSE itself and its publications, was a formal structure to promote Anglo-Jewish history. Whilst the objective of a Jewish Museum was a goal of many of the early enthusiasts, this was not created until 1932 and even then within a small and largely inaccessible communal context.[6] Furthermore, there were no academic posts devoted to the study and promotion of Anglo-Jewish history and the small centres of Jewish studies in Britain did not consider it a worthy subject to research and teach. Cecil Roth was the first professional historian with expertise in Anglo-Jewish history to be appointed to a position in a British university – indeed, he dominated its study from the inter-war years until his death in 1970. It was not especially for his knowledge in this area, however, that he was appointed in 1939 as Reader in Post-Biblical Jewish Studies in 1939 – a post created through private benefaction. Indeed, Roth had trained as an Italianist. But as Elisa Lawson has illustrated, both before and after his Oxford appointment, 'Roth spent much of his career battling against and attempting to correct the belittling and perceived insignificance of British Jewry and British-Jewish history'.[7]

Roth, his protégé V.D. Lipman, and Israel Finestein were isolated practitioners within Britain of Anglo-Jewish history in the first decades after the Second World War. In his ninth and final Presidential address to the JHSE on 17 September 1968, Roth returned to the question of 'Why Anglo-Jewish history?'[8] Following his mentor, Wolf, Roth focused in this lecture on the medieval and early modern eras. Yet trying to answer his own question, Roth seemed at a loss other than to suggest that the subject had not yet been exhausted in terms of detail. He thus argued 'that much remains to do, and that even the most minute aspects of our research forms an integral part of the wide picture – of Jewish history, of British history, even in some measure of the history of humanity'.[9] Ultimately, Roth's reason for studying Anglo-Jewish history was non-intellectual: 'Because', he said, 'it is fun.'[10]

In a British higher education context in which efforts are made to measure everything, especially now against the vague concept of 'impact', Roth's justification for such research would not be taken seriously in the early twentieth century. The current focus on the short term and the utilitarian does not undermine his response in itself – indeed, there is a great need to return to the *joy* of scholarship in the humanities. If, as has been suggested, on a popular level history is the 'new rock 'n' roll',[11] those that govern its purse strings at an academic level are in danger of policing it out of creative existence by demanding that it should be for the greater public good and quantifiably so. The criterion 'Value for money' that every research proposal now needs to meet is perhaps best answered by the Beatles in 'She's Leaving Home' in a line written just a year before Roth's justification: 'Fun is the one thing that money can't buy'.[12] The danger in Roth's answer is not that it fails on Benthamite principles, but that it is in danger of confirming those who accuse the practitioners of Anglo-Jewish studies of antiquarianism – perfectly acceptable as a private pastime, but not the task of a serious/professional scholar.

Sadly, when Roth was fading away from the scene at the time of this Presidential lecture – he would die two years later in Jerusalem – there were few who were taking Anglo-Jewish history and culture as a subject of major consequence. Within the world of British historiography, as well as within British Jewry as a whole, apart from a score of amateur enthusiasts there was little impulse from within Britain. It is thus significant that it was the work of two American historians – first Lloyd Gartner in the 1960s and then Todd Endelman in the 1970s – which attempted to give significance to national (or, more precisely, London-focused) Anglo-Jewish studies within both British and wider Jewish history.[13] Indeed, it was only in the last two decades of the twentieth century that a new, locally-based, momentum was achieved.

The transformation of Anglo-Jewish historiography and heritage work from the 1980s has been much noted if not ever fully explained. It is hard to connect it to inter-generational mentoring. It is true that Geoffrey Alderman was inspired by Cecil Roth, but the former, whilst opening up for the first time the study of Anglo-Jewish political history in a critical manner, was of an older generation to the so-called 'new school' of historians.[14] Certainly, two of the older inspirational figures of new approaches to history and heritage – Bill Fishman in London and Bill Williams in Manchester – were independent of the JHSE circle.[15] Both were part of the social history revolution in British historiography and, for them, the study of ordinary Jews in Britain – mainly immigrants – needed no defensive justification, nor did their emphasis on communal and wider power politics. The 'history from below' movement was one in which minority history was not marginal but was in fact at the forefront of research and methodology. The work of Williams especially inspired a new generation of Anglo-Jewish scholars in the fields of both history and culture.[16]

The new work from the late 1980s onwards was innovative and self-reflexive, exemplified by two key edited collections – first David Cesarani's *The Making of Anglo-Jewry* (1990) and second Tony Kushner's *The Jewish Heritage in British History* (1992).[17] These volumes and related monographs from the scholars represented within them reflected a sea change in Anglo-Jewish historiography. As a more recent collection of essays, *New Directions in Anglo-Jewish History* (2010) from academically younger scholars assembled by Geoffrey Alderman, proclaims: 'The past two decades have witnessed a remarkable renaissance in the academic study of the history of the Jews in Great Britain and of their impact upon British history.' The collection rightly states that the essays within the volume reflect 'that regeneration, which could scarcely have been imagined a generation ago'.[18] As Todd Endelman notes, 'The health of Anglo-Jewish history writing is strikingly robust when viewed in the light of its condition a half century ago.'

On the surface, it would appear that all has been progress since the 1980s. A significant number of those featuring in *The Making of Modern Anglo-Jewry* and *The Jewish Heritage in British History* have developed long-standing academic careers and have nurtured a new generation of scholars themselves – thus four out of the seven contributions in *New Directions in Anglo-Jewish History* are completing or have recently completed doctorates under the supervision of the editors of the two earlier collections. Moreover, there is now an institutional framework to complement the work of these young scholars. In London, Rickie Burman developed the

Museum of the Jewish East End which was to evolve into the Museum of London Jewish Life and then become amalgamated into the London Jewish Museum. Even earlier, in the north-west of England, the Manchester Jewish Museum opened in 1984, growing out of the Manchester Studies Unit of Manchester Polytechnic headed by Bill Williams and supported by Rickie Burman and Rosalyn Livshin. The University of Southampton and what became London Metropolitan Archives, alongside local repositories across the country, began to actively collect Jewish communal and individual records, and, with the support of English Heritage, Jewish Heritage UK was created to promote buildings preservation. The appendixes to this volume outline in each case the progress made as well as the challenges still ahead in these various forms of heritage and rescue work.

Moreover, building on the work of informal workshops held in the late 1980s and the first half of the 1990s, the journal *Jewish Culture and History* was launched in summer 1998. In its first editorial, Nadia Valman explained that it sought 'to build on and nurture the work of a new generation of scholars whose innovative research and new interpretative models have offered a dynamic challenge to the old teleologies'.[19] Valman added that the aim of the journal was 'to explore previously neglected areas of the Jewish experience, with a particular, though not exclusive, interest in British Jewry'.[20]

The journal, in which these essays originally appeared is now entering its thirteenth year. The essays come from established scholars at all stages of their careers as well as those carrying out doctoral research. Although the range is wide and the numbers represented plentiful, many others could have been included here – it provides an overview of recent scholarship and approaches but is far from exhaustive. The question bringing these essays together, 'Whatever Happened to British Jewish studies?', would evidently seem to be superfluous, or rather it could be answered, as with the Alderman volume, positively that there is no need to be concerned – the study of British Jewry was in the best possible health.

A different perspective is, however, possible and perhaps necessary for the future well-being of the subject matter, as Todd Endelman's contribution implies. This volume is partly based on a conference of the same title held at the Parkes Institute for the study of Jewish/non-Jewish relations at the University of Southampton in July 2008. On the one hand, the discussion over several days provided a showcase for recent, sophisticated and nuanced research, highlighting that more such work was taking place on British Jewish history, heritage and culture than ever before. On the other hand, there was acknowledgment that there had been a loss of clear purpose that typified the forming of *Jewish Culture and History* ten years earlier and in the workshops that pre-dated the journal.

In itself, this possible loss of identity as scholars of British Jewry might not necessarily be a negative development. It might, for example, reflect a greater sense of security and less of a need to justify and explain apologetically the focus on a relatively small minority group in a society and culture still coping with ethnic pluralism. The response to the question: 'why Anglo-Jewish history?' might simply be – in a world of increasing Balkanisation of the study of the past – 'well, why not?' And even within her introductory editorial highlighting the importance of *British* Jewish studies, Nadia Valman was keen to emphasise that she looked 'forward to publishing work on the *global* contexts of Jewish culture and history'.[21]

It is an indication of the quality of some of the best recent work on British Jewish studies that it is not confined to the nation state, reflecting the wider tendency to explore the importance of diasporic and transnational linkages within both majority and minority communities. A recent and sophisticated example of this has been provided by Abigail Green's remarkable study of Moses Montefiore in which she concludes that his life 'highlights the international dimension of Jewish emancipation and the emergence of a new sort of Jewish politics, rooted in transnational Jewish activism'.[22] Susan Tananbaum's essay in this volume on Norwood Jewish orphanage, whilst not ignoring the British context and British (non-Jewish) comparisons, also suggests the importance of providing a comparative model on an *international* level. Likewise, Nadia Valman's introduction to the chapters in the 'Culture' section, whilst not understating the importance of the 'local', points out that in the nineteenth century 'English, French and German Jewish literature adapted and borrowed widely from each other'. The same, it could be argued, is true of the twentieth and twenty-first centuries when truly global influences in national Jewish cultural production can be located.

There are, however, still good reasons to be concerned about the loss of identity, partial or otherwise, in British Jewish studies. First, the apologetic tendency has still not been overcome, as Endelman persuasively argues. It must be strongly argued that its persistence, albeit in a different form to the early decades of the JHSE, reflects the ongoing antipathy within Britain of the historical mainstream (though perhaps far less the literary mainstream) to take minority studies seriously. It is significant, for example, that David Feldman, perhaps the scholar of British Jewry who has been taken most seriously by general historians in Britain, spends much space and thought in the introduction and conclusion to his classic study *Englishmen and Jews: Social Relations and Political Culture 1840–1914* (1994) justifying his subject matter. He argues, as Endelman notes, that 'By illuminating the history of the nation, the Anglo-Jewish past has a significant contribution to make to our understanding of English history'. Ultimately, his work is vindicated in Feldman's words for the light it will shed on 'the development of political culture and politics in Britain'.[23]

Whilst the 'local' contextualisation emphasised by Feldman is crucial, it does reveal the wider pressure to make sure that minority history is not, using the particular case study of this volume, 'too Jewish' – that is too parochial in its focus. Thus a regional study of British Jewry from medieval to modern was rejected by the Arts and Humanities Research Council, the major funding body in Britain, because 'the focus on Jews without the inclusion of other communities could be too narrow'.[24] In a world of scarce funding in academic and heritage work, such responses are hard to ignore. This 'reality' differs greatly from the world of the JHSE, Anglo-Jewish Archives and the Jewish Museum several generations earlier in which the objectives were modest and the work carried out largely voluntary. Professionalisation has brought more opportunities but also greater dilemmas when confronting the broadly defined marketplace.

Second, whilst much British Jewish scholarship has been comparative, as represented in some of the essays here, the attempt to treat Jews as one of many immigrant and minority groups in Britain, or even more controversially, to apply postcolonial theory to the Jews, has rarely been reciprocated and indeed, in many cases has been rejected in a hostile way. Ironically, whilst the historical mainstream still has a tendency to reject British Jewish studies as a minority subject and marginal, those within other ethnic studies rarely consider the Jewish case to be of relevance, perceiving Jews to be 'white' and part of the majority culture and power bases of society and sometimes, through reference to the Middle East and Israel/Palestine, even imperialist. Mark Levene opens up this question provocatively within this volume, but from one rooted in an understanding of British Jewish history and culture. Those less aware can resent any work comparing and contrasting Jews to former colonial subjects. As one reviewer of such an attempt warned, 'one needs to be very careful not to homogenise the diasporic experience of Jews with the post-slavery and Empire experience of Black British citizens'.[25] Scholars such as Paul Gilroy who *have* made such connections within postcolonial studies are unfortunately rare.[26] The essays by Gavin Schaffer and Didi Herman especially, but many others as well in this collection, show the importance of increasing the dialogue promoted by Gilroy.

Whilst Todd Endelman argues that such attempts to link to other experiences suggests that the 'study of Jews is validated by reference to what it can do or the study of something else', the argument is surely that what is required are conversations to show both linkages and dissimilarities. If such an approach leads to a richer understanding of British Jewry, then it is a two-way exchange and not simply a new form of seeking outside approbation. And if, as Endelman argues, Anglo-Jewish historiography risks being cut off from the Jewish historiographical mainstream, there is an equal and ongoing danger of the latter being cut off from wider theoretical perspectives.

Todd Endelman suggests that, placed in an international context, the health of Anglo-Jewish historiography 'seems less robust'. The lack of dialogue between its practitioners within the UK concerning praxis, methodology and context (and, to follow Endelman, with those studying Jewish history and culture beyond its shores) suggests that taking stock at this point in time is a matter of some urgency. But before introducing the major themes explored by the essays in this collection, a study of current museology inside and outside the Jewish sphere in Britain will analyse further the tensions that exist within contemporary British Jewish studies. The prism of the museum has not been chosen at random – here, it could be argued, is an ideal observatory enabling an overview of both academic and popular understandings and representations of Anglo-Jewry.

II

The year 2010 marked the 250th anniversary of the founding of the
Board of Deputies of British Jews, perhaps the oldest ethno-religious
body in Britain. That this milestone was only met by the production
of an internally produced hagiography, rather than a critical academic
text, reflects the lack of self-confidence, as well as the continued
marginality of professional historians within British Jewry.[27] It is not
for this anniversary that 2010 was chosen for a brief overview of
museology in Britain but because three landmark exhibitions took
place within weeks of each other. Two relate to major museum
redevelopments (the London Museum and the London Jewish
Museum). The third exhibition, at the Manchester Jewish Museum,
was designed to take it back to its original mission when it opened
over a quarter of a century earlier.

On one level this coincidence of exhibitions was accidental – there
were no *direct* factors linking the three. At another, they reflect
changes over a generation when new approaches to the
representation of the past became established in the 1980s. In the
cases of the two London museums, national funding, especially in the
form of the Heritage Lottery Fund, have enabled the extension and/or
re-building of galleries and space. The absence of such support at the
Manchester Jewish Museum has necessitated a more modest
approach but its temporary exhibition – 'In the Red. Redbank – A
Seedbed of Modernity' – is both reflexive and aimed as a precursor to
changing the permanent displays which have remained unchanged
since the opening in 1984.

The analysis that follows relates to what are significant heritage
sites: the two Jewish museums of Britain and what is the leading and
most extensive 'local' museum in the country (and indeed one that as
it is in the capital city, has national/international scope and
ambitions). Through them it will be possible to chart what has
changed since the 1980s and whether indeed there have been
dialogues between 'margins' and 'mainstream' or indeed within the
'margins' themselves. It will also allow a further probing of Todd
Endelman's concern – has the global Jewish experience been
downplayed in favour of the 'local' and, if so, is this *necessarily*
problematic?

The Museum of London's 'Galleries of Modern London' opened
in May 2010. The galleries reflected three years of building work
costing £20 million. They also reflected a desire to present the history
of London less homogeneously than in the mid-1970s when the

museum first opened. The change was reflected in the landmark exhibition, 'The Peopling of London: 20,000 Years of Settlement' (1993–94), still the largest ever attempting to show the scale and range of immigration to Britain.[28] With its 7,000 artefacts covering aspects of London's history from the mid-seventeenth century onwards, the extensive 'Galleries of Modern London' provide an ideal opportunity to assess the representation of Jews, especially as their chronology corresponds exactly with the formal readmission of the Jews to England.

It is surprising, therefore, that in this respect the major feature of the 'Galleries' is the *absence* of Jews within them. It is not a total lacuna – Jews as individuals do appear, but as with the impresario Imre Kiralfy, it is a visitor and there is no reference to his Hungarian Jewish background. It may appear that Kiralfy's statement, blown up on one of the gallery walls, that 'London seemed to offer the greatest chance of the last success I sought' had little to do with his Jewishness and thus required no further gloss by those creating the new galleries. But it has been argued that his creation of world fairs in England was 'as though his Jewish origins, in a country which was part of an unstable empire, had filtered through to the very core of his psychological make-up, to surface in a manic involvement with the empire of his adopted home'.[29] The opportunity here and elsewhere in the galleries to reflect on Jews making and re-making London and the city's identity is thus squandered.

There are occasional and passing references to Jewish refugees, especially the *Kindertransport* before the Second World War and alien internment in 1940.[30] There is, however, only one small, poorly presented and obscure section on the Jewish community as a whole, and that focusing on east European immigrants from 1880 to 1914. The text is short, consisting of several vague sentences, outlining that the migration was 'massive' and that the Jewish East End 'was a microcosm of London itself, with all its divisions of class'. In a dark corner, and with the text close to the ground, it is hard to read. Furthermore, it and the small display of objects relating to Jewish housing, education, marriage, religion, work and the Yiddish theatre give no indication of the dynamism of this lost world.[31] This small display gives the impression of being perfunctory and unrelated to more recent migrant presences in the capital city or even the Jewish worlds that were to come out of the East End and other centres of immigrant settlement.

Even more troubling is the reproduction of antisemitica from the

British Union of Fascists (BUF), a Mosleyite stencil designed for wall graffiti: 'Keep out Alien Jews'. It is accompanied by the inaccurate statement that 'By the late 1930s [in fact it was there from the start of the movement in 1932] the British Union of Fascists had adopted a policy of anti-Semitism'. No indication is provided of the impact of the street anti-Semitism of the BUF on ordinary Jews in the East End and without any real sense of context the 'alienness' of Jewish East Enders (the large majority by the 1930s were British-born) is unchallenged.[32]

Throughout these new permanent galleries a timeline is provided of key dates. None of them relate to Jews – whether marking their readmission, emancipation, mass arrival, the Aliens Act and so on. If anything, material relating to the Jews is less prominent and substantial than in the original displays.[33] In a museum that is committed to present the diversity of London past and present this is, to say the least, curious. Put into a context of the representation of some other immigrant/minority groups in London's history, the Jewish case is not massively different. The sections on the Italians and Irish are perhaps a little more energetic, but they are not much more extensive. It could also be argued that by focusing on Huguenot entrepreneurs in the early section of the galleries, with luxury artefacts relating to the production of watches and silk, immigrant/refugee presence is reflected, being true to the goals of the earlier 'Peopling of London' exhibition. But, Huguenots aside (for so long regarded as the 'acceptable' face of past migration, especially in debates about more recent and supposedly less 'desirable' immigrants), 'white' migrants to London are not prominent in the new galleries. The narrative that is to the fore, however, relates to the black presence in London, which is extensive and wide-ranging in chronology and diversity. No linkages are drawn between it and earlier (non-black) migrants, including the Jews. The relative absence and marginality of Jews in the new galleries is especially disturbing given the overarching aim of the museum in redeveloping its displays was to look 'critically at the story of London we tell, and how we can best fit ourselves to the 21st century'.[34]

The contemporaneous re-opening of the London Jewish Museum might on the surface justify why there is a paucity of material in the larger museum. More convincing as an explanation is the resistance to considering Jews (and other 'white' groups of migrant origin) within an agenda set by a particular postcolonial reading of history. It is thus a reflection of the dominant historiographical and theoretical tendency to refuse to make linkages in the experiences of and responses to ethnic minorities in Britain. If Jews are mentioned, it is in passing and rarely in relation to contemporary debates or concerns. A dialogue is made difficult if the dominant museum has to refer to a specific and very much Jewish site if visitors want to find out about London's Jewish history.

Ironically, when the London Jewish Museum received a Heritage Lottery Fund grant of £4.2 million in 2005, enabling the major extension and rebuilding to take place, the justification for such funding three years earlier highlighted the important part it played 'in presenting the experience of one of Britain's oldest established minorities. It makes a positive contribution to cultural diversity and anti-racist education. By learning more about one another, barriers of ignorance, misunderstanding and racism can be overcome.'[35] Such reasoning has not been accepted in the new Museum of London galleries, also part-lottery funded.

The London Jewish Museum's desire to 'increase knowledge and understanding of Jewish history, culture and religious life, as part of Britain's diverse cultural heritage' also had an 'internal' justification. It was hoped that 'preservation of artefacts and memories [will give] British Jews a sense of identity, vision and continuity with the past, as well as immense pride'.[36] How successful has it been in realising that aim and what is the dominant narrative presented by the new London Jewish Museum?

For the first time since the idea was first mooted in the late nineteenth century, London now has a professionally presented Jewish museum using modern technology and bringing together the older elite artefacts of its predecessors alongside more 'everyday' material from the twentieth and even twenty-first centuries. It is indeed a successful melding of the very best of the old museum and its display dominated by religious ceremonial objects and the social history displays originating in the Museum of the Jewish East End. Exhibitions over the past quarter-century covering subjects such as the Yiddish theatre, the *Kindertransport*, the wedding photographs of 'Boris', the Holocaust, and emigrants from the Yemen, Iraq, Iran, Morocco and elsewhere have been distilled and presented in an engaging fashion. The elitist limitations of the original Jewish Museum have been overcome, as has the focus on east European Jewish migrants in the Museum of the Jewish East End which ignored

those from central Europe and beyond Europe itself. A deep history
of Anglo-Jewry is provided, aided by the evocative presence of a
medieval *mikvah* found during excavations of the City of London in
2001 and believed to belong to the prominent and wealthy Crespin
family.

The photographs and artefacts collected by the Museum of the
Jewish East End in the 1980s – part of what was seen as the 'last
opportunity to recover and record an account of the social history of
London Jewry'[37] – are prominent, as are more recent video
testimonies of refugees from Nazism, Holocaust survivors and anti-
fascist veterans. The methodology, evidence and interests of the 'new'
generation of Anglo-Jewish scholars is clearly present in the museum
displays. If not on the grand scale of some of its recent continental
sister museums, the London Jewish Museum is still an impressive
achievement. Nevertheless, its skill in fusing so smoothly the 'old' and
the 'new', the religious and the secular, brings its own tensions and
reveals some of the dilemmas already raised within this introduction.

First is the issue of conflict. It has somewhat harshly been
suggested that 'An overriding characteristic of the museum is a
pervasive poignancy: there is little that either questions or is critical
of Judaism today.'[38] In response, it might be said that by showing the
diversity of British Jewry, religiously, politically and in terms of origin,
the Jewish Museum – whilst not referring directly to internal divisions
– emphasises the heterogeneity of the community. This is particularly
the case with the 'Welcome Galleries' which feature ten interspersed
video interviews ranging from a gay youth worker, to a Jewish woman
born in India but of Baghdadi origin, to a strictly orthodox rabbi from
Stamford Hill.[39] Nevertheless, the emphasis is ultimately on *one*
community, admittedly made up of 'different backgrounds and
cultures of life'.[40] Historic conflict within Anglo-Jewry, which has
been outlined without apology by the 'new' school of historiography,
is not ignored but it is generally downplayed in contrast to the
emphasis placed on communal solidarity and the importance and
positive influence of philanthropy. This is revealed in what might
appear a whimsical item – a game of snakes and ladders representing
the 'ups and downs' of the 'great migration' from eastern Europe to
the western world. Being greeted by an Anglo-Jewish organisation at
the docks leads to a 'move forward', not the move backwards
experienced by tens of thousands of *ostjuden* confronting the Jewish
Board of Guardians. Sooner or later, the immigrant will get through

and the final space redemptively praises the game player: 'You've made it.'[41] Ultimately, as with the production of many other forms of ethnic minority heritage, the representation of communal life is consensual. Similarly, there is not much 'dirty linen' on display. There is passing reference to Jewish 'petty criminals' within eighteenth century England but this is safely in the deep past. The dominant tone is not purely celebratory, but it is a generally uplifting one of 'survival and success, challenge and contribution'.[42]

Second, the narrative is very much a national one – it is 'Britain's Jewish story'. It is made up of 'many people's stories', ones which share 'common threads' which are 'woven into the history of Britain – the place that has become home'.[43] The Jews of Britain are not presented in isolation – there is some material on all the many countries and regions from which they or their ancestors came – 'a story of diverse roots from around the world, journeys begun in hope or despair'.[44] But rather than being interwoven through ongoing diasporic networks, the narrative is focused on the local with the global represented more through the commonality through time and space expressed through religious identity. Thus at the start of the exhibition, the visitor confronts the *mikvah* which 'links the long history of Jewish people in Britain to a religious practice still shared by Jews across the world'.[45]

Whilst always in the background, the global never dominates the permanent exhibition and it is the island story that is to the fore. Nevertheless, the new museum is not defensive about national belonging in the same way as its forerunners in the late nineteenth century were at a time of growing anti-alienism directed at both foreign and British-born Jews. Even so, it is to be ideologically located in the later years of 'new Labour' and its concern about national belonging, especially articulated by Gordon Brown during the first decade of the twenty-first century. It respects diversity *within* British Jewry but, as a product in part at least of the post-9/11 world, understates the importance of diaspora and the emergence of transnational communities. It also presents journeys in a way that downplays their complexity and temporariness – transmigration, for example, is hardly referred to. Owing much to the 'new' Anglo-Jewish historiography, Endelman's critique is manifested in the new museum's localism.

More positive, however, is the ability to make connections to other minorities through a critical approach to Britishness. This is achieved through a section 'The Same Old Story', which follows on from an earlier landmark exhibition 'Closing the Door' (2005) held at the London Jewish Museum to mark the centenary of the 1905 Aliens Act. The timing of that exhibition was remarkable as it coincided with the blatant and crude use of immigration in the 2005 General Election. That exhibition, which showed the continuities in anti-alien discourse, is continued in the new permanent display. Visitors have to guess the date and source of racist comment which cover the period from the 1900s through to the first decade of the twenty-first century. No punches are pulled in outlining the venom that has been produced by both mainstream newspapers and prominent politicians: 'Britain is now open house to the scum of the Earth. We have become the world's dustbin.' Whilst this easily could have been part of the discourse at the time of the Aliens Act it in fact came from the *Sun* in 1998 to describe the alleged 'flood' of east European Gypsies. The display is brought up to date with an excerpt from the *Express* railing against the entry of east European migrants.[46] It is genuinely difficult, even for students of immigration restrictionism, to find the right chronology and the right group being attacked. Yet it is disappointing that such connections are made only through the exposure of xenophobia and racism: there is little explicit linkage made in the exhibition between the experiences of Jews and other minorities in Britain. As the 'only [museum] in London dedicated to a minority group' parallels (and dissimilarities) with other ethnic and religious communities is implicit and for the visitor to make (or not make). In this respect, Endelman's critique that recent Anglo-Jewish historiography has been validated 'by reference to what it can do for the study of something else' is questionable.

London now has a Jewish Museum that deserves to be taken as seriously as any other on an international level. It represents, in perhaps a largely unthreatening way, the strengths and some of the limitations of the 'new' Anglo-Jewish historiography. There is a particular emphasis on religion and on the Holocaust which partly reflects the power of the marketplace and the need to meet the requirements of the national school curriculum. Yet in both cases there is a wider justification. Religion is presented, in contrast to much recent Anglo-Jewish history writing, as core to Jewish identity and thus is prominent throughout the exhibition. And the Holocaust, as David Cesarani's contribution to this volume illustrates, was more of a feature of post-war British life and culture, including Anglo-

Jewry, than has previously been recognised. Cesarani's call for more detailed work in this field finds a positive response through the material in the museum devoted to the experience of Holocaust survivors in Britain and the lives they rebuilt. Similarly, the essays by James Jordan and Tony Kushner in this collection are steps in the direction posted by Cesarani, even if their conclusions on the place of the Holocaust in post-war British society and culture point in slightly different ways.

But if the London Jewish Museum has now presented a new and exciting face to the world, the same cannot be said of the Manchester Jewish Museum, the permanent display of which is now over a quarter of a century old. Nevertheless, its 'In the Red' presents perhaps the most radical Jewish display that has been created since the celebratory Anglo-Jewish Exhibition held at the Royal Albert Hall in 1887. Bill Williams, in his afterword to this volume, outlines this exhibition's objectives which are also made explicit in the exhibition's conclusion:

> From its outset the Museum hoped to represent the lives of 'ordinary' Jewish residents of Manchester; to tell the stories of their relationships, religion and work patterns. It has collected the belongings, voices and images of all sections of Manchester's Jewish Community. With the lack of physical resources of the old Jewish Quarter we are able to put on an exhibition that hopefully sheds some light on the history of the community and its importance to the development of modern Manchester.[47]

Just as the London Jewish Museum's new permanent exhibition represents a distillation of a quarter of a century of research and presentation, so 'In the Red' highlights the work and collecting pattern of the Manchester Jewish Museum, and especially its founder and leading force, Bill Williams, over the same period. More than its sister museum in the capital, this temporary exhibition illustrates the radical edge of the 'new' Anglo-Jewish historiography, especially in acknowledging the importance of class, class conflict and left-wing politics in the east European Jewish community in Britain. In both 2010 exhibitions poverty is not ignored, but in Manchester its depth in what was one of the most notorious areas of any industrial city – Red Bank – is emphasised throughout, especially through the use of oral testimony. Even so, reflecting Williams' work more generally, the variations in poverty are made clear with the wider social implications drawn out in terms of the evolution of Manchester Jewry. Similarly, social mobility is acknowledged but not overstated. Religion is not made separate from class – national origins in the formation of *chevra* are acknowledged, but their socio-economic foundations are never ignored. Social control, including the pressure from the elite Jews of Manchester for their poorer 'brethren' to assimilate, especially with regard to the removal of Yiddish, is a major feature and one that is only touched upon in the new London exhibition. Philanthropy is put into the context of a large and expanding industrial city. Whilst its specifically Jewish origins are noted, its Manchester bourgeois inspiration is given greater stress. 'In the Red', as its title more than hints, is not ashamed to present Karl Marx and Friedrich Engels (the latter of whom wrote of the area in his *The Condition of the Working Class in England in 1844*) in its poster and throughout the exhibition. It is proudly local, emphasising the importance of Red Bank in the life of Manchester without doing so in the 'cheerleader' school of minority contribution history. Its lack of apologetic tone is illustrated by the inclusion of a police notebook including 'mugshots' of Jewish criminals from the 1900s and the recognition in the text that extreme poverty pushed some of the immigrants into breaking the law.

The exhibition concludes that its goal has been to 'highlight the significance of Red Bank and demonstrate its impact on a national and even global stage'. Again, using the Endelman critique it could be argued that the global influence on the local is not sufficiently highlighted, yet there is throughout an awareness in the exhibition of the world the east European immigrants brought with them and transformed in Manchester, albeit against the desire of the anglicised elite in the city. Moreover, flow through transmigrancy and step migration *is* acknowledged and, through the inclusion of several Yiddish 'penny dreadfuls', including *Life Amongst the Cannibals*, published in America but for sale in Manchester, the existence of a transnational Jewish world reinforced by internationally circulating popular culture is documented.

More could have been made of these global connections, and we still need to know far more about Jewish family networks in the age of mass migration – how much contact was maintained between the 'old' world and the 'new'? But this exhibition, as well as Bill Williams' oeuvre as a whole, including his contribution to this volume, exemplifies what can be achieved by knowing the 'local' intimately. It is perhaps this 'local knowledge', then applied to the national and global, that makes the new Anglo-Jewish historiography, of which Williams is the father figure, special and significant.

Anthropologist Clifford Geertz is right to warn that 'We need, in the end, something rather more than local knowledge. We need a way of turning its varieties into commentaries upon another, the other lighting what the other darkens.'[48] If Todd Endelman is correct in his assessment that British Jewish history is not featuring in Jewish studies outside Britain itself, then this is not necessarily the fault of its specialists who have, as with the Parkes Institute 'Port Jews' project, worked increasingly at an international and comparative level.[49] More, no doubt, could be learnt by British Jewish scholars from those working on other communities and across borders, but the reverse is perhaps even more the case. 'In the Red' is a fine and beautifully executed example of all that has recently been achieved in British Jewish studies. The section that follows provides further evidence of that claim from both new and established scholars, especially in social history and cultural studies, the areas in which British Jewish scholarship has excelled and been world-leading.

III

In the introduction to his recent edited collection *New Directions in Anglo-Jewish History*, Geoffrey Alderman commented that Jews in Britain at the *fin de siècle* were 'obsessed with considerations of image, and with the management of that image'.[50] A powerful statement indeed, and yet, as the essays throughout this collection demonstrate, it is one which – with some necessary qualification – might be more forcefully and broadly applied even further still to define the British Jewish condition in both a historical setting as well as up to the present day. Mark Levene opens his contribution to this collection, for example, lamenting the docility and submissiveness which, he argues, has and continues to characterise the 'hegemonic centre' of British Jewry as they aspire to be neither seen nor heard. In his assessment of contemporary Anglo-Jewish historiography, as with Cesarani's earlier one, Todd Endelman illuminates a similarly worrying trait, pointing to the 'apologetic dimension' which underpins much current research into the history and culture of that community. The popular tendency within that type of scholarship to argue 'that Anglo-Jewish history is important because it serves British history, because it sheds light on the history of Gentile Britons' is a position which makes Endelman – a frank and unapologetic American Jew – distinctly uncomfortable.

Yet perhaps these perspectives are unnecessarily pessimistic. The British Jewish academic community has come a long way from the days of Lucien Wolf and his 'Plea for Anglo-Jewish History'. Certainly much of the recent work conducted within the field of British Jewish literary studies, as Ruth Gilbert suggests, would argue that 'British-Jewish writers today are shaking off a culture of reticence and self-censorship born of anxiety and embarrassment, which arguably inhibited previous generations of Anglo-Jewry'.[51] It is, according to Gilbert and others, a time of hopeful 'revival' – the era of 'shouty Jews'.[52] Indeed the 'blossoming' of a more candid style amongst British Jewry can also be found well beyond the bounds of literary studies. In his century-long view of research into Jews and race science, Gavin Schaffer rather exasperatedly declares 'enough already with the Jewish difference debate', concluding that because scholars 'are no closer to the truth about what makes a Jew' than they were 100 years ago, perhaps the time has come to stop agonising over it.

Thus, invariably, this is not a matter only of image but one also of identity. There may be much to be hopeful about in this period of an apparent 'renaissance' of British Jewish studies, but, as stressed in the opening section of this introduction, there are also the pressing issues of direction and objective which remain matters of some concern. British Jewish studies, Anne Kershen fears, have 'becom[e] lodged in a cul-de-sac' which, according to Kershen, might only be successfully navigated out of if those engaged in this type of research ensure their work is seen as 'part of the bigger picture', and do so confidently. This hesitancy to adopt such an assured tone is, however, also discernable within the wider community, and might in fact contribute to this – if not identity crisis – then certainly this case of assiduous low self-esteem. British Jewry may or may not have reached a point where they are able to 'let go' of the composed communal face which they have nurtured for so long for the benefit of the Gentile world as well as their own, and yet they cannot relinquish their own unrelenting need to understand that face – its many contours and crevices, its place within the world around it, the justification for its very existence.

This preoccupation, of course, has a long history. As Kathrin Pieren shows in her exploration of two turn-of-the-twentieth-century exhibitions of Jewish art and history which took place in London in

1887 and 1906 respectively, British Jewry has long been engaged in the act of shaping, remoulding, preserving and assessing their own cultural identity. Museum displays were not only a way for the British Jewish community to control and communicate their own self-image to a Gentile audience but also offered an opportunity for heritage conservation, the transfer of cultural knowledge, and, above all, self-reflexivity. Thus in this way, the production and dissemination of a communal identity by British Jewry was as much a constructive act as it was a defensive one. This too can be seen in the philanthropic endeavours of the British Jewish community in that same era. As Susan Tananbaum, in her comparative exploration of late nineteenth and early twentieth century Christian and Jewish orphanages in Britain makes clear, the primary motivation for Jewish philanthropists orchestrating and supporting such institutions was not (or not only) to safeguard their image by being seen to be taking care of their own, but rather was part of a deliberate policy to ensure the preservation and perpetuation of Jewish religious and cultural life.

Of course, such seemingly uninhibited expressions of communal self-confidence and identity 'ownership' have not consistently typified the British Jewish experience. As often as Jewish cultural and historical traditions were tentatively celebrated, so too was there an accompanying insidious anxiety that any overly exuberant signs of 'difference' must be contained. This tendency certainly seems to have characterised the long and uneven process through which Jewish food identity in Britain was forged. Publications by key Jewish cookery writers in Britain throughout the nineteenth and twentieth century, so argues Jane Gerson, often chose to downplay, dilute or disguise the rich cultural heritage of their Jewish recipes. Hence the anglicisation of the much-loved Yiddish dish *lokshen* pudding, renamed 'a Rachael' in Judith Montefiore's *The Jewish Manual* (1846), and the denigration of the iconic Chicken Soup to a chapter on 'invalid cookery' by Montefiore's successor Florence Greenberg (1934), all point to an objective of assimilation and Anglicisation of Jewish cultural identity by culinary means. By 'conferring Jewish food identity with the attributes necessary to be esteemed in well-to-do Victorian (and, later, twentieth century) society', these writers, it seems, had few qualms disrupting the integrity of certain Jewish dishes and along with it, Jewish food culture to achieve that objective.

So too was this the case amongst some Jews serving in the military during the First World War. Albeit a markedly different setting to that of the British Jewish kitchen, Jews volunteering for service, so argues Anne Lloyd, 'preferred to be integrated throughout the army rather than separated in a way which marked their "difference"'. The increasingly ambivalent and lax attitude of many Jewish servicemen towards *Kashrut* was just one way in which such 'concealment' tactics were attempted. Although the scarcity of *Kosher* food provisions for Jewish servicemen, as well as a reluctance by any Jews within a position of authority to campaign for a re-evaluation of the situation, meant that all but the most Orthodox were forced by necessity to transgress Jewish dietary laws, as Lloyd suggests many quite willingly accepted and even embraced the practice of eating *trifah* army rations.

In this way then, this predilection to conceal, or, at the very least, qualify Jewish difference favoured by some British Jews both past and present was a compunction generated not only from within but also in response to perceived pressures from beyond the bounds of the community. Hannah Ewence, in her contribution to this volume, shows how the desire to reaffirm 'the Jew' as the eponymous 'other' in the wake of the arrival of thousands of 'alien' Jews from eastern Europe, was a marked feature of late nineteenth century British literary culture – a trend which ultimately manifested itself in the best-selling gothic horror novel of the era: *Dracula*. In light of such a vivid and disturbing publication – although, as Ewence argues, one which can be read as a partly sympathetic analogy for the aliens' 'crisis' – the anxiety amongst assimilated and long-established British Jews to temper all displays of 'un-British' Jewishness, when seen in the context of a growing body of anti-alien press articles and political comment, was more feverish than ever. Even in a post-war and post-Holocaust Britain, visibly 'Jewish' Jews – essentially those whose 'difference' from British society was tangible – could still be cause for concern. As James Jordan shows, the viewing public of the latest media technology – television – tended to be wary or even suspicious of any programmes that dealt explicitly with 'Jewish' subjects. As one comment from a viewer of *The Dybbuk* (1952), a play which dealt with *shtetl* life in eastern Europe, wrote:

> This might have had some significance for members of the Jewish communities but I am sure for the ordinary viewer it was pointless and afforded no relaxation in a dreary evening's television. There arc surely plenty of good English dramatists without resorting to this type of hocus-pocus![53]

Jewish religious and cultural life was not a topic that was considered to be of general interest, and, in the minds of some viewers of that era, was even considered to be subversive. Such programmes underscored the presence of socio-cultural difference which, far from evoking a sympathetic or empathetic response, was deemed to be largely incomprehensible and thus deeply unsettling for the 'ordinary' viewer. In this light, the tendency amongst British Jews to downplay distinctly 'Jewish' elements of their identity seems unsurprising.

Certainly, despite the supposed advent of the age of 'tolerant multiculturalism' in contemporary Britain, that ambivalence towards and mistrust of both overt and covert signs of 'ethnicity' persists. The controversy in 2009, for example, surrounding the decision by London's Jews' Free School to refuse entry to a child whose Jewish matrilineal descendancy credentials were not deemed 'authentic' enough, exposed the British Jewish community once again to uncomfortable and unwelcome scrutiny. Discussed by both Didi Herman and Gavin Schaffer, the case reaffirmed the invasive need of both state and society in Britain to categorise and quantify Jews – to be clear on exactly who they were dealing with and how best they might be defined. Ironically, however, as Herman argues, by treating the case judiciously under the Race Relations Act, the confusion and prejudices surrounding Jewish identity remained as pronounced as ever. What is more, that confusion was not only confined to the non-Jewish world. In fact, as Schaffer remarks, the case 'illuminated brightly the ongoing inability of Jewish communities to agree about what constitutes a Jew'.

The continuation of such apprehensions over identity amongst British Jews when dissected and laid bare within a complex legal framework such as this is certainly understandable, but in purely practical terms, such definitional ambivalences are worrying because it can (and already has had) very real consequences for the heritage of the community. As the contributions from Lawrence Cohen and Tony Kushner make clear, vital and exceedingly 'rich' areas of memory work – typically histories belonging to those on the margins of British Jewish society such as orphans and refugees – have been all but neglected. Without Cohen's painstaking efforts with fragments of oral history, for example, the story of the 'Norwood Rebellion' – a staged protest by a minority of the institutions' 'inmates' over the meagre food provisions and harsh discipline regime – would have been lost. Official records fail to make mention of the incident, and indeed it was quite probably intentionally omitted from those records because that type of counter-history disrupted the more polished image of institutional care which Norwood preferred to cultivate. Neither tales of insurrection nor anarchic young Jews belonged in the overarching narratives constructed by British Jewry. The same too seems to have been the case with the memory of young Jewish Holocaust survivors, brought to the English countryside in 1945–46 to recuperate. Unlike the vast quantity of scholarly research, memoirs and public history products and output that have been generated about the *Kindertransport*, the story of these child refugees, some housed in the Lake District, has 'hardly been remembered', probably, offers Kushner, because '[t]hese children do not "fit" easily into wider narratives, whether Jewish or non-Jewish, or whether local, national or global'. However, whilst British Jewish history remains all too frequently excluded from the mainstream, British Jews themselves must take responsibility for the archaeology and preservation of such narratives, refashioning their approach to both heritage and identity in the spirit of inclusion.

IV

Finally, what direction could/should British Jewish studies take? In her introductory editorial to *Jewish Culture and History*, Nadia Valman listed areas of interest for the journal. This included

> the history of Jews in society and in relation to other ethnic and historical minorities, cultural representations of Jews, oral history, historiography, history and memory, Yiddish culture, gender, life-cycle experience, class, consumption and life-styles, Jewish identities, Jews and modernity, geography and place.[54]

Whilst not explicitly so, this list has a clear bias towards the modern Jewish experience and the essays in this volume likewise cover the period from the late nineteenth century through to the present day. Such a chronological focus in no way implies that exciting work is not being carried out into earlier periods. Patricia Skinner's landmark edited collection, *Jews in Medieval Britain* (2003), significantly subtitled 'Historical, Literary and Archaeological Perspectives', and a similarly wide-ranging interdisciplinary conference held at the University of York in 2010 on the same theme reveal the intellectual vibrancy in the pre-expulsion Anglo-Jewish communities.[55] Eliane

Glaser's provocative work on the readmission of the Jews in the mid-seventeenth century, following on from that of David Katz, shows similar dynamism, and there have been excellent studies of the place of Jews in early modern English culture from James Shapiro, Michael Ragussis and Frank Felsenstein, and David Ruderman's study of the 'Jewish Enlightenment in an English Key'.[56] In relation to Victorian Britain, the work of Abigail Green has already been referred to and Michael Clark has added rich detail to our knowledge of the politics of emancipation and especially its aftermath.[57]

The decision to focus on the post-1880s period is twofold. First, it reflects that this is the period that still attracts the greatest scholarly attention, especially from younger scholars, with the chronology as reflected in several of the essays now covering the post-1945 era. Second, and more importantly, it is to provide the volume with greater coherence. This is not to suggest that linkages cannot and should not be made between the different chronological stages of British Jewish history and culture – work in the area of memory and history is perhaps a particularly rich seam that can be mined in this respect.[58] With Anglo-Jewish specialists in medieval, early modern and modern eras having recently taken stock of the current state of historiography and research, it is perhaps possible that stronger links between them can now take place with more sophisticated and multi-layered approaches than have so far been attempted.

Are there areas to add to Nadia Valman's introductory list? Bill Williams emphasises the importance of studying what he terms 'nonconformity' in British Jewry. Whilst some of the essays in this volume point in this direction, there is still much more to be done in breaking down the idea of a 'normative' Jewish experience. And if the essays in this collection have not broken down chronological barriers, they illustrate that at its best, disciplinary fences, especially between history and culture, *have* been overcome. Jewish studies is inherently interdisciplinary but British Jewish studies has shown the potential of bringing in new theoretical and methodological approaches that can act as a model to the area as a whole as well as to other 'minority' studies.

One area that is not covered explicitly in this volume is the subject of British anti-Semitism. Indeed, many of the authors would be hesitant to use the term, viewing it as too crude a tool to investigate British responses and attitudes towards 'the Jew'. In this respect, Anthony Julius' *Trials of the Diaspora: A History of Anti-Semitism in*

England (2010) has been an unwelcome and polemical intervention, taking scholarship back a generation, unaware, as Nadia Valman suggests, of the work of literary critics who have viewed 'semitic representations as metaphors for larger questions specific to time and place'.[59] The best work in the field, as exemplified by Bryan Cheyette, still needs to be taken further.[60] What is also needed is research that explores the impact of hostility and negative imagery on British Jews, including, as in Cesarani's contribution to this volume, the impact of anti-Semitism elsewhere in extreme form, most traumatically in the Holocaust, on those away from mass murder.

British Jewish studies can lose out on a simplistic comparative level – no great disasters, at least since the medieval period, compared to the rest of Europe, and few great theological figures since the readmission. From this, a more sensitive and subtle approach has emerged, with the emphasis on ordinary lives and everyday culture as well as religious praxis studied from 'below'. Rather than a limitation, it is still an example for other historiographies to emulate – the challenge now is for 'mainstream' British history (but far less literary and cultural studies), Jewish studies, and ethnic and racial studies to take note and to engage in greater dialogue. And that this volume represents the fourth major set of essays on British Jewish history in a 20 year period suggests that there is much life in the subject yet.

Lastly, the essays presented here are not intended as the final word on their subject matter – it is to be hoped that a successor collection will emerge in the not too distant future, perhaps dominated by the younger scholars in *Whatever Happened to British Jewish Studies?* and those yet to emerge. Indeed, this volume will have succeeded only if a new generation emerges to challenge the approaches adopted within, and to further analyse the tensions – between the 'inside' and the 'outside', the 'local' and 'global' – in the search for the 'right' context to study British Jewry.

NOTES

Sections 1, 2 and 4 of this introduction were written by Tony Kushner and section 3 by Hannah Ewence.

1. Lucien Wolf, 'A Plea for Anglo-Jewish History', *Transactions of the Jewish Historical Society of England*, 1 (1893–94), 1–7 (p.1).
2. Ibid.
3. Ibid. pp.2–3.

4. On the more positive symbiosis with local historians, see Tony Kushner, *Anglo-Jewry since 1066: Place, Locality and Memory* (Manchester: Manchester University Press, 2009), passim.
5. See David Cesarani, 'Dual Heritage or Duel of Heritages? Englishness and Jewishness in the Heritage Industry', in *The Jewish Heritage in British History: Englishness and Jewishness* ed. by Tony Kushner (London: Frank Cass, 1992), pp.29–41.
6. See Rickie Burman, 'The Jewish Museum, London: Introduction and History', in *Treasures of Jewish Heritage: The Jewish Museum London* ed. By Rickie Burman, Jennifer Marin and Lily Steadman (London: Scala Publishers, 2006), pp.10–19; David Clark, 'Viewing the Past with Vision', *Jewish Renaissance* (Summer 2002), 10–11; and Tony Kushner, 'Anglo-Jewish Museology and Heritage, 1887 to the Present', *Journal for the Study of British Cultures*, 16.1 (2009), 11–25.
7. Elisa Lawson, 'Cecil Roth and the Imagination of the Jewish Past, Present and Future in Britain, 1925–1964' (unpublished PhD thesis, University of Southampton, 2005), pp.12–13.
8. Cecil Roth, 'Why Anglo-Jewish History?', *Transactions of the Jewish Historical Society of England*, 22 (1968–69), 21–9.
9. Ibid. p.29.
10. Ibid.
11. Peter Mandler, *History and National Life* (London: Profile Books, 2002), p.1.
12. From the 1967 album *Sgt. Pepper's Lonely Heart Clubs Band* (EMI, 1967), written by Paul McCartney with John Lennon.
13. Lloyd Gartner, *The Jewish Immigrant in England* (London: Allen & Unwin, 1960); Todd Endelman, *The Jews of Georgian England, 1714–1830* (Philadelphia: Jewish Publication Society of Philadelphia, 1979). It should be noted, however, that whilst Gartner was trained in America in both immigration and Jewish history, Endelman also studied at Warwick where he experienced the new developments in British social history.
14. Geoffrey Alderman, *The Jewish Community in British Politics* (Oxford: Clarendon Press, 1983). See also idem, 'The Young Cecil Roth, 1899–1924', *Transactions of the Jewish Historical Society of England*, 34 (1994–96), 1–16.
15. Bill Williams, *The Making of Manchester Jewry, 1740–1875* (Manchester: Manchester University Press, 1976); William Fishman, *East End Jewish Radicals, 1875–1914* (London: Duckworth, 1975).
16. Tony Kushner, 'Bill Williams and Jewish Historiography: Past, Present and Future', *Melilah*, 1 (2006), 1–14.
17. David Cesarani, ed., *The Making of Modern Anglo-Jewry* (Oxford: Blackwell, 1990); Kushner, *The Jewish Heritage* (see note 5).
18. Inside cover blurb in Geoffrey Alderman, ed., *New Directions in Anglo-Jewish History* (Brighton, MA: Academic Studies Press, 2010).
19. Nadia Valman, 'Editorial', *Jewish Culture and History*, 1.1 (1998), 1.
20. Ibid. p.2.
21. Ibid. p.2 (emphasis added).
22. Abigail Green, *Moses Montefiore: Jewish Liberator, Imperial Hero* (Cambridge, MA: Belnap Press of Harvard University Press, 2010), p.421.
23. David Feldman, *Englishmen and Jews: Social Relations and Political Culture 1840–1914* (New Haven, CT: Yale University Press, 1994), p.13.
24. AHRC communication to Tony Kushner, 8 July 2005.
25. Anonymous reviewer response for *Journal for the Study of British Cultures*, October 2009.
26. See, for example, Paul Gilroy, *Between Camps: Nations, Cultures and the Allure of Race* (London: Allen Lane, 2000).
27. Raphael Langham, *250 Years of Convention and Contention: A History of the Board of Deputies of British Jews, 1760–2010* (London: Vallentine Mitchell, 2010). For critical comment, see Geoffrey Alderman, 'Sweeping the Board – after 250 Years', *Jewish Chronicle*, 16 July 2010.
28. See David Kahn, 'Diversity and the Museum of London', *Curator: The Museum Journal*, 37.4 (1994), 240–50.

29. Within the 'People's City, 1850s–1940s' section. Tony Kushner, site visit, 14 July 2010. For Kiralfy, see Paul Greenhalgh, *Expositions Universalle, Great Exhibitions and World Fairs, 1851–1939* (Manchester: Manchester University Press, 1988), p.93.

30. In section on 'War'.

31. In 'Struggle', part of the 'People's City, 1850s–1940s'.

32. Unlabelled section on the inter-war period within the 'People's City'.

33. This is especially disappointing as the lavish book that now is marketed alongside the new displays – Cathy Ross and John Clark, *London: The Illustrated History* (London: Allen Lane, 2008) – includes much more on the history of London Jewry and responses to its presence. The book was intended as part of the museum's process of redevelopment. See the preface (p.7) by its director, Professor Jack Lohman.

34. Lohman, 'Preface' in ibid. p.7.

35. Jewish Museum 'Look into the Future' (unpublished pamphlet, 2002).

36. Ibid.

37. First mission statement of the Museum of the Jewish East End, quoted by Tony Kushner, 'Looking Back With Nostalgia? The Jewish Museums of Britain', *Immigrants and Minorities*, 6 (July 1987), 200–211 (p.207).

38. Sara Selwood, review of the Jewish Museum in *Museums Journal*, 110.6 (June 2010), 49.

39. Tony Kushner, site visit, 10 August 2010.

40. From the entrance to the 'Welcome Galleries'.

41. 'Snakes and Ladders' game in section outlining the arrival of east European Jews.

42. 'Britain's Jewish Story', Jewish Museum.

43. Ibid.

44. Ibid.

45. Mikvah at the entrance to the museum.

46. 'The Same Old Story', Jewish Museum.

47. Conclusion to 'In the Red: Red Bank – A Seedbed of Modernity', Manchester Jewish Museum 18 May to 29 September 2010, visited by Tony Kushner, 12 August 2010.

48. Clifford Geertz, *Local Knowledge* (London: Fontana, 1973), p.233.

49. See, for example, David Cesarani, ed., *Port Jews: Jewish Communities in Cosmopolitan Maritime Trading Centres, 1550–1950* (London: Frank Cass, 2002); and David Cesarani, Tony Kushner and Milton Shain, eds., *Place and Displacement in Jewish History and Memory* (London: Vallentine Mitchell, 2009).

50. Geoffrey Alderman, 'Introduction', in *New Directions in Anglo-Jewish History* ed. by Geoffrey Alderman (Boston: Academic Studies Press, 2010), pp.vii–x (p.ix).

51. Ruth Gilbert, in her contribution to this volume, cited Donald Weber, 'Anglo-Jewish Literature Raises Its Voice', *JBooks.com*, 12 July 2007, as having written of the 'flowering' of 'an Anglo-Jewish literary "revival"'.

52. This is a term coined by Linda Grant, *The People on the Street: A Writer's View of Israel* (London: Virago, 2006), p.5, and quoted by Gilbert.

53. BBC WAC Audience Research VR/52/474: The Dybbuk, quoted by James Jordan in his contribution to this volume.

54. Valman, 'Editorial' (see note 19), p.2.

55. Patricia Skinner, ed., *The Jews in Medieval Britain: Historical, Literary and Archaeological Perspectives* (Woodbridge: Boydell Press, 2003). The conference 'York 1190 – Jews and Others in Wake of Medieval Massacre' was held at the University of York in March 2010 under the auspices of the Centre for Medieval Studies.

56. Eliane Glaser, *Judaism without Jews: Philosemitism and Christian Polemic in Early Modern England* (Basingstoke: Palgrave, 2007); David Katz, *The Jews in the History of England, 1485–1850* (Oxford: Clarendon, 1994); James Shapiro, *Shakespeare and the Jews* (New York: Columbia University Press, 1996); Michael Ragussis, *Figures of Conversion: 'The Jewish Question' and English National Identity* (Durham, NC: Duke University Press, 1995); Frank Felsenstein, *Anti-Semitic Stereotypes: A Paradigm of Otherness in English Popular Culture, 1660–1830* (Baltimore, MD: Johns Hopkins University Press, 1995); and David Ruderman, *Jewish Enlightenment in an English Key: Anglo-Jewry's Construction of Modern Jewish Thought* (Princeton, NJ: Princeton University Press, 2000).

57. Michael Clark, *Albion and Jerusalem: The Anglo-Jewish Community in the Post-Emancipation Era* (Oxford: Oxford University Press, 2009).
58. See, for example, Kushner, *Anglo-Jewry since 1066* (see note 4).
59. Anthony Julius, *Trials of the Diaspora: a history of anti-Semitism in England* (Oxford: Oxford University Press, 2010).
60. Bryan Cheyette, *Constructions of 'the Jew' in English Liberalism and Society: Racial Representations, 1875–1945* (Cambridge: Cambridge University Press, 1993).

SECTION 1

HISTORY

Anglo-Jewish Historiography and the Jewish Historiographical Mainstream

TODD ENDELMAN

The health of Anglo-Jewish history writing today is strikingly robust when viewed in light of its condition a half century ago. There is a flurry of activity: conferences, publications, dissertations, debates. To observers who recall the somnolence of the field in the 1960s and 1970s, the current scene is, in contrast, bustling and animated. Those who identify themselves as Anglo-Jewish historians enjoy an audience of sympathetic but critical readers both inside and outside the academy. To be sure, research and teaching in Jewish studies in Britain remain underfunded, certainly in comparison to North America, but this reflects in large part the indifference of successive governments to the needs of higher education more generally (as well as, of course, the proverbial unwillingness of the community to fund Jewish scholarship).

Viewed from a vantage point outside the British Isles, however, the scene is less remarkable. The health of Anglo-Jewish historiography, when seen within the context of modern Jewish historiography more generally, seems less robust. The reason, I will argue, is its isolation from the mainstream of Jewish historical writing and research. By this, I mean that its practitioners seem unaware of, indifferent to, or reluctant to engage with the concerns that animate those who write the histories of other western Jewish communities. For their part, historians of other western communities, wherever they live and teach, take little interest in Anglo-Jewish history. It is not a subfield that generates excitement outside Britain, attracting new students and sparking debates. In North America, for example, where doctoral programmes in modern Jewish history flourish and where candidates for the degree must demonstrate familiarity with the sweep of European and American Jewish history from the eighteenth century to the present (whatever the focus of their dissertation research), no student in the last 20 years, to the best of my knowledge, has chosen to write on an Anglo-Jewish topic. Similarly, with two exceptions,[1] modern Jewish historians in North America and Israel rarely contribute to the writing of Anglo-Jewish history (as distinct from historians of modern Britain, like Peter Stansky, Eugene Black, and David Katz, who occasionally venture into the field). A search in the on-line catalogue of the Harlan Hatcher Library at the University of Michigan – as well as, more unsystematically, a search of my own bookshelves – yielded nothing on Anglo-Jewish history published by Jewish historians outside Britain (excepting David Ruderman and myself) in the last 15 years.

One sign of the marginal position of Britain within modern Jewish historical scholarship is the need that Anglo-Jewish historians feel to justify what they do. When I wrote *The Jews of Britain* in the late 1990s, I could not assume that other academic historians were prepared to see the links between Anglo-Jewish history and their own work, whether in modern Jewish history or modern British history. So, unlike other authors in the series, I began in an apologetic vein – with a discussion of why most Jewish historians view Anglo-Jewish history as peripheral or irrelevant to major trends in their fields and why British historians tend to ignore Jews altogether or, on the occasions when they do note their presence, cast them in a few, well-known roles (chiefly as immigrants or aliens).

The marginalisation of Anglo-Jewish history in centres of research and teaching outside Britain means that its writing is largely (but not exclusively) a monopoly of historians who are themselves British-born and British-educated and who live and work in Britain. (In contrast, writing about German Jews is an international endeavour, in which historians from Israel, North America, and Western and Central Europe participate more or less equally). Because the Ph.D. or D.Phil. in Britain is a research degree requiring no coursework (and thus exposure to the sweep of Jewish history), and because the setting in which most Anglo-Jewish history writing is produced is 'local' rather than 'European' or 'western', the framework in which its practitioners locate their work is that of British, rather than Jewish, history. No longer concerned, as were their predecessors, with presenting Anglo-Jewish history in a benign, rose-tinted light, as a counterweight to contemporary Jew-baiting, they seek instead to address pressing questions in the field of British history. They thus realise what the first cohort of Jewish historians to enter the American academy (those who began teaching in the late 1970s) ardently desired: a mainstreaming of Jewish historical writing and a break with master narratives that plotted the flow of Jewish history as a uniform process, driven by its own dynamics, with perhaps minor local variations here and there. An example of this is David Feldman's *Englishmen and Jews*, in which he retells the story of Anglo-Jewish emancipation as a chapter in the conflict 'between proponents of the confessional state and those who wanted to reform or dismantle it' and of the emergence of a Jewish Question later in the century as an episode in 'attempts to redefine the national community according to new criteria'.[2]

This kind of contextualisation serves two different purposes – one intellectual and the other apologetic or strategic. First, it makes comprehensible – in a way that the old, inward-looking Jewish master narratives failed to do – the ups and downs and twists and turns of European-wide processes in specific national contexts. It offers nuance, texture, and complexity while explaining why Anglo-Jewish history – or any other national Jewish history – was no mere variation on a standard, linear course of development. It reveals the limitations of assuming that there is a pan-Jewish paradigm that is the measure of variations everywhere. In concrete terms, to take one example, it explains why Benjamin Disraeli was able to climb 'the greasy pole' of politics to the office of prime minister while not even the most ambitious and talented German Jewish convert – or even son of a convert – ever entertained the hope of heading a German government.

The insertion of Anglo-Jewish history into a British context also serves a strategic end that is distinct from whatever scholarly work it performs. It seeks to make Anglo-Jewish history 'relevant' to the history of Britain by asserting that the latter needs the former in some way to be completely comprehensible. It does this by arguing that it illuminates, perhaps uniquely, corners of Britain's history that are otherwise in the shadows. Thus, David Feldman writes in the concluding paragraph to his book that his 'overarching claim' is that 'some of the central issues in modern English history, such as the nature of Victorian liberalism, the growth of the collectivist state and the history of the working class, can be seen in a new light by closely examining their relation to the Jewish minority'.[3] For example, British attempts to fix the social and legal place of Jews in British society also 'shaped conceptions of the [English or British] nation'. These conceptions were not pre-existing, reflecting 'beliefs and solidarities that were already in place'. Rather, the very act of asking where Jews belonged enabled Englishmen to constitute and develop 'conceptions of the nation'. Thus, by illuminating the history of the nation, 'the Anglo-Jewish past has a significant contribution to make to our understanding of English history'.[4]

My point is not to take issue with Feldman's assertion – who would disagree? – but, rather, to note its apologetic dimension: its argument that Anglo-Jewish history is important because it serves British history, because it sheds light on the history of Gentile Britons – their institutions, values, and culture. As Moshe Rosman notes in his collection of essays *How Jewish Is Jewish History?*, those who point to the instrumentality of Jewish history mimic the 'contribution' discourse of historians like Cecil Roth, who emphasised the worthiness of Jews – their patriotism, their scientific and artistic creativity, their philanthropy, their contributions to the common weal – to counter the anti-Jewish hostility of the time.[5]

The persistence or re-emergence of this discourse is surprising or even counterintuitive. In theory, the triumph of the multicultural ethos in the academy should have made this kind of defensiveness redundant, for the logic of multiculturalism rejects cultural hierarchies, celebrates diversity and devalues acculturation. It trumpets the intrinsic value of the history of any group of men and women seeking to negotiate and make sense of the world in which they live. In practice, however, the most ardent promoters of academic multiculturalism are uninterested in the culture and history of the Jews because Jews are no longer a stigmatised, persecuted minority but, instead, a materially comfortable, socially acceptable, well-connected group for the most part. Moreover, because western Jews are 'white', they are *ipso facto* complicit in the racist socio-economic arrangements that keep 'people of colour' in their place, be they African-Americans in the United States, South Asians in Great Britain, or Palestinians in the State of Israel. The logic of multiculturalism, in other words, extends only to 'unsuccessful' minorities, those still mired in poverty, suspected of violent or 'unsocial' behaviour and victimised by exclusion and discrimination.

Excluding Jews from the universe of multiculturalism in this way challenges the *bona fides* of scholars of Jewish history and literature, whether in Britain or America, who teach in settings where postmodern and multicultural sentiments are well entrenched. Not wishing to be seen as complicit in the oppression of others, they frequently invoke an updated version of 'contribution' discourse to validate what they study. One form that this takes is the argument that knowledge of the Jewish experience brings to the multicultural table something that would otherwise be missing. For example, Jonathan Freedman writes in the introduction to his recently published *Klezmer America*: 'It's the central thesis of my project that dealing with the collective fictions that accrete around the examples of Jews, Jewishness, and Judaism can unsettle even the most seemingly secure of the seemingly calcified categories by which our culture parses otherness', in which he includes immigrant and ethnic otherness, racial alterity, gender difference, and sexual dissidence.

> Perhaps more important, they can do this in such a way as to reveal what was at stake in the making of those categories in the first place. When we place the Jew and all the things associated with that figure into such culturally powerful if resolutely multiple conceptual contexts, the things we 'know' about all of these categories becomes less certain.[6]

Or, to take a British example, Bryan Cheyette and Laura Marcus justify studying Jews, in the introduction to the collection *Modernity, Culture, and 'The Jew'*, by reference to their creative disruptiveness and lack of fixity. 'What is at stake', they ask, 'when Jewish history and culture are inserted into current feminist, gay and lesbian, post-colonial and postmodern revisions of modernity?' Doing so, they answer, unsettles both 'the new orthodoxies' spawned by 'the radical reconstruction of modernity' and 'the desperate bid' of liberal humanists 'to signify the universality of the modern project'.[7] However admirable the intent, once again, the study of Jews is validated by reference to what it can do for the study of something else – in these examples, the study of race, gender, and ethnicity and the terms and concepts on which their study proceeds.

While validating the study of Jewish history by reference to something else may be only a strategic nod to current fashion and the foibles of all-too-human colleagues, it does have substantive consequences that transcend matters of style and technique. It is a historiographical move that shapes how we narrate events, how we contextualise and explain them, and how we assess their significance (what weight we assign to them). As a rule, the more one roots Anglo-Jewish history in the history of Britain, the greater the temptation to view it only in that context, and not simultaneously in the context of a transnational Jewish history as well. While it is a truism that modern Jewish history makes sense only when it is fully contextualised, it is also true, I would argue, that detaching and isolating the history of any Jewish community or subcommunity from its transnational context has a downside as well. In the case of British-based Anglo-Jewish history, resistance or indifference to its presentation within a pan-European or trans-Atlantic context has contributed to its neglect by modern Jewish historians more generally.

I could illustrate this point by referring to the tendency to measure and judge British anti-Semitism, especially from the mid-nineteenth to the mid-twentieth centuries, by reference to Britain's self-professed ideals of tolerance and fair play rather than by reference to patterns of exclusion, stigmatisation, and persecution elsewhere. In the first instance, the picture that emerges is bleak and unflattering; in the second, when the frame of reference is broader, the result is more favourable, perhaps even inspiring. I have written about this elsewhere[8] and there is no need to repeat myself here. It is sufficient to note that British-born historians trained at British universities tend to invoke the first frame of reference and Israeli- and American-trained historians the second.

Instead, to illustrate the point, let me turn to a now prominent topic on the Anglo-Jewish historiographical agenda: the chief rabbinate, Orthodox Judaism, and religious polarisation in the twentieth century, or what is often described as the shift rightward away from the tolerant, inclusive, middle-of-the-road Judaism of the United Synagogue in the Victorian era. Between 2006 and 2008, two book-length studies of this subject were published – Miri Freud-Kandel's *Orthodox Judaism in Britain since 1913* and Meir Persoff's *Faith against Reason: Religious Reform and the British Chief Rabbinate* – and one doctoral dissertation – Benjamin Elton's at Birkbeck College[9] – was successfully defended.

The impetus for this direction in historical research is no mystery. Denominational polarisation is a hallmark of Anglo-Jewish religious life at the start of the twenty-first century. This, in turn, has led historians to wonder (a) whether religious harmony or consensus was ever the rule, and (b), if it was, what upset it, sowing ill-will and dissension. In trying to answer these questions, Freud-Kandel, for example, focuses on the influence that chief rabbis Joseph Hertz and Israel Brodie (and to a lesser extent Immanuel Jakobovits) were able to exert over the religious direction of the community, examining in particular their theological views through a close analysis of their sermons. One can question whether this is the best way to understand the weakening of centrist orthodoxy in Britain, but this is not the issue here. It is rather the frame of reference in which to set the examination and analysis. For the revival of orthodoxy, its ability to influence Jewish life beyond its own walls, and the growth, in particular, of *haredi*, or ultra-orthodox sectarian Judaism, are not peculiar to Britain. These trends characterise religious life in the United States, France and the State of Israel as well – that is, wherever Jews live in large numbers, orthodoxy and especially strict orthodoxy are flourishing in ways that were unimaginable at the end of World War II. Remember that at mid-century social scientists in the United States were predicting the demise of orthodoxy in the future, viewing it as an immigrant, Old World phenomenon that would fade away – as its constituents died and their children and grandchildren increasingly moved to the suburbs, mixed socially with Gentiles, and acquired a taste for upper middle class comforts. Their predictions – we now know – were wrong.

Freud-Kandel's presentation of the rightward shift of Anglo-Jewish orthodoxy is firmly rooted in Anglo-Jewish soil. She endorses the widely accepted view that Hertz's theological outlook was 'progressive conservative', that he embraced both sacred tradition and secular wisdom (*Torah im derekh erets*) without compromising the former and that he laboured to embrace and reconcile both the East and West End communities. She presents him, above all, as a man of moderation, as a 'mediator' and 'bridge-builder', rejecting the extremes of both reform and fundamentalism in order to fight for 'the validity of the middle ground that could encompass both immigrant and native Jews'.[10] In her reading, the shift began imperceptibly and unintentionally with the appointment of Yehezkiel Abramsky in 1935 to the *bet din* (at a time when it was a low-profile body with little influence) and picked up steam after the death of Hertz in 1946 and the appointment of Brodie in 1948. In her view, Brodie's inability to articulate 'a comprehensive theological system' and his willingness to delegate halakhic authority to the *bet din* allowed Anglo-Jewry to fall under the influence of sectarian orthodoxy, thus propelling it rightward.

Clearly, there is more to the story than this. While it would be foolish to ignore the foibles of leaders, they cannot bear the explanatory weight that Freud-Kandel assigns them. Implicit in her telling of the story is the conclusion that, if Brodie had been born with a stiffer backbone and a suppler mind, Victorian orthodoxy –

tolerant, inclusive, latitudinarian – would have survived until the end of the twentieth century and would perhaps still be with us today. Given the renaissance of sectarian orthodoxy everywhere, this seems unlikely. I would argue that Freud-Kandel could have avoided this improbable conclusion if she had cast her project in a broader context – that is, in the context of modern Jewish history as well as Anglo-Jewish history. Then her account of the decline of *minhag angliyyah* would be richer, more credible and more compelling. It also would speak to historians outside the Anglo-Jewish historiographical fold who grapple with similar phenomena in other contexts. Whatever its merits, in its current form, her account of 'an ideology forsaken' looks inward rather than outward.

Freud-Kandel's book is symptomatic of a broader trend: the divorce of Anglo-Jewish history from the mainstream of Jewish historical writing. The causes of this disconnection are multiple. First, in Britain, there are no historians of Anglo-Jewry who were trained as modern Jewish historians in the way that Jewish historians are trained in Israel and North America. While the research of the latter may be as narrowly focused as the research of the former, it is presented frequently in a transnational context. Second, teaching and writing in Britain encourages, not surprisingly, the writing of an Anglo-Jewish history that speaks to British problems. In the not-too-distant past, the writing of Anglo-Jewish history was a parochial, self-congratulatory project, often hitched to communal tasks. While this is no longer true, old perceptions die hard. Since those who write about Jews in Britain do not want their work to be branded parochial, they seek to present their work in such a way that it connects to the work of British historians in their own and other institutions. Three, the very content of Anglo-Jewish history – its freedom from the worst excesses of anti-Semitism, its intellectual poverty (no Mendelssohns, Geigers, Rosenzweigs, or Bubers), its lack of dramatic triumphs and tragedies, its island setting and distance from much larger centres of Jewish life – works against its easy inclusion in a pan-European or trans-Atlantic Jewish framework. Anglo-Jewish events, while not uniquely different, encourage their disassociation from Jewish events elsewhere by virtue of their difference. At the same time, the 'calm' of Anglo-Jewish emancipation and integration and the absence of intellectual and religious breakthroughs have discouraged historians of modern Jewry from turning their attention to events in Britain (unless, perhaps, they are working on the history of Zionism). The problem is not that

Anglo-Jewish history is intrinsically dull and unrewarding, but that the master narratives that dominate the writing of modern Jewish history – stories about political emancipation, religious modernisation and ideological strife – are too narrowly imagined to encompass Anglo-Jewish transformations.

These matters aside, there is also an ideological dimension to this historiographical divorce. Under the influence of postmodernist currents, some in the academy now ask whether there is a coherent, unified, transnational Jewish historical experience into which local Jewish histories can be integrated and whether the very notion of Jewish history may not itself be culturally constructed for an ideological end. One of the themes of Moshe Rosman's recent collection is how postmodernism problematises the existence of the collective entity 'the Jewish people' and the very word 'Jewish'. In his words: 'If the word "Jewish" signifies no essential features continuous over time and place, if it can be – or if it has been – constructed in an infinite number of ways, if it is always and everywhere contingent, then, as a practical matter, how do we go about defining the subject which we seek to research and write about? ... If Jewish can be everything, is it anything?'[11] In other words, perhaps Jewishness is in the eye of the beholder and Jews are an 'imagined community' (to reference Benedict Anderson). If so, the correct framework for understanding Anglo-Jewish history may indeed be British history. (Of course, this begs the question of what is 'British' – or 'English' for that matter – and why one collectivity is described as 'imagined' while the other is not.)

Reasoning thus, opting for British rather than Jewish historical contextualisation, brings with it a bonus: it aligns research on Jews, always vulnerable to the charge of parochialism, with two powerful currents of thought in the contemporary academy. The first current is the belief that nationalism is a destructive but increasingly anachronistic force in human history, called into being by earlier but now disappearing historical circumstances, and that the nation-state is on its last legs (as the history of European integration seemingly demonstrates). Historians and other scholars who view the present in this way encourage us to transcend the time-bound, ideologically generated category of 'the nation' and to embrace global, transnational perspectives. For example, David Schneer, a historian, and Caryn Aviv, a sociologist, argue in *New Jews: The End of the Jewish Diaspora*, that globalisation, economic prosperity and political stability have created 'a new Jewish map', one that transcends the notion of periphery (the Diaspora) and centre (the

Land of Israel). The old binary, they believe, prevents us from understanding the ways in which Jews craft their identities wherever they make their homes.[12] Of course, it could be argued that Jewish historians embedded their work in transnational perspectives long before the recent vogue for the global, but in the current climate it is assumed that to write Jewish history is to posit the existence of a Jewish people or nation whose centre is in the Land of Israel.

The repudiation of nationalism intersects with another current, one that singles out the State of Israel as illegitimate and Jewish nationalism as racist and exclusionary. While these notions are far from triumphant in the academy, they are powerful and seductive, especially since they come bundled with other postmodern attitudes that are widely seen as being on the cutting edge of scholarship. In extreme cases – for example, in the writing of Daniel and Jonathan Boyarin – the postmodern critique of the nation and visceral anti-Zionism combine to empower a privileging of Diaspora – 'a disassociation of ethnicities and political hegemonies as the only social structure that even begins to make possible a maintenance of cultural identities in a world grown thoroughly and inextricably interdependent'. They seek to replace 'national self-determination' as a 'theoretical and historical model' with the idea of Diaspora (which, in my view, is no more or less historically and culturally constructed than 'the nation').[13] In much less explicit ways, the ideological assault on 'the nation' and the demonisation of Jewish nationalism may discourage (and I emphasise *may* for this is speculation) the contextualisation of Anglo-Jewish history in a 'national' (pan-Jewish) context. At a minimum, studying British Jews in a British context alone avoids the potential for awkward confrontations.

Were Anglo-Jewish historians to forge closer ties with modern Jewish historians in Europe, North America and Israel, the work of both parties to the conversation would benefit. Anglo-Jewish historiography would be enhanced by perspectives drawing on the experiences of Jews elsewhere, Jews whose histories were at once both similar and dissimilar to the history of Jews in Britain. A more comparative perspective would encourage Anglo-Jewish historians to question (but not necessarily reject) the categories, terms of analysis and explanatory devices they conventionally invoke, as I suggested earlier in regard to the history of Orthodox Judaism in Britain. Ironically, the use of a comparative context would also highlight what is quintessentially or specifically English about Anglo-Jewish developments and events, for it is comparison alone that can define what is similar and dissimilar. At the very least, engagement with the work of historians who grapple with similar problems in communities elsewhere would inject new energy into Anglo-Jewish historical writing. Optimally, it would also make historians elsewhere take notice of new work in the field and lead them to conclude that they cannot go about their business without knowing what Anglo-Jewish historians are up to. In time, perhaps, the field would attract as diverse a group of historians as does Polish Jewish history or French Jewish history or German Jewish history.

On the other side of the equation, historians of other Jewish communities have much to learn from the best Anglo-Jewish historical writing. Foremost is the robust sense of place that permeates Anglo-Jewish historiography – that is, its acute sensitivity to the ways in which urban landscapes, architectural settings, and social arrangements structured how Jews lived, both expanding and constraining the choices available to them. In Anglo-Jewish historical writing, London, Manchester, Leeds, and Birmingham (their streets, schools, markets, clubs, parks) – as well as the countryside, where urban Jews peddled, rambled, rode and hunted – are lively presences. By contrast, the historiography of Jews in Berlin and Paris lacks colour and specificity. One would think that how and where Jews lived in these two metropolitan centres – the topographical, material and social *realia* of their day-to-day lives – were irrelevant to their histories.

Historians of other Jewish communities could also learn from the prominent role that Anglo-Jewish historical writing assigns to social and economic activity. While historians of other communities tend to privilege the life of politics and the life of the mind over other spheres of activity, Anglo-Jewish historiography accords a respected place to the material and social worlds. Recall V.D. Lipman's study of the social history of English Jewry, published half a century ago, or Bill Williams's account of the growth of the Manchester community, published a quarter century ago.[14] Both were in advance of their time; neither has received the acknowledgment it warrants from historians of modern European Jewry. To be sure, cynics might say that what Anglo-Jewish historians have done is to make a virtue out of a necessity, given the relative impoverishment of Anglo-Jewish intellectual life and the relative calm of Anglo-Jewish political circumstances. But I would argue, on the contrary, that historians of other communities have overvalued the power and reach of formal politics, intellectual creativity and ideological ferment, assigning them a weight in human affairs that they do not warrant. Anglo-Jewish historical scholarship not only restores balance to the scale of forces that determine human behaviour but also demonstrates that social conflict and religious discord can flourish in the absence of self-conscious ideological activity.

I am not suggesting that writing Anglo-Jewish history is an either/or proposition – that the historian must choose one, and only one, framework in which to present his or her story. The challenge, rather, is to invoke two contexts more or less simultaneously. Each context, after all, the pan-Jewish and the British, accesses a different dimension of the past and thus highlights what the other might obscure. As I noted above, the historian needs to explain both why Disraeli succeeded in Victorian politics and why, at the same time, he was dogged every step of the way by anti-Semitism. The challenge is to keep two contexts in play more or less simultaneously – to juggle them, keeping both aloft. The task is challenging, but not impossible.

NOTES

1. I am thinking of David Ruderman's two books on Anglo-Jewish intellectual history – *Jewish Enlightenment in an English Key: Anglo-Jewry's Construction of Modern Jewish Thought* (Princeton, NJ: Princeton University Press, 2000) and *Connecting the Covenants: Judaism and the Search for Christian Identity in Eighteenth-Century England* (Philadelphia: Princeton University Press, 2007) – and my own work.
2. David Feldman, *Englishmen and Jews: Social Relations and Political Culture, 1840–1914* (New Haven, CT: Yale University Press, 1994), p.379.
3. Ibid. pp.387–8.
4. Ibid. p.13.
5. Moshe Rosman, *How Jewish Is Jewish History?* (Oxford: Littman Library of Jewish Civilization, 2007), chapter 4.
6. Jonathan Freedman, *Klezmer America: Jewishness, Ethnicity, Modernity* (New York: Columbia University Press, 2008), p.15.
7. Bryan Cheyette and Laura Marcus, eds., *Modernity, Culture, and 'the Jew'* (Cambridge: Polity Press, 1998). pp.2–3.
8. Todd M. Endelman, *England – Good or Bad for the Jews?*, The Jubilee Parkes Lecture, May 2002, Parkes Institute Pamphlet No.3 (Southampton, 2003).
9. Benjamin James Elton, 'Britain's Chief Rabbis, the Jewish Encounter with Modernity and the Remoulding of Tradition, c. 1880–1970' (Ph.D. diss., Birkbeck College, University of London, 2007).
10. Miri J. Freud-Kandel, *Orthodox Judaism in Britain since 1913: An Ideology Forsaken* (London: Vallentine Mitchell, 2006), pp.63, 108–109.
11. Rosman, *How Jewish Is Jewish History?*, p.4.
12. Caryn Aviv and David Shneer, *New Jews: The End of the Jewish Diaspora* (New York: New York University Press, 2005). Shneer summarises their argument in 'We Are All Global Jews Now' in the *Jewish Chronicle*, 15 August 2008, p.29.
13. Daniel Boyarin and Jonathan Boyarin, 'Diaspora: Generation and the Ground of Jewish Identity', *Critical Inquiry*, 19 (Summer 1993), 693–725 (pp.717, 723).
14. Vivian David Lipman, *Social History of the Jews in England, 1850–1950* (London: Watts, 1954); Bill Williams, *The Making of Manchester Jewry, 1740–1875* (Manchester: Manchester University Press, 1976).

WAR, CONFLICT AND THE NATION

Between Integration and Separation: Jews and Military Service in World War I Britain

ANNE LLOYD

The scale and duration of World War 1 forced the state to place unprecedented demands on the British population, not least on the Jewish community which, since the eighteenth century, had led a largely self-regulatory existence under the guidance of its first national communal body, the Board of Deputies of British Jews, drawn from the Anglo-Jewish hierarchy.[1] By the late nineteenth century, a complex infrastructure of inter-related organisations, both secular and religious, had been established in the attempt to control the wider community.

In the four decades before August 1914, both majority/minority relations and intra-communal harmony had become more problematical for the traditional leadership to negotiate. Rapid, large-scale migration of Eastern European Jews to Britain had placed severe social and economic strains on London's East End and other areas of immigrant settlement in Britain's larger cities, resulting in growing public antagonism towards the alien sector of the community.[2] Anglo-Jews feared that this hostility would escalate to eventually compromise their own hard-won place in the nation, and the economic, political and social advances achieved since emancipation. Anxious to dissuade the government from direct intervention, and to retain their own 'policing' role in the community, positive action was taken through their network of philanthropic bodies. They attempted to deter further immigration through publicity within the Russian Pale, encouraged the transmigration of 25,000 new arrivals, mainly to the United States and secured the repatriation to Russia and Poland of over 30,000 aliens who had arrived within the previous seven years.[3]

For the many thousands of immigrants who remained, a major aim of Anglo-Jewry's charitable initiatives was to effect their rapid

Anglicisation, particularly by targeting the young. By the 1870s the Jews' Free School, which had been opened in 1817 and was largely financed by the Rothschilds, encouraged the wiping away of 'all evidence of foreign birth and foreign proclivities' from the 1,700 boys and 1,000 girls on its roll.[4] In the late nineteenth and early twentieth centuries, a variety of clubs had been established to transform working class immigrant youths into fit and respectable 'Englishmen of the Mosaic persuasion'.[5] While earlier literature assessed community relations as relatively free from conflict, it has more recently been suggested that the decades before World War 1 witnessed not only the polarisation of the so-called 'West End' and 'East End' Jews but an increasing resentment between the two groupings.[6]

In academic debate in 1831 Germany, the Jewish lawyer Gabriel Riesser had stated that 'There is only one baptism that can initiate one into a nationality, and that is the baptism of blood in the common struggle for a fatherland and for freedom'.[7] Ricsser's pronouncement resonated for Jews in Britain nearly a century later. During a rather piecemeal emancipation process, the nation had remained free of major conflict and hence the expectation of military service. Even so, over 1,200 Jews had voluntarily offered themselves to auxiliary units of the British Army in the Boer War.[8] When HMG declared war on the Central Powers on 4 August 1914, Anglo-Jews had already voiced their repugnance for Britain's ally, Russia, in the marginalisation and persecution of its Jewish minority.[9] But they fully recognised the imperative of military service to their own emancipation contract, and the pressing challenge to Britain's Jews of a war that was engulfing much of Europe.

The uneasy balance of the community which had evolved during *fin de siècle* came under increased pressure from the demands of the British state at war, particularly over military service. The British government also became aware that its Jewish minority contained an immigrant sector which had become less pliable and responsive to its own traditional leadership. Anglo-Jews were forced to confront the complexities of identity in their conspicuous co-operation with the machinery of state while being all too aware of the reactions to army service of a gamut of young Jewish men whose social, cultural, religious and political consciousness diverged so widely from their own. The activities of the principal Anglo-Jewish wartime committees concerned with military service, and their effects on Jews of military age, form the basis of exploration of such dilemmas. Their independent campaigns to enlist British and foreign Jews, together with their role as advisor to the military authorities on the army's first significant inclusion of Jewish soldiers, expose the essential dichotomy of integration and separation at a time of national crisis.

Anglo-Jews and the Voluntary Enlistment Campaign

An estimated total of 41,500 Jews from Britain were serving in His Majesty's Imperial Forces by 1918.[10] A little over 25 per cent, mostly young men from long-established Jewish families, had joined up during the period of voluntary enlistment which ended in early 1916.[11] By far the greater proportion were conscripts and more 'recent' British citizens: 20,000 army recruits were naturalised British subjects, and many others were first generation.[12] Also included in the overall community contribution were 8,000 Russian Jews conscripted in 1917/18.

Before World War 1 most 'new' British Jews had continued to work and live in London's East End and other urban immigrant areas where shared history and tradition played an important part in their self-perceptions of identity. This included a historic antipathy towards warfare and warriors, rooted in experiences in Russia, which remained significant in their collective memory.[13] The transition period from ethnicity to a sense of 'national belonging' remains highly controversial in terms of time lag, and it has been suggested that many Jews in early twentieth century Britain led 'a double life' in their notions of identity.[14] For the majority of 'newer' British Jews, their sense of 'citizenship' was less developed, and they consequently felt less compelled to join up as an expression of national identity. Many had struggled economically since their arrival in Britain, and could anticipate the demands of a rapidly growing army for uniforms, boots and saddles, and wooden camp furniture, which their traditional trades could profitably supply.

Most assimilated Jews joined the army with similar attitudes and expectations to their non-Jewish fellow recruits. Many young men from immigrant families who had come under the anglicising influence of the Jews' Free School and the Jewish youth movement in their formative years were swift to enlist.[15] By contrast, prior to 1914 the domestic lives of thousands of other more recent arrivals in Britain had centred on 'indoors' and family, far removed from the 'threats and practices of the Gentile world'.[16] Military service, with the probability of isolation from their co-religionists in a masculine, Spartan environment with its outdoor drills and military customs, quite apart from the horrors of front-line battle, was an intimidating prospect. Many elite Anglo-Jews, such as Basil Henriques, who served as a Tank Corps officer in World War I, were convinced that pre-war segregation and ignorance of English customs had done much to aggravate ill feeling against the alien sector of the community, and hoped that army life would encourage greater cohesion.[17] Immigrant military service appeared to offer Anglo-Jews the completion of their own anglicising efforts, which had often been rejected and resented in the past.

In the first weeks of the war the British government established a national cross-party Parliamentary Recruiting Committee (PRC), which quickly realised not only that the initial rush to volunteer for military service was dwindling but that the public anticipated a short-lived war requiring minimal numbers of new recruits.[18] To raise national awareness, a Householders' Return of males between the ages of 19 and 35 was carried out, and in the following six months a publications sub-committee issued 20 million rallying leaflets and two million posters in Britain and the Empire.[19] The PRC appealed to British Jews to join up in November 1914, as they did to other religious groups. The Chief Rabbi, the Very Reverend Joseph Hertz, immediately issued a leaflet which was widely circulated in the community calling for it to perform the supreme duty and prove the old Maccabean spirit was still alive.[20] A further direct approach by the PRC was made to young Jewish workers a year later. The appeal, in Yiddish, cited past support by the British labour movement for their welfare and called upon their sense of honour and gratitude to defend the civil rights granted to them in Britain.[21]

Accusations that Jews were shirking their obligations as citizens appeared from the early weeks of the war, as indeed they had done in the Boer War.[22] These stemmed to a considerable extent from *fin de siècle* pseudo-science which purported to classify the Jewish male as feminised, physically and psychologically unfit for soldiering, with the implicit association of cowardice: indeed, Sharman Kadish has suggested that the 'image of the Jew as a soldier jarred in the eyes of both Jews and non-Jews certainly until the creation of the State of Israel in 1948'.[23] Before the passing of the first Military Services Act in January, 1916, a succession of Anglo-Jewish recruiting initiatives, independent of the national campaign, had been undertaken to exhibit the community's loyalty by maximising its voluntary contribution. The majority of assimilated Jews were anxious to emphasise their Britishness at a time of national crisis, but some, in particular those with Zionist sympathies, such as Dr David Eder, wanted the Jewish identity to be openly displayed through the creation of a distinctly Jewish unit:

> The idea of a Jewish Battalion had been accepted in the first weeks of the war by Zangwill, Greenberg, Joseph Cowen and myself ... We meant Jews to play as Jews any part for which they were called, so that the Jewish nationality and the Jewish nation should not be left out of the final adjustment. It was left to me, as the most detached from the groupings, to start a campaign. The military first welcomed, and, when success seemed assured, converted the scheme, under Anglo-Jewish influence, into futility.[24]

As a result of Anglo-Jewish intervention at the War Office by Michael Adler, the Senior Chaplain, Jews were invited to serve together in special units similar to the ethos of the Pals' Battalions but with no specifically Jewish identity. Ironically, Eder was invited to open the first Jewish recruitment office in Aldgate East in December, 1914, and the *Jewish Chronicle* published the call: 'Jews! Fall In!! Serve with your fellow Jews'.[25] Unsurprisingly, there was little interest in the scheme either from the majority who wished to be fully integrated into Regular Army regiments or from those who had pressed for a Jewish military identity. According to Adler, the army authorities considered themselves misled by Eder's group and 'withdrew all their official sanction'.[26]

Prompted by growing Anglo-Jewish concern over poor enlistment levels in the East End among naturalised and first-generation British-born Jews, the Jewish Recruitment Committee was formed a few weeks later. It was largely composed of those Anglo-Jews who had been figureheads in the immigrant youth organisations, and included Denzil Myer, Honorary Secretary and Chairman of the Stepney Jewish Lads' Club, Sir Frederic Nathan, Commandant of the Jewish Lads' Brigade, Charles Sebag-Montefiore, Honorary Secretary of the Victoria Boys' Club and Arthur Joseph, Chairman of the Brady Street Boys' Club.[27] Past members of such clubs had readily responded to the call to arms in the first weeks of the war, and it was presumably hoped that the Committee members' previous experience would bear further fruit among the more reluctant young men of the East End. Success appears to have been somewhat limited as at the end of June 1915 Lord Kitchener asked the committee why young and suitable men were not 'availing themselves of the opportunity to see service'.[28] Broadening the scope of its activities, the Committee encouraged Jewish soldiers to canvass for recruits during home leave, and large employers of labour were urged to release some of their young workers for the army.[29] The Jews' Free School provided an exemplar, granting their teachers every opportunity to enlist by guaranteeing reinstatement without loss of salary and status after the war, and the maintenance of full pension arrangements.[30]

When Lord Derby, the new Director-General of Recruiting, introduced his national plan to secure group attestations of future military service rather than pressing for immediate enlistment, he gave an undertaking that Jews who joined up together in batches before 30 November would be kept together in the army.[31] Following the overall failure of the Derby Scheme and in the vanguard of the conscription, the War Office established an official Jewish link to continue to press for voluntary enlistment until the implementation of the Military Service Act and to advise the army authorities on the implications of military service for Jewish recruits.[32] The new body, the Central Jewish Recruiting Committee, later renamed the Jewish War Services Committee (JWSC), was led by members of the Anglo-Jewish hierarchy prominent in British civic and political life, notably Edmund Sebag-Montefiore and Major Lionel de Rothschild, MP, and established its offices at New Court, the premises of the N.M. Rothschild Bank. There appears to have been little response to Derby's invitation as, anxious to ameliorate the immigrants' continuing reluctance to serve, the committee informed the War Office that many had been willing to enlist under the scheme but had been refused because their names 'sounded foreign'.[33]

Increasingly anxious about the negative perceptions of the War Office, the press and the British public, the Anglo-Jewish recruiting committees had worked independently, and with mounting fervour, to improve the community's enlistment record. It would appear that the reluctance of much of the immigrant sector to join up can be partly attributed to cultural and economic factors, as well as to its still nascent sense of Britishness. Although the Anglo-Jewish monopoly of independent recruitment initiatives was a natural extension of their traditional role in the community, it may also have deterred those who had resented efforts to re-direct their private lives away from ethnic custom and tradition in the years before the war.

The campaigns also present a certain paradox. Anglo-Jewry's over-arching concern for the community to be regarded as an integral part of the nation at war might suggest that the voluntary enlistment of British Jews should have rested purely in the hands of the state, namely the PRC and the army. Their anxiety to be seen as fulfilling the ultimate responsibility of citizenship clearly overrode this consideration, but may have served to endorse national perceptions of Jewish exclusivity and separation.

The JWSC and the Recruitment of Russian Jews

By far the greater challenge to Anglo-Jewry arose over the British government's *volte face* in 1916 over 'friendly aliens' of military age, which included about 30,000 Russian Jews. In August 1914 they had been officially barred from voluntary enlistment by state legislation, but in November 1915 Lord Derby advised Anglo-Jewry of an imminent policy reversal, and warned that in the event of conscription Russian Jews would be forcibly recruited into the army.[34] Reflecting its responses to government concerns at *fin de siècle*, the leadership immediately lent active support to the change in policy. Even before the matter came into the public arena, the JWSC had lobbied the army Adjutant-General on several occasions, urging the military inclusion of Russian Jews, and offering its administrative machinery to investigate immigrant *bona fides*.[35] It also set the expectation that Russian Jews were only awaiting the opportunity to serve, having felt previously 'snubbed in their desire to show gratitude to the country which had offered them safe shelter'.[36] However, Herbert Samuel, the newly appointed Jewish Home Secretary, described by David Cesarani as occupying 'an exquisitely agonising position', was warned by the editor of the *Jewish Chronicle* that the British public made no differentiation between Jew and Jew, and that 'to have left the Russian born Jew in our midst outside service to this country must have fixed that sentiment to the permanent hurt of the Anglo-Jews'.[37]

The JWSC, well aware of the bitter opposition of Russian immigrants to its pro-government stance, was obliged to adopt a low profile in the enlistment drive in the East End, and its role was taken up briefly by Lucien Wolf, Secretary of the Conjoint Foreign

Committee of British Jews. In addition to his own initiatives, Wolf encouraged the JWSC to take covert action and issue rallying leaflets and posters in Yiddish in the immigrant areas, but to 'let it be a bolt from the blue, quite anonymous'.[38] By this time, Edmund Sebag-Montefiore had become a member of the government's Alien Enlistment Committee, established in June 1916, to progress the forthcoming conscription of Russian Jews.

During a short period of voluntary enlistment as the precursor to conscription, Police Alien Records of male Russians between the ages of 18 and 41 were used to compile lists for perusal by the JWSC. By 25 October, the committee had issued over 1,500 certificates of eligibility, although they eschewed to recommend military suitability.[39] Only 400 or so volunteers came forward. While the JWSC remained largely *sotto voce* in the East End, Secretary Stephany officially informed the Home Secretary that it was 'the unanimous desire of HM subjects of the Jewish faith that the services of their Russian born co-religionists should be placed at the disposal of the Imperial Government at this time'.[40] This recommendation formed part of Cabinet deliberations on 31 October. The legal mechanism to conscript took almost a year to accomplish, and during this time the JWSC continued to encourage alien enlistment, sometimes indirectly through association with Russian Jews, but with virtually no success.[41] Meanwhile War Office officialdom professed itself increasingly exasperated with the 'opinions of prominent, over-age Jews'.[42] Gentile political supporters of the Russian Jews in Parliament, such as the Liberal MP Joseph King, railed against the army's partnership with the JWSC

> It was a fatal mistake to put the recruiting of Russian Jews into the hands of the people at New Court in the City. The Army should use people who know the psychology and mentality of the people affected.[43]

Through their pre-war charitable work in the East End, Anglo-Jews had become well aware of the psyche of the Russian Jews. But any sympathy they might have had for Jewish foreign nationals being forcibly inducted into another country's army was sublimated by their fear of adverse public reaction directed at the whole community.

When the Convention with Russia was signed in July 1917, legalising the conscription of Russian immigrants in Britain, both Anglo-Jewry and the army were under the impression that recruits would be trained together before being drafted to regiments throughout the army, wherever needed. Indeed the JWSC was invited to recommend suitable officers for such training units. The government's sudden announcement of a new, discrete Jewish battalion, principally it now appears for geo-political propaganda reasons, shocked many Anglo-Jews, and Leopold Greenberg professed his astonishment that Lionel de Rothschild, 'virtually an adjunct of the War Office', had been entirely ignored.[44] Anglo-Jews were to be further disillusioned by HMG's decision in March 1918 to relegate large numbers of Russian Jews to the Labour Battalions, which appeared to stigmatise them as 'hewers of wood and drawers of water', a derogatory image of inferiority which they feared would reflect on the whole community.[45]

Throughout the war, dilemmas of identity faced the wartime organisations over the integration of Jews into British military service. Anglo-Jewry's dominance over the lines of communication between the army and all Jewish soldiers, many of whom perceived their identity in ways far removed from that of assimilated Jews, lay at the root of further dissension.

Faith under Fire: Jewish Chaplains and the London Committees

In the early summer of 1916, the JWSC became the sole liaison body with the War Office on all matters of military service. Prior to conscription, the Visitation Committee of the United Synagogue, whose members had no direct connections either with the military authorities or state departments, had acted as an intermediary between the Jewish soldier and the War Office for all matters other than recruiting. The wide scope of the committee's work encompassed meetings with War Office officials, the selection of Jewish chaplains, the negotiation of special leave for the major Jewish festivals, the visit of the Chief Rabbi to the Western Front in 1915, the compilation and issue of a Jewish prayer book and other religious literature to troops, and the appropriate marking of Jewish graves on the battlefields.[46]

For the first few months of the war, the Visitation Committee's responsibilities for the religious welfare of Jewish soldiers were restricted to the needs of servicemen in training camps in Britain where the War Office had authorised 'special religious ministrations' for regiments containing sufficient numbers of Jewish soldiers. The only channel of religious support for those on the battlefields was through correspondence with the Senior Jewish Chaplain. Complaints soon appeared in the Anglo-Jewish press that there were no ministers at the Front to conduct burial services for fallen soldiers or to offer spiritual comfort to the wounded.[47]

Due to the influence of the Jewish MP Sir Charles Henry, and with the approval of the army Chaplain-General, Adler was permitted to visit Jewish troops in France to explore the possibilities for padres of their faith to support them on the battlefields. Following his investigations, and notwithstanding some War Office delay in permitting chaplains to work on the battlefields, not confined to Jews alone, in mid January 1915 he was given leave of absence by the Visitation Committee and appointed Chaplain, 4th class, with the equivalent army rank of Captain, and left for France shortly afterwards.[48] He was the first Jewish chaplain to minister on the battlefield, and wore the Star of David on his uniform in *lieu* of the traditional chaplain's badge. By 1918, there was a total of 18 padres on active service throughout Salonika, Palestine and Egypt as well as on the Western Front, with an additional chaplain on Home Service stationed with Southern Command at Aldershot.[49] They formed part of the body of over 4,500 padres of all denominations as commissioned officers in the army Chaplains' Department between 1914 and 1919.[50]

The Christian *credo* played a prominent role in the army's management of morale in World War 1. It was perceived both as an opiate and a source of ideological uplift in the brutalising context of killing and suffering, and measures to strengthen religious feeling were regarded as highly desirable to justify the necessity and justice of the allied cause.[51] Field Marshal Haig, Commander-in-Chief of the British Expeditionary Forces from 1915, had recommended that every chaplain should be a vehicle for patriotic instruction so that, as a result of their teaching, all ranks would come to know and understand the 'great and noble objects' for which they were fighting.[52] In the opinion of many Jewish 'Tommies', this message, which glorified war and personal sacrifice, was contemptible to their own religious faith, and a snare to be guarded against.[53]

Adler's background before 1914 was one of scholarship and a commitment to narrowing the Jewish/Gentile divide. His ecumenical interests had been guided by Chief Rabbi Herman Adler, who encouraged Jewish scholars to address learned Gentile societies on all manner of Jewish topics. Having served the Hammersmith synagogue for 13 years, he found preferment in 1903 in the Central Synagogue, which he was then to serve for 31 years. He was commissioned into the Territorial Army in 1909, and ministered to the small number of Jews then serving in the Regular British Army.[54] His continuing interest in promoting an understanding of Jewish history and the spirit of Judaism to non-Jewish troops and padres, most of whom had little or no contact with Jews before the war, formed an important facet of his wartime ministry in France and that of his colleagues, all largely based in Casualty Clearing Stations.[55]

Throughout the war and on all battlefronts, the common complaint of Jewish soldiers was the dearth of chaplains of their own faith and the resulting lack of religious services, particularly when contrasted with those available to their Christian comrades.[56] Of the total number of chaplains serving overseas by the Armistice, a third were not appointed until 1918.[57] On average, an Anglican padre in the British Army supported about 1,000 troops compared with a Jewish chaplain's responsibility for twice that number under the stewardship of the Visitation Committee and subsequently the JWSC.[58] In 1918, when the number of Jewish chaplains serving on the battlefields had reached its maximum, a soldier with the 10th Royal Fusiliers on the Western Front complained

> I have been out here for three years and do not think we have had more than five services in the whole period. We see our Christian colleagues attending services every week and it makes us Jews feel we are being neglected.[59]

The shortage of chaplains resulted from a combination of factors: a reticence by the Anglo-Jewish military *liaison* committees to press for them with army authorities, occasional War Office refusal to sanction, and a lack of volunteers to serve in combat zones.[60] Adler was acutely conscious of the privations this caused to Jewish servicemen and made numerous appeals to the JWSC in London for additional support but he was equally concerned that the reputation of Jews and Judaism among non-Jews would be damaged.[61] Exacerbating the lack of religious support for Jewish soldiers was the absence of motorised transport for chaplains, obliged to cover wide distances between servicemen, who were often isolated in their units. Anglican padres were attached to specific regiments and were automatically carried with them on the battlefields while their Jewish colleagues were obliged to walk, ride or hitch lifts on army lorries. Only the Senior Chaplain had the use of a car and a military driver given to him by Field Marshal French, which he acknowledged as essential to his duties.[62]

It was not just the paucity of religious support that angered many Jewish troops. Some more orthodox soldiers were also critical of what they considered to be 'adapted services', conducted by chaplains in English rather than Hebrew.[63] The different practices and patterns of religious observance followed by the United Synagogue, from which Jewish chaplains were largely drawn, was a cause of dissension among those immigrant troops accustomed to the form of synagogue and *chevra* services in the Federation of Synagogues, formed in 1887. Some complained that Jewish chaplains had assumed a mandate to introduce certain reforms at the Front, which they feared would inevitably lead to a dilution of Judaism after the war. The accusation was strongly refuted by Adler, who claimed that the chaplains' primary concern was to keep Jewish consciousness alive in adverse conditions.[64]

The problem over the form of services was circumvented by the 38th battalion RF (later gazetted as the Judaeans). Rejecting the JWSC's recommendation, it made its own choice of chaplain to accompany the men to Palestine, and selected the Reverend Lieb Falk, a recent immigrant and rabbi at a local Plymouth synagogue, who had to be naturalised before he could become an officer in the army Chaplain's Department.[65]

Supporting troops on the battlefields as part of an integrated body within the British Army's infrastructure was a totally new experience for Jewish padres to negotiate. But the often disparate responses of Jewish soldiers to their efforts appears to underscore the religious diversity which flourished within the community in civilian life before 1914, a factor to which the London Committees' provision and selection of chaplains appears to have paid little heed.

Queens Regulations for the British Army were revised in 1886 to officially recognise Judaism, largely through the efforts of Colonel Albert Goldsmid, co-founder of the Jewish Lads' Brigade, and Private Woolf Cohen.[66] Since then it had been accepted army practice to grant leave for major religious festivals to the small number of Jewish troops in HM Forces. During the war, the committees' leave applications were usually granted for troops on Home Service, although not always to the full extent requested, and often included the proviso of 'circumstances permitting'.[67] The *Jewish Chronicle* consistently acknowledged 'the thoughtful regard always extended to members of the Jewish faith' by the army authorities, and on the first Christmas of the war encouraged Jewish soldiers to offer duty in return for their own special privileges.[68] In times of military crisis, while the War Office expressed sympathy, leave was refused, e.g for the celebration of Passover in 1915.[69] And in 1917, the War Office refused the JWSC's request for Passover leave for Jewish soldiers in Britain for reasons of equality. Due to the curtailment of railway transport for troops, all leave was cancelled and it was considered to be 'inequitable to make a concession to one body of men in the Army which would have to be denied to the rest'.[70]

On the Western Front, Adler remained concerned throughout the war that the issue of leave for Jewish soldiers might be perceived as a special privilege by their Christian comrades, and become a marker of separation. On one occasion he overruled General Birdwood's sanction for Passover leave for ANZAC soldiers, much to the chagrin of the Australian padre, the Reverend Freedman, and the troops concerned.[71] It would seem that Adler's anxieties were not unfounded as a young British soldier, George Coppard, testified:

> There was only one person I knew whose professed religious beliefs did him any good, and that was a Jew named Levinsky. He came to our company on a draft, and had only been with us for about four weeks when he was given a week's leave in Blighty to attend ceremonies in connection with the Passover. It is not difficult to imagine the feelings of the Gentiles in the company who had been in France for a year with no leave, or any hope of any in the foreseeable future.[72]

Behind battlefield lines, Adler's services in celebration of the major festivals, for which he had taken a portable Ark and the Scrolls of Law from England, attracted large numbers of soldiers from a wide area. Two services were held in a cinema in Baupaume for Jewish troops of the 3rd Army in September 1917, attended by over 2,700 men.[73] During 1915 the army had devised a system to advise soldiers of such services: specially printed invitation cards were sent by General Headquarters, British Expeditionary Forces, to those registered as Jews in army records, who were required to apply for permission to attend from their commanding officers. Notices of Services were also published in Army Orders.[74] Occasionally the army provided transport to bring the troops to services, such as for Yom Kippur near Arras in 1916, when Divisional HQ allotted lorries which, Adler acknowledged, 'saved them the fatigue of a long tramp'.[75]

It appears that Jewish servicemen in training camps in Britain were not officially excused military duties on Saturday mornings, and a considerable number chose not to attend religious services in the afternoons, preferring to go to football matches with their friends or to the cinema.[76] How far this was religious disinterest or fear of being regarded as an 'outsider' by Christian comrades is debatable. However, there would appear to be some latitude on the issue at the regimental level and many Jews were excused Sabbath duties by their unit officers to attend local synagogues.[77]

For the first few months of the war, fallen Jewish soldiers were frequently buried, either in ignorance or through insensitivity, under improvised crosses, a matter of distress to their co-religionist comrades, which filtered back to the community at home. Through the auspices of the Visitation Committee, Adler, in consultation with Major Fabian Ware of the Graves Registration Commission, made arrangements in mid-1915 for Jewish graves to be marked, wherever possible, with a wooden Star of David. The Christian symbol was also removed from existing graves and replaced with the Jewish memorial peg.[78]

The London committees were never successful in securing the provision of *kosher* food for Jewish troops in Regular Army regiments. JWSC leaders who liaised directly with the War Office may have transmitted, consciously or unconsciously, a measure of religious ambivalence based on their own practices. In the decades preceding the war, Todd Endelman has suggested that the elite of Anglo-Jewry had become content to observe religious traditions that did not overly inconvenience them, preferring a Judaism that stressed 'reasonable behaviour, fraternal responsibility, intellectual courtesy and communal charity'. In this, they echoed the dilution of Victorian religiosity, where the old routines of Christianity became transmuted into a matter of good taste.[79]

This hypothesis may extend to observations and comments by Jewish chaplains and soldiers that officers, drawn almost entirely from the Anglo-Jewish middle class, rarely attended religious services either on Home Service or on the battlefields. At the Jewish Chaplains' Conference in 1918, it was noted that officers were 'conspicuous in their anxiety not to be recognised as Jews, or at least not to be identified with their religious practices'.[80] Although padres generally attributed their absence to 'pure moral cowardice', it may rather have reflected a more relaxed approach to religious observance among the middle and upper classes of Anglo-Jewry.

At the beginning of the war Lord Kitchener had given an undertaking that where Jews chose to serve together in army units, appropriate food would be provided. In the event, most volunteers preferred to be integrated throughout the army rather than separated in a way that marked their 'difference'. As a result, the army authorities claimed that the provision of *kosher* food was impractical due to 'military exigencies'. This decision had undoubtedly deterred some from enlisting voluntarily, but became more crucial when conscription forced military service on orthodox British Jews for whom dietary laws were fundamental to their religious observance. Anticipating the distress this would cause, a serving chaplain, Reverend Lipson, had suggested to the Chief Rabbi that he declare a temporary dispensation on *kosher* food for the duration of the war.[81]

Shortly after the JWSC became the sole medium between the Jewish soldier and the War Office, the Chief Rabbi expressed his concerns over *kashruth* to its Vice President, Lionel de Rothschild, and his strong desire that appropriate food should be made available, at least for those in training. Rothschild's views on Jewish religious observances in the army plainly aligned with those of the military authorities

> I do not understand your requirement that men should be able to observe the Sabbath. The disadvantages in Jews not training on a Saturday would be very great and would cause confusion. Nor is it possible for *kosher* food to be provided in this country because Jews are spread throughout all regiments.[82]

Whether the army was unconvinced of the need, unable or unwilling to provide appropriate food for observant Jews, it had no objection to arrangements 'for *matzos* being sent to Jewish soldiers or brought back by them on return from leave and to their using them in place of bread during Passover'.[83] In the early months of the war there had been a Jewish plan for *matzos* to be distributed to troops in France through a society in Paris, funded either by private sources or through an appeal in the Jewish press, but this failed to materialise and it appears that no further attempts were made.[84]

The issue of *kosher* food for Jewish servicemen came into the public domain in the spring of 1917, after it was raised in Parliament by Sir John Randles, MP. Comparisons were drawn in the press with the special provisions made for Indian troops in France but their argument was unsound as discrete Indian regiments were not part of the Regular British Army, and were provisioned and financed by the *Sirkar*, the Indian government.[85] In response to Randles' questioning, the House of Commons was informed by MacPherson, Under-Secretary of State for War, that while the supply of *kosher* food was impractical, army authorisation would be given for Jewish troops on Home Service to receive a monetary allowance in *lieu* of rations in connection with Jewish festivals. He claimed that 'this had gone a long way to meet the requirements of the Jewish religion'.[86] In practice, this small gesture proved largely futile as 'appropriate food' was generally unavailable for purchase in many isolated training areas.

Strictly orthodox Jews found army life demanded great sacrifices. In training in Britain they were often sent food by their families, and on combat duty went to great lengths to avoid transgressing their Judaic principles. Some openly decried the acceptance of *trifah* army rations by their co-religionists, one soldier commenting that he

> always found it tragic to reflect that compulsory Christian food and atmosphere, which was to my own father the worst thing of service in the Russian Army, should be accepted, even welcomed, in England by conscripts and volunteers who surely could have made their own conditions.[87]

When the War Cabinet pressed the army into creating a separate battalion of Russian Jews in the summer of 1917, Lord Derby, then Secretary of State for War, acknowledged that special dietary provision, where possible, and a rest day on the Sabbath was a 'coveted privilege', unavailable to all other Jewish troops.[88] *Kashruth* remained a highly vexed question to the large number of orthodox conscripts throughout the army, and in March 1918 the JWSC was urged to approach the War Office to request the transfer of such men to the two special Russian battalions, 38th and 39th Royal Fusiliers.[89] By this time the 38th was at full strength, and the 39th awaited the arrival of Russian Jewish troops from the United States.[90]

How far *kashruth* actually prevailed for troops of the Jewish battalions remains questionable. One recruit in training claimed that the food was no different to that in other army regiments, apart from

Holy Days when *matzos* and wine were made available, and there was an option of buying fish from a trader on the periphery of the camp.[91] He also admitted that 'everyone was glad to eat non-*kosher* food', an observation reinforced by Horace Samuel's memories of his service in Palestine where the Jewish lines were littered with empty bacon tins (army breakfast rations).[92]

There had been little precedent of Jewish military service in the Regular Army before 1914 and it follows that the military authorities had limited experience of accommodating religious and cultural difference. This implies that the advisory role of the United Synagogue Visitation Committee and the JWSC in wartime was seminal to the military lives of a significant and diverse body of Jewish troops. While some anomalies were addressed by the JWSC, such as the proper marking of war graves, many soldiers remained dissatisfied with the committee's provision of religious support in comparison with their Christian comrades. They also resented the direction of the chaplains' services, which appeared to diminish their own ethnic practices in favour of those of Anglo-Jewry. The committees' monopoly in representing Jewish interests to the military authorities was matched by their ready deference to War Office views, possibly reflecting Anglo-Jewish insecurities in wartime but also their own integration into the customs and *mores* of British society. Nevertheless, this resulted in War Office responses, at times insensitive, even dismissive, which ignored the concerns of many Jewish troops. At a lower level in the army many regimental commanders were empathetic with the problems of 'difference' for Jewish soldiers. Private Hyam, who served with the RAMC in Italy, commented that 'the army authorities are anxious to do a hundred-fold more for us to live as Jews than are some of our own people'.[93]

Conclusions

By November 1918, the status of the Anglo-Jewish leadership had been diminished both within the community and in its relationship with the state, in part through the activities of its newly created wartime committees. The problem posed by the conscription of Russian Jews remains central to the literature, and was a major cause of friction and fracture within the Jewish minority.[94] Much to its distress, Anglo-Jewry's support of state policy, albeit in its own interests, had unpalatable outcomes. Despite the pro-active part played by the JWSC in progressing the government's *volte face*, the results fulfilled the worst fears of most Anglo-Jews. Their desire for Jews to be seen by the government and British public as united and fully integrated into the nation's war effort was met with the separation and marginalisation of a sector of the community. The assimilated Jews' *bête noire* of a discrete Jewish military identity crystallised in the shape of the separate battalions of the Royal Fusiliers, which they perceived as a threat to their own reputation as loyal subjects and worthy warriors. Similarly, the *fin de siècle* Gentile image of the Jew as the inferior soldier appeared to be confirmed in the army's deployment of many thousands of Russian Jews in the non-combat role of the Labour Corps.

From the start of the war, Anglo-Jewry's independent efforts to press the community's young men to volunteer and so exhibit their Britishness had distanced them from many in the immigrant sector. When conscription inexorably drew the more reluctant into the army, ethnic identity, which many Jewish soldiers were determined to maintain and protect in military service, was a reality the Visitation and Jewish War Services Committees appeared loath to acknowledge in their advisory capacity at the War Office. By the end of the war, many Jewish servicemen had become disillusioned by the London committees' lack of sensitivity to the sacrifices military service required of them.

NOTES

1. Geoffrey Alderman, 'English Jews or Jews of the English Persuasion: Reflections on the Emancipation of Anglo-Jewry', in *Paths to Emancipation: Jews, States and Citizenship* ed. by Pierre Birnbaum and Ira Katznelson (Princeton, NJ: Princeton University Press, 1995), p.130. The Board was awarded statutory recognition in Britain in 1836.
2. Lloyd Gartner, *The Jewish Immigrant in England, 1870–1914* (London: Vallentine Mitchell, 2001), Appendix. Immigrant numbers from Russia, Russian Poland and Romania rose from 9,574 in 1871 to 99,263 in 1911, the vast majority being Jewish.
3. David Feldman, *Englishmen and Jews: Social Relations and Popular Culture, 1840–1914* (London: Yale University Press, 1994), p.303.
4. Geoffrey Alderman, *Modern British Jewry* (Oxford: Clarendon Press, 1998), p.139.
5. Sharman Kadish, *A Good Jew and a Good Englishman. The Jewish Lads' and Girls' Brigade, 1895–1995* (London: Vallentine Mitchell, 1995), p.39.
6. See Vivian Lipman, *A Century of Social Service, 1859–1959. The Jewish Board of Guardians* (London: Routledge & Kegan Paul, 1959); Mordecai Rozin, *The Rich and the Poor. Jewish Philanthropy and Social Control in Nineteenth century London* (Brighton: Sussex Academic Press, 1999), pp.2–4.
7. Paul Mendes-Flohr and Jehuda Reinharz, *The Jew in the Modern World. A Documentary History* (Oxford: Oxford University Press, 1995), p.145.
8. 'Jews as Soldiers', *The Spectator*, 3 January 1903, in *A Documentary History of Jewish*

Immigration in Britain, 1840–1920 ed. by David Englander (Leicester: Leicester University Press, 1994), p.343.

9. *JC*, 31 July 1914, p.7. At that time, the editor of the *JC* had also expressed the community's abhorrence at the possibility of England going to war against Germany 'with whom she has no quarrel'.
10. Alderman, *Modern British Jewry* (see note 4), p.235.
11. Harold Pollins, 'The Rothschilds as Recruiters for Buckinghamshire in the First World War', http://www.hellfire-corner.demon.uk/snillop.htm.
12. *JC*, 22 January 1922, p.13. The *JC*'s figure may well include approximately 3,000 post-war naturalisations granted to Russian Jewish servicemen, who were offered *gratis* citizenship in return for Army service at the end of the war, National Archives, HO 144/13352, 3 June 1921: certificates of naturalisation granted 1919–21.
13. See Olga Litvak, *Conscription and the Search for Modern Russian Jewry* (Bloomington: Indiana University Press, 2006).
14. Deborah Cohen, 'Who was Who? Race and Jews in Turn of the Century Britain', *Journal of British Studies*, 41.4 (2002), 460–83 (p.479).
15. *JC*, 14 August 1914, p.9; Julia Bush, 'East London Jews and the First World War', *London Journal*, 6.2 (1980), 147–61 (p.148); Kadish, *A Good Jew* (see note 5), p.55.
16. D. Boyarin, '*Goyim Naches* or Modernity and the Manliness of the *Mentsch*, in *Modernity, Culture and 'the Jew'* ed. by Brian Cheyette and Laura Marcus (Cambridge: Polity Press, 1998), p.72.
17. B. Lammers, 'A Superior Kind of English: Jewish Ethnicity and English Identity in London's East End, 1905–1939' (unpublished Ph.D. thesis, Rutgers University, 1997).
18. British Library, MSS 54192A, PRC Minute Book, 21 October 1914.
19. R. Douglas, 'Voluntary Enlistment in the First World War and the Work of the Parliamentary Recruiting Committee', *Journal of Modern History*, 42 (1970), 564–85 (p.568).
20. Southampton University Library, Anglo-Jewish Archives (hereafter AJA), Papers of Chief Rabbi J.H. Hertz, MS 175 AJ 141/2, PRC leaflet 22.
21. Imperial War Museum, Poster PST 12101, February 1916.
22. *JC*, 28 August 1914, p.5: 'critics in certain quarters are asking impatiently what Jews are doing in this crisis to help the motherland'; S. Bayme, 'Jewish leadership and anti-Semitism in England, 1898–1918' (unpublished Ph.D. thesis, Columbia University, 1977), pp.83–4, 87.
23. Sander Gilman, *Franz Kafka, the Jewish Patient* (London: Routledge, 1995), pp.58, 61–2; Kadish, *A Good Jew* (see note 5), p.57.
24. Joseph Hobman, ed., *David Eder. Memoirs of a Modern Pioneer* (London: Victor Gollancz Ltd., 1945), p.135. Joseph Cowen was Eder's brother-in-law, Israel Zangwill a writer and political commentator, and Leopold Greenberg was editor of the *Jewish Chronicle*.
25. *JC*, 25 December 1914.
26. London Metropolitan Archives (hereafter LMA), papers of the Office of the Chief Rabbi, ACC/2805/4/4/1, Adler to Hertz, 26 February 1915. See also David Cesarani, 'An Embattled Minority: the Jews in Britain during the First World War', *Immigrants and Minorities*, 8.1–2 (1989), 61–81 (p.70).
27. LMA, ACC/2805/4/4/6, Denzil Myer to Hertz, 23 March 1915.
28. *JC*, 9 July 1915, p.6.
29. Ibid. 8 October 1915, p.16.
30. Ibid. 21 April 1916, p.6.
31. Ibid. 19 November 1915, p.16, Interview with Lord Derby.
32. Ibid. 10 December 1915, p.9.
33. National Archives (hereafter NA), WO 32/4773, 23 March 1916.
34. *JC*, 19 November 1915, p.16.
35. NA, HO 144/13362, Lord Derby to Herbert Samuel, 17 July 1916, 'As you know, Russian Jews may be accepted for military service on production of a certificate from the Jewish War Services Committee'.
36. NA, WO 32/4773, Edmund Sebag-Montefiore to War Office, 23 March 1916.
37. Ibid. 21 July 1916, p.9; Cesarani, 'An Embattled Minority', p.67.
38. LMA, ACC/3121/C/11/2/9, Wolf to Sebag-Montefiore, 8 September 1916.

39. NA, HO 45/10818/317810, Memo, 24 October 1916.
40. NA, HO 45/10819/318095, JWSC to Home Secretary, 25 October 1916.
41. NA, WO 32/11353, 3 April 1917. One initiative was through 'a very respectable and pleasantly spoken Russian Jew, Morris Aaron, who was prepared to canvass his Socialist friends in the East End' which, to the embarrassment of the JWSC, yielded no volunteers.
42. Ibid. 10 May 1917.
43. Ibid. 15 June 1916.
44. JC, 10 August 1917, p.7. For new insights into the creation of the Jewish battalions, see Martin Watts, *The Jewish Legion and the First World War* (Basingstoke: Palgrave Macmillan, 2004), and James Renton, *The Zionist Masquerade. The Birth of the Anglo-Zionist Alliance, 1914–1918* (Basingstoke: Palgrave Macmillan, 2007), chapter 7.
45. JC, 12 April 1918, p.5.
46. LMA, papers of the United Synagogue, ACC/2712/6/34/7, Committee Secretary to Chairman, 12 November 1915.
47. JC, 4 September 1914, p.10; ibid. 13 November 1914, p.11.
48. LMA, ACC/2712/01/008; Council Minute, 18 January 1915. Anglican and Non-Conformist chaplains were also forbidden passage from England at the beginning of the war by army order; see C. Kerr, 'A Consideration of the Service of British Army Chaplains in WW1, 1914–1918, with reference to War Expectations and Critical Elements in the Literature of Disenchantment' (MA dissertation, University of Birmingham, 1982), p.69.
49. Michael Goldberger, 'An Englishman and a Jew. Reverend V.G. Simmons, ACD', *Medal News* (December 1993), p.14.
50. Kerr, 'A Consideration of the Service of British Army Chaplains' (see note 48), p.145.
51. D. Englander, 'Discipline and Morale in the British Army, 1917–8', in *State, Society and Mobilisation in Europe during the First World War* ed. by John Horne (Cambridge: Cambridge University Press, 1997), p.137.
52. Ibid. p.140.
53. JC, 5 January 1917, p.17; Soldier's letter from France.
54. Arthur Barnett, 'Memorial Address in Honour of Past Presidents, the Reverend Michael Adler, DSO, SCF, BA (1848–1944)', *Transactions of the Jewish Historical Society of England, XV (1939/45)* (London: Edward Goldston, 1946).
55. AJA, Papers of Rev'd Michael Adler, 1915–18, MS 125, AJA 16/4; Diary entry, 12 October 1917, records 'A Lecture on Jewish History' at a CCS in Buisans, and on 6 March 1918, 'A Lecture on the Jews of England'.
56. JC, 3 May 1918, p.24.
57. Goldberger, 'An Englishman' (see note 49), p.14.
58. Joanna Bourke, *An Intimate History of Killing: Face to Face Killing in Twentieth Century Warfare* (London: Granta, 1999), p.258.
59. JC, 22 March 1918, p.14; Letter from Stanley Solomon, 10th Royal Fusiliers.
60. Ibid. 25 October 1918, p.15.
61. LMA, ACC/2805/4/4/1, Adler to Hertz, 19 August 1917.
62. Ibid. Adler to Hertz, 8 February 1915.
63. JC, 19 November 1915, p.23; ibid. 5 October 1917, p.9.
64. Ibid. 26 January 1917, p.17, letter from Lt. Loewe to Editor; ibid. 16 February 1917, p.15, Letter from Senior Chaplain.
65. Cambridge University Library, Papers of Redcliffe Salaman, ADD 8171, Box 4, 10 November 1917.
66. Cecil Roth, 'The Jews in the Defence of Britain, 13th to 19th century', *The Jewish Historical Society of England Transactions, 1939–1945*, XV (London: Edward Goldston, 1946), p.26.
67. LMA, ACC/2805/4/4/1, WO to Adler, 26 January 1915.
68. JC, 4 December 1914, p.16.
69. Ibid. 19 March 1915, p.24.
70. Ibid. 16 March 1917, pp.19–20, letter from B. Cubbit to Secretary, JWSC.
71. AJA, MS 175 AJ 141/2, Adler to Hertz, 12 April 1917.
72. David Lister, *Die Hard, Aby. Abraham Bevistein – the Boy Soldier Shot to Encourage the Others* (Barnsley: Pen & Sword Books Ltd., 2005), p.128.
73. AJA, MS 125 AJ 16/4, diary entries 26 and 27 September 1917.
74. AJA, MS 125 16/1, December 1915.

75. Michael Adler, ed., *British Jewry Book of Honour* (London: Caxton Press, 1922), p.49.
76. LMA, ACC/2805/4/4/1, Chaplain Vivian Simmons to Hertz, 29 April 1918.
77. *JC*, 22 December 1916, p.17, letter from Gunner J. Mendelowitch.
78. *JC*, 2 July 1915, p.12.
79. T. Endelman, 'Communal Solidarity among the Jewish Elite of Victorian London', *Victorian Studies*, 8 (1985), 491–526 (p.501).
80. *JC*, 1 March 1918, p.6.
81. LMA, ACC/2805/4/4/10, 17 March 1916.
82. LMA, ACC/2805/4/4/12, Rothschild to Hertz, 3 April 1916.
83. LMA, papers of Board of Deputies, ACC/3121/A16, letter to WO, 15 March 1915.
84. LMA, ACC/2805/4/4/1, 7 May 1915, letter from Adler.
85. David Omissi, *Indian Voices of the Great War. Soldiers' Letters, 1914–18* (Basingstoke: MacMillan Press, 1999), pp.295, 322.
86. *JC*, 27 April 1917, p.20.
87. Ibid. 27 July 1917, p.10, letter from Pte. Eli Vogel; ibid. 19 October 1917, p.15.
88. Ibid. 14 September 1917, p.8.
89. Ibid. 1 March 1918, p.14.
90. Watts, *The Jewish Legion* (see note 44), Appendix 1, p.244.
91. Imperial War Museum, Sound Archives, 12506, Reel 2, Joseph Plotzker.
92. Horace Samuel, *Unholy Memories of the Holy Land* (London: Hogarth Press, 1930), p.19.
93. *JC*, 30 August 1918, p.9.
94. See Julia Bush, *Behind the Lines: East London Labour, 1914–1919* (London: Merlin Press, 1984); Julia Bush, 'The Ghetto and the Great War', *Jewish Socialist*, 4 (1985/86), 23–4; Sharman Kadish, *Bolsheviks and British Jews: the Anglo-Jewish Community, Britain and the Russian Revolution* (London: Frank Cass, 1992); Harold Shukman, *War or Revolution. Russian Jews and Conscription in Britain, 1917* (London: Vallentine Mitchell, 2006).

Jews, Britons, Empire: And How Things Might be Very Different

MARK LEVENE

'It is a kind of special wisdom with English Jews to be as docile and submissive as only good children should be.'[1]

David Mowschowitch, 1917

'I felt injustice was wrong and that you had to do something about it ... Being Jewish you had this sense of moral responsibility.'[2]

Jude Bloomfield, 1997

Does Anglo-Jewish history operate in parallel universes? The juxtaposition of the two above statements might suggest so. Alas, the *actual* universe that the Jewry of Britain both historically and contemporaneously inhabits has at its hegemonic centre those of the former ilk. Only at its margins does the latter tendency have purchase. Yet if this contribution begins thus by signalling its dissatisfaction with the communal status quo it also does so in the wake of a signal collective protest against that authority. Only some years down the road will historians be able to gauge whether the publication of *A Time to Speak Out* amounted to a paltry ripple in Anglo-Jewry's languid pond, or marked a wave of change dramatically invigorating the pond's potential for life. The book brought together a variety of views from Independent Jewish Voices (IJV) which was originally launched in 2007 to contest the notion that there is consensual British Jewish support for Israel, Zionism, or, more particularly, Israeli policy and behaviour to Palestine and the Palestinians.[3] Against this backdrop this piece seeks to comment on the historic relationship between British Jews and the 'state' and how things might have been – or yet may still become – very different.

*   *   *

In recent years Jewish/non-Jewish interaction, across time, has been increasingly framed in British Jewish studies through the prism of ethnicity. This reflection of a newly vibrant, multicultural Britain is positive and laudable. However, by locating Anglo-Jewry amongst the many migrant communities, even if as something of a forerunner, it runs the danger of misplacing what was *peculiar* to the Jewish relationship to the British state and more exactly that between an elite Jewry and an aggressively expanding military-industrial polity. In part this is a matter of context. Modern British Jewish history happens to be chronologically situated within the confines of a major state building project, one which for a considerable century or more made 'Great Britain' not only a key player in the rise of a globalised Western system/society but in its own right *the* major political and economic power on the world stage. Yet something is clearly more at stake here than the good fortune of British Jews being born and raised under the self-confident flag of the Union Jack: even if much of the old liberal Anglo-Jewish historiography – following in the footsteps of Cecil Roth who sought to celebrate the supposed convergence between British and Jewish 'civilisations' – would like to tell it to us that way.[4]

Rather the issue is of a two-fold variety. Firstly, what brought elite Anglo-Jewry into close proximity to the state apparatus, even to the point – without wishing to overdo the case – of a shared outlook and symmetry of interests? Secondly, and this is ultimately more relevant to the direction of this contribution; in what form did this state: communal-plutocratic nexus impact upon a broader, grass-roots communal self-understanding, and to what degree did this stultify, or more exactly submerge its truly *Judaic* potential?

Of course, one can garner much of the answer to the first question by way of a recent historiography of Anglo-Jewry, including a slew of highly valuable monographs which have concentrated on the Victorian period and beyond.[5] Paradoxically, however, one might still have to reach beyond the specific island story to studies of a Jewish engagement with other European societies to get a handle on some of the forces and factors creating both synergy and tension between Jews and non-Jews in Britain. Yuri Slezkine's recent characterisation of this interplay as one between Mercurians and Apollonians, that is between an intermediary ethno-religious grouping of 'service nomads' and ruling polities, the latter deriving their power by way of extracted revenue from largely land-based peasant societies, has done much to clarify and indeed illuminate the ubiquitous nature of Jewish proximity to centres of dominant power across time and space.[6] The thesis works as much for an emerging English Angevin empire as for later on while also reminding us of the perilous Jewish status as insiders/outsiders. The very fact that Anglo-Jewish existence had to 'resume' almost 400 years on from a caesura to which ritual murder accusation, massacres and total group expulsion were all part of the backdrop may itself suggest how the medieval legacy cast a long shadow across the behaviour and actions of a successive wave of early modern Jewish migrants to these north Atlantic shores.

One paradox of the Slezkine thesis, in fact, is that its Mercurian–Apollian dynamic works best in a traditional corporate state–communal framework. More contemporary concepts of citizenship should in theory make the distinction between different social and religious groups, or classes, as indeed between *indigenes* and incomers, *politically* redundant, just as the very nature of Britain's avant-garde, and indeed accelerated trajectory towards a capitalist-industrial society, should equally suggest foreclosure on any specific Jewish *economic* role in the face of a more generalised Mercurianism.

That the process of eighteenth and nineteenth century British transformation into a modernised polity/society proved altogether more complex and entirely less streamlined than a simple *marxisant* model would allow, has stood as an element of the challenge to those who have to date charted the slow and convoluted path of British Jewish legal integration.[7] Yet the residual hold of quasi-feudal elements within the English or British political and economic order – itself the subject of some famous if sometimes perplexed Marxist studies[8] – has been less readily acknowledged as a factor which might throw further light on the significant role of a largely metropolitan Anglo-Jewish banking and mercantile elite as set against a traditional-cum-modern British ruling class. To be sure, this hardly amounts to an argument for an English *sonderweg*. Jewish plutocracies played even more seminal roles in modern French, German, Italian, Austrian, even Russian state formation, especially when it came to the financing and development of key modernising infrastructural projects, including railways. Yet, arguably, we would need to turn to Pierre Birnbaum and Ira Katznelson's 1995 comparative examination of nineteenth century Jewish elites and their role in communal emancipation within a wider range of European polities, rather than to any British-centred study, to more fruitfully pursue the implications of this communal-cum-state nexus.[9]

One can see too obviously why students of Anglo-Jewry have largely fought shy of this potential line of inquiry. The very notion that some wealthy Jews *were* important economic and – sometimes – political actors in the rise of imperial Britain seems to offer an open invitation to any number of anti-Semitic accusations. And, as we know, especially from the work of Tony Kushner and others, these accusations as expressed especially from the late Victorian period onwards were not simply marginal (the standard liberal apologia) but rather part of a wider, more mainstream British political culture, indeed one which made 'Great Britain' much more *like* continental Europe.[10] Paradoxically, it has become safer from a scholarly standpoint to delimit any analysis of actual elite relationships to a sole examination of the persistence of prejudice. Even the Birnbaum–Katznelson study which in its introduction upped the ante with its suggestion that Jewish 'admission to citizenship ... also implied access to state power and the control of capital'[11] largely failed to goad its other contributors into properly pursuing this promising theme.

The consequences of such avoidance, however, carry their own historiographic deficit. It may, for instance, be difficult in J.A. Hobson's influential 1902 study on imperialism to disentangle that part which by way of accusation against the role of the Rand Lords in the making of the second Boer war is pure anti-Semitism and that part which is a legitimate, often profoundly piercing critique of imperial expansion – and in which the role of – some – 'Jewish' capital was an undoubted factor.[12] The key question for us is whether in the evolution of banking house portfolios, boardroom decision making and state–corporate agendas we might actually be able to garner insight into the nature – or not – of elite communal-cum-state interactions. Looked at from this perspective Hobson's *fin-de-siècle* spotlight on a key South African moment may be particularly apposite. This, after all, was also the moment when New Court – in other words the British Rothschilds – represented 'the biggest concentration of financial capital in the world', in which Lord Rothschild himself was not only leading shareholder in De Beers Consolidated (diamond) Mines, and effectively 'unpaid financial adviser' to Cecil Rhodes' overtly expansionist British South Africa Company (BSAC), but also the crucial backer in the financing of the production of the Maxim automatic machine gun – the same gun which enabled Rhodes' 1890s conquest of Matabeleland. Rothschild also happened at the time to be hugely well connected to some of the most senior British politicians of the day, including former Prime Minister Lord Rosebery, none other than Rothschild's son-in-law.[13]

Again, the question arises: how should we interpret these interrelationships? Through the prism of anti-Semitism what we obviously end up with is a narrative of malevolent international Jewish conspiracy. Through a thoughtful, empirically-driven approach what we might more fruitfully discern is a critical sequence (or is it actually apotheosis?) in the capitalisation of the British imperial project, among whose key underwriters were Jewish banking houses whose role in this development had been both ongoing and arguably fundamental since the mid-eighteenth century, if not earlier. Yet what is notable is that where there have been studies which have dealt with this significant arena of interaction they have rarely been from the standpoint of British Jewish studies, and where the latter has been the case, almost always in order to place a celebratory or alternatively, exculpatory gloss on particular events, or incidents.[14] Perhaps it is time that the field, through its own maturity, as well as growing distance from the worst Judeophobic horrors of the twentieth century, might be able to make one final leap towards a much more complete and detached sense of sociologically-informed scrutiny and scholarship, disencumbering itself in the process of any last traces of the apologetic and setting itself to consider squarely the course and consequences of a plutocracy-led communal development.

Let me throw in some immediate caveats so that what I propose here is understood – not misunderstood. The Jewish community in Britain and its wider imperial realm, then as now, was no more monolithic than any other Jewish, or other minority, diaspora community worldwide. High-risk entrepreneurs of the ilk of Beit, Barnato, Lippert and Albu who came to dominate Rand gold production at *fin-de-siècle* were of a radically different, mostly Eastern European background, hue and education, from the highly acculturated London-based Jewish grandees who, as a tightly intermarried, self-perpetuating (if not entirely closed) grouping had come to be known as the 'Cousinhood'. Even then, what we know to date about the latter's roles as financiers to high business and the Crown does not suggest they in any sense acted as a 'Jewish' bloc or cartel: the notion of some phalanx of 'Jewish' capital per se was essentially the chimera of fevered gentile perception. And where some of the grandees did, on occasion, individually or collectively, attempt to use their financial muscle to influence British policy making on *Jewish* matters, as for instance did the English Rothschilds in their refusal to participate in a loan to tsarist Russia in the wake of the Anglo-Russian *entente*, their efforts proved futile.[15]

Two things from this litany might provide us, however, with grounds for reflection, and from that, perhaps, a basis for further academic consideration. Firstly, as a major, discrete, if not uniform group – broadly confirming Slezkine's Mercurian characterisation – there remains (despite some earlier, worthy studies)[16] a lacuna in our proper understanding of the nature, interactions and consequences of an elite Jewish role in the development of Britain's imperialising political economy: to what degree did it operate within a given Jewish sphere, to what extent was it advanced though specific Jewish communal, social activity and relationships, where were its Jewish/non-Jewish boundaries; in other words, to what extent, and for how long, was it – or has it been – able to operate as a separate or specialised adjunct to the dominant culture? However, this very description is predicated on conditions determined by that dominant culture. If there was synergy or a degree of nexus, it was always highly dependent on the good will of the British ruling elite. Or, put more precisely in Gramscian terms, the British Jewish plutocracy was always *culturally* subordinate to the hegemonic, necessarily materialistic values of the system.

But this second point must excite a further issue. How did this unequal relationship impact upon and inform the nature of British Jewry's *own* communal interactions? Did the imbibing of the values of state and empire by a British Jewish elite have knock-on consequences in its relationship to its self-appointed constituency. And if so, to what extent was a much wider British Jewish *demos* also internally colonised by such values?

At issue here is not so much the nature of plutocratic efforts to *socially* anglicise the post-1880 wave of eastern European immigrants, a subject which has been comprehensively mined and exhaustively analysed. Rather, I would propose what remains an open question is whether traditional *Judaic* values were either fractured or destroyed in the light of the new statist imperatives or were somehow reformulated – perhaps by a dissenting minority – in other, perhaps not overtly *Jewish* guises. Again, Birnbaum and Katznelson, rather than scholars closer to home, may offer the most pertinent guidance on how this question might be further explored. Their *Paths of Emancipation* both picked up on Albert Hirschman's famous loyalty, voice, and exit triad as subaltern strategies in the face of state, organisation, firm, or community, as modes highly applicable to Jewish diaspora contexts, while also noting that the choices involved could be combined in the latter two options.[17] Yet in the British Jewish case something more reveals itself.

Certainly, when it has come to the British state and its interests, Anglo-Jewish loyalty would appear to be the dominant and persistent elite mode. Indeed, the more the leaders of the community *qua* community have walked down the corridors of Whitehall, the more they have attempted to convince themselves of some special consonance of interests between themselves and the Crown. David Mowschowitch, whose comments open this piece, went so far as to propose that the Conjoint Foreign Committee (CJC), the pre-1917 body authorised by the communal leadership to speak on its behalf with government on Jewish matters abroad, sometimes conveyed its expressions of loyalty to the Foreign Office 'in forms that are monstrous'.[18]

The obvious retort to this statement is to say: what about Zionism? Surely the very fact that the CJC was trumped by Weizmann and his British Jewish followers in 1917 demonstrates that loyalty was very far from the only available communal strategy and that with the public pronouncement of the Balfour Declaration, a complete paradigm shift in British-Jewish relations, now at least geared in (long-term) principle towards 'exit', actually replaced 'loyalty' as the standard operating wisdom.

There is no doubt that the Declaration is the seminal moment in British state–communal relations and with internal ramifications – not least the crisis of community as supposed old-time 'assimilationist' plutocrats collided with supposed new-style pro-Jewish nationalist 'democrats' – which have again been exhaustively studied for every last detail. Except, one might argue, that while the pieces on the chessboard had changed the board itself had not. One 'loyal' Jewish elite had simply been replaced by a new 'loyal' elite and even then, if one examines the lead composition of bodies such as the Board of Deputies only in part: the pace of departure of the Jewish grandees from communal office rather mirroring that of Etonians and Harrovians from British governance. Moreover, the supposed new dispensation, Zionism, under the auspices of British rule in Palestine, simply became a more firmly embedded basis for Anglo-Jewish adherence and allegiance to empire. In other words, exit became the new loyalty, albeit more forthrightly articulated by communal spokespeople of the ilk of Selig Brodetsky, at the Board, Weizmann in his still Whitehall-based incarnation as head of the Jewish Agency – and apparently more representative of a now predominantly Eastern European-descended community.

I say 'apparently' because this statement simply mimics without qualification a standard Zionist narrative in which after 1917, and then all the more firmly after 1948, Jewish nationalism supposedly triumphed within the community. Zionist historiography has reinforced the point, as we have already inferred, by reading the internal division as that between assimilationists wedded to being British and Zionists committed to being Jews. However, Michael Berkowitz in his important 1993 study on western European Jewry has rather deftly shown how sentimental or cultural attachment to the idea of Zion could still be reconciled with an ongoing civic commitment to the terms of liberal emancipation through the notion of having a 'supplemental' (Jewish) nationality.[19]

In fact, in the specific case of Anglo-Jewry, one could take the argument one step further. Because of Britain's modernising trajectory as *both* avant-garde liberal state and expansionist globalising empire – which after 1917 included Palestine – the new version of communal elite narrative was able to merge the otherwise irreconcilable strategies of exit and loyalty and so provide British Jewry with their own two-state solution. They could be both loyal to Britain and loyal to Israel, thus having their cake and eating it. Indeed, given the growing tendency of both British Jews and Israeli Jews (especially after 1967, and increasingly in future decades all the way through to our present day) to reposition themselves mentally, culturally and emotionally somewhere in the mid-Atlantic, they might conceive of themselves as loyal to three states, the USA included. Each, after all, had become central players in the dominant geo-politics which reached its zenith in the decade after 1990. Living within Britain as a Jew, the need to think of oneself in specifically statist terms could even be dispensed with altogether: under the terms of the new hegemonic dispensation is one not encouraged to think of oneself as a global citizen anyway? (The world is one's oyster: it just happens that Hendon, Netanya and Palm Beach are 'natural' points of departure or return in one's incessant criss-crossing of the globe for work, family or leisure.)

And so, with the community encased within in its self-congratulatory logic and political myopia, is it any wonder that there is nothing much to inspire about its own past history or culture? If this is truly where British Jewry has arrived, if indeed its national organ, the *Jewish Chronicle*, is an honest reflection of what, contemporaneously, it is, then clearly either the long-term impact of British state and society on its Jews has been as some sort of anaesthetic, or British Jews themselves have voluntarily chosen to surrender their critical faculties in line with the dominant mode. We have had our chances, the Jacobs affair, now more than 40 years on, being one key turning point.[20] The disappointment of the result can only confirm the overriding analysis. Even a leading scholar of British Jewry not so long ago claimed that 'the offspring of the immigrant generation left no collective mark on cultural or intellectual life'.[21]

Yet what about Hirschman's 'voice'? Has it really been so utterly stifled by the collusive and corrosive influence of state and communal policy makers and opinion formers? The writer Michael Kustow, one of the contributors to *A Time to Speak Out*, neatly turns the tables on the negative verdict thus. Yes, he agrees:

> One must behave. One must strive ... to be accepted into the host country without fear that its order will be transgressed. One must be a Good Boy. The trouble with this logic is that there is an alternative tradition in which the best in Jewish culture – indeed in Western culture – has been produced by Bad Boys and Bad Girls not by unthinking solidarity with 'the community.[22]

So, if Kustow is correct, then what *really* matters in being Jewish in Britain can be found not within the community, but outside it. This is indeed a paradoxical conclusion, not least because it would seem to imply not so much voice but, instead, a different version of exit. That would also seem to imply problems for the researcher. If 'Jews', however interesting they may be, have left the community, how can one define them as such if they themselves do not choose to maintain religious or institutional affiliation?

The problem is not an entirely novel one for the Jewish historian. There have been, after all, many historical, so-called crypto-Jews who researchers of the stature of Gershom Scholem have felt it worthy to pursue.[23] And not just as exotic oddities but rather for the ongoing Judaic ideas they carried into 'internal exile' with them. Could it be, indeed, in the British Jewish case that fiercely Judaic ideas of social justice, speaking 'truth to power' and 'creating a society based on harmony and equality in which every single individual would be respected'[24] have operated most successfully off the communal radar screen precisely because they have not been able to operate in clear, categorical and unambiguous terms within it?

Paradoxically, this might seem to suggest that finding Jewish voice might require searching for it in places which are not overtly Jewish. Actually, though, one would not have to look too far, or too laterally. My own personal experience in the peace and environmental movements suggests an abundance of passionate, radical, thinking *yidn*, and – as always – entirely disproportionate to their demographic base. Rarely do these good people bare their Jewish breasts. But nor, on the other hand, if you speak to them about background, do they claim to have disassociated themselves from their origins, or culture. True, again, they may often be stridently secular in outlook, yet at the same time their sense of right and wrong and of the need to be active agents in the creation of a better world has a peculiarly familiar ring about it.[25] They are thus not going down a 'radical assimilating' route. On the contrary, they are, as Isaac Deutscher might put it, speaking of an earlier generation of Jewish-born revolutionaries, 'very Jewish indeed'.[26]

This, I propose, hardly amounts to a verdict of Jewish intellectual sterility in Britain but rather to the submerged persistence of a vibrant and authentically universalised Judaic world view. And one which we can clearly chart back through earlier generations. It was there in the women and men who were often at the forefront of the radical socialist and feminist movements, through *History Workshop*, the *Universities and Left Review*, through critical academic and cultural questionings of conventional societal wisdoms, especially in BBC drama, and the radical theatre of the 1960s. A specific South African variant necessarily took on a much more overtly radical and entirely politicised direction in the face of apartheid and of the unwillingness of the South African Jewish community to openly speak truth to power. In the previous generation, Jewish prominence in anti-fascist circles was not just a reaction to Hitlerite persecution of the Jews: at every turn, Jewish worker activists and intellectuals, whether born in Britain or from émigré or refugee circles, were at the forefront of communism and direct involvement in the fight against Franco. A generation earlier still, it was Bundists, anarchists and, in the most trenchant repudiation of the plutocrats' bidding in British Jewish history, droves of ordinary immigrants who refused to don uniform or participate in the carnage of the Great War.[27]

Again, at issue here is not whether there was a skein of oppositionism within modern Anglo-Jewish life. This is well known and well explored. Nor is it a revelation that it has operated across time and space from an earlier moment when it was still hovering at the margins of Jewish communal existence to a later period when it was largely being articulated either entirely outside of, or with no direct reference to that existence. More intriguing is how the skein was kept alive as the generational shift from communal to non-communal became pronounced. Clearly the figure of the ubiquitous Jewish radical is very much a facet of modernity. Yet one might equally argue that the very success of Anglo-Jewry's conformist project deprived emerging generations, step by step, of the social marginality often seen as the necessary underpinning to *their* radicalism.

This would contrast, for instance, with conditions in inter-war Central Europe where the failure of progressive communal assimilating agendas in the face of Nazism and other ultra-nationalisms also produced the most marked effulgence of the Judaic subterranean tradition in largely secularised form. One would have to reach for Michael Löwy's wonderful *Redemption and Utopia* to get a taste of the small galaxy of intellectuals who most keenly represented these antinomian, utopian, even messianic tendencies.[28] Clearly, their context is important. Yet what one also derives from the study is the very consciously self-willed rejection of normative, German-Jewish mantras by the likes of Buber, Benjamin and Bloch. Already heavily immersed in dominant German culture, these intellectuals managed the feat of critically distancing themselves from *both* tendencies, the outcome of which was their critical re-engagement with biblical Judaism as if it was something entirely new and fresh to them. And what did they most particularly alight on in this process? Its millenarianism: that essentially subversive, anti-statist element within the prophetic texts which spoke of a thoroughly humanistic social and cultural transformation: not in some obscure and distant future but in one's own time – and for all humankind.

There is no corpus of dissenting Anglo-Jewish writing which articulates these tendencies as does the inter-war Central European pantheon. But that is not to say it never happened or existed here. It came through in nooks and crevices, to be sure it was moulded by a different set of cultural conditions, was hence more empirical and activist, less theoretical or self-reflective. It was also more demotic and diffused: though less a matter of class consciousness, more of an interiorised, spiritual one.

While it makes it more difficult to empirically study, that does not in itself represent a good reason for not doing so at all. And also not least because while, on the one hand, its primary expression was outside the community, on the other, it also tenaciously hung on at its margins. We can discern it in the loose campaigning networks which formed in the 1970s and 1980s, such as the Jewish Socialist Group (JSG), and Jews Organised for a Nuclear Arms Halt (JONAH), who resisted the easy allure of loyalty to state/s (Israeli or British), neo-empire or the military-industrial complex, and instead began challenging first principles. More recently it emerged in Jews for Justice for Palestinians (JFJFP), for which we can thank especially the late Irene Breugel. The naming of names is surely relevant here: voice is an individual talent, especially when it involves going fearlessly against the grain of the compact majority. In Irene's case 'the power of one' involved speaking out against a Western-backed or condoned violence done by Jews as Israelis to other human beings who happen to be Palestinians. Now, too, we have Independent Jewish *Voices*, in effect a diverse collectivity of all the emerging dissenting voices both within and without the community.

There is surely something genuine to celebrate here as well as to investigate for its historic roots. But in Jewish studies as in Jewish life there is little point in all this if it cannot be more practically applied. And 'my G-d', we need that practical application now. Let us be absolutely clear that if the thrust of this piece has been to propose that Jewish voice is the most potent resource the community has – indeed, the one true Judaic gift it can offer to humanity at large – if this cannot be applied purposefully in present conditions then British Jewry must share responsibility for the ongoing cultural and political *deformation* of *this* society as it continues to abdicate responsibility in the face of its ultimate challenge. Another IJV writer and thinker, Anthony Rudolf, has described anthropogenic climate change as 'the invasion from Mars',[29] conjuring up brilliantly just how serious that threat is. In another sense, though, the metaphor is inapt. The danger comes neither from Martians nor the Gods: it is human beings in their wanton greed and stupidity who have created the seeds for this self-inflicted Nemesis. Only prescience of the biblical kind, as translated into collective human action, can save us now.

In the final chapter of *A Time to Speak Out*, IJV co-founder, Brian Klug, quotes one of the great tannaim, Rabbi Tarfon: 'The day is short, the task is great.' Rabbi Tarfon's words from the first century should now quite literally be deafening. But where is the uptake? Never before has Judaic voice been so necessary right here in Britain. But to begin its proleptic task for humankind the community first will have to undergo its own utter transformation, in the light of the new Carbon-informed reality. Before it can even prophetically speak truth to power it will have to be reformed into a community which practices what it preaches. Said Rabbi Tarfon: 'You are not obliged to complete the task, but neither are you free to give it up.'[30] If our guide, however, remains a history of Jewish communal subservience to statist, corporate and, by implication, conventional wisdoms of the neo-imperial kind, then, truly, all that is left is the sackcloth and ashes.

NOTES

1. David Mowschowitch. 'Notes', 30 March 1917, quoted in Mark Levene, *War, Jews and the New Europe: The Diplomacy of Lucien Wolf, 1914–1919* (Oxford: Littman Library of Jewish Civilisation and Oxford University Press, 1992), p.150.
2. Quoted in Phil Cohen, *Children of the Revolution, Communist Childhood in Cold War Britain* (London: Lawrence and Wishart, 1997), pp.69–70.
3. Anne Karpf *et al.*, eds., *A Time to Speak Out, Independent Jewish Voices on Israel, Zionism and Jewish Identity* (London: Verso, 2008).
4. For more on Roth see Elisa Lawson, 'Cecil Roth and the imagination of the Jewish past, present and future in Britain, 1925–1964' (Ph.D. thesis, Southampton University, 2005). See also W.D. Rubinstein, *A History of the Jews in the English-Speaking World: Great Britain* (London: Macmillan, 1996), for a contemporary restatement of the congratulatory meta-narrative.
5. See notably Geoffrey Alderman, *Modern British Jewry* (Oxford: Clarendon Press, 1998);

Todd M. Endelman, *The Jews of Britain, 1656–2000* (Berkeley, CA; University of California Press, 2002); Eugene C. Black, *The Social Politics of Anglo-Jewry, 1880–1920* (Oxford: Blackwell, 1998); Daniel Gutwein, *The Divided Elite, Economics, Politics and Anglo-Jewry, 1882–1917* (Leiden and New York: Brill, 1992); David Cesarani, *The Jewish Chronicle and Anglo-Jewry, 1841–1991* (Cambridge: Cambridge University Press, 1994).

6. Yuri Slezkine, *The Jewish Century* (Princeton, NJ and Oxford: Princeton University Press, 2004).

7. David Feldman, *Englishmen and Jews, Social Relations and Political Culture, 1840–1914* (New Haven, CT: Yale University Press, 1994).

8. See most famously the debates which swirled around E.P. Thompson, 'The Peculiarities of the English' (1965), in idem, *The Poverty of Theory and Other Essays* (London: Merlin Press, 1978), pp.35–91.

9. Pierre Birnbaum and Ira Katznelson, eds., *Paths of Emancipation, Jews, States and Citizenship* (Princeton, NJ: Princeton University Press, 1995).

10. See Tony Kushner, *The Persistence of Prejudice: Antisemitism in British Society during the Second World War* (Manchester: Manchester University Press, 1989); Bryan Cheyette, *Constructions of the 'Jew' in English Literature and Society, Racial Representations, 1875–1945* (Cambridge: Cambridge University Press, 1993).

11. Birnbaum, and Katznelson (see note 9), p.4.

12. John A. Hobson, 'The Scientific Basis of Imperialism', *Political Science Quarterly*, 17 (1902), 460–89.

13. Niall Ferguson, *Empire: How Britain Made the Modern World* (London: Penguin, 2004), pp.221–4.

14. Ibid.; Geoffrey Wheatcroft, *The Randlords* (London: Weidenfeld & Nicolson, 1985), for examples of the first category

15. See A.J. Sherman, 'German-Jewish Bankers in World Politics: The Financing of the Russo-Japanese War', *Leo Baeck Year Book*, 28 (1983), 59–73; C.C. Aronsfeld, 'Jewish Bankers and the Czar', *Jewish Social Studies*, 35 (1973), 87–104.

16. Chaim Bermant, *The Cousinhood* (London: Eyre and Spottiswoode, 1971) for the classic, if heavily anecdotal study. Harold Pollins, *Economic History of the Jews in England* (Rutherford, NJ: Littman Library of Jewish Civilisation and Farleigh Dickinson University Press, 1982), for the more empirically informed, solid but not notably illuminating discussion.

17. Birnbaum and Katznelson (see note 9), pp.30–31; Albert Hirschman, *Exit, Voice and Loyalty* (Cambridge, MA: Harvard University Press, 1970).

18. Quoted in Levene (see note 1), p.150.

19. Michael Berkowitz, *Zionist Culture and West European Jewry before the First World War* (Cambridge: Cambridge University Press, 1993).

20. See Chaim Bermant, *Troubled Eden, An Anatomy of British Jewry* (London: Vallentine Mitchell, 1969), chapter xix, 'The Jacobs Affair'.

21. Todd M. Endelman, *Radical Assimilation in English Jewish History, 1656–1945* (Bloomington and Indianapolis: Indiana University Press, 1990), p.187.

22. Michael Kustow, 'Last Straws', in *A Time to Speak Out* (see note 3), p.217.

23. See, for instance, Gershom Scholem, *Sabbatai Sevi, The Mystical Messiah* (Princeton, NJ: Princeton University Press, 1973).

24. Gillian Slovo, 'South Africa and Israel: A Dialogue', quoting South African chief rabbi, Cyril Harris, on the occasion of Joe Slovo's burial, 1995, in *A Time to Speak Out* (see note 3), p.58.

25. See for a classic recent example, that of Dan Glass the young man who glued himself to PM Gordon Brown for his failure on climate change, http://news.bbc.co.uk/1/hi/uk_politics/7520401.stm.

26. Isaac Deutscher, *The Non-Jewish Jew and Other Essay* (London: Oxford University Press, 1968), p.27.

27. Anne Patricia Lloyd, 'Jews under Fire: The Jewish Community and Military Service in World War One Britain' (Ph.D. thesis, Southampton University, 2009), sheds new light on the intensity of this struggle. See also Sharman Kadish, *Bolsheviks and British Jews, The*

Anglo-Jewish Community, Britain and the Russian Revolution (London: Frank Cass, 1992).

28. Michael Löwy, *Redemption and Utopia, Jewish Libertarian Thought in Central Europe, A Study in Elective Affinity*, trans. by Hope Heaney (London: The Athlone Press, 1992).

29. Anthony Rudolf, 'Paths of Peace: A Personal Trajectory', in *A Time to Speak Out* (see note 3), p.205.

30. Pirke Avot 2; 20-1, quoted in Brian Klug, 'A Time to Move On', in *A Time to Speak Out* (see note 3), p.289.

RACE AND ANTI-SEMITISM

Dilemmas of Jewish Difference: Reflections on Contemporary Research into Jewish Origins and Types from an Anglo-Jewish Historical Perspective

GAVIN SCHAFFER

In 2009, London's Jews' Free School (JFS) found itself at the centre of national controversy over its admissions policy. A year before, on the recommendation of Britain's Chief Rabbi, Jonathon Sacks, the school had declined entry to a pupil whose mother was a non-Orthodox convert to Judaism.[1] Although the woman's conversion had been endorsed by comparable Israeli rabbinic authorities, it was deemed insufficiently rigorous according to the strictures of the Chief Rabbi's rabbinic court in London, the Beth Din. Consequently, the woman's child was considered non-Jewish according to the principle of matrilineal descendency which sits at the core of Orthodox Jewry's concept of religious inheritance, and JFS refused admission.[2] The family responded with a legal challenge, arguing that the school's decision was based on a perception of (the mother's) ethnicity in breach of the 1976 Race Relations Act.[3] After a series of rulings, Britain's new Supreme Court agreed that this indeed was the case, forcing JFS (and other Jewish schools) into a speedy re-working of their admissions criteria based on practice (like synagogue attendance) and not inheritance.[4]

Aside from raising important questions about the relationship between church and state, the JFS case was significant because it illuminated the ongoing inability of Jewish communities to agree about what constitutes a Jew and, in particular, about what ideas of ethnic or racial origin may or may not have to do with it. It is a discussion that makes awkward bedfellows of science and religion, as Judaism (or perhaps, more accurately, Jewishness) becomes increasingly discussable in terms of roots, inheritance and genetics. If you are a Jew because your mother is a Jew, it is arguable that the science of DNA renders a lab-worker, not a Rabbi, best equipped ultimately to say who is Jewish and who is not.[5]

Moreover, if Jewishness is understood as a genetic inheritance, further questions arise about the role of science in constructing and understanding both the Jewish past and the Jewish present. Most pressingly, recent years have seen an explosion of research into the specifics of disease occurrence and cure among Jews, a valuable body of work, but one which has served to entrench Jews in both social and scientific thought as an homogenous scientific group (or more often as two groups, Ashkenazim and Sephardim).[6] Over the same period, a whole host of scholars, across a range of scientific disciplines, have begun to hypothesise about the ability of genetics to develop historical understanding of Jewish roots and history.[7]

This article will consider the history of some of these arguments about Jewish ethnic and racial difference over the last century in an attempt to weigh up the potential and/or wisdom of encouraging scholarly interventions into the question of what constitutes, and marks out, Jews as a distinct group. It will argue that for all the scientific innovation and achievement of the last 50 years, much of the core agenda of these debates remains unchanged. It will also argue that the terrain of research has consistently been so clearly demarcated by intransigent ideological positions that discussions of this nature are unlikely to come to synthesis any time soon and instead are destined to remain bogged down in religious dogma and political agendas.

The prominence of Jews themselves at every level of these debates about Jewish racial difference is hardly surprising. Scholars of race and racism have frequently argued that ethnic minority groups are as susceptible to the lure of racial research as anyone else; and, indeed, have frequently seen the potential for communal advancement and defence in the seductive subjectivity of racial categorisation. In this context, Gilroy reminds us, that:

> People who have been subordinated by race thinking and its distinctive social structures ... have for centuries employed the concepts and categories of their rulers, owners, and persecutors to resist the destiny that 'race' has allocated to them and to dissent from the lowly value it placed upon their lives.[8]

Building on this theory, I have argued elsewhere that scholarly interventions (on behalf of Jews) in debates about Jewish difference have tended historically to fall into two categories: those who have accepted the idea of Jewish racial difference and championed positive constructions of Jewish type in order to cement Jews as worthy citizens in western societies and as a national community, and those who have attempted to pull Jews from the glare of racial scholarship by refuting the idea of a distinct Jewish racial type (or types).[9] These contrasting perspectives can be seen as a matter of tactical conflict or as rooted in different belief systems, although I would argue that it is usually impossible to prise exigency from ideology. As a dispute, it is neatly illustrated by a spat between two doctors and scholars in the inter-war period, Redcliffe Salaman (1874–1955) and Charles Singer (1876–1960), who were both caught up in the acrimonious atmosphere of racial science in 1930s Britain. Both men were Jews, trained in medicine, and scholars of genetics; both were forceful defenders of Jewry in the face of European anti-Semitism and the emergency of Nazism. However, the nature of their strategies towards Jewish defence was very different.

For most of his career, Charles Singer lectured in the history of medicine at University College London and other leading academic institutions in Britain and the United States.[10] As a trained doctor and zoologist, he repeatedly focused his intellectual gaze on the issue of race, especially as it related to the Jewish past and present. The rise of the Nazi regime brought forth a new level of commitment from Singer, who contributed substantially to major popular scientific studies which were written to refute Nazi racial theory. In particular, Singer's long-standing friendship with zoologist and broadcaster Julian Huxley led to his participation in the writing of *We Europeans*, perhaps the most famous scientific contemporary critique of Nazism.[11] Almost certainly because of his Jewishness, Singer's contribution to the writing of *We Europeans* was never publicly acknowledged but archive records reveal that in this project, and in Huxley's anti-Nazi pamphlet *Argument of Blood* in 1940, his contribution as a writer and researcher was paramount.[12]

While this body of work fell well short of refuting the idea of race as a useful scientific concept (the emphasis in these studies was very much on the Nazi corruption of racial scholarship), the scientific idea that Jews comprised a homogenous racial type was repeatedly attacked, especially in *We Europeans*, as scientifically untenable. This text argued that European Jewry was made up of racially tangled, eclectically rooted groups which could not be described as a race in any sense. Jews, it asserted, 'rank neither as nation nor even as ethnic unit, but rather as a socio-religious group carrying large Mediterranean, Armenoid, and many other elements, and varying greatly in physical characters'.[13] The concept of Jewish variety was central to the *We Europeans* argument. 'Jews of different areas', it informed its readers, were 'not genetically equivalent ... in each country the Jewish population overlaps with the non-Jewish in every conceivable character.'[14] Jewish people, *We Europeans* concluded, 'vary as much as, if not more than, any people in Europe'.[15]

Singer's own papers reveal the extent to which the *We Europeans* stance on Jewish racial origins and difference was his own. In a letter to Salaman in the midst of the war, Singer forcefully argued that it was wrong to construct Jews as sharing an ancient racial origin or as representing a distinct national community. Instead, he told Salaman that while Eastern European Jews may share racial characteristics, these had little to do with Western European Jewish communities who were, to Singer's mind, not part of the racial group at all:

> is there a Jewish nation at all? Surely there is in Eastern Europe where Jews differ from (say) Poles as much as Poles differ from Germans. They differ too, in the same superficial as well as deeper ways, language, social customs, religion, art, philosophy, laws, historical outlook, occupations etc. Agreed. But the majority of westernised Jews in this country can never belong to this nation, however much they may think they may.[16]

To regard Jews as one group was, to Singer, not only a scientific error but a sop to Hitler's racial platform. He told Salaman: 'Is Judaism then no more than the "call of the blood", or no more than that call plus the call of the Rabbis? If so Hitler is right'. Jews were, he joked, only a nation in the sense 'that they are a social aggregate sharing a common error as to their origin and a common dislike of their neighbours'.[17]

At the core of Singer's argument here were ideas which were to have a wider resonance beyond resistance to Hitler's genocidal racism. To Singer, Judaism was a practice, a way of life, which said plenty about an individual's culture but nothing significant about either his character, physique, or his racial origins. Singer clearly found it distasteful, as well as scientifically erroneous, to regard Jews as a racial group in this sense and did not hold back from telling Salaman what he thought of his racialised presentation of Jewishness.

It is as though Judaism were an impulse of persons with a particular type of nose (for example) to huddle together. If so, then I have to say that I do not suffer from that particular kind of itch, whatever my nose and whether it be shaped by genetic or social history or both.[18]

One of the central areas of dispute between the two men related to the Jewish claim to Palestine, specifically to the role of racial science in justifying the Zionist cause. To Singer, there was no Diaspora nation waiting to be re-formed, as a whole, in Palestine or anywhere else. Believing as he did that Jews were comprised of numerous different racial groups, Singer could not see how the Zionist agenda could speak to Jews like himself and Salaman, who were, to his mind, Britons to the core. He told Salaman:

You and I for example, even were we 50 years younger, could not give up our language, social customs, religion, art, philosophy, law, historical outlook, occupations and habits of life. We could not form part of a Jewish nation which must, in any event, be reconstituted from excessively debased remains by borrowing from the stores of other nations.[19]

This stance, although not opposing Zionism, was anathema to Redcliffe Salaman, a scholar who saw the idea of the Jewish state in exactly the terms ridiculed by Singer, as a restoration of Jewish racial unity and the logical racial conclusion of Jewish diasporic existence.

Salaman was a medical doctor and keen geneticist, a specialist in Jewish racial types who had gathered data and observations on his subject as a medical officer in the British Army's 2nd Judean Battalion in Palestine in the First World War.[20] Although he was as strong an opponent of Nazism as Singer, Salaman bitterly objected to the scientific tendency, in opposition to Hitler, to deny the existence of a Jewish race, believing Jewish racial difference to be an observable fact. Salaman did not think that all Jews were the same. As Falk has noted, he was sure that Ashkenazi Jews had been, in his words, 'less subject to local intermarriage during their sojournings' and were therefore purer Jewish types than their Sephardi co-religionists.[21] And in the purer specimens of Ashkenazi Jewry, Salaman saw the potential for a bright Jewish future based upon the inherent strengths of the Jewish racial character.[22] This belief in a Jewish future was firmly rooted in Salaman's understanding of the Jewish past in Palestine.

'Reclaiming' this land for its racial progeny, he thought, would enable the next generation of Jews to reach new heights, according to an ancient racial destiny. In his 1920 memoir, *Palestine Reclaimed*, Salaman asserted that Ashkenazi Jews were undergoing a 'metamorphosis' as a result of their contact with the land of Palestine. 'What is vital', he told his readers, 'is that there in Palestine is a body of young people whose parents were just ordinary Russian Jews whom a new life, in contact with the land they love and cultivate, has transmuted into real men and women.'[23]

The transformative power of Palestine was crucial within Salaman's thinking. He believed that it was 'only here in Palestine that the re-birth of our people can take place'.[24] The Jewish transformation of Palestine into a national home was, to Salaman, a racial return. The colonist, whose strength was in 'his Jewishness, and his blood', behaved as he did as the product of a historical racial space, like the return of an animal to its natural habitat. Thus, the Jewish *chalutzim* were now 'carrying on, as if the two thousand years of separation had not taken place'.[25] Underpinning this belief in a racial continuity was the idea that Jews (or Ashkenazi Jews at least) had retained their racial integrity by shunning intermarriage with non-Jews. To illustrate the idea in a lecture, Salaman pointed a Jewish audience in 1913 to the example of the *Cohanim* (the Jewish priests). These men, he argued, lived as part of 'an unfailing tradition that they are descended from the priests who performed in the temple 2000 years ago and who, anyhow up to quite recent times, had in their veins not a single admixture of alien blood'.[26]

Salaman's belief in Jewish racial type outlasted Hitler and the Holocaust, and left him (like many other biologists and physical anthropologists) feeling isolated in a post-war atmosphere where there was an increasing tendency to minimise the importance of race, epitomised in the UNESCO First Statement on Racial Difference in 1950.[27] In the face of these intellectual currents, Salaman defended the idea of race as important and obvious.[28] In a paper to the Anglo-Jewish Association, in the same year as the first UNESCO Statement, he complained that he found it 'rather humiliating to watch the frantic appeal to scientist and journalist alike to help them prove that they [Jewish racial types] have no distinctive corporeal existence. Any evidence which might support this theory is welcomed. The only testimony refused is that of their own mirror'.[29] Even in the face of Hitler, Salaman had not been able to bring himself to abandon his belief in Jewish racial difference. In a letter to Lilly Montagu, he declined to write a propaganda piece to undermine the Nazi belief in the racial differences between Jews and non-Jews, telling Montagu that he feared that 'in the end, my views might not be just those which you would least desire to see expressed'.[30]

Ultimately, disagreement between Salaman and Charles Singer, as representative of a broader intellectual schism among Jewish thinkers on race, hinged on two key matters; the unity of an ancient Jewish past and the location of this past (and often by implication of the Jewish future) within the land of Israel. To Singer, Jews emanated from different places, and their future needed to be rooted in their integration into the broader populations of which they were a natural racial part. To Salaman, Jews came from the land of Israel, 2,000 years ago, and their ability to contribute to world society hinged upon their being given the right to return to this land, the only place where they could truly fulfil a distinct racial destiny.

While it is always difficult to build bridges between very different historical contexts, and while there is no doubt that the successor protagonists in contemporary debates about Jewish difference have an altogether different armoury of evidence, it is the contention of this article that present-day debates about what it means to be a Jew continue to hang on the issues that divided Salaman and Singer, specifically on the origins of the Jews, Jewish racial difference, and the implications of these origins and differences on the modern state of Israel.

No doubt, in the wake of the Holocaust, there was a scientific turn against the racial classification of groups, particularly with regard to Jews.[31] Elsewhere, I have argued at length that this swing was neither universal nor permanent, and in particular that it involved a reorientation of the study of race from the natural to the social sciences.[32] While the social anthropologists and sociologists that were signatories to the UNESCO statement were happy enough to argue that race was a 'social myth' more than it was a 'biological phenomenon', biologists and physical anthropologists were generally not in agreement; a disaffection epitomised in Salaman's complaint that post-war scientists were, for political reasons, ignoring what was in 'their own mirror'.[33] However, in the wake of Nazi racism, it was the social scientists who held the upper hand. For their part, geneticists tended to re-focus their research into a quieter discourse which did not inflame the anti-Nazi sentiments of the period. As Falk has put it, 'overt eugenic language' was replaced by 'notions of population genetics, of gene frequencies and their dynamics often expressed in statistical terms'.[34]

In this climate, it is perhaps understandable that negative constructions of Jewish racial difference became particularly taboo. Indeed, it is arguable that those scholars who displayed a desire to continue to work on the idea of group racial differences tended to extol the racial virtues of Jews, particularly the idea that Jews (or usually, more specifically, Ashkenazi Jews) were more intelligent than other peoples.[35] The championing of Jewish quality in racial science has been a notable post-war tendency which, I would argue, has not been unrelated to the desire of racial scientists not to be labelled as Nazis. However, it would be a gross over-simplification to argue that this desire has been the only driver of post-war research on Jewish racial difference and intelligence. Instead, research of this kind needs to be seen as part of a longer tradition, exemplified by the continuation of debates like those of Salaman and Singer, and again often steered by Jewish scientists. Indeed, such research into Jewish difference has witnessed something of a recent renaissance.

Firstly, improved understanding of genetics has led to an avalanche of scientific interest in Jewish susceptibility to certain diseases and the potential of genetics to offer a cure.[36] As geneticist David Goldstein has asserted: 'The Jewish share of the overall burden of genetic disease is probably no greater than that of Africans, Arabs, Icelanders, or anyone else, but I wouldn't blame you if you came away from the biomedical literature with a different impression'.[37] But newly heightened genetic interest in Jews has not only been focused on disease and cure. Since the late 1990s, the developing study of DNA has propelled forward scientific ability to wade into discussions about Jewish origins. The study of the Jewish Priests (*Cohanim*) which so interested Salaman have again been given centre stage, inspiring the research of scholars such as Michael Hammer, Neil Bradman and Karl Skorecki. These men have all used the potential to locate genetic similarities on the Y chromosome to attempt, in varying ways, to explore Jewish lineage, arguing that the traditional Jewish hypothesis, that priestly status has been conferred from father to son since ancient times, can now be tested by secular science. These researchers have claimed extraordinary results, seemingly revealing that the Y Chromosomes of those *Cohanim* tested indeed show a degree of familial similarity which seems to confirm the oral Jewish tradition and pre-dates the geographical split of Ahkenazi and Sephardi Jews, results which John Entine has seen fit to describe as 'pure dynamite'.[38] Work off the back of these results has attempted to date the origins of the genetic roots of the *Cohanim* more clearly, leading some, like Mark Thomas, Neil Bradman and David Goldstein, to use detailed analysis of the Y Chromosome (specifically, the identification of the Cohen Modal Haplotype) to speculate that priestly origins may indeed be sufficiently ancient to confirm (possibly) Jewish founding narratives. In Goldstein's words: 'the figure we got is about three thousand years before the present, or right about the time that Solomon is thought to have been building the Temple in which the priests would serve'.[39] While Goldstein and his team have never overtly claimed to have dated the priestly haplotype to the exact time and place specified by Jewish religious tradition, neither have they intellectually discounted the possibility. Goldstein has concluded: 'There's no way to know, but while we have certainly not shown that to be true, neither can I or anyone else say it is impossible.'[40]

Aside from allowing scientists to speculate on the accuracy or otherwise of Jewish religious narratives, the identification of Jewish genetic markers has led to the testing of various African and Asian communities who seem to have Jewish cultural traditions and/or claim Jewish ancestry. Thus substantial work has been conducted into the origins of the Lemba, a Southern African tribe who believe themselves to be descended from the Middle East, whose own priests (the Buba) have been found to carry the Cohen Modal Haplotype in similar quantities to *Cohanim*.[41] Excitement concerning this new evidence of the Lemba's Jewishness has led to Jewish missions being sent out to them (even though most Lemba are Christians) and to calls for the tribe to be granted the 'Right of Return' to Israel.[42] All in all, there is little doubt, as Tudor Parfitt has concluded, that 'these "scientific" findings will have an overwhelming impact upon the narratives of the Lemba community ... upon their sense of where they belong and indeed upon the way in which the communities are regarded by other people'.[43]

At its most controversial, new genetic ability to read the Jewish body has even led to claims that Ashkenazi Jews were selected for intelligence in medieval Europe. As has been argued above, claims of Jewish superior intelligence have been made repeatedly in post-war science, and recently such claims have been explained in terms of genetic makeup. The idea that, in a Darwinian sense, the history of Jews has been one of intelligence selection, has been made most notably by Cochran, Hardy and Harpending in a controversial 2005 article which suggested that the conditions of Jews in medieval Europe ensured a need for the clever to thrive, as Jews were forced into various intelligence-related professions as a result of persecution.[44] This argument further contends that this 'fitness payoff to intelligence' may also explain the high prevalence of Tay Sachs, Gaucher's disease, and other lysosomal storage diseases among Ashkenazi Jews. Jews may suffer these illnesses more than most other groups, the authors think, as 'a by-product of this selective regime'.[45] The idea behind this theory mirrors scientific understanding of the relationship between malaria and sickle cell anaemia in Africa. Just as, in that instance, two copies of a mutant globin gene causes sickle cell anaemia while one offers a desirable immunity from malaria, so these lysosomal storage diseases only occur when Jews carry two copies of the lysosomal enzyme gene. Carrying one, Cochran, Hardy and Harpending speculate, improves life chances in a hostile environment by increasing intelligence, a payoff not unlike the African malarial immunity.[46] With this comparison in mind, the authors' comment: 'Selection has imposed a heavy human cost: not crippling at the population level, cheaper than the malaria-defence mutations like sickle cell … but tragic nonetheless.'[47]

Looking broadly at this extraordinary body of work poses challenges to the historian of racial science. For one thing, it is not initially clear that it is the historian's business to comment on any of these claims. For sure, this author has neither the expertise nor the experience to critique the science behind theories of Jewish origins, Jewish intelligence or disease susceptibility. However, it is perhaps pertinent to make a few observations as an outsider in these discussions, the first of which relates to the patterns of continuity that are shared by contemporary researchers and scholars of previous generations. Looking at the work of Cochran, Hardy and Harpending, for example, one cannot fail to think of Salaman, who told the Jewish Health Organisation of Great Britain, 80 years prior to their article, that Jews had indeed bred for intelligence:

> The old custom of marrying the rich man's daughter to the most promising student of the chevra was one of the most successful and illuminating eugenic experiments ever conceived, and we can never be too grateful to our forebears for thus artificially breeding an aristocracy of brains.[48]

Similarly, arguments of contemporary researchers of Jewish origins seem to hang on the same questions as their predecessors. In particular, the importance of Zionism to these sets of discussions is key, and seems to raise bigger questions about the objectivity of science and the sagacity of work of this nature.

Accusations of partiality and bias have generally received short shrift from scholars of Jewish difference who have tended to argue that their work is objective and that their science speaks for itself. This reflects a broader trend; in the post-war climate of anti-racism, the swing of racial studies into social science has often led scholars of natural science to invoke their objectivity in opposition to what they believe has been an unscientific silencing of academic truth about race among social scientists. These new experts, the natural scientists contend, are determined, whatever the evidence, to seek explanations which do not entertain the idea of racial difference. This posturing can be seen in Salaman's contention that social scientists were failing to look in their own mirrors, and it was a repeated theme in criticism of the first UNESCO statement on race. For example, Julian Huxley argued that the anti-race line taken by UNESCO was 'coloured by wishful thinking'[49] while the *Mankind Quarterly*, beyond the margins of most acceptable scientific discourse, told the world that they were now the only scholars not displaying bias in the face of the anti-racial opposition that had ascended as a result of the Holocaust. In this way, one early article of the journal argued: 'Until recently, memories of Hitler with his untenable racial theories and abhorrent practices were so fresh in people's minds that the further exploration of ethnic group differences was almost taboo' and that racial equality was no more than 'a beautifully consoling illusion'.[50]

Similarly, those geneticists who have recently weighed into debates about Jewish difference have been keen to highlight the irrationality of those who cannot accept the premise of Jewish racial differences and who do not respect the possibility of scientific objectivity on this subject. For example, David Goldstein launched his book on Jewish genetic history, *Jacob's Legacy*, with a typical attack on social scientists who, he perceives, have tried to close a subject which is built from facts that speak for themselves.

> Social scientists in particular have shown a willingness to extrapolate from Lewontin's study that race and ethnicity are biologically meaningless, hence the refrain that 'we are all the same'. The data I present here, however, showing clear genetic

differences among the members of population after population, as well as hundreds of other published studies on the genetics of disease, drug response, and human variation, argue otherwise.[51]

In debate with the author, Goldstein outlined even more clearly his opinion on the role of the scientist as objective investigator and its moral implications:

> I believe scientists fundamentally lack the authority, both moral and practical, to decide what the public can and cannot know. In the case of studies of human genetic variation, however, I go even further. Not only do I believe that we scientists lack the authority to camouflage, whitewash, or 'spin' what we know about human genetic variation, I don't think we have any reason to do so.[52]

Armed with this worldview, Goldstein absolves himself from responsibility for the consequences of his discoveries. Describing ethical worries over his work on the Lemba, he notes that he has 'concluded that it is just not possible to control' how his work is presented.[53] But scientists do not sit outside society in this way, and everything in the cannon of work on Jewish racial difference indicates that scholars enter these discussions as political protagonists at every stage. That natural scientists often do not agree with this contention, especially as regards race, reflects broader inter-disciplinary disagreement about the relationship between facts and ideology. When Gary Werskey, historian of science, interviewed the cytologist J.R. Baker about his views on race, Baker's reaction highlighted this academic schism: 'Werskey thinks people's backgrounds have a profound influence on what they think. I tried to persuade him that some things are thought by some people because they happen to be true.'[54]

However, the historical record suggests that, on the subject of race, scientists do not deal in clear-cut truths but do 'spin' and do 'whitewash', albeit often subconsciously, presenting findings that are in line with personal beliefs and ideology, not set apart from social racial discourse in any clear sense.[55] In Jewish difference debates, this is nowhere clearer than on the issue of Israel and Zionism.

In his latest book on race, David Theo Goldberg has highlighted a link between racial research into ancient origins and contemporary land disputes.

> Those whose 'racial origins' are considered geographically somehow to coincide with national territory (or its colonial

extension) are deemed to belong to the nation; those whose geo-phenotypes obviously place them originally (from) elsewhere are all too often considered to pollute or potentially to terrorize the national space, with debilitating and even deadly effect.[56]

In this way, potential links between theories of an ancient Jewish past in Israel and contemporary conflict in the Middle East become important. In the face of a generally hostile international media, which often constructs Jews in Israel as colonisers and occupiers, scientific proofs of Jewish indigeneity in Israel confer legitimacy on Zionists and their sympathisers.[57] This being the case, it is equally unsettling and significant, to the author at least, that the leading investigators of Jewish genetic roots frequently seem to be largely uncritical supporters of Israel.[58]

In *Abraham's Children*, Entine has noted that the pioneering scholar of the Priestly gene, Karl Skorecki, was 'motivated as much by his commitment to Israel as by scientific curiosity'.[59] Similarly, David Goldstein states clearly and openly his attachment to Israel in *Jacob's Legacy*, describing his romantic ideological connection to the country as a Jew at an Israeli rock concert:

> Surrounded by rowdy young Israelis boisterously singing along, I felt a part of it all, even able somehow to understand the lyrics. The connection with that community that night, hard to define but tangible, told me something about how the Jews had survived all that they had and somehow remained a people. I often think back to that concert and those kids taking off their shirts and swirling them around, those Cohen Y chromosomes and varied mitochondria that may have started there and somehow found their way back after two millennia.[60]

In many ways, Goldstein's putting of his ideological cards on the table in this way is laudable and certainly negates any claim that could be made that he is attempting to hide his own opinion or disguise his ideological baggage. Nonetheless, the idea that this kind of ideological starting point has not had an impact on research, that facts speak for themselves around belief systems of this nature, is unconvincing.[61]

Ultimately, all of this research hinges on the ability of scientists to cast generations backwards into a useable historical past. It frequently presupposes, with theological writing at the core, that Jewish history occupied certain spaces and times, and extrapolates scientific possibilities around these narratives.[62] These are, at once, comforting and self-fulfilling, 'proving' with science what generations have always held to be true about Jews and their antecedents. The problem is that historical debate is fundamentally a secular matter, fraught with disagreement and debate at every juncture, and there is little written in this vibrant field which lends itself to the creation of any such kind of usable past. When Cochran, Hardy and Harpending assert that life in Medieval Europe shaped Jewish genetics, surely it is important to question exactly what these scholars know about life in Medieval Europe. Are they engaging with history or merely with folkloric constructions of the Jewish past?[63] Similarly, while scientists of Jewish origins may believe themselves to be partaking in the business of history, they too are mostly only engaging with theological narratives, leaving professional historians to argue in a different part of the university.[64] Here, traditional historical approaches are usurped by genetics, which becomes a new evidence base and source in and of itself, reinforced by an unholy alliance with theology. However, this is not to say that professional historians have been silenced or 'gone quietly' in recent Jewish difference debates. Indeed, the intervention of Israeli Professor of European History Shlomo Sand in the debate over Jewish origins has caused ripples across disciplines and borders in the last year, and reminds us that debates on Jewish difference are by no means the preserve of geneticists.[65]

Like the writers of the Jewish genetic histories that have been discussed here, Shlomo Sand brings to the table his own set of agendas and prejudices. If the writers above offer arguments that are reminiscent of Redcliffe Salaman, then Sand takes a perspective which has strong echoes of Charles Singer. As with Singer, who questioned whether there was 'a Jewish nation at all', Sand has similarly argued that Jewishness is not a racial issue but a matter of faith and culture which extends to numerous, racially unconnected, populations. Judaism, to Sand, needs to be historicised as a faith 'that bridged the diverse linguistic-cultural groups that arose in far-flung lands and followed different historical paths'.[66]

If the seekers of the priestly gene have an openly Zionist agenda, Sand too makes no effort to hide the desired political implications of his research, to reset the Israeli state on a path towards 'democratic multiculturalism', a 'republic for its citizens', where 'Palestino-Israelis' have their rights protected and, crucially, are embraced within the state's conception of itself.[67] This is not the case in modern Israel,

Sand believes, specifically because the state's dominant narrative of Jewish history erroneously emphasises a common and ancient Jewish heritage, which he describes as the 'active myth of an eternal nation that must ultimately foregather in its ancestral land'.[68] To debunk this myth, and liberate the nation from its 'ethnocratic' chains, Sands pours over the *longue duree* of Jewish history, arguing that Jews did not generally emerge from ancient Israel, were not expelled from the land, and in fact are comprised of racially disparate faith communities, which have evolved over centuries, from a variety of starting points.[69] The book closes with a political call to arms as Sand challenges Israelis to re-think their past in order to re-negotiate their future: 'If the nation's history was mainly a dream, why not begin to dream its future afresh, before it becomes a nightmare?'[70]

Sand's book has created an enormous storm, leading to accusations within Israel that he is a traitor and a self-hater. One review in leading newspaper *Haaretz* noted: 'From all the sound and the fury you might think that his agenda is to expel all Jews from Israel, or to abolish the Jewish state.'[71] But given Sand's clearly political goals, this is perhaps not too surprising. Patricia Cohen, in the *New York Times*, has stressed the role of personal ideologies in shaping the reception of *The Invention of the Jewish People*. The book has, she argues 'been extravagantly denounced and praised, often on the basis of whether or not the reader agrees with his politics'.[72] Put simply, Sand has become something of a *bête noire* to many Zionists (who feel he is fuelling the agenda of Israel's enemies) and has been praised by others (from leftist Zionists to extreme anti-Zionists) who welcome any critical engagement with the intellectual foundations of the state.

However, it is particularly interesting that some of the criticism levelled at Sand has come from the scholars of Jewish genes. For example, a recent interview with Harry Ostrer of New York University about his own study, *Abraham's Children in the Genome Era*, soon turned into an attack on Sand's history of Jewish origins. Speaking to the *Jewish Chronicle*, Ostrer introduced his new research as a study which 'disproved' Sand's theory, as well as debunking the work of Arthur Koestler (who had earlier argued, like Sand, that Jewish origins were not largely rooted in the Middle East).[73] Sand's book, Ostrer told the *JC*, was simply 'bad genetics', an interesting comment because, aside from six sides of synthesis, Sand's book is not genetics at all, but traditionally sourced history.[74] Indeed, the nature of Ostrer's criticism of Sand speaks of a wider disciplinary dispute, long-standing and un-resolved, about who has the right to work and pronounce on racial origins and difference.

I have argued above that natural scientists largely lost authority on racial matters in the wake of the Second World War. Marginalised by the clarity and dogma epitomised in UNESCO's anti-racial stance, they disappeared to the margins of popular scholarship on race, while social scientists (a group in which I am including historians of race) were ascendant. However, breakthroughs in scientific research into genetic makeup and the Human Genome have increasingly turned the tables on this state of affairs to the extent, as we have seen here, that Ostrer, the geneticist, now feels that he has the authority to accuse Sand, the historian, of acting beyond his knowledge as regards Jewish origins.

But this turn back to natural science is not only, perhaps even not primarily, a disciplinary matter. Instead it represents broader political shifts in discussions about race, identity and roots. As we drift further away from the horrors of the Holocaust, ideas which were once taboo, or at least unfashionable (such as trying to pinpoint common Jewish ancestry), are now all the rage, as Jewish agendas have moved on from trying to prove sameness with European neighbours to wanting to highlight a distinct space and place for Jewish people. The irony has been noted by Sand, who has contended:

> there were times in Europe when anyone who argued that all Jews belong to a nation of alien origin would have been classified at once as an anti-Semite. Nowadays, anyone who dares to suggest that the people known in the world as Jews (as distinct from today's Jewish Israelis) have never been, and are still not, a people or a nation is immediately denounced as a Jew hater.[75]

There is nothing particularly Jewish in this new interest in pinpointing racial roots. As Kenan Malik has pointed out in his study of race from 2008, across society there has been a recent heightening of interest in racial origins emerging from the liberal politics of multiculturalism, confounding traditional categories of racism and anti-racism and taking the study of race onto a new and complex terrain. In Malik's words: 'Out of the withered seeds of racial science have flowered the politics of identity. Strange fruit, indeed.'[76]

Yet there are continuities and these are well borne out by the Jewish difference debate. Looking at the differing perspectives of Singer and Salaman, and at how closely their positions have been reconstructed in contemporary research, one cannot escape the conclusion that little has changed. Like Salaman, many present-day scholars of Jewish genes conduct their science in the belief that there is nothing to be feared from identifying distinctly Jewish racial origins and that these will legitimate the rightful future of Jews in Israel as a nation state. Like Singer, scholars such as Shlomo Sand remain convinced that the well-being of Jews in the future will hinge on recognition of their essential racial oneness with their international neighbours. In both cases, ideology takes the lead in driving science, narratives dictate the paths of supposedly objective research, leaving the public, frequently interested as they are, to pick from the bookshelves the science and history that affirms their world view, beliefs, and sense of self. Any fragments of objectivity are lost in the hyperbole, so that we can rest assured that we are no closer to the truth about what makes a Jew than when Singer and Salaman were arguing it out nearly 100 years ago.

This is perhaps all to the good, the healthy debate of vibrant intellectual communities; but the history of racial science suggests that we would be wise to proceed with caution. In particular, the language and tone of discussions about Jewish origins should be tailored to a recognition that the Israel/Palestine conflict is bloody and ongoing, and riddled with protagonists who would be extremely glad to have their positions legitimised by scientific proof of ancient Jewish presence (or absence) on the land. In this atmosphere, academic research has a real social impact and scholars need to tread carefully past the boundaries of evidence and medical necessity. In the words of Israeli poet Yehuda Amichai: 'In this burning country, words need to be shade.'[77]

NOTES

1. For the background of this case see G. Alderman, 'Not Strictly Orthodox', *Guardian Online*, 28 November 2007, http://www.guardian.co.uk/commentisfree/2007/nov/28/notstrictly orthodox.
2. For analysis of these Jewish laws see M. Konner, *The Jewish Body* (New York: Schocken, 2009), pp.230–31.
3. For analysis of the Race Relations Act see H. Goulbourne, *Race Relations in Britain since 1945* (London and New York: Palgrave, 1998); J. Hampshire, *Citizenship and Belonging: Immigration and the Politics of Demographic Governance in Postwar Britain* (Basingstoke: Palgrave, 2005); and Z. Layton-Henry, *The Politics of Immigration* (Oxford: Blackwell, 1992).
4. The Court of Appeal found against JFS on 25 June 2009 and the decision was upheld by the Supreme Court on 16 December 2009. For the most thorough analysis of the ruling see *Jewish Chronicle*, 26 June 2009 and 18 December 2009.
5. For a thoughtful survey of the impacts of research into Jewish genetics see T. Parfitt and Y.

Egorova, *Genetics, Mass Media and Identity: A Case Study of the Genetic Research on the Lemba and Bene Israel* (Oxford and New York: Routledge, 2006), pp.29–43.

6. For analysis of this body of research see J. Entine, *Abraham's Children: Race, Identity, and the DNA of the Chosen People* (New York: Grand Central Publishing, 2007), pp.270–89; S. M. Kahn, 'The Multiple Meanings of Jewish Genes', *Culture, Medicine and Psychiatry*, 29 (2005), 179–92; and D. Goldstein, *Jacob's Legacy: A Genetic View of Jewish History* (New Haven, CT and London: Yale University Press, 2008), pp.100–114.

7. Most notably, several scholars have argued that genetics is on the way to authenticating, at least partially, Jewish folkloric narratives of Middle Eastern origins and the racial homogeneity of the Jewish Diaspora. This work has been pioneered by scholars like Ariella Oppenheim, Michael Hammer, Neil Bradman and Mark Thomas and popularised in books like Goldstein's *Jacob's Legacy* (see note 6) and Entine's *Abraham's Children* (see note 6).

8. P. Gilroy, *Between Camps: Nations, Cultures and the Allure of Race* (London: Penguin, 2000), p.12. With specific regard to Jews see J. Efron, *Defenders of the Race: Jewish Doctors and Race Science in fin-de-Siecle Europe* (London: Yale University Press, 1994); T. Endelman, 'Anglo-Jewish Scientists and the Science of Race', *Jewish Social Studies*, 11.1 (2004), 52–92; and G. Cantor and M. Swetlitz, *Jewish Tradition and the Challenge of Darwinism* (Chicago and London: University of Chicago Press, 2006).

9. See G. Schaffer, 'Assets or Aliens: Race Science and the Analysis of Jewish Intelligence in Interwar Britain', *Patterns of Prejudice*, 42.2 (2008), 191–207.

10. See G. Cantor, 'Presidential Address: Charles Singer and the Early Years of the British Society for the History of Science', *The British Journal for the History of Science*, 30 (1997), 5–23; and Anna-K. Mayer, 'When Things Don't Talk: Knowledge and Belief in the Inter-war Humanism of Charles Singer (1876–1960)', *The British Journal for the History of Science*, 38.3 (2005), 325–47.

11. For the history of *We Europeans* (J. Huxley and AC Haddon, *We Europeans: A Survey of Racial Problems* (London: Jonathon Cape, 1935)), see E. Barkan, *The Retreat of Scientific Racism: Changing Concepts of Race in Britain and the United States Between the World Wars* (Cambridge: Cambridge University Press, 1992); and G. Schaffer, *Racial Science and British Society: 1930–62* (Basingstoke and New York: Palgrave, 2008).

12. Both texts went out under Julian Huxley's name. *We Europeans* (see note 11) was presented as co-written by Huxley and the anthropologist Alfred Cort Haddon (later the role of Alexander Carr-Saunders was acknowledged) and *Argument of Blood* (London: Macmillan, 1941) as Huxley's alone. For analysis of the writing of these anti-Nazi texts see Schaffer, *Racial Science* (see note 11), pp.32–4.

13. Huxley and Haddon, *We Europeans* (see note 11), p.182.

14. Ibid. p.96.

15. bid. p.184.

16. Charles Singer MSS, Wellcome Library and Archive, Euston Road, London, PP/CJS/A.16, Singer to Salaman, 2 November 1943.

17. Ibid.

18. Ibid.

19. Ibid.

20. For analysis of Salaman see D. Stone, 'Of Peas, Potatoes and Jews: Redcliffe N. Salaman and the British Debate over Jewish Racial Origins', *Simon Dubnow Institute Yearbook*, 3 (2004), 221–40; Endelman, 'Anglo-Jewish Scientists' (note 8); and R. Falk, 'Zionism and the Biology of the Jews', *Science in Context*, 11.3–4 (1998), 587–607.

21. R. Salaman, 'The Inheritance of Facial Features', *Modern Science* (October 1926), p.8. For analysis see Falk, 'Zionism and the Biology of the Jews' (note 20), pp.594–5.

22. These constructions of Ashkenazi superiority would, in this period, have stood in contrast to a more traditional body of scholarship which maintained that Sephardi Jews were racially superior. For analysis see T. Endelman, 'Benjamin Disraeli and the Myth of Sephardi Superiority', in *Disraeli's Jewishness* ed. by T. Endelman and T. Kushner (London: Vallentine Mitchell, 2002), pp.23–39.

23. R. Salaman, *Palestine Reclaimed: Letters from a Jewish Officer in Palestine* (London: Routledge, 1920), p.37.

24. Ibid. p.64.

25. Ibid. pp.202 and 163–4.

26. Salaman MSS, Cambridge University Central Library, Cambridge, Box 13, Speech to the Maccabeans, 26 October 1913. Also see Falk, 'Zionism and the Biology of the Jews' (note 20), p.591.

27. See Schaffer, *Racial Science* (note 11), pp.120–32; Barkan, *The Retreat of Scientific Racism* (see note 11), pp.341–3; and M. Brattain, 'Race, Racism and Anti-Racism: UNESCO and the Politics of Presenting Science to the Postwar Public', *The American Historical Review*, 112.5 (2007), 1386–413.

28. See Endelman, 'Anglo-Jewish Scientists' (see note 8), p.84.

29. Redcliffe Salaman MSS, Box 22, Lecture on 'The Jews: Race, Nation, Religion', for the Anglo-Jewish Association, 19 December 1950.

30. Salaman MSS, Box 1, Salaman to Montagu, 29 January 1934.

31. See M. Kohn, *The Race Gallery: The Return of Racial Science* (London: Jonathon Cape, 1995), pp.40–47.

32. See Schaffer, *Racial Science* (see note 11); and G. Schaffer, '"Scientific" Racism Again? Reginald Gates, Mankind Quarterly and the Question of Race in Science after the Second World War', *Journal of American Studies*, 41.2 (2007), 253–78.

33. 'The UNESCO Statement by Experts on Race Problems', 18 July 1950.

34. Falk, 'Zionism and the Biology of the Jews' (note 20), p.599. Also see S. Sand, *The Invention of the Jewish People* (London: Verso, 2009), p.272.

35. See for example the championing of the intellectual virtues of Ashkenazi Jewish intelligence in Murray and Herrnstein's highly controversial *Bell Curve* study and the treatment of Jewish difference in the *Mankind Quarterly* journal in articles such as N. Weyl, 'The Jewish Role in the American Elite', *Mankind Quarterly*, 3.1 (July–September 1962), 26–36; and N. Weyl, 'The Ethnic and National Characteristics of the US Elite', *Mankind Quarterly*, 1.4 (1961), 242–52. See R. Herrnstein and C. Murray, *The Bell Curve: Intelligence and Class Structure in American Life* (New York: The Free Press, 1994), p.275. Sander Gilman has rightly noted that these positive constructions of Jewish intelligence are not necessarily less problematic than more obviously hostile constructions. See S. Gilman, *Smart Jews: The Construction of the Image of Jewish Superior Intelligence* (Lincoln and London: University of Nebraska Press, 1996).

36. See Konner, *The Jewish Body* (note 2), pp.232–43.

37. Goldstein, *Jacob's Legacy* (see note 6), p.100. For broader criticism of the *Bell Curve* see P. Knapp, J. Kronick, R. William Marks and M. Vosburgh, *The Assault on Equality* (Westport, CT and London: Praeger, 1996) and S. Fraser (ed.), *The Bell Curve Wars: Race, Intelligence and the Future of America* (New York: Basic, 1995).

38. See M. Hammer *et al.*, 'Y Chromosomes of Jewish Priests', *Nature*, 385 (1997), 32–3. The report asserted: 'This result is consistent with an origin for the Jewish priesthood antedating the division of world Jewry into Ashkenazic and Sephardic communities, and is of particular interest in view of the pronounced genetic diversity displayed between the two communities'. For Entine's account see *Abraham's Children* (note 6), pp.78–9. For academic analysis of these scientific developments more generally see Parfitt and Egorova, *Genetics* (note 5), pp.29–43.

39. Goldstein, *Jacob's Legacy* (see note 6), pp.37–8. These claims relate to research announced as 'Origins of Old Testament Priests', *Nature*, 394 (1998) by M. Thomas *et al.* The report claimed: 'We trace the origins of Cohen chromosomes to about 3000 years before present, early during the Temple period.'

40. Goldstein, *Jacob's Legacy* (see note 6), p.39. Also see Entine, *Abraham's Children* (see note 6), pp.81–90; and Konner, *The Jewish Body* (see note 2), p.232.

41. See Parfitt and Egorova, *Genetics* (note 5), pp.51–88; and T. Parfitt, *The Lost Tribes of Israel: The History of a Myth* (London: Weidenfeld and Nicolson, 2002), pp.200–202.

42. Goldstein, *Jacob's Legacy* (see note 6), pp.57–9.

43. Parfitt and Egorova, *Genetics* (see note 5), p.125.

44. G. Cochran, J. Hardy and H. Harpending, 'Natural History of Ashkenazi Intelligence', *Journal of Biosocial Science*, 38 (2006), 659–93.

45. Ibid. p.659. The more conventional explanation for these illnesses among Jews is that of 'genetic drift'. See N. Risch, H. Tang, H. Katzenstein and J. Elstein, 'Geographic Distribution of Disease Mutations in the Ashkenazi Jewish Population Supports Genetic Drift Over Selection', *American Journal of Human Genetics*, 72 (2003), 812–22.

46. For analysis of this theory see Konner, *The Jewish Body* (note 2), pp.239-40.

47. Cochran *et al.*, 'Natural History' (see note 44), p.667.

48. Salaman MSS, Box 13, Lecture to the JHOGB, 'Heredity: A Factor in Public Health', 5 December 1925.
49. Julian Huxley MSS, Rice University, Houston, Box 19, Huxley to Alfred Metraux (UNESCO), 23 February 1951.
50. S.D. Porteus, 'Ethnic Group Differences', *The Mankind Quarterly*, 1.3 (1960), 187–200 (p.187).
51. Goldstein, *Jacob's Legacy* (see note 6), p.9.
52. G. Schaffer vs. D. Goldstein, 'Jews and Race: Should we be Researching Jewish Genetic Origins', *Jewish Renaissance* (April 2009), 6–7.
53. Goldstein, *Jacob's Legacy* (see note 6), p.59.
54. CP Blacker MSS, Wellcome Archive, Wellcome Institute, London, Box 2, Baker to Blacker, 17 August 1969. J.R. Baker wrote perhaps the most controversial book on race of his generation. See J.R. Baker, *Race* (London: Oxford University Press, 1974).
55. For analysis of the interactions of science with society on the subject of race see K. Malik, *The Meaning of Race: Race, History and Culture in Western Society* (Basingstoke: Macmillan, 1996); N. Stepan, *The Idea of Race in Science: Great Britain 1800–1960* (London: Macmillan, 1992); H. Nowotny, P. Scott and M. Gibbons, *Re-Thinking Science: Knowledge and the Public in an Age of Uncertainty* (Cambridge: Polity, 2001); H. and S. Rose, *Science and Society* (London: Allen Lane, 1969); and T. Duster, *Backdoor to Eugenics* (New York and London: Routledge, 1990).
56. D.T. Goldberg, *The Threat of Race: Reflections on Racial Neoliberalism* (Malden, MA and Oxford: Blackwell, 2009), p.7.
57. See Sand, *The Invention* (note 34), p.279.
58. Kahn has noted various trajectories of Jewish genetics, citing one as: 'Using the haplotype to legitimate historical claims to the land of Israel' in 'The Multiple Meanings of Jewish Genes' (see note 6), p.180. On the importance of Zionist ideology in early Israeli genetics see N. Kirsh, 'Population Genetics in Israel in the 1950s: The Unconscious Internalization of an Ideology', *ISIS: Journal of the History of Science*, 94 (2003), pp.631–55.
59. Entine, *Abraham's Children* (see note 6), p.66.
60. Goldstein, *Jacob's Legacy* (see note 6), p.xiii.
61. Also see K.G. Azoulay, 'Not an Innocent Pursuit: The Politics of a "Jewish" Genetic Signature', *Developing World Bioethics*, 3.2 (2003), pp.119–26.
62. See Sand, *The Invention* (note 34), pp.127–8.
63. This article engages with literally a handful of historical sources and with next to no up-to-date scholarship on the subject of Jews in medieval Europe.
64. For a particularly clear example of slippage between theology and history see Konner, *The Jewish Body* (note 2), pp.231–2.
65. Sand's book (*The Invention*, see note 34), was published in Israel in 2008, one year before its English publication. It is translated by Yael Lotan.
66. Ibid. p.248.
67. Ibid. pp.310–13.
68. Ibid. p.22.
69. Interestingly, Sand re-invigorates Arthur Koestler's theory of Jewish origins in Central Asia, made famous in Koestler's controversial *The Thirteenth Tribe: The Khazar Empire and its Heritage* (London: Hutchinson, 1976). Koestler's motivations in originating Europe's Jews in Khazaria were connected to his belief that it would reduce allegations of deicide, which are predicated on the belief that modern Jews descend from ancient Israel.
70. Sand, *The Invention* (see note 34), p.313.
71. C. Strenger, 'Shlomo Sand's "The Invention of the Jewish People" is a Success for Israel', *Haaretz*, 27 November 2009.
72. P. Cohen, 'Book Calls Jewish People an "Invention"', *New York Times*, 24 November 2009.
73. P. Berger and M. Dysch, 'Jews Share a Genetic Signature', *The Jewish Chronicle*, 18 June 2010.
74. Sand deals with genetic constructions of Jews and their significance in *The Invention* (see note 34), pp.273–9.
75. Ibid. p.21.
76. K. Malik, *Strange Fruit: Why Both Sides are Wrong in the Race Debate* (Oxford: Oneworld, 2008), p.5.
77. Y. Amichai, 'Love Song', in *Love Songs* (Tel Aviv: Schocken, 1986), pp.72–3.

How Post-war Britain Reflected on the Nazi Persecution and Mass Murder of Europe's Jews: A Reassessment of Early Responses

DAVID CESARANI

Until the 1990s few historians paid much attention to the various ways in which societies during the post-war era reflected on the persecution and mass murder of the Jews that had occurred between 1933 and 1945. Judith Miller's journalistic investigation *One by One by One*, which appeared in 1991, was one of the earliest and most influential attempts at an international assessment.[1] Annette Wieviorka's seminal study of how different segments of French society filtered the memory of the deportations and integrated them into narratives of the war years provided a model that was to be widely adopted for other national contexts.[2] Then, in 1994, Tony Kushner published his ground-breaking work charting and comparing pre-war, wartime, and post-war responses in Britain and the United States. *The Holocaust and the Liberal Imagination* inspired generations of researchers and created a template for subsequent projects in the UK and elsewhere.[3] By the end of the decade key studies had appeared on most of the relevant countries and a rough consensus had emerged concerning the social, cultural and political reckoning that took place from 1945 to the early 1990s. The findings are conveniently summarised in the compendium *The World Reacts to the Holocaust*, edited by David Wyman, which appeared in 1996.[4]

Historians generally agreed that the liberation of the concentration camps in April–May 1945 provoked intense media coverage and public outrage in the allied countries. This was replicated at certain points during the war crimes trials in 1945–46, with the spotlight on the International Military Tribunal at Nuremberg. However, during these periods in both Britain and America the public got a very partial account of Nazi atrocities. News reports and judicial investigations tended to highlight the concentration camps rather than the death camps and tended to gloss over the mass murder of Jews in eastern Europe.[5]

Furthermore, thanks to the predominance of a liberal-universalist or left-wing anti-fascist agenda, the identity of the Jews as the chief victims of Nazi racial policy was frequently blurred, while their suffering tended to be subsumed into the plight of other national, ethnic, or religious groups who had suffered Nazi brutality. Indeed, so few Jews had survived the round-ups and deportations to the death camps that they tended to get lost amongst the far greater numbers of non-Jews who returned from the concentration camps. Throughout western Europe little distinction was made between Jewish and non-Jewish survivors of Nazi persecution even though Jews had been deported, murdered by poison gas, or shot to death because of their 'race' and not because they had resisted the Nazis as citizens of occupied countries.[6]

This confusion was perpetuated by the war crimes trials and embodied in many early accounts of the camps. Jewish survivors found little interest in their stories; few of them published memoirs and soon they fell silent.[7] During the 1950s the need to rehabilitate West Germany and integrate it into the anti-Soviet bloc added to the pressure on Jews living in NATO countries to hold their piece and avoid making a now valued ally feel uncomfortable by adverting to the dreadful past. Hence, the 1950s were a decade of indifference and ignorance. It was not until the capture of Adolf Eichmann and his spectacular trial in Jerusalem in 1961–62 that the world finally heard the story of Jewish suffering in full, from the mouths of the survivors themselves.[8] Even then, a further 15 to 20 years would elapse before 'the Holocaust' as a fully formed and comprehensive narrative, embracing the time span and the subject matter we know today, entered into public discourse and featured as a subject for cultural explorations. It was generally agreed that the transmission of the TV mini-series 'Holocaust' in the United States in 1978 and across Europe in 1979, marked the watershed.

This, at least, was the consensus. However, at the end of the century a number of books appeared that radically re-interpreted the alleged post war indifference and the reasons for its rupture. With varying emphases and for different motives Tim Cole, Peter Novick, and Norman Finkelstein argued that there had been a virtual conspiracy of silence, and that it was deliberately broken at the instigation of the Jewish leadership in the USA in the wake of the June

1967 Arab–Israel war. Awareness of 'the Holocaust' was deliberately built up and thrust into the public sphere in order to foster sympathy for Jews in the diaspora and for Israel, specifically.[9] These controversial arguments helped to stimulate a re-examination of the late 1940s and 1950s. As a result, over the last few years fresh research has challenged the notion that during this phase survivors held their tongues, that little was published in the way of memoirs, that historical research was both sporadic and patchy, and the subject barely figured in films or other mass media.[10]

This contribution is an attempt to re-assess recent trends in the scholarship concerning post-war responses in Britain to the Jewish catastrophe of 1933–45, such as it is. While it may be a tribute to the quality and comprehensiveness of Tony Kushner's study it is nevertheless surprising that there has not been more historical research, in particular, into the period after 1950. The standard histories of British Jewry hardly mention the impact of the war years except in demographic terms or with reference to the rise of Zionism and fluctuations in Jewish identity.[11] Instead, the 1950s and beyond have been left mainly to sociologists, geographers, and practitioners of cultural studies. A cottage industry has developed around the memory of the war and the destruction of Europe's Jews, its commemoration and explanation, as well as the development of 'Holocaust consciousness', although the focus is almost entirely on the period after 1979.[12] This work builds on the foundations laid by Tony Kushner but frequently exceeds his measured conclusions regarding the patchiness of awareness as against a complete absence of a response. Anne Karpf, for example, writes: 'Again and again, the stereotype of the survivor who didn't want to talk about his or her experience was (and still is) invoked as justification for the silence greeting Holocaust survivors in Britain.' Rather than integrating this dreadful history, 'in post-war Britain silence took up residence instead'. Andy Pearce grants that there was 'more than a kernal of truth' to Yehuda Bauer's accusation in 1979 that in Britain 'nothing at all has been done' in the fields of education or commemoration.[13]

In short, much of the current work on awareness of 'the Holocaust' assumes that there was a 'silence' in the first 15 years after the war and that the subject, in any form, was absent from the public sphere. However, the notion of 'silence' or 'absence' needs to be qualified. Kushner stresses that survivors *did* want to talk, and points out that 'It was not the shortage of information but the unwillingness to accept the uniqueness of the Jewish plight during the war which acted as a barrier to comprehension'.[14] Bloxham, like Kushner, indicates that the scholarly as well as the popular narratives of the war did not entirely exclude Jewish suffering, but simply pushed it to the margins and misconstrued the machinery of persecution and destruction that was responsible.[15] Thus the literature on the post-war era is varied. It spans the analysis of partial and confused narratives which misplaced or marginalised Jewish suffering, popular representations in which the identity of the Jews as victims of a specific genocide is blurred, and blunt assertions that there was a complete 'silence' or an 'absence'.

The central argument here is that we are mistaken if we look in the past for representations of what we recognise today as 'the Holocaust'. It is anachronistic to expect journalists, war crimes investigators, and even survivors of the camps to have had any inkling of the scope and complexity of Nazi anti-Jewish policy between 1933 and 1945, let alone discrete events or sites, many of which were deliberately rendered ambiguous or actually concealed. Moreover, at such close proximity to the undiscriminating horrors of the war and the metastasation of Nazi barbarity, it was not self-evident that the Jews had been differentiated from all other victims. Patchiness or 'marginalisation' may have seemed to contemporaries like the proper perspective – in rather the same way that critics of Holocaust memorialisation today who plead for a less Judeocentric approach, calling for more attention to the non-Jewish victims of Nazi racial-biological persecution as well as to other genocides of the twentieth century, insist on contextualising Jewish suffering.

Even so, time and again, contemporaries remarked on the singularly appalling treatment of the Jews by the Nazis. What is more, by late 1945 it was almost universally accepted that up to six million Jews had perished as a result of deliberate Nazi policy, abetted by their allies and collaborators. It may have been familiarity with these facts that led witnesses to refer to the anti-Jewish atrocities in an almost perfunctory fashion, for at the time they needed little explanation or expansion. The methodology reflects the argument. If we should not expect to find a fully formed historical narrative of 'the Holocaust' or a focus on Jewish victimhood, we have to consult a wide and sometimes unusual range of contemporary sources for traces of a reaction and to treat marginal comments by non-Jews less as a sign of indifference than as a mark of engagement. We also need a more nuanced approach to public discourse, treating it less as a monolithic, centralised stream of rhetoric than a multiplicity of diverse discourses that only occasionally overlapped or combined in the public sphere. Hence statements made in media that are not national or by persons who are not in the public eye may still be public discourse, reaching significant sections of the entire population.

II

Thanks to research by Tony Kushner and others we now have a fair picture of how people in Britain may have learned about Nazi atrocities through the press, newsreels at the cinema, and radio reports. However, as Kushner observed, the liberal-universalist understanding of anti-Semitism and the position of the Jews in society generally tended to dictate that Jews should be treated as citizens of the countries from which they came and not identified as a religious or 'racial' group. Consequently, narratives and analysis in all three media frequently masked the identity of the Jewish victims behind their nationality (which was largely irrelevant to their plight) and misunderstood the nature of the crimes that were now being exposed. It was common, for example, to see the liberated camps as a continuation of the police-terror system of the 1930s rather than constituent parts of a genocide launched during the war. The prevailing liberal-universalist approach made it hard for observers to comprehend a genocide that was irrational, leading instead to narratives that were comprehensible in their own terms even if the explanations that underpinned them were grotesquely inappropriate.[16]

However, certain groups learned much more because of their professional engagement with the consequences of genocide. Thousands of officers and soldiers from almost every branch of the armed forces encountered the camps or the survivors.[17] Dozens of military medical personnel were involved in the relief operations. In the case of Belsen, 97 medical students were flown from Britain to assist in the care of the sick. They joined dieticians, nursing teams from the Red Cross, a Quaker ambulance unit, and medical contingents from several other nations.[18] Moreover, awareness of Belsen was disseminated well beyond the circle of those who directly confronted its horrors. The relief effort was such an extraordinary

medical and social challenge that those involved in it, especially the
health and medical professionals, wanted to share their experience
with others of their calling. This led to a stream of articles in specialist
publications that extended well beyond the initial wave of general
press reports.[19]

Between May 1945 and June 1953, 11 items on Belsen and other
concentration camps appeared in *The Lancet*, the leading journal of
the medical profession in Britain. Four were major articles. In 1946
the *British Medical Journal*, the 'trade paper' of British doctors,
carried six items, including four substantial reports. Articles
appeared in a dozen other medical publications in the UK between
1945 and 1947, usually written by medical students for the journals
of the medical schools and hospitals to which they were attached.
These articles merit close attention because they reveal how medical
relief workers perceived the victims of Nazi policies and whether
there was a 'silence' around their identity.

The Lancet carried one of the earliest detailed accounts of the
medical relief effort on 12 May 1945, beginning with the story of
how Belsen was handed over, a description of the camp layout and
an account of the conditions therein. It recorded the nature of the
diseases and health problems afflicting the survivors, but did not
identify them by nationality or otherwise. In this sense they were
indeed rendered 'invisible' and 'anonymous'.[20] However, a fuller
report by Lieutenant Colonel F.M. Lipscombe that appeared on 8
September 1945, stated that 'Russians and Poles predominated.
Czechs, Belgians, French, Italians and Yugoslavs were also present.
The great majority were Jews'.[21]

In March 1946, the journal carried a special article by Lucie
Adelsberger that gave a concise, powerful and moving account of her
experiences in Auschwitz and Birkenau. Adelsberger commenced by
introducing herself: 'I was arrested in May 1943, and was sent to
Birkenau concentration camp. This was the climax to a series of
restrictions that began in March, 1933, with my removal from a post
at the Robert Koch Institute, Berlin, because I was a Jewess.' She
thereby put the span of Nazi anti-Jewish policy in a nutshell.
Adelsberger then described what she had witnessed in the course of
her employment as an 'internee woman doctor', including selections
from Jewish transports from Italy and Norway. She recalled the
summer of 1944 when Hungarian Jews were being transported to
Birkenau: 'At this time the children in the camp containing gipsies

[sic] played "burning the Jews".' Adelsberger depicted the selections within the camp and remarked that 'Every Jewish prisoner regarded his life as already forfeit, and merely awaited his turn.'[22]

In August 1948, *The Lancet* carried a long notice of a work by Dr Wolff-Eisner who had ended up in Theresienstadt after he, too, was dismissed from the Robert Koch Institute. The notice, which reflected the subject matter of the book, was mainly about the effect of starvation on health but left no doubt about the role of the ghetto-camp, even if the writer located it in the wrong place. 'Theresienstadt, an old fortress near Vienna [sic], was a "privileged" concentration camp intended primarily for elderly Jews.' The piece described how the camp functioned, the plight of the inmates, and reported that 80,000 were 'taken off to Birkenau and Auschwitz for extermination'.[23]

The *British Medical Journal* on 9 June 1945 included a report from Belsen by the Irish paediatrician W.R.F. Collis. It contained graphic descriptions, but the victims were anonymous and mute. Yet the report was preceded by a striking editorial that stated:

> Accounts in the lay press of German concentration camps and the report of the Parliamentary delegation have confirmed what many people knew years ago – namely, that the Nazis, with cold inhumanity, were systematically torturing and slowly exterminating Jews and political enemies.

The editors, who said they felt compelled to publish the medical dispatch, had no illusions about the scope of the disaster. 'Apparently only a small proportion of the inmates of Belsen were German Jews. The rest were Jews from various countries occupied by Germany at the height of her recent expansion.'[24]

As in *The Lancet*, the contributors to the *BMJ* who wrote about the camps did not describe the victims uniformly. Collis blurred their identities, perhaps because he did not place much value on Judaism or Jewishness. In the course of reflecting on the plight of an orphan survivor he asked: 'Is he to be brought up Jew or Catholic?' as if the choice did not much matter.[25] Henri Rosenacher, a French doctor writing on medicine in Dachau, commented that 'Of 293,000 French people deported to Germany 42,000 came back, and 65% of these were found to be in bad health on their arrival in France'.[26] He made no distinction between the types of deportees. However, P.L. Mollinson, writing about starvation in Belsen, was specific about the camps and its victims.

> Belsen was a detention and not an extermination camp – that is to
> say, not a camp where organised extermination was carried out.
> … At its peak it is said to have contained over 66,000 persons.
> The majority of these were Jews of Polish and Hungarian origin,
> but almost all countries were represented.

Many had come from other camps, 'such as the notorious one at
Auschwitz'.[27]

Articles about the camps appeared in other publications serving
health professionals. The *British Dental Journal*, the dentists'
equivalent of the *BMJ*, carried an exhaustive study of facial gangrene
amongst inmates of Belsen. The research by Major J. Dawson was
based on ten case studies, each of which opened with a brief
biographical comment. Dawson identified eight as Jews, of whom six
were Hungarian.[28] A study of psychological breakdown amongst
Belsen camp inmates by M. Niremberski that appeared in the *Journal
of Mental Science* was based on interviews with 60–70 survivors.
Niremberski set down 20 brief case histories of which 11 were
identified as Jewish (including Belgian, Romanian, Polish, Czech,
Dutch and Hungarian Jews). The author summarised the appalling
stories that explained the 'reaction types' and gave his fellow
psychologists an insight into the camps.[29]

It is hard to estimate the impact of these publications, beyond the
likelihood that they were read by numbers of doctors, nurses,
dentists, and psychologists. However, it is possible to surmise that
they were noted by a significant section of the medical and health
community and had an effect. Indeed, several generated subsequent
correspondence. Such was the interest in the health consequences of
the Nazi camps that in 1947 the Royal Society of Medicine convened
an Inter-Allied Conference on War Medicine that included a special
section on 'the physical and psychological problems arising out of
the concentration camps, DP camps, Belsen and Buchenwald'.[30]

These medical reflections were not about what we call 'the
Holocaust' and they often failed to specify the identity of the victims.
Yet they appeared against a background of common knowledge
about Nazi anti-Jewish policies. It is therefore not unreasonable to
assume that the readers connected the spare medical prose about
epidemics and famine with the Nazi persecution and mass murder of
Europe's Jews. But this readership was hardly a cross-section of the
population. They were overwhelmingly male, middle and upper
class, and highly educated. Their professional interests and training

may have made them aware of Nazi crimes against the Jews while others around them had at best a general knowledge and at worst remained oblivious.

III

Psychologists were another professional group that shared this knowledge and propagated it within their own disciplinary community. However, whereas the medical literature focussed on the victims, psychological discourse embraced both victims and perpetrators. Psychologists had long been employed by the Allied armies and intelligence services to draw up psychological profiles of enemy leaders, field commanders, troops, and populations. Some of those employed in these roles went on to interview captured enemy personnel and an elite group monitored the mental welfare of the prisoners at Nuremberg. They published their findings in journals and more accessible publications in a steady stream throughout the late 1940s and 1950s. This body of work, which has been neglected for too long by historians, constitutes the first oral history of the Second World War and the Third Reich.[31]

Saul Padover was an American-born Jew who had lived in Germany in the 1920s and early 1930s. During the war he served in the Psychological Warfare Division of the US Army and followed the allied invasion force into north-west Europe and occupied Germany where he interviewed German civilians in order to assess their psychological resilience. Whenever he confronted Germans he asked them about the persecution of the Jews and noted their responses. His questions showed a significant knowledge about the systematic annihilation of the Jews and, in turn, he learned more as he progressed. Eventually he arrived at Buchenwald where he noted testimony from Auschwitz survivors. A Viennese Jew pleaded with him: 'Please tell them in America one thing, that all the people the Germans burned were Jews. They burned only the Jews. All these bones and ashes are Jewish bones and ashes.' Padover fulfilled this plea, but his book was also published in London in 1946. While it is not solely about the destruction of Europe's Jews, unlike the books published by some British doctors, notably W.R.F. Collis, it clearly and forcefully differentiates them from the other victims of Nazi persecution.[32]

Indeed, by the time that Elie Cohen completed his account of

Human Behaviour in the Concentration Camps, published by
Jonathan Cape in London in 1954, there had been so many medical
and non-medical reports about the camps that interest was flagging.
Cohen, a Dutch Jewish survivor of Westerbork and Auschwitz, wrote
his medical thesis as much to exorcise his own feelings as to inform
a professional and general audience. However, in his introduction
he remarked:

> Any writer of a book on German concentration camps is under no
> delusion that nowadays there is a great deal of general interest in
> the subject. Though it is only a very few years ago, that the
> survivors left these camps, thanks to the military defeat of
> Germany, and the world learned of the horrors that had occurred,
> interest in them is very much on the wane.

This syndrome was not simply due to indifference: it was a reaction
to the first wave of camp literature. Book after book came out
recalling terrible things and demanding the attention of the public.
He explained, 'the reader who has thus had to take the author's
burdens upon his shoulders very soon felt he had enough'.[33]

Criminology was heavily influenced by psychology and there is an
overlap between psychological and criminological literature written
under the impact of Nazi crimes. These works explored the criminal
mentality allegedly bred by Nazism but also served as a conduit for
exploring the crimes themselves.

During the war Alex Comfort, a left-wing, pacifist doctor who
was later to achieve fame as the author of the *Joy of Sex*, had
expressed scepticism about news of Nazi atrocities. He then believed
them to be propaganda manufactured to incite support for an
imperialist war. By the end of the war his views about the capitalist
state had not altered but he now gave credence to the scale of Nazi
brutality. In 1950 he published *Authority and Delinquency in the
Modern State. A Criminological Approach to the Problem of Power*
which attempted to explain how states generate and patronise men
pathologically inclined towards violence. As he explained:

> Refusal to participate in the persecution of a racial minority, or in
> the military destruction of civilian populations, have recently
> figured as crimes in civilized Western societies. Under these
> conditions the independent tradition of the psychiatrist must lead
> him to decide at what point the psychopathy of the individual
> exceeds that of society, which he should attempt to fortify, and by

what standards. More important perhaps is the growing awareness that, great as is the nuisance-value of the criminal in urban society, the centralized pattern of government is to-day dependent for its continued function upon a supply of individuals whose personalities and attitudes in no way differ from those of admitted psychopathic delinquents.[34]

Comfort's study was associated with an international research programme on the 'causes of international and intra-national hatreds and tensions' sponsored by UNESCO. It is spattered with reference to Nazism and Nazi crimes and resonates as a response to National Socialist genocide.[35]

In 1957, Giles Playfair and Derrick Sington published *The Offenders. Society and the Atrocious Crime*. Sington had worked for a British army psychological warfare unit during the war and was one of the first British officers to enter Belsen. He later wrote a powerful account of his experiences, *Belsen Uncovered*, and testified in the trial of the camp commandant and guards. During the 1950s he became interested in criminology and penal policy, but his reflections on these issues were permeated by memories and lessons drawn from the war. So although *The Offenders* is not about Nazi mass murder per se, it contains long sections on the relief of Belsen, Irme Grese, and the Belsen trial.[36]

In these passages, Playfair and Sington reflect on the political, social, and psychological influences that turned Grese and other Germans into mass murderers. They also describe her crimes and the victims, which leads them ineluctably to focus on Jews and to sketch out the genocide in which Grese played her part. Describing her experiences when she was transferred to Auschwitz they write: 'Trainloads of Jews, in tens of thousands, were arriving from France, Belgium, Greece, Bulgaria and Poland to swell the vast queue for the gas chambers.' Thus although the book is not about 'the Holocaust' it contains crucial elements of the narrative with which we are familiar today. *The Offenders* thus contributed to informing a readership that, ironically, had probably not expected to learn from it about Nazi racism and its effect on Europe's Jews.[37]

The traditional discourse of legal studies and law reports was another important medium for conveying information about the origins and impact of Nazi anti-Jewish policy. The law reports from the Nuremberg Tribunal are well known: the proceedings and document collections provided the main source for historical

research for over two decades.[38] However, many other trial reports
were published in Britain. Sir David Maxwell Fyfe edited the *War
Crimes Trials* series published in London between 1948 and 1952,
running to nearly 20 volumes. The series included the trial of Josef
Kramer and SS guards captured at Belsen, which was of special
interest in Britain and contributed to knowledge of both Auschwitz
and Belsen, as well as the trial of the Hadamar murderers, the
Natzweiler trial, and the proceedings against Germans accused of
shooting escaped Allied POWs.[39] The controversial Trial of William
Joyce (Lord Haw Haw) shed light on pre-war British fascism as well
as Nazi propaganda.[40] From 1946 to 1951, the great juridical theorist
and pioneer of international law Sir Hersch Lauterpacht edited the
regular section on the punishment of war criminals that was a feature
of the *Annual Digest and Reports of Public International Law Cases*.

In addition to this discourse of case law there were numerous
commentaries on Allied laws for the restitution of property, the UN
Genocide Convention, the UN Universal Declaration of Human
Rights, and the debates around the aborted establishment of an
international criminal court.[41] It may be fashionable to denigrate the
relevance of these legal discourses and point up the meagre Jewish
content, but Jacob Robinson and Philip Friedman placed the highest
value on legal discourse. In their view it was the only objective
record of events at a time when testimony was distrusted for being
too emotional and unbalanced, and even professional historians were
thought to be too close to events to be sure of impartiality. In their
eyes deliberation on laws against genocide and efforts to entrench
human rights were inseparable from historical research and analysis
as a response to Nazi crimes.[42]

Yet legal discourse, like its medical and psychological counterpart,
was overwhelmingly elite and male. If law courts and legal journals
functioned as sites of memory, they were predominantly male sites.[43]
They were also class specific: vast swathes of the population would
have been ignorant of these intense debates. To those on the outside
it might well have seemed as if there was nothing but 'silence'.

IV

As we have seen, even if 'the Holocaust' as a fully formed event is not
present in the news media or professional publications of the late
1940s and 1950s, awareness of the persecution and slaughter of

Europe's Jews permeated a number of discourses. References to the fate of Jews in the concentration and death camps may have been oblique and partial, but these passing mentions may actually have assumed the existence of a wider body of knowledge gained from other sources. This is not the same as expecting readers to have had the sort of comprehensive, structured understanding that we possess. It was, if anything, reliant on an exclusively visceral understanding of Nazi atrocities centred on certain tropes such as Belsen, a camp, and Lidice, a massacre. Yet the period also saw the publication of a surprisingly large number of reports about the destruction of Jewish communities in eastern Europe as well as memoirs and testimonies from the camps. Few of these early memoirs have been noted or examined in detail, possibly because only a fraction were written by or exclusively about Jews.[44] Nevertheless, these non-Jewish memoirs of incarceration and torture almost always contain reflections on the appalling situation of Jews in the 'concentrationary universe'. Neglecting them has thereby had the double effect of ignoring a considerable source and reinforcing the false impression of a 'silence'.

Contrary to the notion that Auschwitz and German crimes in 'the east' were shrouded in mystery and occluded by the attention paid to concentration camps liberated in western Europe, detailed reports of the killing sites located in Poland reached England very quickly.[45] The Yiddish version of Philip Friedman's summary history of Auschwitz, originally written for the official Polish Commission for the Investigation of German Crimes in Poland, was translated into English by the poet and writer Josef Leftwich, and published in London as *This Was Oswięcim* in 1945. The booklet was issued by a Polish Jewish relief organisation rather than a mainstream publisher, but it carried a foreword by the Polish Ambassador which lifted it above the level of ephemera.[46]

The findings of the Polish state Commission for the Investigation of German Crimes in Poland were themselves translated into English for use by the Nuremberg Tribunal and published in several volumes. Copies made their way to libraries in England (notably the Wiener Library) and were consulted by the first UK-based historians of the 'Final Solution', notably Gerald Reitlinger. These early studies, which remain valuable sources, were produced with the help of the Jewish Historical Commissions in Poland and utilised the testimony of Jewish survivors. Thanks to them anyone who wanted to find out about Auschwitz, Majdanek, Chelmno, Belzec, Sobibor, and Treblinka had an excellent source of information. If there was widespread ignorance in Britain about the death camps in 'the east', it was not for lack of material.[47]

From 1948 onwards historical works, often utilising testimony, appeared almost annually. That year Victor Gollancz published Marie Srykin's path-breaking overview of Jewish resistance, *Blessed is the Match*. Syrkin, who was fluent in Yiddish despite living most of her life America, made extensive use of interviews she had conducted with survivors who reached Palestine. They included Renya Kulkielko, a courier for the Zionist underground in Poland (who went on to publish her own memoir), fighters in the Warsaw ghetto, Abba Kovner, who led the partisans in the Vilna area, and Tuvia Bielski, creator of the famous family camps in White Russia (dramatised in the film *Defiance*). Syrkin was the daughter of a leading Zionist-Socialist thinker, so it is hardly surprising that she stressed the role of Palestinian Jews in resisting the Germans. However, she wrote about Jewish reactions to persecution in Poland, Russia, France, and the Netherlands. Nor did she deal only with resistance: she asked the hard questions about why so many Jews had apparently succumbed without fighting back. Her answers, informed by her interviews with survivors, bear revisiting today. Jews, she noted, were the victims of an elaborate German strategy of deception. Even when the extermination policy was clear, the Germans always offered hope to a portion of the trapped Jewish communities. She also wrote about non-violent resistance, describing how the Warsaw ghetto leadership sought to 'live with honour', providing education and welfare services, as well as finally deciding to 'die with honour' in the revolt.[48]

That the book was not better known at the time may owe something to the odd title, which did little to inform the curious or library cataloguers that it was about the persecution and mass murder of the Jews. This misnomer was a curious characteristic of many early accounts and may help to explain their lapse into obscurity. It is also true of Bernard Goldstein's memoir of the Warsaw ghetto uprising, published by Gollancz two years after Syrkin's book appeared, under the title *The Stars Bear Witness*. Goldstein was the most senior surviving figure of the Bund's leadership in Warsaw and he had a unique perspective on the fate of the city's Jews. The title of his book when it was originally published in Yiddish was, quite sensibly, *Five Years in the Warsaw Ghetto*. In the

English translation by Leonard Shatzkin, a rising star of the New York publishing scene, it became something more poetic but also more enigmatic.[49]

Goldstein afforded readers who got beyond the title a detailed insight into the first years of the ghetto, including sketches of all the major figures in the leadership. He recorded the struggle for survival and the efforts of the Bund to organise welfare for the disease-ridden, starving ghetto inhabitants. Goldstein brilliantly captured the terror and chaos of the 'Great Aktion' from July to September 1942, explaining how it was impossible to think of anything other than personal survival let alone resistance. Finally, he described the emergence of a concerted resistance organisation in the calm that followed, when the Jews were no longer under the illusion that they could survive by cooperating with the Germans. According to the reviewer Michael Zylberberg, writing in the *Jewish Monthly*, the book's appearance created a 'sensation' because it was the first in English 'by a survivor of the great Warsaw catastrophe'. Zylberberg elaborated that although there was already an extensive 'catastrophe literature' it was mainly in Yiddish and other languages so had not yet reached an Anglo-Saxon readership. Hence the interest in *The Stars Bear Witness*.[50]

Yet two issues earlier in the same journal, November 1950, Leftwich had constructed a review article on 'The Tragedy of Warsaw' around the *New York Times* best-seller *The Wall* by John Hersey. Hersey, an American journalist and novelist, had employed teams of researchers to translate sources from Yiddish and Polish to produce an astonishingly accurate, vivid, and frankly didactic documentary novel of the uprising. The book was a critical and commercial success when it appeared in Britain, too. Thus, on both sides of the Atlantic, the suffering and resistance of Warsaw Jewry had registered with a mass readership. If anything, Goldstein's memoir may have benefited from the prior appearance of Hersey's novel which had created an appetite for a more 'authentic' eye-witness report.[51]

There is certainly evidence of a market for such testimony. In 1950, Secker and Warburg published the English translation of Eugen Kogon's account of the Nazi concentration camp system. Kogon was a German Catholic who was held in Buchenwald from 1938 until the liberation as a consequence of his anti-Nazi views. His report on the camp was initially written at the request of a US Army

Psychological Warfare unit, but Richard Crossman, then serving in an equivalent British army team, recommended that it should be published as a book. Kogon subsequently broadened the report into an analysis of the camp system as a whole. It appeared under the title *Der SS-Staat* and was hugely successful, becoming the standard work on the subject for many years. Although it was not about 'the Holocaust' and discussed the Jews as just one element of the camp population, Kogan made it abundantly clear that Jews followed a different path through the *Konzentrationslager* (concentration camp) system and were doomed from the start. He perceptively identified the different phases of Nazi anti-Jewish policy culminating in 'systematic extermination of the Jews, especially in the East' in 1942–45. Although he admitted that he had no direct experience or knowledge of the extermination camps, he drew on the testimony of Jewish survivors from them who had ended up in Buchenwald and included testimony by survivors who recalled experiences in Treblinka, Auschwitz, and the Riga ghetto. Philip Friedman, reviewing the book for the New York-based journal *Jewish Social Studies*, was especially appreciative of the way in which Kogon framed the plight of the Jewish inmates.[52]

Friedman had immigrated to the USA from Europe in 1948, bringing with him direct knowledge of the Nazi destruction of east European Jewry. Indeed, the migration of survivor-historians and writers was crucial for the global dissemination of information about the catastrophe. By an irony of fate, the fact that Zdenek Lederer, a survivor of Theresienstadt, was forced to emigrate to Britain from his native country after the Communists took control in Czechoslovakia meant that his history of the ghetto-camp was quickly translated and published in London. Lederer combined a personal memoir with scrupulous research. As he explained in the introduction:

> I have striven to write a narrative in which sentimentality would not be substituted for feeling, which would not be a mere description of horrors and suffering, but a balanced account of what happened during the years 1941–5 in a small Czech town transformed by the Nazis into a ghetto.

Lederer's history was intimate, insightful and wholly Jewish in orientation. It provided a first-rate history of the annihilation of Czech Jewry, the organisation of the camp-ghetto, daily life within the walls, and, above all, the function of Terezin as a way-station towards Auschwitz-Birkenau.[53]

The following year, Jonathan Cape published Elie Cohen's hybrid memoir and medical history of the camps. By this time so many books on the subject had appeared that he anticipated a lukewarm response to his own contribution. He was also keenly aware that the first wave of memoirs had been so graphic that readers were deterred from tackling any more. Consequently, he adopted a cool tone, although this did nothing to blunt the force of his personal recollections or the testimony he garnered from other witnesses and evidence from trial documents. *Human Behaviour in the Concentration Camps* gives a sound overview of the development of the KZ system and the evolution of the genocide against the Jews in which Auschwitz, the focus of the book, played a central role. Cohen described every aspect of the camp, including the selections, before he homed in on the medical dimension. He concluded with a neo-Freudian analysis of prisoner behaviour and an attempt to explain the mentality of the SS guards.[54]

Cohen's admonition concerning the plethora of memoirs was directed at readers in the Netherlands, but it applied equally to Britain. Shocking testimony to Nazi mass murder of the Jews in eastern Europe had been published here even during the war. One of the first was Stefan Szende's *The Promise Hitler Kept*, a curious and possibly fabricated account of a Polish Jew evading the German occupiers. Even if Szende invented the survivor, named Adolph Folkmann, on whose experiences the book was based, it was a reasonable approximation to what was happening and was intended to alert public opinion to the genocide.[55]

There was no question about the authenticity of Jean-Jacques Bernard's memoir of his imprisonment in the Compiegne internment camp near Paris in 1942, which Gollancz also published in 1945. Bernard was a popular playwright in inter-war France. His father, who was Jewish, had been an even more famous dramatist during the Belle Époque. Both men faced Nazi persecution, but it was the son who was arrested in a round-up of French Jewish intellectuals on 12 December 1941. Bernard found himself sharing the camps with hundreds of Jews of east European origin whose accent made him wince and with whom he initially felt he had little in common. Paradoxically, by virtue of treating them all as Jews, the Germans had only made him and his Jewish compatriots feel more French. 'Let it be understood', he announced, 'that if I have to die in this business, I shall have died for France; I don't want to be claimed by Judaism as a martyr.' Bernard was lucky: he was set free when the Germans released those who were sick or elderly. His memoir is a fascinating insight into French Jewish identities and the chasm that opened between the Jews in wartime France. It is also a brilliantly written account of one more ante-chamber to Auschwitz.[56]

The ability of someone who was not Jewish to give readers an insight into the Nazi treatment of the Jews was underlined in Christopher Burney's thinly disguised reminiscences of his imprisonment in Buchenwald after he was caught while on a mission for the SOE. Burney began *The Dungeon Democracy* with a brief resumé of the history of the concentration camps in Germany. He informed readers about the internal dynamics of prisoner society, concentrating on the drive by the communist political prisoners to establish informal control over the inmates. He also offered short descriptions of each national group, mentioning what made them distinctive. 'No history', he wrote, 'however superficial, would be complete without mentioning the Jews.' He observed that the surviving remnant of German Jews had managed to claw their way into relatively protected positions in the camp hierarchy, but the Polish and Hungarian Jews evinced 'by far the most glaring examples of Nazi brutality'. In both cases, 'the attitude of the SS was that Jews were only fit to die'. While Burney was critical of the conduct of Jews towards the SS, wondering somewhat insensitively why they were 'obsequious', he concluded sympathetically and with no ambiguity that the vast majority of Jews in Europe had been murdered and the remnant reduced to a state of 'physical and mental depravity'.[57]

Burney's memoir is in some senses complemented by the publication in England of Denise Dufournier's account of her imprisonment in Ravensbrück following her arrest for resistance work in France. In the style typical of the moment, Dufournier prefaced her memoir by telling readers that 'the story of my exile at Ravensbrück could be that of any other prisoner'. But gradually differences emerge between her experiences and those of other groups of women in the camp. Having described the journey, the reception and processing, she explains the different categories of prisoners and the system of badges, including the yellow star for Jews. Repeatedly she mentions that Jews arrived in the worst state, were most afflicted by disease, and were kept in the worst block. Chapter 6 is titled 'Extermination', although it refers to the last phase of Ravensbrück and not gas chambers. Yet this is not as misleading as it seems: Dufournier comments that the women in the camp were terrified by the reports of the evacuation of Auschwitz brought into the camp by survivors of the notorious death march.[58]

If the memoirs by Burney and Dufournier shed light on conditions in the concentration camps in Germany, readers who wanted to find out about Auschwitz had two outstanding testimonies to refer to by the start of the 1950s. Both were by women, one non-Jewish and the other Jewish, although she chose to write as if she were not. In 1942 Ella Lingens-Reiner was practising as a doctor in Vienna when she was arrested by the Gestapo for resistance activities and sent to Auschwitz-Birkenau. In the camp she worked in the women's infirmary where she performed abortions on Jewish women to save their lives and witnessed infanticide. Initially Lingens-Reiner found it hard to believe that Jews were being murdered on an industrial scale, but 'slowly, we all grew blunted and saw the mass murder of the Jews as something that was horrifying but immutable'. In her book, like Burney, she included a nation-by-nation assessment of the camp inmates, devoting a separate section to the Jews. Amongst them 'the best and the worst survived'. She did not blur their destiny or the role of Auschwitz: it was 'the stage of the greatest tragedy of the Jewish people, the cruellest and most extensive persecution of their race in history'.[59]

Unlike Lingens-Reiner, Krystyna Zywulska was Jewish. She was born Sonia Landau in Lodz and was working as a para-legal before the war. Following the German occupation of western Poland she fled to the Soviet zone but returned to Warsaw in 1941 and entered the ghetto. She later escaped and lived underground on the 'aryan side' working with the Polish resistance and assisting other Jews in hiding. She was arrested by the Germans in June 1943 and eventually sent to Auschwitz-Birkenau. Following her liberation Zywulska retained her *nom de guerre* and assumed persona for her memoir of the camp, translated into English as *I Came Back*. She nevertheless made many observations about the Jews she encountered in Birkenau and was brutally frank about their singular destiny. She made the point with black humour in a comment addressed to survivors of the Warsaw uprising who poured into the camp in summer 1944. When they expressed apprehension about what might happen next,

Zywulska reassured them: 'They only burn Jews. Don't worry.'[60] *I Came Back* was a great success when it was published in London in 1951 and quickly went through three printings.

As Elie Cohen had predicted, in the mid 1950s there was a lull in the appearance of memoirs – although the steadily increasing success of Anne Frank's diary, first published in 1952, to some extent filled the vacuum.[61] A second wave became evident around 1958, well before the publicity attendant on the capture and trial of Eichmann. In 1958 Leslie Hardman combined with the writer Cecily Goodman to produce *The Survivors*, a passionate account of the liberation and relief of Belsen. It was the first of its kind. Alan Moorehead had published a superb description of the liberation in a compilation of his wartime journalism, *Eclipse*, as long ago as 1945 and there were several accounts of the relief effort, notably Derek Sington's *Belsen Uncovered*. But there was no single book on the history of the camp and none written from a Jewish point of view.[62]

Hardman provided the narrative strand for the book, weaving into it various testimonies by survivors, some covering several pages. They included a variety of voices such as Dr Leo Fritz, a German Jewish doctor who survived Sachsenhausen and Belsen, and 'Sima' who had come from the Vilna ghetto via camps in Estonia where she encountered captured Jewish partisans who told her about the battles in the forests. It was a hybrid book, but Goodman and Hardman cleverly wove a tapestry of experiences within the frame of the Belsen story. However, it is worth noting that in his foreword to *The Survivors* Lord Russell, author of the *Scourge of the Swastika. A Short History of Nazi War Crimes* (1954), commented that 'So many books have been written about the German concentration camps that it may be wondered whether there is room for yet another'. Thus, even a well-read author of a best-selling work on Nazi atrocities thought that the appetite for another was not self-evident.[63]

The same year saw the publication of *Advocate for the dead* in which Alex Weissberg, a scientist and writer who had achieved literary success with an account of his experiences in Stalin's Russia, redacted Joel Brandt's recollections of the desperate efforts to save the Jews of Hungary in spring 1944. The book was written in a dramatic style, but offered genuinely new insights into the destruction of the Hungarian Jews and the ambivalent response of the British when offered the possibility of rescuing thousands of victims.[64] Brandt's searing personal history was translated from the

German by Constantine FitzGibbon who had just completed the translation of the memoirs of Rudolf Hoess, commandant of Auschwitz, published in London by Weidenfeld and Nicolson.[65] Unlike many of the other memoirs that George Weidenfeld published at this time, mainly by German military and diplomatic figures, this one was inescapably concerned with the 'Final Solution' – even if the reader had to cope with Hoess' miserable attempts at self-exculpation (largely by blaming Adolf Eichmann for the mass murder of the Jews sent to Auschwitz-Birkenau).

By coincidence, the next Jewish memoir to appear was Eugene Heimler's *Night of the Mist*. It told the racy tale of a young Hungarian Jew who was deported to Auschwitz-Birkenau where he was adopted by a kapo in the so-called Gypsy camp. Heimler had emigrated to England after the war and trained as a psychiatric social worker, a profession in which he built a considerable reputation. His memoir of Auschwitz and his time in other camps is shot through with his later-developed philosophy of life and social-psychological observations. But it is largely memorable for recording his ability to indulge a healthy sexual appetite in the most adverse conditions, even after the murder of his wife and all of his family.[66]

One book that defies almost every category is *Follow My Leader*, written by Louis Hagen. It was, however, an important contribution to knowledge of the Nazis and the Third Reich and deserves to be better known today. Hagen was a German Jew from a wealthy banking family who migrated to Britain in 1936 after a spell in a concentration camp. During the war he served as a glider pilot and later wrote a gripping account of the battle of Arnhem, in which he won the Military Medal. After the war Hagen returned to Germany with the idea of tracking down people he had known and through interviews with them reconstructing what life was like under Hitler. In effect he embarked on one of the first oral histories of everyday life in the Third Reich. He did not set out to write what we would understand as a 'Holocaust book', but his interviewees constantly shed light on anti-Semitism, the attraction of Nazism, and the resistance to Hitler. One reason Hagen did not write explicitly about Jews was that none survived in Germany from his immediate circle. 'There are no Jews among the biographies', he explained in the foreword, adding that 'Much has been written about the Jews, and those who are left are being well looked after'.[67] In a few words his aside captured the extent of the desolation visited upon German

Jewry and the reparative impulse that followed the end of the war.

At this point it may be apposite to offer some interim conclusions about this neglected memoir literature. It is clear that the *Diary of Anne Frank* was not the only book about the Nazi persecution and mass murder of the Jews. There were many more, several of which were about Auschwitz and the destruction of Polish Jewry. Whereas Anne Frank's diary ended before the worst horrors of the camps began, these memoirs tended to be harsh and graphic. Of course, whereas we know a great deal about the escalating sales of the diary and its rapidly expanding school-age readership, there is a question over the reception of these other works and the size of their audience.

It is also puzzling why certain works were translated quickly while others were overlooked. Victor Gollancz went to the trouble and expense of translating the memoirs by Jean-Jacques Bernard and Ella Lingens-Reiner, but several acclaimed accounts that were translated into English and published in the United States were not even taken up by a UK publisher.[68] 'Jewish' publishing houses in London clearly took the lead in publishing survivor memoirs: Victor Gollancz, Secker and Warburg, Andre Deutsch, Vallentine Mitchell, and Edward Goldston account for the majority of them. Yet non-Jewish publishers were obviously also willing to take a punt in this area and include Heinemann, Allen and Unwin, Dennis Dobson, Bodley Head, and Jonathan Cape. Most of these books were reviewed, especially in the Jewish press, including The *Jewish Chronicle*, the *Jewish Monthly*, the Association of Jewish Refugees *Information*, and the *Wiener Library Bulletin*. However, the *New Statesman* was no less assiduous and many received notices in *The Times* and *The Observer*. It would require a full-scale reception study to evaluate just how widely they were reviewed, what reviewers said, and how well they sold. Some went through a number of printings; others seem to have appeared in a small run and then vanished. But the late 1940s and early 1950s were a period of austerity and book sales need to be calibrated to those conditions. More pertinently, we need to measure the reception of concentration camp memoirs against the hugely popular genres, such as prisoner of war sagas and accounts devoted to the fate of SOE operatives.[69]

What can be said with some assurance is that for the idly curious alongside serious researchers there was already a significant library of historical studies and testimonies. In fact, by the mid 1950s there were so many books on Nazi atrocities that authors and publishers felt the need to apologise for the appearance of yet more. If anything, the rush to publish in the immediate aftermath of the war glutted the market and prevented better works making their way to the public. As early as 1948, the jacket description of Denise Dufournier's memoir of Ravensbrück stated that 'This is one of the many books on the concentration camps that have been published in countries occupied by the Germans. Of Belsen, Buchenwald and Dachau we have already heard much, but of Ravensbrück ... we have been told very little.' So, although it may seem a mystery why people who lived through the period recall that little was said or written about what we recognise as 'the Holocaust', the truth may be that there had been too much, too soon. The 1950s may have turned into a relatively barren decade, but not as result of indifference. If anything, the opposite was the case.

V

After 1945 every country touched by the Second World War and the genocide against the Jews had its own reasons for wanting to ignore, marginalise, or simply move on from the Jewish cataclysm. However, Britain was a special case. Britain held Palestine under a mandate from the League of Nations and the Zionist campaign for an independent Jewish state in the country led to an insurgency that targeted the British security forces and colonial administration. Jewish terrorists even struck at British targets in Europe and on the British mainland. In the United Kingdom, 'compassion fatigue' converged with deep irritation over the behaviour of Jews in Palestine and those in the diaspora supporting their struggle for independence. It led to indignation and occasionally to violent expressions of anger.[70]

One of the main causes of contention between the Jews and the British was Britain's refusal to increase the quota for Jewish immigration into Palestine. This policy condemned tens of thousands of survivors of the ghettos and camps to languish in Displaced Person's (DP) camps in central Europe. The Zionist organisations orchestrated protests amongst the Jewish DPs, making full use of their tragic stories. They also staged spectacular attempts to run the British naval blockade of Palestine, drawing further attention to the miserable condition of the survivors of Nazi persecution. To underline the point, Zionist propaganda routinely depicted the British as anti-Semitic and compared them to the Nazis.[71]

Hence, from November 1945, when the issue first exploded, until May 1948, when the mandate was wound up, Jews were in the news and usually in a confrontational role. Yet the Zionist insurrection in Palestine was the mirror image of the Jewish fate under the Nazis. The two things were so intimately connected that events in Palestine ineluctably dragged in memories of and references to the Nazi persecution of the Jews in Europe. Hence, when Richard Crossman and Michael Foot collaborated in June 1946 to write a polemic against the Labour government's betrayal of pledges to the Jews they entitled it *A Palestine Munich*, linking the decisions that helped lead to war with its ultimate consequences for the Jewish people.[72]

Arthur Koestler, the Hungarian Jewish writer and author of *Darkness at Noon*, worked closely with Crossman and Foot on the polemic although his name was kept off it because his allegiances were well known. At around the same time he published a best-selling novel, *Thieves in the Night*, which dramatised the Zionist struggle and showed how the memory of Nazi persecution fed Zionist ardour. The novel is set in Palestine in 1937–39 and one of the leading characters, Baumann, is a Viennese Jewish socialist who had fought the Nazis and fascists in Austria and Spain before arriving in Palestine where he joined the Jewish underground. The message of the book was transparent: a Jewish state was the answer to centuries of anti-Semitism and a refuge for persecuted Jews.[73]

Koestler rammed home this point unremittingly in his advocacy of Zionism. In August 1947, after a vicious round of Jewish terrorism against the British and no less ferocious counter-measures, he published in the *New Statesman* a 'Letter to a Parent of a British Soldier in Palestine' in which he summarised the Jewish case for statehood and reminded readers of what the Jews had experienced in Europe. 'If, instead of Smith, your name was Shmulewitz, it might have happened to you.'[74] His account of the Jewish struggle for statehood, *Promise and Fulfilment*, published two years later, established the model for later histories by setting the efforts of the Zionist movement in the 1930s and 1940s against the backcloth of the Nazi persecution of the Jews. The chapter on 'The Little Death Ships', the rickety vessels that sought to carry 'illegal' Jewish immigrants to Palestine during the war years, directly linked the rise of Jewish terrorism in Palestine to the frustration of attempts by Jews to escape the genocide in Europe.[75]

Meanwhile the British government tried to involve the United States in solving the dilemma of Palestine. In November 1945 the two countries set up an Anglo-American Committee of Inquiry.[76] Its terms were

> To examine the position of the Jews in those countries in Europe where they have been the victims of Nazi and Fascist persecution, and the practical measures taken or contemplated to be taken in those countries to enable them to live free from discrimination and oppression and to make estimates of those who wish or will be impelled by their conditions to migrate to Palestine or other countries outside Europe.

Thus the Inquiry explicitly linked Nazi persecution of the Jews to the situation in Palestine. Furthermore, members of the Inquiry toured Jewish DP camps, visited Poland, and took evidence from Jewish survivors. Their report contained a stark summary of what they saw and heard:

> In the cold print of a report it is not possible accurately to portray our feelings with regard to the suffering deliberately inflicted by the Germans on those Jews who fell into their hands. The visit of our subcommittee to the ghetto in Warsaw has left on their minds an impression which will forever remain. Areas of that city on which formerly stood large buildings are now a mass of brick rubble, covering the bodies of numberless unknown Jews. Adjoining the ghetto there still stands an old barracks used as a place for killing Jews. Viewing this in the cold grey light of a February day one could imagine the depths of human suffering there endured. In the courtyards of the barracks were pits containing human ash and human bones. The effect of that place on Jews who came searching, so often in vain, for any trace of their dear ones, can be left to the imagination.
>
> When we remember that at Maidanek and Oswiecim and many other centers a deliberate policy of extermination, coupled with indescribable suffering, was inflicted upon the Jews, of whom it is estimated that certainly not less than five millions perished, we can well understand and sympathize with the intense desire of the surviving Jews to depart from localities so full of such poignant memories. It must also be understood that this happened in what were regarded as civilized communities.[77]

The Committee's report received huge publicity in Britain, mainly thanks to its contentious recommendation that 100,000 Jewish DPs should be allowed to enter Palestine immediately. The Labour government was appalled by the implications and felt let down by the conduct of the Labour MP Richard Crossman who had been selected for the Committee by the Foreign Secretary, Ernest Bevin, himself. But in a powerful book Crossman went on to explain his role in the inquiry and defend his decision to back the report. *Palestine Mission*, published by Hamish Hamilton in 1947, became a best-seller. It is not 'Holocaust literature' but it is laced with reflections on the war, anti-Semitism, and offers glimpses into the experiences of Jewish survivors. In several heart-rending passages Crossman recalled his interviews with survivors of Auschwitz and retold their graphic stories about the camps. It was a sort of oral history, albeit in the service of the Zionist cause.[78]

The debate about Palestine in 1945–48 inexorably tapped an awareness of the Jewish catastrophe and ensured that for a further three years the fate of the Jews echoed in the mass media, sometimes in unexpected ways. Tony Kushner, using reports compiled by Mass Observation and other sources, first observed that British commentators and members of the public who were enraged by Jewish behaviour did not balk at comparing Zionist atrocities to Nazi misdeeds.[79] His evidence has been reinforced by the publication of extracts from some of the diaries kept for Mass Observation in 1945–48. Edie Rutherford, a housewife in Sheffield, was so exercised by events in Palestine that on 3 December 1946 she wrote: 'As more and more lads are killed there, I begin to wish we had started the war a bit later, so that Hitler would have exterminated a few more Jews.' On 4 August 1947, in the wake of a much publicised Zionist outrage climaxing in the hanging of two kidnapped British sergeants, B. Charles, an antiques dealer living in Edinburgh, wrote: 'The Jews are a scourge to mankind. I should rejoice to know that every Jew – man, woman, and child – had been murdered. We ought to drop six atomic bombs on six different cities in Palestine and wipe out as many Jews as possible.'[80] It is surely not too fanciful to suspect that the six cities/bombs summoned up by Mr Charles echoes the figure of six million already murdered Jews that was by now established currency.

If studies of 'Holocaust literature' and 'Holocaust historiography' in Britain have scarcely noted the nexus between the 'Palestine emergency' and the war years, they have also overlooked the extent to which anti-fascist rhetoric and the fight against anti-Semitism pulled in references to the genocide against the Jews. Yet the revival of fascism in Britain and the return of Oswald Mosley could not be dissociated from the memory of Nazism. The Jews and non-Jews who rallied against the fascists inevitably had in their minds the events that had occurred just a few years earlier in Europe. Recalling the formation of the anti-fascist 43 Group in 1947, Vidal Sassoon, said:

> I do not know the exact day when we decided to return the hate in kind, but the horror of the images coming from Auschwitz, Dachau, Buchenwald and seemingly so many other places triggered a sense of survival within the remaining Jewish population of Europe. Hearing of the heroics of Mordechai Anielewitz and his few thousand followers in the Warsaw ghetto nurtured our mood. ... 'Never Again!' became a command not a slogan, and so the 43 group was born.[81]

Sassoon's memories may have become adulterated over time (as his impressive list of references suggests), but Morris Beckman, a founder of the 43 Group, vividly recalled how ex-servicemen at the time collapsed the partition between war and post-war, between Nazism and British fascism:

> Going from a cinema showing newsreel of piles of Jewish men, women and children being bulldozed into lime-pits in the concentration camps, and then passing an outdoor fascist meeting or seeing swastikas whitewashed on Jewish homes and synagogues affected these ex-servicemen with emotions ranging from choleric anger to cold hard desire to kill the perpetrators.

Beckman illustrated the chain of thought linking Palestine with street-fighting in Britain and the still fresh impressions of Nazi genocide:

> Dominating the conversations was Palestine; the flood of Jewish survivors trying to reach there, and the efforts of the British armed forces to reduce the flood. There were continuous heated arguments between those who were more conscious of being British than Jewish, and those whose solidarity was wholly with the Jewish survivors. It was a painful dual loyalty. But all, no matter what their views, were painfully sensitive to the knowledge that too many Jews had perished during the previous six years.[82]

Not only Jews were haunted by the past or capable of making these connections. After a weekend of anti-Jewish rioting in British cities in August 1947, triggered by news of the atrocity against the two British sergeants in Palestine, many politicians and newspapers recoiled in alarm. The *Evening Standard* warned: 'There is no place in Britain for the apostles of Hitler's satanic creed.' The *Spectator* magazine admonished that 'chains of events of this kind have led in the past to mass-murder and the gas chambers'. Showing that awareness of wartime Jewish suffering existed only in order to condemn the Zionists for occluding it by their antics, the communal activist Harold Soref, writing in the *Jewish Monthly*, complained that 'the sympathy aroused by the massacre of the six million Jewish martyrs and the concentration camp atrocities have been eclipsed by happenings in Palestine. Belsen, Auschwitz and Dachau have slipped from public memory'.[83]

However, they did not. Jews and non-Jews, pro-Zionists and anti-Zionists, fascists and anti-fascists were irresistibly led back to the terrible past in their pursuit of future political objectives. The arguments were rehearsed endlessly and the images that reinforced them recurred until they became clichés. If the wartime plight of the Jews was spoken of less often in public discourse from the early 1950s onwards it may have been because it was too well known to bear reiteration. Furthermore, with the creation of the State of Israel in 1948, the issues that had given rise to this discourse were superficially resolved. Decades would pass before the partial and unsatisfactory nature of post-war retribution, restitution and reparation could be detected and revealed. In the meantime, however, it was not unreasonable for people to believe that they had heard and knew enough. It was perhaps sufficient for them not to want to know anything further: knowing a little acted as a barrier to learning more.

VI

There is no doubt that many Jewish survivors of the ghettos and camps, as well as refugees who arrived in Britain before the war, felt that their experiences were not recognised in the public arena for decades after the Second World War. With good reason Kushner places importance on the recollections of survivors who attested to the ignorance, insensitivity or lack of curiosity they encountered in post-war Britain. Gena Turgel, liberated in Belsen, remembered: 'When I first came to England, people seemed very preoccupied with themselves. Some said: "We also had a hard time. We were bombed and had to live in shelters. We had to sleep in the Underground."'[84] Kitty Hart, a survivor of Auschwitz, recalled that

> I was soon to discover that everybody in England would be talking about personal war experiences for months, even years, after the hostilities had ceased. But we, who had been pursued over Europe by the mutual enemy, and come close to extermination at the hands of that enemy, were not supposed to embarrass people by saying a word.[85]

At the opening of her memoir, *Inherit the Truth*, Anita Lasker-Wallfisch remarks: 'When we first came to England, Renate [her sister] and I badly wanted to talk, but no one asked us any questions.'[86]

Such examples could be multiplied. But countervailing experiences should not be ignored. When Gena Turgel arrived in England in November 1945, 'All of Fleet Street had heard that we were coming, and dozens of reporters and photographers were waiting for us at St Pancras Station'. True, the reason for this attention was less to do with interest in the Nazi genocide than in the mawkish appeal of Turgel's marriage to a Jewish soldier who had been amongst the liberating force. Turgel resented this clamour, but even if their interest was perverse, the pressmen did convey something of the horrors so recently experienced by the Jews. As she remembered: 'The papers were full of banner headlines: "The Bride from Belsen is here."'[87]

Another Belsen survivor, Paul Oppenheimer, recalled that

> As far as I can remember, nobody asked us about our experiences during the war, and we were not anxious to remember all these horrible events. At that time in 1945/6, Belsen was a very high profile subject and it did not require any contributions from us to explain what had happened there.[88]

Yet Oppenheimer's observation offers a key to unlocking the conundrum of simultaneous presence/absence. Nazi atrocities were 'very high profile': they were lodged in the popular imagination and featured in public discourse. Whether Jews were specifically identified as victims may not have mattered. The very anonymity of 'the victims' allowed an identity to be assumed or projected onto them and it is hardly likely that in the context of 1945–50 when people saw newsreels, or heard radio broadcasts, or read news reports about the concentration camps and Nazi crimes, they identified the dead or the survivors as, say, Croatians or Belgians. In this sense, universalisation provided a tabula rasa onto which the Jewish experience could be inscribed.[89]

Nor is public discourse (a tricky and ill-defined concept at the best of times) monolithic. It comprises many discourses that mingle in the public sphere, not all of which are equally accessible. In post-war Britain, the persecution and mass murder of the Jews was conveyed in numerous professional discourses that included some groups in the distribution of knowledge and awareness while excluding others. It is thus possible to point out locations of intense research and reflection on the fate of the Jews – they might be described as sites of memory – that were sharply circumscribed by class, occupation, age, and gender. The subject was being broached, but the 'reception' was patchy. For an observer in one place at that time it might have seemed as if there was nothing but 'silence' about the fate of the Jews, while for another person in a different location the facts of the catastrophe may have been glaringly obvious and not in need of reiteration. These perceptions were then carried forward and reified as memories of the period.

Age was as important as class and gender. Most of the survivors who have been interviewed since the 1980s about their post-war experiences were young at the time they arrived in Britain. Although we have derived much from their testimony and recollections, they may not be the best barometer of public feeling or awareness within and beyond the Jewish communities of the late 1940s and 1950s. Many were initially sundered from the surrounding population by language barriers. They were young men and women in a society that tended to believe teenagers should be seen and not heard, least of all young girls. It took several years before they attained a position from which to fully engage with the surrounding society, and by that time (usually the early 1950s) the experiences that were fresh and urgent for them had become yesterday's news for everyone else. Indeed, even those who did care about the fate of the Jews may have become fatigued by constantly hearing of it in the late 1940s. The demonstrable reluctance of many Jews, and non-Jews, to hear their stories is a puzzle and seems morally repugnant to us today. Yet we have to remember that for a brief, intense period 'Jews were news', an experience that British Jews did not relish at the best of times. These were the worst of times, when reports about the genocide jostled with stories from Palestine; when memoirs about the Warsaw ghetto uprising collided with news stories about the insurgency in the Yishuv, when coverage of massacres in Jerusalem overlapped accounts of massacres in Poland. In these circumstances it may be understandable that by the end of the 1940s, within and beyond the Jewish community, people were sick and tired of hearing about Jews fighting and dying.

To conclude, between 1945 and 1960 an awareness of the Nazi persecution and mass murder of the Jews was maintained through a variety of discourses and disciplinary fields beyond the commemorative activity of the Jewish community, refugees, and survivors. This historical consciousness was rooted in a media bombardment during the spring of 1945 that created an imperishable store of memories and images. It was reinforced and refreshed by a string of events and news stories relating to the trial of Nazi war criminals and the conflict in Palestine from 1947 to 1948. The collective memory of the Allies' war and the Nazi war against the Jews was shaped in a matrix of discourses that flowed together in the public sphere. These discourses were often partial, and they were class, gender, and age specific. Yet in combination they were responsible for a breadth and depth of understanding that is easy to miss if we look only for something that resembles 'the Holocaust' as it exists today in public discourse, popular cultural representations, literature, or historiography.

Pro-Zionism and anti-fascism were shot through with a historical consciousness. In comparison with what is now known about Nazi anti-Jewish policy and its implementation, the data that supported this awareness was flawed and shallow. But throughout the 1950s there was, nonetheless, a dim awareness that something terrible had happened in Europe under the Nazis as a result of which six million Jews perished and the State of Israel came into existence. People knew enough to know this much. They did not think they needed to know more; some may even not have wanted to; for both groups the 'silence' was a result of partial knowledge rather than complete ignorance. This may explain the curious phenomenon whereby 'the Holocaust' was simultaneously present and absent.

It would be possible to comb through the novels and films of this period, as Lawrence Baron has done for the United States, to find evidence of this peculiar awareness and, if nothing more, I hope my contribution will inspire further, much-needed research on the 1950s and 1960s in Britain.[90] For current purposes, however, one British film may be taken to exemplify the presence of the past. The film *Dunkirk* was directed by Leslie Norman and opened in Britain in 1958. It had a large cast and many plots that converged on the evacuation of the BEF in June 1940. One strand concerns a team of doctors in a field hospital in the port. When the time arrives for the final evacuation they draw lots to determine who will stay with the wounded who cannot be moved. One member of the team is identified by his name, Dr Levy, as a Jew. It falls to him and another doctor to stay behind while the Germans close in. The look of tragic stoicism in his face and the anxious, compassionate glances from his more fortunate comrades tells the audience everything it needs to know about the fate of Jews who fell into the hands of the Germans. The soundtrack in the background punctuates the scene with long bursts of machine gun fire, echoing the mass shooting of Jews. The scene has almost no dialogue and could not have been understood without the benefit of a rich historical subtext. It is not a scene from a 'Holocaust' movie, but it is a scene about 'the Holocaust'. It is in a film that premiered in 1958 when, supposedly, a pall of 'silence' hung over a plain of ignorance.[91] Yet the scene could only have been interpreted by an audience aware of the unspoken implications for the Jewish doctor. They may not have had detailed knowledge of Auschwitz or been able to identify Treblinka or to differentiate Belsen from Buchenwald, but nor were they unaware or uncaring that a genocide had been inflicted on Europe's Jews.

ACKNOWLEDGEMENTS

I would like to thank Tony Kushner for his perceptive and constructive comments on a draft of this contribution. An earlier version entitled 'Israel, the Diaspora and the Emergence of "the Holocaust" as a Cultural Construct' was delivered to the conference on 'War, Holocaust, State: Sixty Years since the end of World War II', Tel Aviv University, 15 June 2005 and I would like to thank the organisers and participants, particularly Professor Anita Shapira, for their remarks on the paper.

NOTES

1. Judith Miller, *One, By One, By One. Facing the Holocaust* (New York: Simon and Schuster, 1991).

2. Annette Wieviorka, *Deportation et Genocide. Entre la memoire et L'Oubli* (Paris: Plon, 1992). See also Dienke Hondius, 'A Cold Reception: Holocaust Survivors in the Netherlands and Their Return', *Patterns of Prejudice*, 28.1 (1994), 47–65.
3. Tony Kushner, *The Holocaust and the Liberal Imagination* (Oxford: Blackwell, 1994).
4. David S. Wyman, ed., *The World Reacts to the Holocaust* (Baltimore, MD: Johns Hopkins University Press, 1996).
5. Donald Bloxham, *Genocide on Trial. War Crimes Trials and the Formation of Holocaust History and Memory* (Oxford: Oxford University Press, 2001).
6. Pieter Lagrou, 'Victims of Genocide and National Memory. Belgium, France and the Netherlands, 1945–1966', *Past and Present*, 154 (1997), 181–222. See also his *The Legacy of Nazi Occupation. Patriotic Memory and National Recovery in Western Europe, 1945–1965* (Cambridge: Cambridge University Press, 2000).
7. Wieviorka, *Deportation et Genocide* (see note 2), pp.161–328 on France; and Manuela Consoni, 'The Written Memoir: Italy 1945–1947', in *The Jews Are Coming Back. The Return of the Jews to their Countries of Origin after World War Two* ed. by David Bankier (New York: Yad Vashem/Berghahn, 2005), pp.169–80. See also note 5. On the impact of trials see David Bankier and Dan Michman, eds., *Holocaust and Justice. Representation and Historiography of the Holocaust in Post-War Trials* (Jerusalem: Yad Vashem/Berghahn, 2010).
8. Annette Wieviorka, *The Era of the Witness* trans. by Jared Stark (Ithaca, NY: Cornell University Press, 2006 [first published in 1998]), pp.56–95.
9. Tim Cole, *Images of the Holocaust. The Myth of the 'Shoah Business'* (London: Duckworth, 1999); Peter Novick, *The Holocaust in American Life* (Boston: Houghton Mifflin, 1999); Norman Finkelstein, *The Holocaust Industry* (London: Verso, 2000).
10. Lawrence Baron, 'The Holocaust and American Public Memory, 1945–1960', *Holocaust and Genocide Studies*, 17.1 (2003), 62–88; Alan Rosen, *Sounds of Defiance. The Holocaust Multilingualism and the Problem of English* (Lincoln, NE: University of Nebraska Press, 2005), pp.6–33; idem, 'Comme si e'etait hier. David Boder et l'histoire des temoignages sur l'Holocaust', in *Je N'ai Pas Interroge Les Morts* ed. by Alan Rosen and Florent Brayard, trans. by Emmanuel Dauzel (Paris: Tallandier, 2006), pp.11–37; and idem, *The Wonder of their Voices. The 1946 Interviews of David Boder* (New York: Oxford University Press, 2010); Zoë Waxman, *Writing the Holocaust: Identity, Testimony, Representation* (Oxford: Oxford University Press, 2006), pp.100–112; Hasia R Diner *We Remember With Reverence and Love. American Jews and the Myth of Silence After the Holocaust, 1945–1962* (New York: NYU Press, 2009). See also David Bankier and Dan Michman, eds., *Holocaust Historiography in Context. Emergence, Challenges, Polemics and Achievements* (New York: Berghahn/Yad Vashem, 2008), parts II and III. See also Jeffrey Shandler, *While America Watches. Televising the Holocaust* (New York: Oxford University Press, 1999).
11. V.D. Lipman, *A History of the Jews in Britain since 1858* (Leicester: Leicester University Press, 1990), pp.229–30; Geoffrey Alderman, *Modern British Jewry* (Oxford: Clarendon Press, 1992), p.314; Todd Endelman, *The Jews of Britain 1656 to 2000* (Berkeley: University of California Press, 2002), pp.229–31.
12. Efraim Sicher, *Beyond Marginality. Anglo-Jewish Literature after the Holocaust* (Albany: State University of New York, 1988), pp.153–57; Tony Kushner, 'The Impact of the Holocaust on British Society and Culture', *Contemporary Record*, 5.2 (1991), 357–61; Anne Karpf, *The War After. Living With the Holocaust* (London: Heinemann, 1996); David Cesarani, 'British War Crimes Policy and National Memory of the Second World War', in *War and Memory in the Twentieth Century* ed. by K. Lunn and M. Evans (Oxford: Berg, 1997), pp.27–42; Steven Cooke, 'Negotiating Memory and Identity: The Hyde Park Holocaust Memorial, London', *Journal of Historical Geography*, 26.3 (2000), 449–65; Tom Lawson, 'Constructing a Christian History of Nazism 1945–49: Anglicanism and the Memory of the Holocaust', *History and Memory*, 16.1 (2004), 146–76; idem, 'Shaping the Holocaust: Understanding the European Jewish Tragedy in Christian Discourse, 1945–2005', *Holocaust and Genocide Studies*, 21.3 (2007), 404–20; Andy Pearce, 'The Development of Holocaust Consciousness in Contemporary Britain, 1979-2000', *Holocaust Studies. A Journal of Culture and History*, 14.2 9 (2008), 71–94.
13. Karpf, *The War After* (see note 12), pp.166, 204; Pearce, 'The Development of Holocaust Consciousness in Contemporary Britain' (see note 12), p.72.

14. Tony Kushner, '"I Want to go on Living after my Death": The Memory of Anne Frank', in *War and Memory in the Twentieth Century* (see note 12), p.6.
15. Bloxham, *Genocide on Trial* (see note 5), pp.153–81, 185–218.
16. See Kushner, *The Holocaust in the Liberal Imagination* (note 3). I contributed to reinforcing this impression: see David Cesarani, 'British War Crimes Policy and National Memory of the Second World War', in *War and Memory in the Twentieth Century* ed. by K. Lunn and M. Evans (Oxford: Berg, 1997), pp.27–42; idem, 'Great Britain', in *The World Reacts to the Holocaust* (see note 4), pp.599–641; idem, '"Le crime contra l'Occident": les reactions britanniques a la "liberation" des camps de concentration nazis en 1945', in *La Liberation des camps et le Retour Des Deportes* ed. by E. Lynch and M.-A. Matard-Bonnuci (Brussels: Editions Complexe, 1995), pp.238–49.
17. For the military, see Paul Kemp., ed., *The Relief of Belsen. April 1945. Eye Witness Accounts* (London: Imperial War Museum, 1991).
18. See Ben Shephard, *After Daybreak. The Liberation of Belsen, 1945* (London: Jonathan Cape, 2005).
19. For a comprehensive account of media responses see Joanne Reilly, *Belsen. The Liberation of A Concentration Camp* (London: Routledge, 1998), pp.50–77. See also Toby Haggith, 'The Filming of the Liberation of Bergen-Belsen and Its Impact on Understanding of the Holocaust', in *Belsen 1945. New Historical Perspectives* ed. by Suzanne Bardgett and David Cesarani (London: Vallentine Mitchell, 2006), pp.89–122; and Suzanne Bardgett, 'What Wireless Listeners Learned: Some Lesser Known BBC Broadcasts about Belsen', in ibid. pp.123–36.
20. 'Belsen Concentration Camp', *The Lancet*, 12 May 1945, pp.603–5.
21. 'Medical Aspects of Belsen Concentration Camp', *The Lancet*, 8 September 1945, pp.313–15.
22. 'Medical Observations in Auschwitz Concentration Camp', *The Lancet*, 2 March 1946, pp.317–19. Lucie Adelsberger later published an important memoir: *Auschwitz. A Doctor's Story* trans. by Susan Ray (Boston; Northeastern University Press, 1995; first published in Germany, 1956).
23. 'Life and Death in a Concentration Camp', *The Lancet*, 7 August 1948, pp.228–9.
24. *British Medical Journal (BMJ)*, Editorial note and 'Belsen Camp: A Preliminary Report', 9 June 1945, pp.813–16.
25. 'Some Pediatric Problems Presented At Belsen Camp', *BMJ*, 23 February 1946, pp.273–5. In fact, Collis adopted four orphaned Jewish children and raised them as Christians. See Robert Collis, *To Be A Pilgrim. An Autobiography of Robert Collis* (London: Secker and Warburg, 1975).
26. 'Medicine in Dachau', *BMJ*, 21 December 1946, pp.953–5.
27. 'Observations on Cases of Starvation in Belsen', *BMJ*, 5 January 1946, pp.4–8.
28. 'Cancorum Oris', *British Dental Journal*, 79.6 (21 September 1945), 151–7.
29. 'Psychological Investigation of a Group of Internees at Belsen Camp', *Journal of Mental Science*, 92.386 (January 1946), 60–74.
30. Sir Henry Letherby Tidy, ed., *Inter-Allied Conference on War Medicine 1942–1945* (London: Staples, 1947), section 12.
31. D.M. Kelly, *22 Cells in Nuremberg. A Psychiatrist Examines the Nazi War Criminals* (New York: Greenberg Publishers, 1947); H.V. Dicks, J. Gibson and others, *The Case of Rudolf Hess. A Problem in Diagnosis and Forensic Psychiatry* (London: Heinemann, 1947); G.M. Gilbert, *Nuremberg Diary* (New York: Farrar, Strauss and Young, 1947); L. Alexander, 'War Crimes. Their Social-Psychological Aspects', *American Journal of Psychiatry*, 105.3 (1948), 170–77; Leon Goldensohn, *The Nuremberg Interviews* ed. by Robert Gellately (New York: Knopf, 2005).
32. Saul K. Padover, *Psychologist in Germany. The Story of an Intelligence Officer* (London: Pheonix House, 1946), pp.30–31, 28–50, for question on anti-Jewish policies; for evidence of knowledge of mass murder, pp.90–91, 269–74; on Buchenwald and Auschwitz, pp.284–7.
33. Eli A. Cohen, *Human Behaviour in the Concentration Camps* trans. by M.H. Braaksma (London: Jonathan Cape, 1954), pp.xiii, 4.
34. Alex Comfort, *Authority and Delinquency in the Modern State. A Criminological Approach to the Problem of Power* (London: Routledge and Kegan Paul, 1950), pp.9, 29, 42, 44–5, 46, 60–61.

35. Ibid. pp.ix–x.
36. Giles Playfair and Derrick Sington, *The Offenders. Society and the Atrocious Crime* (London: Secker and Warburg, 1957), pp.149–53, 154–5, 156–63, 165–80.
37. Ibid. pp.161–3, 175, 179–80.
38. For contrasting evaluations of their value and use, see Michael Marrus, 'The Holocaust at Nuremberg', *Yad Vashem Studies*, 26 (1998), 5–42; and Bloxham, *Genocide on Trial* (see note 5). For a short overview of the IMT see Michael Marrus, *The Nuremberg War Crimes Trial 1945–46. A Documentary History* (New York: Bedford, 1997).
39. Sir David Maxwell Fyfe, ed., *War Crimes Trials Series* (London: William Hodge, 1948–52); *The Trial of Josef Kramer and Forty Four Others* ed. by Raymond Phillips (London: William Hodge, 1949).
40. J.W. Hall, ed., *Trial of William Joyce* (London: William Hodge, 1946). See also Rebecca West, *The Meaning of Treason* (London: Macmillan, 1949), pp.11–146.
41. For a list of publications, see Jacob Robinson and Philip Friedman, eds., *Guide To Jewish History Under Nazi Impact* (Jerusalem: Yad Vashem, 1960), pp.216–20.
42. Ibid. pp.176–7.
43. Cf. Anna Reading, *The Social Inheritance of the Holocaust. Gender, Culture and Memory* (London: Palgrave, 2002).
44. An important recent exception is Waxman, *Writing the Holocaust* (see note 10), pp.100–112.
45. '[A]t the end of the Second World War Auschwitz simply had no popular resonance in liberal culture', Tony Kushner, 'The Memory of Belsen', in *Belsen in History and Memory* ed. by Jo Reilly *et al.* (London: Frank Cass, 1997), p.188.
46. Filip Friedman, *This Was Oswięcim. The Story of a Murder Camp* trans. by Josef Leftwich (London: United Jewish Relief Appeal, 1946).
47. It is important to note that Tony Kushner made this point many years ago: Kushner, '"I Want to go on Living after my Death"' (see note 14), p.6. For new research on the activity of Jewish survivors, in Poland and their interaction with war crimes investigations see: Natalia Aleksiun, 'Organising for Justice: Jewish leadership in Poland and the Trial of the Nazi War Criminals at Nuremberg', in *Beyond Camps and Forced Labour. Current International Research on Survivors of Nazi Persecution. Proceedings of the International Conference London, 29–31 January 2003* ed. by Johannes-Dieter Steinert and Inge Weber-Newth (Hamburg: Secolo, 2006), pp.184–94. See also, Natalia Aleksiun, 'The Central Jewish Historical Commission in Poland 1944–1947', *Polin*, 20 (2007), 74–97. For evidence of one historian who bothered to make use of the available research, see section 2 of the bibliography in Gerald Reitlinger, *The Final Solution. The Attempt to Exterminate the Jews of Europe 1939–1945* (London: Vallentine Mitchell, 1953).
48. Marie Syrkin, *Blessed is the Match. The Whole Story of Jewish Resistance in Europe* (London: Victor Gollancz, 1948).
49. Bernard Goldstein, *The Stars Bear Witness* trans. by Leonard Shatzkin (London: Victor Gollancz, 1949).
50. Ibid. passim; Michal Zylberberg review, *Jewish Monthly*, 4.10 (January 1951), 662–5.
51. John Hersey, *The Wall* (London: Hamish Hamilton, 1950); Josef Leftwich, 'The Tragedy of Warsaw', *Jewish Monthly*, 4.8 (November 1950), 502–9.
52. Eugen Kogon, *Der SS-Staat. Das Systems Der Deutschen Konzentrationslager* (Berlin: Verlag des Druckhauses Tempelhof, 1947). See also, Publishers' Introduction to the 1950 US edition, *The Theory and Practice of Hell* trans. by Heinz Norden (New York: Farrar, Straus and Cudahy, 1950), pp.5–12; and Nikolaus Wachsman, 'Introduction', *The Theory and Practice of Hell* (New York: Farrar, Straus, Giroux, 2006), pp.xi–xxi; Philip Friedman and Koppel S. Pinson, 'Some Books on the Jewish Catastrophe', *Jewish Social Studies*, 12.1 (1950), 88–9.
53. Zdenek Lederer, *Ghetto Theresienstadt* trans. by K. Weisskopf (London: Edward Goldson, 1953), p.vii.
54. Cohen, *Human Behaviour in the Concentration Camps* (see note 33).
55. Stefan Szende, *The Promise Hitler Kept* (London: Victor Gollancz, 1945).
56. Jean-Jacques Bernard, *The Camp of Slow Death* trans. by Edward Owen Marsh (London: Gollancz, 1945), pp.9–10, 23–4, 42–4; originally published as *Camp de la mort lente* (Paris: Albin Michel, 1944). See Wieviorka, *Deportation et Genocide* (see note 2), pp.286–8.
57. Christopher Burney, *The Dungeon Democracy* (London: Heinemann, 1945), 105–6, 109, 111.
58. Denise Dufournier, *Ravensbrück* trans. by F.W. MacPherson (London: Allen and Unwin, 1948), pp.vii, 37, 109.

59. Ella Lingens-Reiner, *Prisoners of Fear* (London: Gollancz, 1948), pp.61–2, 69–74, 79, 117–28.
60. Krystyna Zywulska, *I Came Back* trans. by Krystyna Censkalska (London: Dennis Dobson, 1951).
61. For the mediocre debut and increasing success of the book in Britain, see Kushner, "'I Want to go on Living after my Death'" (note 14); and Carol Ann Lee, *The Hidden Life of Otto Frank* (New York: William Morrow, 2002), pp.230–6.
62. Alan Moorehead, *Eclipse* (London: Hamish Hamilton, 1945), pp.250–59. Moorehead's account was also selected for an anthology of the best writing in Cyril Connolly's *Horizon* magazine. Derek Sington, *Belsen Uncovered* (London: Duckworth, 1946), esp. pp.47–8, 64–5, 186–7.
63. Leslie Hardman with Cecily Goodman, *The Survivors. The Story of the Belsen Remnant* (London: Vallentine Mitchell, 1958), pp.3–9, 24–7. For Lord Russell's comments, see p.ix.
64. Alex Weissberg, *Advocate for the Dead. The Story of Joel Brand* trans. by Constantine Fitzgibbon and Andrew Foster-Melliar (London: Andre Deutsch, 1958).
65. Rudolf Hoess, *Commandant of Auschwitz* trans. by Constantine FitzGibbon (London: Weidnefeld and Nicolson, 1959).
66. Eugene Heimler, *Night of the Mist* (London: Bodley Head, 1960).
67. Louis Hagen, *Follow My Leader* (London: Allen Wingate, 1951), p.xi.
68. For example, David Rousset, *The Other Kingdom* trans. by Ramon Guthrie (New York: Reynel and Hitchcock, 1947; first published as *L'Univers Concentrationnaire* (Paris, 1946); US edn Seweryna Szmajlewska, *Smoke Over Auschwitz* trans. by Jadwiga Rynas (New York: Henry Holt, 1947); first published as *Dymy nad Birkenau* (Warsaw, 1946)).
69. Cf. Ken Worpole's pioneering essay 'The Popular Literature of the Second World War' in his *Dockers and Detectives* (London: Verso, 1983), pp.49–73.
70. David Cesarani, *Major Farran's Hat. Murder, Scandal and Britain's War against Jewish Terrorism 1945–1948* (London: Heinemann, 2008).
71. David Cesarani, 'The British Security Forces and the Jews in Palestine, 1945–48', in *Rethinking History, Dictatorship and War. New Approaches and Interpretations* ed. by Claus-Christian W. Szejnmann (London: Continuum, 2009), pp.191–210.
72. Richard Crossman and Michael Foot, *A Palestine Munich* (London: Gollancz, 1946). Arthur Koestler's played a fundamental role in conceiving and drafting the pamphlet.
73. Arthur Koestler, *Thieves in the Night* (London: Macmillan, 1946), pp.45–65.
74. David Cesarani, *Arthur Koestler. The Homeless Mind* (London: Heinemann, 1996), pp.285–6.
75. Arthur Koestler, *Promise and Fulfilment* (London: Macmillan, 1949), pp.45–65.
76. Amikam Nachmani, *Great Power Discord in Palestine. The Anglo-American Committee of Inquiry into the Problems of European Jewry and Palestine 1945–1946* (London, 1987), pp.66–81.
77. The report of the Anglo-American Inquiry, 1946, is available at http://avalon.law.yale.edu/subject_menus/angtoc.asp.
78. R.H.S. Crossman, *Palestine Mission. A Personal Record* (London: Hamish Hamilton, 1947), pp.32, 38–53, 60–65, 82–106.
79. Kushner, *The Holocaust in the Liberal Imagination* (see note 3), pp.226–7.
80. Simon Garfield, *Our Hidden Lives. The Remarkable Diaries of Post-War Britain* (London: Ebury Press, 2005), pp.321, 430.
81. Morris Beckman, *The 43 Group* (London: Centreprise, 1992), pp.5–6.
82. Ibid. p.19.
83. *Evening Standard*, 4 August 1947; *Spectator*, 8 August 1947; *Jewish Monthly*, September 1947.
84. Gena Turgel, *I Light a Candle* (London: Vallentine Mitchell, 1995; first published 1987), p.138.
85. Kitty Hart-Moxon, *Return to Auschwitz* (Laxton: Beth Shalom, 1997; first published 1981), p.2.
86. Anita Lasker-Wallfisch, *Inherit the Truth* (London: Peter Halban, 1996), p.15.
87. Turgel, *I Light a Candle* (see note 84), p.134.
88. Paul Oppenheimer, *From Belsen to Buckingham Palace* (Laxton: Beth Shalom, 1996), p.171.

89. Pietr Lagrou, *The Legacy of Nazi Occupation. Patriotic Memory and National Recovery in Western Europe, 1945–1965* (Cambridge: Cambridge University Press, 2000), pp.250–60, makes a similar point about the much scorned rhetoric of the Left in post-war Western Europe: 'There may have been an ideological hegemony assimilating various experiences to some holistic martyrdom, but this was at the same time what many of the Jewish victims who actively adhered to the anti-fascist paradigm needed at the moment. Anti-fascism as a "universalising" device offered a generous and heroic interpretation.' The anonymity of the victims allowed Jews to project their specific experiences onto the undifferentiated category of 'deportees' and to bask in the sympathy it aroused even if their own journey into and out of the camps had been quite unlike the majority.
90. Lawrence Baron, 'The First Wave of American "Holocaust" Films, 1945–1949', *American Historical Review*, 115:1 (2010), 90–114; idem, *Projecting the Holocaust into the Present. The Changing Focus of Contemporary Cinema* (Lanham, MD: Rowman and Littlefield, 2005), pp.23–40; idem, 'From DPs to *Olim*: Depicting Jewish refugees in American Films, 1946–1949', in *Beyond Camps and Forced Labour* (see note 47), pp.749–58.
91. *Dunkirk*, dir. Leslie Norman (1958), 1:47:45–1:48:55.

'The Wandering Jew has no Nation':[1] Jewishness and Race Relations Law

DIDI HERMAN

This essay examines the interaction between Jews, Jewishness, and English law through a legal framework that explicitly seeks to protect minority groups from discrimination.[2] Unlike other material I have explored elsewhere, in which Jews and Jewishness appeared in a range of substantive legal areas not directly concerned with 'race' or 'religion',[3] UK race relations law, on the other hand, aims to provide redress to minorities who have suffered from negative treatment based on their membership in a protected 'racial group'.

In England, the official history of minority groups is now usually told through this concept of 'race relations', a term in use since the 1960s. It refers to both the state of inter-racial relations, and successive governments' responses to the perception of such relations in legislation and policy initiatives. Until the late twentieth century, the dominant race relations narrative, as I shall discuss further below, was almost exclusively one of 'Black and White'; in other words, the perceived race relations 'problem' was represented as being one of the reception and assimilation of peoples of Afro-Caribbean and South Asian origin by the white English. More recently, this gaze has alighted upon 'the Muslim', a figure where concepts of race and religion cohere (as with 'the Jew'), while popular and governmental perceptions of the 'Afro-Caribbean problem' have honed in on the figure of the 'disaffected young Black man'.

In my wider study of Jews, Jewishness, and English law, of which this is a part, I explore how issues to do with the reception of and assimilation by newcomers arose vis-à-vis the migration of Eastern European Jewish refugees around 100 years ago, tracing briefly some earlier histories of discrimination faced by Jewish people in previous centuries. While the phrase 'race relations' was never in use during these earlier periods, many of its perceived problems, particularly a notion of assimilation failure, are not at all new.

However, for the most part, academic accounts of race and racism in England fail to take account of these older histories, nor do scholars, whether mainstream or critical, usually attend to contemporary racialisation processes that do not conform to dominant narratives of race.[4] Popular and academic accounts of race relations in the UK largely dovetail. Both offer a similar story: the history of race relations begins with Black and Asian immigration in the middle parts of the twentieth century. Popular renditions start with the arrival of Afro-Caribbean immigrants aboard the *Empire Windrush* in 1948, which, for example, is described by the BBC as the first 'seminal moment' in 'UK race relations' (also ignoring the long history of South Asian, East Asian, and African presence in England).[5] Media and other similar accounts then tend to consist of a list of 'riots', racist incidents, and legislative initiatives from the middle and latter parts of the twentieth century, culminating in the *Macpherson Report* in 1999,[6] and reports of further 'racial conflict' in the early years of the new century. The 'race' of race relations means perceived skin colour and/or, more recently, Muslimness, and the 'relations' white vs Black/Asian.[7] Official statistics collection operates more or less on the same basis: 'The ethnic minority population includes many distinct ethnic and religious groups. The original migrants came from different regions including the West Indies, Indian subcontinent and Africa.'[8] It is significant that neither Jews nor Sikhs, the paradigmatic ethnic groups for the purposes of the Race Relations Act (RRA) 1976, are allowed to identify themselves as belonging to an 'ethnic group' in the UK census, only as a religious one.[9]

Most academic accounts in the social sciences do little to trouble this dominant race relations narrative, although some inject much-needed postcolonial perspectives into the frame. However, there is a resounding silence when it comes to racialisation processes involving persons now deemed 'white'. Nor is there any acknowledgment that notions of 'white' and 'black' are not fixed but change over time in response to historical and social conditions. The racialisation of Irish, Jewish, and Roma peoples in England, for example, is almost entirely ignored, including how, historically, they were perceived as 'not white'. Unfortunately, this is largely the case in both socio-legal and critical legal work on 'race' and 'religion', as I have explained elsewhere.[10]

In what follows, I first provide a brief parliamentary history of British race relations legislation. I then examine a number of legal cases in detail, both those involving Jewish claimants, and others ostensibly having nothing to do with Jews but which nonetheless draw on Jewishness in some way. In tracing this discourse, I make four key arguments. First, I show how the abstracted figure of 'the Jew' was deployed by all sides in parliamentary debates about race relations legislation. For supporters of legal intervention, references to Jews and the Holocaust enabled positive analogies with other groups coming under racist fire at various periods. For opponents of intervention, 'the Jew' provided a paradigmatic victim from which other immigrant groups and their experiences could be differentiated (a process similar to some uses of 'the Holocaust').[11]

My second argument is that despite all the talk about Jews in post-RRA 1976 race relations cases, their actual status as a 'racial group' under this legislation has never been adjudicated, only presumed. In other words, no English legal decision has ever elucidated how and why Jews fit into the Act's categories. Third, I demonstrate how, until late 2009, not a single Jewish claimant ever won a reported case under the RRA 1976, and that no Christian has ever been found to have engaged in discriminatory acts against Jewish persons (in reported cases under the RRA 1976). My intention is not to argue that Jews lose more cases than others, but that the contrast between this lack of success and the generic rhetoric about Jews in the cases (as I discuss below) is remarkable.[12] Finally, I reflect on how themes of secularism, Christianity, and conversion play out in this legal context.

'The Jew' in Parliamentary Debate on Race Relations Law

Race Relations Act 1965
The first piece of race relations legislation in the UK was the RRA 1965. While subsequent legislation extended the scope, application, and administrative mechanisms of this Act in various ways,[13] the basic principles of non-discrimination and non-incitement of racial hatred, as well as the grounds upon which discrimination would be prohibited – 'colour, race, or ethnic or national origins' – have remained virtually unchanged ('nationality' was added in 1976, see below). References to 'coloured' people and persons abound in the Home Secretary's speeches and clearly indicate that the driving force behind the government's introduction of race relations legislation were the perceived problems occasioned by growing Afro-Caribbean and Asian 'new arrivals' (and not, as Lady Hale claimed in 2009, 'the

Holocaust'),[14] and, indeed, the 1965 Act had been preceded three years earlier by new, restrictive immigration law.[15]

Nevertheless, and perhaps unsurprisingly, the legislative debates from the mid-1960s are peppered with references to Nazi Germany and the mass killings of Jewish Europeans, demonstrating that these spectres were never far from at least some politicians' minds. While the fullest exposition on German anti-Jewish policies, and their relevance to the need for race relations law, was provided by Barnett Janner, a Jewish MP,[16] others, on both sides of the debate, made similar references. John Binns, while paying lip service to the 'gas chambers of Auschwitz', spent most of his speech outraged about 'Asiatics and Pakistanis who cannot speak a word of English ... and come straight from the tribal villages of Pakistan and their ideas of personal hygiene are absolutely different from ours',[17] suggesting that had he been able to contribute to the aliens debate in 1904/5 he would have said something very similar about the Jewish eastern Europeans arriving on British shores.[18] Henry Brooke noted that 'this House must never forget that about six million Jews were put to death as a result of Hitler', while, at the same time, arguing that anti-Semitism was virtually unheard of in England these days and was therefore no excuse for introducing freedom-infringing legislation of this sort.[19] Other MPs, contrarily, argued that anti-Semitic incidents in England occurred both in the recent past and were currently on the rise, justifying the legislation partly on that basis.[20]

Several MPs, with varying motivations, were concerned as to whether the Act would even apply to Jews, and, in response to a direct question on this matter, the Home Secretary stated an unequivocal 'yes'.

> It is certainly the intention of the Government that people of Jewish faith should be covered ... a person of Jewish faith, if not regarded as caught by the word 'racial' would undoubtedly be caught by the word 'ethnic', but if not caught by the word 'ethnic' would certainly be caught by the word 'national' ... he would certainly have an origin which many people would describe as an ethnic if not a racial one.[21]

The issue of whether the Act would apply to Jews was generally raised in connection with the meaning of the word 'ethnic'.[22] The government's response to questions concerning the meaning of this word was simply to state that it was intended to avoid any ambiguity over the meaning of 'race'; in other words, 'ethnic' was meant to catch anyone it might be argued was not a 'race', but was still 'distinguished by skin colour'.[23] While there were a couple of references to Cypriots and Maltese falling into this category (and an implicit assumption that they would not be caught by 'national origins'), it seems clear that the term was not being used as one of art, but merely as a means of avoiding contentious debates about biological race.[24]

At the same time, the Home Secretary tied the word 'ethnic' to the phrase 'blood origin',[25] demonstrating that the two concepts – race and ethnicity – were by no means theorised or even disentangled at a basic level (witness the reference above to 'skin colour'). As I discuss later, it was left to the judiciary, perhaps unfortunately, to try and work it out. Indeed, when a question about the application of the Act to 'gypsies' was raised, the Home Secretary replied that this 'is one of the fringe questions which it is difficult to answer ... possibly that is one of the puzzles which ultimately will come before the court'.[26] The RRA 1965 received Royal Assent in November 1965; however, within a year, there was a concerted attempt to expand its provisions.

The Racial and Religious Discrimination Bill 1966, introduced by Lord Brockway, a campaigner for race relations legislation for some years previous, sought to expand both the Act's coverage (to housing and employment) and, additionally, include 'religion' in the list of grounds upon which discrimination was prohibited. A series of anti-Semitic incidents in the summer of 1966 was clearly a large part of the motivation,[27] as was a continued anxiety as to whether Jews were covered by the existing Act.[28] Nothing, however, came of this Bill and it was not until the spring of 1968 that legislation was introduced by the government to expand the Act's coverage to housing and employment. Religion, however, continued to remain off the agenda.

Race Relations Act 1968
The new Act extended the remit of the provisions to a wider array of public places, as well as housing and employment. It also made significant changes to the administrative and enforcement mechanisms. 'The Jew' figured once again in debates on the proposed Bill and, as on earlier occasions, was deployed by speakers on both sides of the issue. While by this point virtually no speaker paid attention to anti-Semitic incidents, several continued to make use of the abstracted figure of Jewish victimhood in other ways.

Opponents of the Bill, for example Rees-Davies, an MP not known for his empathy towards racial minorities, argued that the Bill might force Jews to employ Germans in their homes (Jews and Germans being clearly distinct persons in his mind),[29] while Lord Conesford used the example of Jews setting up their own insurance companies in order to avoid discrimination in insurance provision as a reason why legislation was not necessary.[30] On the other hand, Lord Hirshfield, a Jewish peer, spoke of the need for 'the Jew to stand up fearlessly and give an example of humanity towards another minority group',[31] while Lord Walton referred to past anti-Jewish prejudice as a rationale for strengthening the legislation.[32]

By 1968, then, it seemed there was no question (within parliament) that Jews were covered by the Act, and, at the same time, there was a clear perception that anti-Semitic incidents were largely a thing of the past (despite the outcry over them just two years previously). The new Act received Royal Assent in October 1968, and, once again, was accompanied by legislation further restricting immigration.[33]

Race Relations Act 1976

The Bill that passed through parliament in 1976 contained, with some amendment, the provisions that currently govern the field, in so far as my subsequent discussion of race and ethnicity is concerned. Although the Equality Act 2010 repealed the RRA 1976, the definition of 'racial group' remains exactly the same. As explained by government ministers at the time, the impetus for legislating anew in the mid-1970s came partly from assessing the shortcomings of the previous legislation, and partly from the experience of passing the Sex Discrimination Act 1975. The new Act was to be modelled on that one.[34] The Bill included the new ground of 'nationality' and contained provisions for indirect discrimination, large private clubs, and a new Race Relations Commission empowered to take positive action. Once again, the stated motivation for the Act was to further the advancement of 'coloured' people; once again, government ministers tied race relations protections into an agenda of immigration control.[35]

Throughout the debates, the figure of 'the Jew' made several appearances. Enoch Powell, in railing against the Bill, suggested that the low birth rate amongst Jewish immigrants could not be compared to the explosion of the black population,[36] while Thomas Torney referred to Jews, pogroms, and concentration camps to underpin his support of the Bill.[37] Jill Knight, in opposing the entirety of the Bill but particularly a provision requiring employers to keep 'racial records', objected 'to the idea that anyone who is Jewish, for example, shall have this fact put down on his records. That brings back echoes of the 1930s'.[38] More than one member, in a question that appears never to have been answered, again raised the issue of whether Jews were covered by the Act,[39] while others referred to the gradual elimination of anti-Semitism through informal means as reason to avoid legislation,[40] or, in language reminiscent of debates ten years previously, argued that Jewish people should not be forced to employ Germans.[41]

During a Lords debate over an amendment to add 'religion' to the grounds, Lord Hailsham, an outspoken opponent of nearly all aspects of the Bill, had this to say on the subject:

> Now Jews, if the noble Lord, Lord Janner, will forgive me, come all [sic] shapes, sizes and colours. There are black Jews called Falashas in Ethiopia; there are yellow Jews called something else in China; and there are white Jews with fair hair and blue eyes, with the best Aryan characteristics, in Europe. They come [in] all shapes and sizes. They are not a race, and it is folly to believe they are. But some of them – not all of them, I am sorry to say, but some of them – have a religion. If you want to discriminate against Jews, it is no use discriminating against people with long noses; you must discriminate against people who will not eat bacon – and that is a religious discrimination.[42]

Although Lord Hailsham seems clear in this charming passage that if Jews suffer discrimination it is because of their religion, somewhat later in the same debate he remarked: 'Are the Jews a nation? In my opinion, they are not a race but they may be a nation.'[43] Lord Hailsham gave no indication as to how this suggestion might fit with his earlier remarks about race, or whether, if Jews were a nation, they would therefore be caught by the RRA 1976's ground of 'national origins'.

Also on this same day in the Lords, an amendment was introduced to remove the word 'ethnic' from the legislation, thus provoking one of the very few legislative debates on that term's meaning. However, Lord Harris, the Home Office Minster, simply repeated the justification from ten years previously, that its inclusion was intended as a catch-all. However, Lord Harris did slightly elaborate, arguing that 'ethnic' was intended to 'get away from the idea of physical characteristics' and 'introduce the idea of groups defined by reference to cultural characteristics, geographical location, social organisation, and so on'.[44]

Race Relations Amendment Act 2000, Equality Act 2006, and Equality Act 2010

The Race Relations Amendment Act 2000, the first substantive revision to the 1976 Act, imposed a positive duty on the public sector to promote race equality, as well as bringing public authorities within the ambit of the Act's jurisdiction (with some exceptions). Once again, 'the Jew' made several appearances in these debates. In defending the amendments in the Lords, Lord Lester, an architect of the RRA 1976 subsequently appointed to the House of Lords, made the following observation:

> discrimination based on ethnic or national origins is as much racial discrimination as the definition of racial discrimination in Article 1 of the United Nations Convention ... Such discrimination involves treating one individual less favourably than another for what is not chosen by them but for what is innate in them at birth – their genetic inheritance – whether as ethnic Jews, Roma gypsies or Hong Kong Indians. It is as invidious and unfair as is discrimination based on the colour of a person's skin.[45]

While Lord Lester clearly differentiates 'ethnic' from 'skin colour', he nevertheless attaches a required 'genetic' component to it. Lord Peston, arguing the changes did not go far enough, offered a rather confusing narrative of ethnic, race, and religious discrimination:

> I remembered that when I was a young man the Jewish boys at my school had to change their names in order even to secure an interview at medical school. You simply could not even get to the starting point of applying to medical school with a Jewish name. Boys who were called Cohen changed their names to Conn while those named Levi became Lefford. That was religious rather than race discrimination. But that is merely to argue a technicality.[46]

While Hilton Dawson MP made the following observation:

> Recently in Lancaster ... the leader of the city council – became the victim of campaign of abuse and vilification. He is Jewish and he takes his religion seriously ... that campaign was so concerted that the impact it had on that individual was probably

disproportionate to the impact that it would have had on someone from a different racial background.[47]

Stephen Twigg MP, in his speech in support of the Bill, referred to historical anti-Semitism and Holocaust education.[48]

During the debates on this Bill, other parliamentarians, critical of how race relations case law had developed in the intervening years, deployed Jews and Sikhs to demonstrate the incoherence of Muslim exclusion and to argue for a religious discrimination provision:

> The House of Lords made a decision, which I welcome, that Jews and Sikhs constitute a racial group and are entitled to protection under the Race Relations Act. They can be defined by their ethnic as well as their religious identity. So a black Jew from Ethiopia, a white Jew from Russia and a brown Jew from Lebanon are all treated as belonging to the same ethnic race for the purposes of English law, whereas black, white and brown Muslims from exactly the same countries are not.[49]

> [T]he problem [is] how to give British Muslims the right to effective remedies for arbitrary discrimination and unequal treatment of the kind that people like myself have if we are discriminated against as Jews on racial grounds ... When, as an officer in the Army, I experienced discrimination, I could never tell whether the anti-Semitism was on racial or religious grounds.[50]

So, 25 years after the 1976 Act, over 35 years since the original articulation of 'racial groups' in 1965 upon which the 1976 Act relied, parliamentarians seemed no closer to arriving at a coherent understanding of Jewishness (leaving aside, for the time being, whether such an understanding is possible). Lord Lester believes Jewishness to be a genetic inheritance while at the same time acknowledging that the line between racial and religious discrimination is thin and wobbly, Lord Peston claimed the discrimination resulting in the Anglicisation of Jewish names was religious in nature, Hilton Dawson MP refers to a Jewish man taking his religion seriously but then calls the discrimination he faced 'racial', and so on. In a brief comment during the debate on what became the Equality Act 2006, Baroness Scotland remarked: 'The Government believes it is right than an ethnic group is not defined by its religion but that it can in part be so defined'.[51] As mentioned above, the Equality Act 2010 did nothing to change the definition of 'racial group' as originally set out in the RRA 1976.

Part of the story I have explored in this section of the essay confirms a familiar narrative in both popular and academic accounts of race relations in Britain. Key points in the parliamentary debates include that the government's initial motivation for race relations legislation in the 1960s was clearly to do with increased Black and Asian immigration and the perceived 'racial tensions' arising from this, and that legislation restricting immigration accompanied race relations legislation on each occasion. So far, this is a familiar story, and, for the most part, popular and academic accounts of the development of race relations in Britain simply provide variations on this theme.

However, for the purposes of a study on Jews, Jewishness and the judiciary, I wish to draw attention to several additional aspects of the debates that have been otherwise ignored. My second point, then, is that in all of the debates over the 45 years, a number of speakers, on both sides, made use of the abstracted 'Jew' and anti-Semitism. Jews and the German-led mass killings of Jewish Europeans in the 1940s figured as both examples of why new law was needed, and as examples of why it was not. For both supporters and opponents of race relations legislation, Jews were deployed as paradigmatic victims of racism. For supporters, this move enabled positive analogies with groups coming under racist fire at the time; for opponents, the Jew as paradigmatic victim enabled speakers to disassociate 'the Jew' from these other immigrant groups in order to render the latter undeserving.

Third, there was consistent confusion over the meaning of 'ethnic group', 'race' and 'religion' and 'national(ity)'. In the 1960s, 'ethnic', at least within the official discourse of government ministers, was clearly tied to 'blood origin' and 'skin colour'. In 1976, there appeared to be a move away from biological characteristics to cultural ones, while, in 2000, 'ethnic' was once again described as something 'innate'. So far as Jews were concerned, the narratives of MPs contained a wide array of understandings that explicitly (as in Lord Hailsham's speech) or implicitly raised questions about the legal status of Jews and Jewishness. Was Jewishness a faith, a race, an ethnicity, a nationality or perhaps all of these? It remained, then, for the judges to attempt to address this question.

The Case Law

Judicial representations of Jews and Jewishness in race relations law occur in two trajectories of cases. One involves Jewish claimants. Over the course of the 45 years or so that such legislation has been in place, the number of reported cases involving Jewish claimants consists of a small handful, almost entirely concerning claims of employment discrimination. Cases involving other claimants, but where Jews and Jewishness is discussed or alluded to by the judges in some way, comprises the second trajectory. I will explore each in turn.

Cases Involving Jewish Claimants

The first reported judgment, *Seide* v *Gillette Industries*, occurred in 1980, and thus under the 1976 Act.[52] Briefly, the case concerned Mr Seide, a Jewish man, who complained that he had received less favourable treatment at work due to his Jewishness. An industrial tribunal, and an appeal tribunal, disagreed. I do not wish to examine this decision in detail here;[53] however, there are two points to which I would draw attention. First, Slynn J, the judge in the *Seide* case, in upholding the Tribunal's decision that the Jewish claimant was responsible for what had happened to him, set the tone for the cases that follow. Second, in two sentences buried in the judgment, Slynn J pronounced on the meaning of 'Jewish', and this was, eventually, to have some future impact.

> the Tribunal accepted that 'Jewish' could mean that one was a member of a race or a particular ethnic origin as well as being a member of a particular religious faith … It seems to us that their approach to this question was the right approach.[54]

As I explore further below, this unargued and undeveloped remark stands as the sole, explicit judicial articulation concerning whether Jewishness comes within the ambit of the RRA 1976.

Three years later, Browne-Wilkinson J, in the case of *Garnel*, another employment appeal decision I have explored elsewhere, made no reference to *Seide* v *Gillette* in his judgment similarly dismissing the Jewish claimant's argument.[55] Here, there was no question that the Act applied: 'Mr Garnel is, by race, a Jew … As is well known, many of our most talented musicians are, indeed, Jews by race.'[56] Although the judge clearly had firm ideas about racial classifications, and thus the application of the Act was never in question, like Slynn J in *Seide* v *Gillette*, Browne-Wilkinson J nevertheless found that the Jewish claimant had brought his troubles upon himself.[57]

Four years after this, in *Simon v Brimham*, the Court of Appeal upheld an Industrial Tribunal and Employment Appeal Tribunal's rejection of a claim by a Jewish man.[58] Although the judgment consistently refers to the claimant's 'Jewish faith', Lord Balcombe confidently stated: 'It is not in issue before us that, if there had been discrimination against Mr Simon on the grounds of his Jewish faith, that would have been discrimination on racial grounds.'[59] Presumably, the employer had not attempted to argue that any discrimination suffered had been on religious not racial grounds (thus rendering the Act inapplicable); however, the court's repeated references to Mr Simon's 'Jewish faith' suggests judicial confusion. Unlike Browne-Wilkinson J in the *Garnel* case, these Court of Appeal judges appeared reluctant to make racial pronouncements and were, perhaps, relieved to simply repeat the phrase 'Jewish faith' from the tribunals below which had used it without any interrogation.

Simon v Brimham made an appearance two years later, in *Tower Hamlets v Rabin*, another claim of employment discrimination by a Jewish man.[60] Here, the industrial tribunal at first instance had upheld the complaint; however, on appeal, Wood J overturned this decision, ensuring that this case conformed to the pattern initially set by *Seide v Gillette*. In the *Rabin* case, Mr Rabin, the claimant librarian, argued that he had been passed over for certain posts and had, in effect, been discouraged from applying for them, due to his observance of the Jewish Sabbath and consequent inability to work on Saturdays. Wood J found that there was no evidence Mr Rabin had suffered any detriment within the meaning of the Act – that, effectively, there had been no discriminatory treatment and the tribunal had erred in law. In coming to his decision, Wood J made the following observations:

> Before leaving *Simon's* case [i.e. the judge's consideration of *Simon v Brimham*] it is important to remember that although mention is made of 'the Jewish faith', that case had nothing to do with religious tenets, it was purely a question of 'the Jewish race' ... [in the present case] one jury might decide that it was obviously on religious grounds, and another, that although seemingly upon religious grounds it was in fact upon racial grounds. It is however unnecessary for us to decide this interesting issue.[61]

The unsettling question of unpacking the distinction between race and religion was thus, again, avoided.

In *Wetstein* v *Misprestige*, a 1993 decision, Peppitt J described the Appellant, Mrs Wetstein, as 'a Sabbath Observant Jew'.[62] Although the case raised a number of concerns, the only issue before the Employment Appeal Tribunal was whether the employer's Saturday work policy discriminated against Jews on racial grounds. The tribunal at first instance decided that it did not, and the Appeal Tribunal found this decision was not factually 'perverse', despite the tribunal's acknowledgement that fewer members of the group 'Jews' could comply with the policy than the group 'non-Jews'. The question of whether this was a case of racial or religious discrimination was, oddly, not addressed.

In *Highdorn* v *Saleh*, Reid J, on behalf of another Employment Appeal Tribunal, dismissed the allegations of discrimination on the basis that they were out of time.[63] Although the case turned on other issues, the judge had this to say about 'Jewishness':

> Mr Saleh asserts that the non-dismissal discrimination claim was based on a series of acts of discrimination against him as a Jew during his seven years of employment with the company. It was suggested on his behalf that the discrimination in a company which is Jewish-owned arose primarily from this overt Jewishness, he being an orthodox Jew, and a desire in the company to present an [sic] 'white Anglo-Saxon' image to the outside world and that 'no religious Jew could ever be promoted to these front-line positions'. This suggests that his complaint may in reality be one of religious discrimination (which is not at present actionable) rather than racial discrimination (which is). Be that as it may ...[64]

In considering these few reported cases with Jewish complainants, it is clear that they share certain characteristics. First, all Jewish claimants lose their cases, usually at first instance as well as on appeal, and in so doing, as I have discussed elsewhere, they are often spoken of as disruptive and/or paranoid in some way.[65] Second, with the exception of *Seide* v *Gillette*, where the reference is very brief, Slynn J suggesting that Jews can be a race, an ethnicity, and a religion, the decisions contain no discussion of how or why Jews constitute a racial group whatsoever. According to Browne-Wilkinson, in his *Garnel* judgment, Jews are simply and obviously a race; in *Simon* v *Brimham* it is unclear, although the language of 'race' is also used; in *Tower Hamlets* v *Rabin* Jewishness is both race and religion; in the *Wetstein* case the question is not addressed at all; and in *Highdorn* v *Saleh* it is unclear, although implicitly it would appear Jewishness is both race and religion. With the exception of the brief references in the case of *Seide*, not a single judgment discusses whether Jews are an 'ethnic group'. Even the *JFS* case, as I go on to explore later, simply asserts Jewish inclusion. Thus, the inclusion of Jews in the RRA 1976 appears as simply a matter of judicial 'common sense'. I now turn to a series of decisions that deploy 'the Jew' paradigmatically to develop the category of 'ethnic group', despite the absence of actual Jewish persons.

Jews and Jewishness without Jews

In 1983, the House of Lords issued their unanimous decision in *Mandla* v *Dowell Lee*, a judgment that remains to this day the leading one on the meaning of 'ethnic origins' in the Act.[66] The claimant, Sewa Mandla, was the father of a Sikh boy, Gurinder, whose school had refused his request to wear his dastar (turban). The Court of Appeal, upholding Gosling J's decision at first instance, dismissed the Mandla's argument, under the RRA 1976, that Sikhs were an ethnic group, Denning J making liberal use of 'the Jew' in his judgment.[67] In overturning the Court of Appeal's decision, the House of Lords made few references to Jews and Jewishness, although they relied on a New Zealand case about Jews to ground their claim that Sikhs were, in fact, an ethnic group for the purposes of the RRA 1976. The language used by both courts in the course of their decision-making contains nearly the full panoply of judicial approaches to representing Jews and Jewishness, and so I will spend some time unpacking each in turn.

At the Court of Appeal, Denning LJ drew from a series of antiquated dictionaries, trust law cases and other texts to determine that Jews were an ethnic group but Sikhs were not.

> Why are the Jews given as the best-known example of 'ethnic grouping'? What is their special characteristic which distinguishes them from non-Jews? To my mind it is a racial characteristic ... If a man desires that his daughter should only marry 'a Jew' and cuts her out of his will if she should marry a man who is not 'a Jew', he will find that the court will hold the condition void for uncertainty. The reason is because 'a Jew' may mean a dozen

different things. It may mean a man of the Jewish faith. Even if he
was a convert from Christianity, he would be of the Jewish faith.
Or it may mean a man of Jewish parentage, even though he may
be a convert to Christianity. It may suffice if his grandfather was
a Jew and his grandmother was not. The Jewish blood may have
become very thin by intermarriage with Christians, but still many
would call him 'a Jew'. All this leads me to think that, when it is
said of the Jews that they are an 'ethnic group', it means that the
group as whole share a common characteristic which is a racial
characteristic. It is that they are descended, however remotely,
from a Jewish ancestor. ... When Hitler and the Nazis so
fiendishly exterminated 'the Jews', it was because of their racial
characteristics and not because of their religion. There is nothing
in their culture of language or literature to mark out Jews in
England from others. The Jews in England share all of these
characteristics equally with the rest of us. Apart from religion, the
one characteristic which is different is a racial characteristic ...
Jews are not to be distinguished by their national origins. The
wandering Jew has no nation. He is a wanderer over the face of
the earth. The one definable characteristic of the Jews is a racial
characteristic. I have no doubt that, in using the words 'ethnic
origins', Parliament had in mind primarily the Jews. There must
be no discrimination against the Jews in England. Anti-Semitism
must not be allowed. It has produced great evils elsewhere. It
must not be allowed here.[68]

Thus, in reasoning that Jews were clearly covered by the RRA 1976,
Denning LJ relied on their connection to 'a Jewish ancestor',
however 'remote'. This was, according to him, a 'racial
characteristic' which, in turn, also made them members of an 'ethnic
group'. Denning LJ then went on to claim, in distinguishing Sikhs
from Jews, that there were no racial distinctions between Sikhs and
'other peoples of India' and that 'they are only to be distinguished by
their religion and culture'.[69] Effectively, however, Denning LJ was
arguing that there was no distinction between 'race' and 'ethnic
group'.

While the other judges in the court came to the same conclusion
as Denning LJ, and dismissed the Mandlas' case, in insisting on a
biological element to 'ethnic' they did not once discuss Jews or
Jewishness. Kerr J, for example, stated that only orthodox Sikhs
wore turbans and that, 'viewed as a group ... the Sikhs are Indians,

and in particular Punjabis; they are not a people or a group having any ethnic or national origin'.[70]

> It follows in my judgment that Sikhs and Sikhism do not as such fall within the Race Relations Act 1976 at all, any more than members of the Church of England, Catholics, Muslims, Quakers, or Jehovah Witnesses; or any other groups which are only distinctive because they adhere to distinct religious, political or social beliefs and customs.[71]

By omitting Jews from his list, Kerr J may have agreed with Denning LJ that the defining characteristic of 'the Jews' was a racial characteristic that these other groups lacked, or he may simply not have known what to do with them.

Before the House of Lords, the lawyers for the Mandlas rested their main argument that Sikhs were an 'ethnic group' upon the New Zealand case *King-Ansell v Police*, a decision that had, apparently, not been brought to the attention of the Court of Appeal.[72] In this case, under New Zealand's Race Relations Act 1971, that country's Court of Appeal was asked to determine whether Jews constituted an 'ethnic group' for the purposes of that Act. The New Zealand Act similarly excluded a 'religion' ground and gave no more guidance than the RRA 1976 as to the meaning of 'ethnic group'. In coming to their decision, the New Zealand Court of Appeal relied, in part, on the expert evidence of Dr Cluny Macpherson, an anthropologist whose research area was the peoples and cultures of Pacific Islanders. His opinion, that Jews were an ethnic group and not a race, was reproduced fulsomely in the judgment. Although the New Zealand Court found Macpherson's definition of 'ethnic group' too broad:

> Nevertheless the evidence which he gave as to the customs and beliefs founded in an historical background, which in his opinion characterised the Jewish people, was of critical importance to the case ... the concept of a group of persons in New Zealand having common ethnic origins would include a group marked off from the generality of our society by shared beliefs, customs and attitudes of the kind attributed by Dr MacPherson to the Jews.[73]

What these beliefs, customs, and attitudes consisted of was not elucidated by the court (so far as the reported judgment is concerned). In his concurring judgment, Woodhouse J stated that there was a:

depth of Jewish history and the unbroken adherence of Jews to culture, traditions, and a mutually intelligible language, as well as religion, so that they have maintained a distinct and continuous identity as a people for longer perhaps than any other than the Egyptians ... undoubtedly Jews in New Zealand are a group of persons with ethnic origins of the clearest kind.[74]

Near the start of his lead judgment in *Mandla* v *Dowell Lee*, Lord Fraser, in what was, in effect, the only remark (other than paraphrasing from *King-Ansell* v *Police*) on Jewishness in the House of Lords decision, noted that 'it is inconceivable that Parliament would have legislated against racial discrimination intending that the protection should not apply either to Christians or (above all) to Jews'.[75] Lord Fraser elucidated the criteria for 'ethnic group' according to several characteristics, two of which he deemed 'essential': '(1) a long shared history, of which the group is conscious as distinguishing it from other groups, and the memory of which it keeps alive; (2) a cultural tradition of its own, including family and social customs and manners, often but not necessarily associated with religious observance'.[76] Other, less essential, features of ethnicity, according to Lord Fraser, included a common geographical origin, language, and religion, and being an oppressed minority or dominant majority within a larger community. An ethnic group could include both converts and exclude apostates. So long as someone was a part of or joined such a group, and felt themselves to be a member of it, 'then he is, for the purposes of the Act, a member'.[77] Lord Fraser noted that the following passage from the *King-Ansell* decision, in support of the finding that 'Jews in New Zealand' did form an ethnic group, 'summed up in a way upon which I could not hope to improve the views which I have been endeavouring to express':

a group is identifiable in terms of its ethnic origins if it is a segment of the population distinguished from others by sufficient combination of shared customs, beliefs, traditions and characteristics derived from a common or presumed common past, even if not drawn from what in biological terms is a common racial stock. It is that combination which gives them an historically determined social identity in their own eyes and in the eyes of those outside the group. They have a distinct social identity based not simply on group cohesion and solidarity but also on their belief as to their historical antecedents.[78]

As Mr Dowell Lee had conceded that if a broad interpretation of 'ethnic group' was to be taken Sikhs would fit into it, Lord Fraser spent little time assessing whether Sikhs met these criteria. All the other justices concurred with Lord Fraser's approach.[79]

Over the years, *Mandla* v *Dowell Lee*, and, either explicitly or implicitly, *King-Ansell* v *Police*, were cited again and again as authority for the definition of 'ethnic group'. In *CRE* v *Dutton*, both the passage from *King-Ansell* reproduced above, as well as Lord Fraser's set of criteria in *Mandla*, allowed the Court of Appeal to find that 'gypsies' constituted an ethnic group for the purposes of the RRA 1976.[80]

In *Morgan* v *Civil Service Commission*, a non-Jewish man alleged that he was not appointed to a post with the British Library on the grounds that he was *not* Jewish.[81] In other words, he argued that the appointing panel was prepared to hire only Jewish persons to the post. Although he lost his case, the Industrial Tribunal at first instance, and as a preliminary issue, stated unequivocally but without any argument (citing the *Seide* case in a subsequent judgment):

> We conclude that the question of Jewishness or non-Jewishness is a matter relating to 'race' and to 'ethnic and national origins', and that to discriminate against a person on the ground that he is non-Jewish is to discriminate on 'racial grounds' within the meaning of the Act.[82]

The Court of Appeal dismissed Mr Morgan's appeal, in January 1993.[83]

In *Crown Suppliers* v *Dawkins*, the Employment Appeal Tribunal was asked to determine whether 'Rastafarians' qualified as an 'ethnic group'.[84] Tucker J, overturning the decision of the first Tribunal, said no; Rastafarians were not separate ethnically to native or diasporic Jamaicans and hence they did not meet the *Mandla* criteria, most importantly the 'essential' criteria of having a long, shared history (a 60-year tradition was deemed to be not long enough).[85] This decision was confirmed by the Court of Appeal in 1993.[86]

In *BBC Scotland* v *Souster*, the Scottish Court of Session held that English (or Scottish) persons could be protected by the RRA 1976 on the grounds of 'national origins', but not on grounds of 'ethnic group'.[87] The court found that there were clearly distinct, historical nations within Britain, from which a person could claim to derive their origin; however, neither 'the Scots' nor 'the English' qualified under the *Mandla* criteria as 'ethnic groups'. Quoting liberally from both *Mandla* and *King-Ansell*, Lord Cameron argued that:

> while there may be that within Scotland there are groups, for instance, the Gaels, who might lay claim to being an ethnic group, it is within judicial knowledge that the racial group which can properly be described as the Scots has a much wider and broader based cultural tradition than that which would constitute one of the two essential conditions or characteristics for an ethnic group. By the same token, I consider that the same observation applies to the racial group which can properly be described as the English.[88]

Thus, both the Scottish and the English lacked the 'distinctiveness of community' to qualify as 'ethnic'.[89] I return to this below.

In *R v White*, a prosecution under the Crime and Disorder Act 1998, a provision containing the same definition of 'racial group' as the RRA 1976 was in question.[90] Again quoting extensively from *Mandla*, Pill J held that the word 'African' did not denote sufficient distinctiveness to qualify for the term 'ethnic group'; however, he did find that 'African' qualified as a 'race':

> In ordinary speech, the word African denotes a limited group of people regarded as of common stock and regarded as one of the major divisions of humankind having in common distinct physical features. It denotes a person characteristic of the blacks of Africa.[91]

However, lest anyone suggest the judge believed all peoples from any single continent formed a race, he went on to suggest that 'South Americans' would not qualify as a 'race' as there was too great a 'range of physical characteristics in the population of that continent'.[92]

These cases suggest that English judges have as great difficulty coming to terms with processes of racialisation in the 'race relations' field as in any other legal area. Far from the interpretation of the RRA 1976 providing a fruitful jumping off point for the intelligent development of understandings of racial and ethnic categorisation, these cases instead exhibit, for the most part, confusion at best, and appalling ignorance at worst. Lord Fraser's speech in *Mandla*, achieving biblical authoritative proportions in subsequent cases, even states that 'Christians' were protected by the RRA 1976. Did Lord Fraser think Christians were a race, or an ethnic group, or that they shared a national origin? Who knows.

However, my concern here is not with making a general critique of the judiciary's approach in this area, but, rather, to elucidate how the judges understand and represent Jews and Jewishness in these race relations cases 'without Jews'. In furtherance of this objective, I would draw attention to two key points: (1) the *Mandla* case implicitly established Jews (and explicitly Sikhs) as an ethnic group for the purposes of the RRA by adopting evidence about Jews adduced by a New Zealand anthropologist in the case of *King-Ansell*; (2) all other cases attempting to define 'ethnic group' applied this same criteria with varying results, 'Gypsies' faring best, English, Scottish, Rastafarians, and Africans deemed to be non-ethnic for varying reasons.[93] However, the inclusion of Jews as an 'ethnic group' in the RRA 1976 has never been debated or reasoned in English case law – not in cases with Jewish parties, and not in cases without.

The *JFS* Case

In 2009, the Court of Appeal, and then the new Supreme Court (replacing the House of Lords), overturned a decision confirming a Jewish school's right to determine who was Jewish for the purposes of its admissions policy.[94] In *JFS*, the claimant/appellant was a Jewish man claiming discrimination on behalf of his son, and his ex-wife – who was a convert to Judaism. The Jewish school was the respondent being accused of discrimination. The school argued that it had relied on the authority of the Office of the Chief Rabbi (OCR) to determine who was Jewish for the purposes of admission.

The OCR recognises Jewishness matrilineally (as does almost every other branch of Judaism in the UK). The mother must be Jewish, and she can be Jewish in one of two ways: her mother was Jewish (by being born to a Jewish mother or having converted); or, she has converted to Judaism in an appropriate conversion process. This has been the method of determining Jewishness in Jewish religious law for centuries and was not peculiar to the English OCR's requirements. However, the OCR's strict approach to conversion, that they would not recognise conversions performed by any Jewish denomination other their own, Orthodox one, had come under intense criticism within some English Jewish communities for some time.[95] In *JFS*, the OCR did not recognise the mother's conversion as it had been performed by a rival denomination and so did not recognise the son as Jewish under Jewish law; therefore neither did the school, as its admissions policy with respect to the definition of Jewishness was determined by the OCR.

The father argued that the determination of Jewishness through matrilineal descent constituted race discrimination. In other words, the mother and son were being discriminated against because they were not genetically Jewish (in the eyes of the school), Jews were a protected ethnic group under the Race Relations Act 1976, and thus any discrimination on the basis of being Jewish, or, as in this case, not being assessed as Jewish, was contrary to the Act. The school (and the Secretary of State for Education) argued that the reason for the non-admission was religious, and not racial (and, as a 'faith school', they had the legal right to engage in religious discrimination).[96] The JFS did not dispute that the mother and son could be Jewish ethnically; the school's position was that as the mother's conversion was not recognised by the orthodox branch of Judaism to which the school belonged, the son could not be considered Jewish under Jewish law, and the school's admissions policy was explicitly determined by Jewish law as interpreted by the OCR. If the mother had obtained a conversion through a recognised orthodox synagogue then that would have been fine. The Office of the School's Adjudicator agreed with the school, and so the father launched an action for judicial review.

The High Court Decision

Justice Munby's decision at first instance upheld the school's position.[97] The judge first found that *Seide* v *Gillette* was authority for both (i) that Jews were an ethnic group under the RRA and (ii) that ethnicity and religion were two separate things. Munby J thus reasoned that a person could be Jewish by religion and not by ethnicity, and vice versa. While ethnicity involved some element of biological descent the reverse was not necessarily the case – a determination of descent did not necessarily involve a racial or ethnic categorisation. He found that this case was one of Jewish 'status' – descent was being used to determine a child's Jewish status for the purposes of an admissions policy, not their race or ethnicity. According to Munby J, determining this status was a purely religious exercise – was this child Jewish according to orthodox Jewish law? The discrimination was thus religious, and therefore allowed under legal provisions for faith schools.[98]

The Court of Appeal

Sedley LJ, writing for a unanimous Court of Appeal, wrote an admittedly short decision overturning Munby J's.[99] With little reasoning, commentary, or reference to the conversion question, the court found that: (i) citing *Mandla* as authority, Jews constituted a racial group under the RRA 1976 and any discriminatory treatment based on a person's Jewish, or non-Jewish, status was per se discriminatory; (ii) the school clearly engaged in a racially discriminatory act against a person it defined as 'not Jewish'; (iii) such an act could not be justified on any account.

> Applying this [the oft-quoted passage from Lord Fraser's judgment in *Mandla*, see above] to the present case, it appears to us clear (a) that Jews constitute a racial group defined principally by ethnic origin and additionally by conversion, and (b) that to discriminate against a person on the ground that he or someone else either is or is not Jewish is therefore to discriminate against him on racial grounds. The motive for the discrimination, whether benign or malign, theological or supremacist, makes it no less or more unlawful.[100]

The court proclaimed that any test of Jewishness must be religious not racial.

While, in the High Court, Munby J had relied on the brief remarks of Slynn J in the *Seide* case to find that Jews were both an 'ethnic group' under the RRA 1976 and also a religious group and it was for the courts to make a factual determination as to whether the alleged discrimination was on racial or religious grounds,[101] in the Court of Appeal, on the other hand, Sedley LJ claimed *Seide* was of 'no assistance in a case where the religious belief in question is that of the alleged discriminator, not of the victim'.[102] Instead of relying on *Seide*, Sedley LJ found that *Mandla* was authority for the fact that 'Jews constitute a racial group',[103] despite *Mandla* not being any direct authority for this proposition at all (see my earlier discussion of this case). As I noted earlier in this essay, with the exception of brief references in *Seide*, and also in *Morgan* (a case to which no court in *JFS* refers), no English case ever actually determined how or why Jews were covered by the RRA 1976. Only Denning LJ, in his *Mandla* judgment, attempted to do so (see the long extract reproduced earlier), a decision never cited or discussed by subsequent courts in any way (except, interestingly, by Lord Hope at the Supreme Court in *JFS*). There is also Lord Fraser's peculiar remark that 'it is inconceivable that Parliament would have legislated against racial discrimination intending that the protection should not apply either to Christians or (above all) to Jews' (see earlier discussion). That Lord Fraser appeared to consider Christians a racial group seems to have been conveniently forgotten by subsequent courts.

Instead, all the courts in the *JFS* case rely on Lord Fraser's disquisition on ethnicity in *Mandla*, where he discussed the applicability of the RRA 1976 to Sikhs. In doing so, as I traced earlier, he relies on a New Zealand judgment about Jews, in which, as I noted previously, the judges there take their understanding of 'ethnic group' from the testimony of an anthropologist whose special expertise was the history and culture of Samoan peoples.[104]

What is also striking about this line of cases is how the judges deal with the question of conversion, and the relationship between conversion and ethnicity. In *King-Ansell*, the New Zealand case, the court did not address the question of conversion at all. Indeed, to do so would have greatly complicated the court's analysis as its holding about the meaning of ethnic group relegated religious belief to a minor consideration. In *Mandla*, Lord Fraser simply asserted, as if it was uncontroversial, that an ethnic group exhibiting sufficient of his elucidated characteristics 'would be capable of including converts, for example, persons who marry into the group, and of excluding apostates'.[105] In *JFS*, both Munby J and Sedley LJ reproduce these remarks without comment. But surely there is a debatable question as to whether one can 'convert' to an ethnicity? And, what does it mean to be an 'apostate' from ethnicity? These obviously religious terms, combined with Lord Fraser's comment that Christians were protected by the RRA 1976, surely demonstrate that *Mandla* provides questionable guidance on these matters.

In an even more problematic move, Sedley LJ went on to compare the school's policy to apartheid South Africa, arguing that it was no defence to such racism to argue that you might honestly believe black people were inferior to white.[106] The analogy to apartheid is misplaced (at the very least). Apartheid was based on a system of complex racial classification resulting in conditions of extreme social, political, and economic inequality throughout South African society. It also had the backing of the South African courts of the time who found nothing wrong with it. Racial classification and ideology was 'the reason for' the system; for many, their form of Christianity also ordained white superiority. While religion might be a factor in supporting these racial laws, they were, at root, racially motivated and dependent on a system of racial classification and hierarchy. The idea that a black person, in 'apartheid South Africa' could 'convert' to whiteness by undergoing a programme of indoctrination in white superiority, thereby also ensuring their children were classified as 'white', is obviously absurd. Thus, rather than seeing the inclusiveness of Judaism as a strength, that it is open to converts of any 'race' or 'ethnicity' or 'religion', the religious test of matrilineal descent instead here becomes equated with despicable racial classification.[107]

In the court below, it was this obvious judicial meddling in religious law that Munby J recognised would not be appropriate:

> The fact that ... religion is the true focus here is illustrated ... by the very fact that at the heart of all the three cases I am considering is a dispute – a quintessentially religious dispute – about the validity of the conversion of the applicant child's mother. ... a dispute about what constitutes a valid conversion is simply not a matter which engages the 1976 Act at all; it is a question of religious doctrine on which the secular courts should be wary to treat.[108]

Munby's long and detailed analysis leading him to this conclusion stands in stark contrast to the Court of Appeal's unreasoned assertions. In 2009 the Supreme Court upheld the Court of Appeal's judgment.[109]

Concluding Remarks

This essay has proceeded in three parts. In the first, I explored the history and context of UK race relations legislation. I argued there that the abstract figure of 'the Jew' recurred in parliamentary debates over several decades, and that this figure was deployed by both supporters and opponents of legislative initiatives. Supporters drew on a history of anti-Semitism and the mass murder of Jewish Europeans during World War II as evidence of the need for legislative protections. Opponents referred to these same histories to ground their contention that racism was a thing of the past and/or to argue that contemporary groups were not akin to Jews and were thus undeserving of protections. I also argued that throughout these debates a consistent confusion was apparent over the meaning of various terms, including that of 'ethnic group', and also over whether Jews were or were not actually protected under race relations law.

In the second part, I considered the case law where Jews and Jewishness were discussed as a matter of racial equality law. Here I showed that, until 2009, no Jewish claimant had ever won a reported case under the RRA 1976. This outcome needs to be read in conjunction with my other work, where I showed how Jews complaining of race discrimination were usually found to have brought their misfortunes upon themselves.[110] No judge in these cases ever referred to a wider English context of anti-Semitism as being in any way relevant to the Jewish individual's complaint. At the same time, no case ever actually got to grips with whether or not Jews were a protected group under the RRA 1976, and, if so, on what basis. Assumptions, not arguments, were made. I further argued that the leading case on the meaning of 'ethnic group', *Mandla* v *Dowell Lee*, was a poor precedent for anything, being, as it was, filled with confusions, contradictions, and patently bizarre remarks.

Finally, I considered the first two decisions in the *JFS* case. I argued that these judgments throw into relief the confusion between race and religion that characterises so much of English law's approach to Jews and Jewishness. The High Court considered the case to be an internal religious dispute – the Court of Appeal and the Supreme Court considered it without doubt to be a case of racial discrimination. It remains notable that, in English law, a Jewish religious school can be found guilty of race discrimination against Jews (or non-Jews, depending on how you define it) while no Christian person or institution appears to have ever suffered a similar fate. At the start of this essay, I noted that the ostensible purpose of race relations law was to provide redress to certain minority groups who suffered discrimination committed by those in other groups. In *JFS*, we have the irony of the only (reported) successful Jewish RRA 1976 litigant being one who took other Jews to court.

NOTES

1. *Mandla v Dowell Lee* [1982] 3 All ER 1108, per Denning LJ.
2. In April 2010, the Equality Act 2010 received Royal Assent. This Act replaces the Race Relations Act 1976 (as well as a number of other pieces of equalities legislation). In this essay, I continue to refer to the RRA 1976, as all the jurisprudence I discuss arose under this statute. RRA 1976 case law will continue to shape understandings of 'racial' and 'ethnic group' under the Equality Act 2010, as the actual provisions pertaining to these categories remain exactly the same.
3. See Didi Herman, *An Unfortunate Coincidence: Jews, Jewishness, and English Law* (Oxford: Oxford University Press, 2011). This essay, with minor revisions, is re-printed from chapter 6 of that book.
4. Ibid. chapter 1.
5. News.bbc.co.uk/1/hi/uk/1517672.stm (accessed 14 May 2010).
6. *The Stephen Lawrence Inquiry, A Report of an Inquiry by Sir William Macpherson of Cluny*, February 1999, Cm 4262-I.
7. See also the Commission for Racial Equality's 'race relations history': cre.gov.uk/40years/. No longer accessible, copy on file with author.
8. J. Dobbs, H. Green and L. Zealey, *Focus on Ethnicity and Religion, National Statistics* (Basingstoke: Palgrave Macmillan, 2006).
9. The Office for National Statistics decided to continue with the omission of Jews and Sikhs from the 'ethnic group' category in the 2011 Census, however the category of 'Arab' was added, see 'Deciding which tick-boxes to add to the ethnic group question in the 2001 England and Wales Census', Office for National Statistics, 2009; 'Final Recommended Questions for the 2011 Census in England and Wales: Ethnic Group', Office For National Statistics, 2009.
10. Herman, *An Unfortunate Coincidence* (see note 3), chapter 1.
11. See ibid. chapter 5.
12. Unfortunately, a comparison between how Jews have fared under the RRA 1976 with other protected groups is beyond the scope of this project. Certainly, ample evidence suggests that a large proportion of complaints to employment tribunals citing 'racial grounds' are unsuccessful, and more unsuccessful than other types of discrimination cases, see, e.g., A.P. Brown and A. Erskine, 'A Qualitative Study of Judgments in Race Discrimination Employment Cases', *Law and Policy*, 31.1 (2009), 142–59; M. Peters, K. Seeds and C. Harding, 'Findings From the Survey of Claimants in Race Discrimination Employment Tribunal Cases (SETA RRA)', Employment Relations Research Series No.54, Department of Transport and Industry, 2006.
13. This Act, for example, applied only to places of 'public resort' (i.e. hotels and restaurants) and not housing or employment, and, unlike subsequent acts, was largely criminal not civil in terms of enforcement and was in this sense exemplary of the UK's gradual shift from understanding racial discrimination as a public order matter to one of 'race relations'. A general analysis of changes to the specific provisions in various incarnations of race relations law over the last 50 years is beyond the scope of my concerns here; however, where particular developments are relevant to my themes and arguments I will discuss them.
14. Frank Soskice, MP, Hansard, cols.926, 942, 104 (3 May 1965). See Herman, *An Unfortunate Coincidence* (note 3), chapters 5 and 7 for discussion of Lady Hale's comments in the context of the *JFS* case.
15. Commonwealth Immigrants Act 1962. That is *not* to say that this was the primary motivation for those non-Cabinet politicians championing the legislation, in particular the Act's original architects Barnett Janner and Anthony Lester. Indeed, Janner explicitly condemned the link with immigration control in his Commons speech, 3 May 1965, col.960. See also, A. Lester, 'The Politics of the Race Relations Act 1976', in *From Legislation to Integration: Race Relations in Britain*, ed. by M. Anwar, P. Roach, and R.

Sondhi (Basingstoke: Macmillan, 2000), pp.24–39.

16. *Hansard*, HC, cols.956–8, ibid.

17. *Hansard*, HC, col.1005 (16 July 1965).

18. See Herman, *An Unfortunate Coincidence* (note 3), chapter 2.

19. *Hansard*, HC, cols.962–3 (16 July 1965).

20. See, e.g., Freeson MP, *Hansard*, HC, col.965 (16 July 1965); Foot MP, ibid. cols.1039, 1043; Hogg MP, ibid. cols.1062–3.

21. *Hansard*, HC, col.933 (16 July 1965).

22. See, for example, *Hansard*, HC, Buck MP, cols.1029–30 (16 July 1965); Renton MP, cols.969–70 (16 July 1965).

23. *Hansard*, HC, Soskice MP, col.932 (16 July 1965).

24. Ibid. cols.971–2.

25. Ibid. col.933 (16 July 1965).

26. Ibid. col.983 (16 July 1965).

27. *Hansard*, HL, cols.2–4 (14 June 1966); also Lord Russell (7 July 1966); Lord Brockway, cols.1857–59 (19 December 1966).

28. *Hansard*, HL, Lord Soper, col.1862 (19 December 1966).

29. *Hansard*, HC, col.338 (9 July 1968).

30. *Hansard*, HL, col.86 (15 July 1968).

31. Ibid. col.80.

32. *Hansard*, HL, col.1304 (25 July 1968).

33. Commonwealth Immigration Act 1968.

34. See *Hansard*, HC, cols.1547–57 (4 March 1976).

35. Ibid. col.1547 (4 March, 1976); see also M.C. Bamforth, M. Malik and C. O'Cinneide, *Discrimination Law* (London: Sweet & Maxwell, 2007), pp.778–9.

36. *Hansard*, HC, col.1583 (4 March 1976).

37. Ibid. col.1619.

38. *Hansard*, HC, col.1648 (8 July 1976).

39. Ibid. cols.1847–8; HL, col.55 (27 September 1976).

40. *Hansard*, HC, col.1866 (8 July 1976).

41. *Hansard*, HL, col.62 (27 September 1976).

42. Ibid. cols.53–4 (27 September 1976).

43. Ibid. col.67.

44. Ibid. col.74.

45. *Hansard*, HL, col.144 (28 October 1999).

46. *Hansard*, HL, col.565 (11 January 2000).

47. *Hansard*, HC, col.1251 (9 March 2000).

48. Ibid. cols.1265–67.

49. Lord Ahmed, *Hansard*, HL, col.455 (28 October 1999).

50. Lord Lester, *Hansard*, HL, col.471, ibid.

51. *Hansard*, HL, col.665 (9 November 2005).

52. *Seide v Gillette Industries Ltd* [1980] IRLR 427.

53. But see Herman, *An Unfortunate Coincidence* (note 3), Chapter 2 for a discussion of 'character' in relation to this case.

54. *Seide v Gillette* (see note 52), paras.21–22.

55. Herman, *An Unfortunate Coincidence* (note 3), chapter 2; *Garnel v Brighton Branch of the Musician's Union* EAT 682/82 (13 June 1983).

56. *Garnel v Brighton* (see note 55).

57. See Herman, *An Unfortunate Coincidence* (note 3), chapter 2, for further discussion of this case.

58. *Simon v Brimham Associates* [1987] IRLR 307.

59. Ibid.

60. *Tower Hamlets LBC v Rabin* [1989] ICR 693.

61. Ibid. 703–4.

62. *Wetstein v Misprestige Management Services Ltd* (19 March 1993).

JEWISH AND CHRISTIAN 'ORPHANAGES'

63. *Highdorn Co Ltd v Saleh* (16 August 2002).
64. Ibid. para. 20.
65. See Herman, *An Unfortunate Coincidence* (note 3), chapter 2.
66. *Mandla v Dowell Lee* [1983] 2 AC 548.
67. *Mandla v Dowell Lee* [1982] (see note 1).
68. Ibid. 1112–13.
69. Ibid. 1114.
70. Ibid. 1122.
71. Ibid. 1122.
72. *King-Ansell v Police* [1979] NZLR 531.
73. Ibid. Richmond J, 535.
74. Ibid. 535-6, 539.
75. *Mandla v Dowell Lee* [1983] (see note 65).
76. Ibid. 562.
77. Ibid.
78. *King-Ansell* (see note 71), p.543, quoted by Lord Fraser.
79. Lord Templeman issued another, concurring, judgment. See H. Benyon and N. Love, 'Mandla and the Meaning of "Racial Group"', *Law Quarterly Review*, 100 (1984), 120–36; and Bamforth *et al.*, *Discrimination Law* (see note 35) for further discussion of distinctions between the two judgments. Note that Stocker L, who agreed with the decision but 'reluctantly', questions Lord Fraser's reasoning in a way that bears further scrutiny; however, his judgment has been all but ignored in subsequent ones.
80. *Commission for Racial Equality v Dutton* [1989] IRLR 8.
81. (12 December 1989), IT. The full decision was issued on 2–3 April 1990.
82. Ibid.
83. *Morgan v Civil Service Commission* (13 January 1993).
84. *Crown Suppliers (PSA) vDawkins* [1991] IRLR 327
85. Ibid. paras.18–19.
86. *Crown Suppliers v Dawkins* [1993] IRLR 284.
87. *BBC Scotland v Souster* [2001] IRLR 150.
88. Ibid. pp.33–4.
89. See also Bamforth *et al.*, *Discrimination Law* (note 35), pp.818–21.
90. *R v White* [2001] All ER (D) 158.
91. Ibid. para.17.
92. Ibid. para.19.
93. In *Heron Corp. Ltd v Commis* (24 June 1980), a man describing his father as 'Arab' was rejected for a position as chauffeur to a Jewish business couple. His claim under the RRA 1976 was upheld by an Employment Appeal Tribunal. The decision contained no discussion whatsoever of the meaning of 'Arab' or where and how that term might fit into 'race or national or ethnic origins'. The applicability of the Act to the group 'Arab' appears to have been assumed without question – whether 'Arab' is a race, an ethnicity, a national origin; whether the term 'Arab' was irrelevant; or whether the relevant category here was 'non-Jewish' – were all questions left unasked much less pursued. In *Advance Security UK Ltd v Musa* (21 May 2008), the phrase 'Middle-Eastern Arab Jordanian' was considered to be a designation of an 'ethnic group' (although the complainant lost his case). There does not appear to have been any further case law on this question but note that 'Arab' was added as a new tick-box in the 'ethnic group' question on the 2011 Census.
94. *R(E) v Governing Body of JFS* [2010] IRLR 136, SC; *R(E) v Governing Body of JFS* [2009] 4 All ER 375, CA; *R(E) v Governing Body of JFS* [2008] ELR 445.
95. A conflictual relationship between Orthodox and other Jewish denominations goes back to the first synagogues that broke away from the United Synagogues and established themselves as separate to the Chief Rabbi's authority in the late nineteenth century. The *JFS* case and the resulting divisions within Jewish religious communities as a result should be read in this context, but this is not the place to delve more deeply into this matter.

96. Schools officially designated as having a 'religious character' are permitted to discriminate on religious grounds, see Equality Act 2006, Part 2, s.50.
97. *R(E)* v *Governing Body of JFS* [2008] (see note 93).
98. Ibid. para.171.
99. *R(E)* v *Governing Body of JFS* [2009] (see note 93).
100. Ibid. para.32.
101. *R(E)* v *Governing Body of JFS* [2008] (see note 93), para.148.
102. *R(E)* v *Governing Body of JFS* [2009] (see note 93), para.30.
103. Ibid. para.32.
104. I am not suggesting that Dr Macpherson was unable to theorise more widely about ethnicity – only that so much significant English case law can be traced to this one intervention.
105. *Mandla* v *Dowell Lee* [1983] (see note 65).
106. *R(E)* v *Governing Body of JFS* [2009] (see note 93), para.29.
107. I am grateful to Maleiha Malik for helping me to clarify these points. It is also worth noting the symbolic role played by 'apartheid South Africa' in English law, but I cannot pursue that any further here.
108. *R(E)* v *Governing Body of JFS* [2008] (see note 93), para.171.
109. I discuss this final decision in Herman, *An Unfortunate Coincidence* (see note 3), chapter 7.
110. See Herman, *An Unfortunate Coincidence* (note 3), chapter 2.

PHILANTHROPY

Childcare Dilemmas: Religious Discourse and Services among Jewish and Christian 'Orphanages'

SUSAN L. TANANBAUM

Scholarly and popular works regularly praise British Jews for their welfare services. Many of these studies emphasise traditions of *tzedakah* (charity, literally righteousness), the comprehensive nature of assistance, and the sometimes fraught relations between donors and beneficiaries. Early congratulatory studies by Laurie Magnus and V.D. Lipman focused on social services provided by the Jewish Board of Guardians. Lipman views the liberal environment of England as responsible for the successful integration of immigrant Jews. As critics have rightly noted, these works present relations between the poor and the Board of Guardians 'as largely free of conflicts'. There were, however, as Mordechai Rozin notes 'bitter social divisions within the Jewish community in London'.[1] In their histories of British Jews, David Feldman, Todd Endelman, and Eugene Black include nuanced discussions of philanthropy.[2] Endelman and Feldman emphasise history from the bottom up. Black focuses on the motives of the rich and powerful, tending to emphasise the perspectives of the benefactors over the beneficiaries. His study also includes brief but important sections on women's voluntary organisations and services for children and young adults.

Only a limited number of works, however, specifically focus on children. These include studies of maternal and child welfare, education, and recreational programmes for youth. Lara Marks' study of Jewish mothering demonstrates how cultural practices and services contributed to the positive reputation of Jewish mothers and low infant mortality rates among Jews at the turn of the century.[3] Her work also notes tensions between more affluent and acculturated Jews and immigrant women and uses the lens of motherhood to highlight cultural, economic, and religious differences between these two groups of Jewish women. At the same time, she credits Jewish voluntary services for their impressive impact on the health of Jewish mothers and babies.

Several scholars assess the impact of Jewish voluntary schools in London and Manchester. Rosalyn Livshin emphasises the efforts to anglicise Jewish children in Manchester – and notes that neighbourhoods and social activities introduced young immigrants to English culture, and that the very intentional efforts schools to teach English manners and behaviours reflected the anxieties of more established Jews. By the 1920s however, that concern shifted as established Jews came to worry that immigrants had become too anglicised and were losing ties to Judaism. Geoffrey Short is most interested in understanding how the educational success of Jewish immigrants might offer insight into contemporary educational challenges facing migrants from the Caribbean and Indian sub-continent. While complimentary toward the efforts of the Jewish community, Short also credits educational policy. He notes that government-supported 'Jewish' Board schools protected immigrant Jews from the widespread anti-Semitism of the period. Writing in 1993, Short suggests that the presence of racism and low teacher expectations in some contemporary educational settings, have had a negative impact on recent immigrants' scholastic achievements.[4] Gerry Black explores educational, co-curricular, and social services provided by the Jews' Free School (JFS). While he notes some tensions – the overall picture he paints is of a highly successful enterprise – with impressive communal support and progressive educational accomplishments and he is quite complimentary in his assessment of the benefactors, staff, and curriculum of the JFS.

Alongside studies of education, several scholars have turned their attention to the experiences of Jews in sport and youth clubs. Among the histories of clubs, Sharman Kadish for example, has analysed the goals and practices of the Jewish Lads' Brigades (JLB) and their efforts to create physically fit and anglicised Jews. Her study explores the misgivings that some in the Jewish community, especially among immigrant families, had about the Brigade's militarism. Kadish traces the strains between the looser religious practices of much of the leadership of the JLB and the more Orthodox practice among families of the recruits. Her study underscores the growing secularisation that came to characterise the early years of the Brigade.[5] My own research on British Jews traces the anglicisation of women and children through communal organisations and education. The combination of self-consciousness, concern over protecting their fragile status, and ethnic/religious solidarity led to the anxiety of established Jews, but also their generosity. Class and religious tensions permeated the relationship between older and more recently arrived Jews.[6]

While the history of childhood has garnered increased attention among British Jewish historians, the scholarship, both popular and academic, on youth, British Christian and state-sponsored services, as well as American Jewish organisations, is far more extensive, and provides rich comparative material for assessing Jewish institutional care.[7] These studies help establish the British context within which the Jewish community operated and highlight what was distinctive (or similar) about philanthropic services in Britain's Jewish community. Comparison with American Jewish organisations helps us to understand more about relations between hosts (both Jewish and Gentile) and immigrants than we gain by limiting our view to Britain alone.

Dr Barnardo's, for example, has been the subject of several studies.[8] Lydia Murdoch's recent book argues that most 'orphans' were not parentless. Institutions and reformers created a public perception of orphaned and neglected children that intentionally misrepresented the children in their care.[9] Recent works have explored child emigration schemes and the harsh experiences of those sent to Canada and Australia.[10] These studies allow for a comparative approach that brings into relief what is distinct about British Jews – and their social services.

During the mid-nineteenth century, state and voluntary societies, through poor law schools, workhouses, and orphanages took in thousands of orphaned, poor, or neglected children. We lack good statistics – but by the early twentieth century 70,000 to 80,000 children lived under poor law residential care, in voluntary society homes, or boarded out each year.[11] Some children were parentless, others lived on the street, and still others were virtually kidnapped. Religious institutions sheltered many of these children. Once thought instinctive, many commentators came to see parents as the least qualified to parent.[12] Reformers often assumed the working class was guilty of gross irresponsibility: of drink, vice, and abuse – or, more benignly, neglect. Consequently, innocent children became criminal, godless, lazy, and uncontrollable, which necessitated the intervention of orphanages. Religious leaders believed they rescued the wicked and prevented those on the proverbial precipice from sliding into the chasm.[13] Orphanages, then, offered shelter and played a role in defining childhood and child rearing.

Each denomination developed its own goals and institutional

structure. By the nineteenth century Norwood cared for nearly all Jewish orphans.[14] Catholic assistance was the least centralised and included homes run by dioceses and religious orders, each with their own policies. Their small size, and the relatively greater poverty of the Catholic minority, limited their ability to provide services. Most extensive were Protestant homes, both denominational and individually sponsored. Particularly dominant were the evangelical Protestant Dr Barnardo's, founded by Thomas J. Barnardo in 1867, and the Methodist-sponsored National Children's Homes (NCH), founded by Reverend Thomas Bowman Stephenson in 1869. Both mushroomed, adding homes, industrial schools, farm schools, and colonial branches.

Typical for its time, nearly all orphanage records accounted for children's nature with a complicated and sometimes contradictory mix of environmental *and* hereditary explanations. Barnardo's saw children with a near inevitability to become evil and to have a contaminating influence. Pauper children were especially suspect. Their parents' sins – poverty or worse – tainted children from an early age and produced offspring of compromised body and morality. Barnardo's 'believed' however, 'that heredity could be overcome by a change in environment, removing the children from conditions which would inevitably drag them down and placing them in entirely new surroundings'.[15]

Probably the most extreme example of this was Barnardo's separate Rescue Home for girls whom he labelled 'depraved'. As a 'centre of contamination', such girls were not allowed 'to associate with other little ones'. The Rescue Home, 'just within our gates' provided shelter for the

> most pitiable of all rescues: young girls whose minds have been polluted and depraved, and whose language, manners, and conduct would be most evil in tendency and effect. ... This branch is thus for the testing of doubtful cases, and for the correction of those in whom evil habits and tendencies have become more deeply ingrained.[16]

During this era, increasing numbers of philanthropists adopted 'scientific method' to eliminate overlapping relief, prevent 'pauperisation', and to encourage self-help.[17] While ranging in quality and purpose, from the mid-nineteenth century on most Jewish charities accepted the values of science over sentiment, while providing a network of social services that went beyond mere physical needs. Many perceived evangelical Christian charities as far less responsible. Some, though not all, of these differences between Christians and Jews appear greater than the reality. Barnardo's enemies, and he had a long line of them, stressed that he was an irresponsible philanthropist who gave indiscriminate charity. In part, this resulted from Barnardo's very public pronouncements that he first admitted children and *then* investigated their need. Seth Koven has questioned this negative characterisation of Barnardo's, claiming the institution did review each case.[18]

Barnardo's autocratic methods, the size of the virtual empire he created, the numbers of children the organisation sent to Canada and Australia – some 30,000 by 1935 – defied much in the way of scientific method.[19] Arguably, his larger goal of salvation undermined the rigour of investigation; Barnardo did not hesitate to remove children from parents he deemed unfit to rear good Christians. On several occasions, he detailed rescues that read rather more like child snatching, and justified them as essential to the child's moral future, society's advantage, and even imperial good.

Despite many common practices and perceptions about the nature of children and appropriate treatment of the poor, there were subtle differences between Christians and Jews. For evangelical Protestants the bible and spreading the gospel were central.[20] Christian charities regularly privileged salvation over other philanthropic goals. Thomas Barnardo favoured 'the training of all the children in Christian knowledge'. Dismissing the doubts of 'scoffers', Barnardo asserted

> that the RELIGION OF OUR LORD JESUS CHRIST has done and can do more for the children of the slums than any other influence. ... My heart's desire and prayer to God for the children is that they might be SAVED, not only for the present life, but also for the life to come.[21]

Barnardo's and Stephenson's religious goals led them to take in large numbers of orphans, but, generally, to shelter them for fewer years than Norwood. Because good Christian living was at odds with the degraded life of the city, they moved many of their orphans to the rejuvenating English countryside. Owing to the high cost of maintaining orphans over long periods, they sent thousands to the uncrowded and spiritually healthier Empire. Not only was the peopling of Canada and Australia with Britons relatively inexpensive, it was also patriotic.

In contrast to Christians, salvation did not motivate Jewish philanthropists. Safeguarding Judaism and preventing shrinkage of the small community in *this life* were, however, paramount. Unlike Barnardo's, which had a virtually endless supply of destitute youth, the Jewish community dealt in finite numbers, though more than they could help, and fewer had potential supporters. While Norwood had misgivings about 'paupers', the rhetoric had a different tone, thanks in part to Judaism and communal priorities.[22] The language of religious commitment was present – but the pathos associated with total degradation and missionary zeal is infrequent in the Jewish records. While words and deeds reveal a self-consciousness and vulnerability, not surprising given prevailing notions of Englishness, anti-alienism, and anti-Semitism, Jewish philanthropists typically viewed poor children as 'unfortunate' and 'bereft of their natural protectors'. It was their duty 'to save' orphans 'from a life of grinding poverty and distress'.[23]

In 1807, using money collected by the Goldsmids, the Jews' Hospital (JH), *Nevi Tzedek* (Abode of Righteousness), opened at Mile End for the support of elderly Jews and needy children from respectable families. They moved to spacious grounds in Norwood in 1866.[24] The Jews' Orphan Asylum (JOA), which probably originated with the 1830 cholera epidemic, opened in 1831, and merged with the Jew's Hospital, becoming the Jews' Hospital and Orphan Asylum (JHOA) in 1867.[25]

The admissions process at Jews' Hospital was rigorous; applicants needed 'a "shareholder" in the Orphanage' to sponsor them.[26] Initially, to qualify, a child had to be able to read Hebrew and English.[27] JHOA, popularly known as Norwood, resisted accepting illegitimate, deserted, and destitute Jews – Anglo-Jewry's most needy. The absence of a Jewish charity to serve such children meant some received care from Parish Unions.[28] Worship services took place twice daily and children who did not attend received punishments, such as loss of meals.

Norwood children remained at the orphanage until their family's situation improved or they completed school. The institution provided 'a sound and practical education to numbers of the children of our poorer brethren' and took credit for 'diminish[ing] the amount of pauperism amongst us, and has been the means of assisting many hundreds to elevate themselves from want to a respectable position in society'.[29] Jewish communal leaders wanted to reduce the numbers of those who might become a long-term economic burden to the Jewish community or the state (which fed into the hands of anti-alienists) and produce respectable anglicised youth. These values suffused nearly all Jewish philanthropy and demonstrate the complex intermingling of altruism, anxiety, and religious obligation so common to British Jewry. In 1868, the Jewish Board of Guardians pressed the Jews' Hospital to change its admissions and accept children from parish workhouses.[30] Two years later, it reluctantly admitted five 'Poor Law' children. The

Norwood Committee concluded that it was their 'positive moral duty ... to rescue them [children] from the associations with which they were surrounded, and to restore them to the knowledge and practices of their religion'.[31] The community felt caught between the potential loss of Jews raised in poor law institutions and the debasing influence of Jewish paupers on otherwise poor or orphaned, but respectable, children.

In an effort to accomplish their goals, orphanages developed programmes of work, schooling, vocational and moral training. Orphanage staff sought to break bad habits and mould children into their version of responsible, obedient charges. All homes put children to work and taught skills they believed would result in self-sufficiency. The NCH and Barnardo's expected especially rigorous labour. At the NCH farm school in Lancashire, the children cleared fields and assisted with construction. The 20th *Annual Report* noted:

> The changed landscape has an unknown beauty and an enhanced value ...; but who can assess the value of the changed lives of those rescued and reclaimed youths, who with pick, crowbar, shovel, spade, plough and harrow, have transformed the barren moorland into a thriving colony, with the important adjuncts and appliances for its educational and Christian work.[32]

The rural setting and manual labour was to serve as an antidote to the evils the charity battled. After rescuing children, institutions sought to keep children from backsliding by providing housing and work placements far from relatives.[33]

Norwood too believed life beyond the crowded East End was restorative, but applied the principle less literally. Donation of the West Norwood property enabled the orphanage to build a new home and 140 boys and 40 girls moved to the country in 1866.[34] The regular enlargement of the institution did not receive universal approval. In 1869, Sir George Jessel, Vice President of the JOA, cautioned against a large institution, advocating personal, 'homely' attention for each child. In 1893, a former headmaster pleaded against plans to enlarge the orphanage, fearing it would 'convert ... the Asylum into a species of barracks filled with little automata'.[35]

By the end of the nineteenth century, Norwood's leadership was well aware of the perceived liabilities of institutional life. The staff, committee members, and volunteers were concerned that the children lacked contact with, and knowledge of, the outside world and increasingly saw the importance of providing experiences similar to those of children living with families. The orphanage used cultural, athletic, and intellectual programmes, as well as education to expose children to typical hobbies and sports and increase the children's sense of themselves as individuals. In 1895, for example, Sergeant O'Keefe was hired as Drill and Gymnastic Master.[36] After a visit in May of 1897, Gertrude Spielman, an active supporter of Norwood, suggested that it would be 'a great boon' for the girls to get seats in their playground. She also recommended painting glass panes to keep the sun from disturbing sleeping children.[37] From 1904, until the outbreak of World War I, all Norwood children travelled to the orphanage's holiday home at Margate. Norwood never adopted the military-like approach implemented by Louis Aufrecht during his years at the Cleveland Orphan Asylum. He required Cleveland children to eat their meals in silence and listen to moralising sermons.[38]

Similar to all orphanages, Norwood emphasised skills that increased the 'efficiency' of the institution. The boys, for example, worked in the gardens, which reduced the size of the staff, improved the practical and economical management of the garden and grounds, and enabled them to supply more vegetables to the 'inmates'.[39] Girls' education included many domestic subjects. Norwood added a laundry (as did Barnardo's in the 1870s), which was considered successful, because it saved money and taught useful skills. Norwood managers hoped the girls' training would qualify them for better paid positions in wealthy Jewish homes.[40] Domestic service, they argued, was 'more conducive to their permanent improvement than returning to poverty stricken homes, where the drawbacks to their future advancement are but too palpable'.[41] Jewish girls and young women, however, tended to shun domestic service. Many parents wanted daughters to help at home and girls preferred poorly paid trades such as tailoring and cigar-making, 'which offer them the attraction of that freedom which is not found in domestic service and it is to be feared they soon forget the careful training which they have received at Norwood'.[42] By the early twentieth century, girls moved into retailing and clerical work.[43]

Norwood's academic programme occupied the children for a larger portion of the day than among Barnardo boys and girls. By 1861 the orphanage became the first Jewish institution in England to train and supply Jewish religious leaders. A number of especially gifted children were identified and supported during more advanced training.[44]

Christian and Jewish homes directed their 'inmates' to similar trades, though a much larger percentage of Barnardo's schooling seems to have been more vocational than Norwood's. Norwood placed boys in apprenticeships at school-leaving age, while Barnardo boys trained while in residence. Barnardo himself concluded that

> only the rudiments of a very plain English education can be aimed at in the school of the various Homes: I have no time, in the interests of the children themselves, to attend to the ornamental adjuncts of an advanced education. The three R's are the chief subjects, with a little grammar, geography, and history. The Scriptures are also reverently read and taught daily.[45]

The NCH, like Barnardo's did not see education as their sole, or arguably, their most important task.

> As important as the schoolroom is in the matter of elementary education, unquestionably the great purpose of these Institutions is to promote the formation of character – to help the children to feel the necessity of breaking away from those habits of moral debasement with which they have so unhappily associated. ... We rejoice in the fact, therefore, that so many of our boys who have left our control, now testify in manly and convincing terms to the success of our labour in this direction. Many of them have avowed their determination to submit themselves to the guidance of their best Teacher and Friend, and serve Him continually.[46]

Over time, the NCH, Barnardo's, and especially Norwood, increased the range of occupations in which they placed their former residents. Boys, whom they generally identified as the primary wage earners of a family, received training in areas such carpentry and agriculture. As early as the 1870s, the list of boys' occupations at Norwood included diamond cutting, scientific instrument-making, and lithographing. They also placed boys with butchers, occasionally as school teachers, and rabbinical students at Aria College. Norwood, unlike Christian institutions, sent very few children overseas. But 'experience' taught that 'boys put to work in London, who ..., when forced to live in degrading and miserable surroundings in the East End, sadly degenerate, and quickly lose all benefit of the education and training given them at Norwood'.[47] Thus, Norwood often tried to secure work for school leavers that minimised contact with families or circumstances that were deemed unacceptable.[48]

Christians and Jews alike sought to keep in touch with those who left their institutions. They wanted to make sure their investments paid off.

They realised their former inmates were young and had tenuous support systems. Both to guide former inmates and to assure each child of individualised attention, Norwood established an after-care Committee in 1883 and assigned guardians to former inmates as they began their working lives. Norwood's aftercare was more comprehensive than other institutions. Certainly, the smaller number of inmates and their placement in England enhanced Norwood's ability to remain in contact. For the Jewish community, immorality, apostasy, or indifference to their Jewish roots, reflected badly on all Jews and demanded prevention.

Norwood wanted to produce able-bodied individuals who would contribute to British Jewry. In 1895, in response to stunted growth, doctors and other institutions were consulted. Hoping to eliminate the children's 'deplorable' physical conditions, more cocoa, milk, and cheese were added to the diet.[49] It was also decided that poorly developed boys would be kept a little extra time.[50] Poor health remained a concern. In 1910, the Honorary Physician, Dr Bertram Soper, and the Matron recommended another dietary increase, this time in the form of fruit, sugar, and jam.[51] Just a year later, the orphanage got a night stoker to improve the heating, purchased automatic fittings for the outer doors to reduce drafts, reorganised games and increased hot food and butter. Additional blankets were provided to decrease cases of chilblains, from which many children suffered.[52] These expenditures suggest problems needing attention, but also a programme of long-term care, and appear to have been more extensive than those undertaken by the NCH and Barnardo's.

Although Barnardo did not implement the same kind of multi-faceted programme as Norwood, he was ahead of his time in other respects.[53] By 1873–74, he established a Girls' Village at Barkingside. It utilised the 'Cottage System', with homes for 15–20 girls and a 'mother', long before most charities moved in that direction. By 1887–88, it boasted 49 cottages and five larger households that accommodated nearly 1,000 girls 'who are trained in domestic service and brought up in Christian ways'.[54] In this period, most of the boys over 14 lived in Stepney, which despite its location and barrack design, received Dr Barnardo's regular praise. The school, military drill, games, swimming bath, and cricket all led the Medical Officer who inspected the boys' home to conclude, 'I could not desire a healthier place than Stepney'.[55] In 1908, as soon as Barnardo's could afford to move the boys out of the slums, they did, and expressed wonder that the lads had managed so well in the large impersonal, dirty, and crowded Stepney facility.[56]

The years after World War I brought extensive change to Norwood and saw increased emphasis on the children as individuals. Beginning in the 1920s, Norwood began to alter its practices with regard to contact with parents and relatives. While the orphanage had, for some time, permitted visits from family members, regular home visits began in 1922 and children would go to suitable homes for a month's visit. For those who remained behind, the staff made special arrangements. Some went off to the Jews' Free School hut at Seaford or to Girl Guide or Jewish Lads' Brigade camps. After the war, the controversy over illegitimate children re-emerged and finally in 1926, after receiving letters from two influential supporters of the orphanage, the General Committee concluded they would no longer refuse admission because of illegitimacy.[57] Major changes continued through the twentieth century. World War II led to evacuation and after the war, Norwood moved with the times and made extensive changes in housing and schooling.

Conclusion

Orphanage leaders came to see themselves as the guardians of children, society, even the empire, yet offered a controversial form of protection and often worried at least as much about promoting good Christian or Jewish living, controlling crime or morally suspect activities, as they did about helping vulnerable children make their way in Britain – or the Empire. Focus on religiously sponsored institutions provides insight into the efforts of Christians and Jews to define and create respectable young adults.[58]

Drawing on the rhetoric of orphanages to understand notions of the child is tricky. There is a complex relationship between social evils – perpetuated by humans – occasionally even young humans – and the notion of a child's innocence. Youthful innocence provided only a limited buffer from a life of crime; corruption was always a latent threat. James Kincaid's exploration of Victorian attitudes toward children notes the same paradox – many writers assumed the innocence of children, maintenance of which justified 'protection' and intervention. For Kincaid, 'the child as holy (or potentially so), as sanctified (if perilously) is an image as important as that of the depraved child'. This, according to Kincaid, led to a 'manic insistence on obedience' – supposedly, according to Victorian commentators, as a route to faith, but not for parents' (and I might add wardens') convenience.[59]

While comparisons may be misleading because of differences in the source material, Norwood, at least during the nineteenth century, seems to have provided children with a somewhat higher standard of living than did either the NCH or Barnardo's. Catholics and Protestants served many more children and solved some of their domestic challenges by sending thousands of children to Canada, and later Australia. They intentionally severed familial ties with great regularity. Child savers claimed emigrating orphans gave them opportunities undreamt of in Britain; the clean living and Christian environment were appealing to Protestants and Catholics alike.[60]

Norwood sought to raise Jewishly literate children and pre-empt potentially disreputable behaviour. As a Jewish institution involved in a religiously sanctioned charitable activity, it could centralise care of orphans, count on numbers remaining manageable, and rely on financial support and voluntary involvement from Britain's Jews. Over time, Norwood implemented changes in child rearing techniques that meant its 'inmates' had experiences more like children raised by their biological parents. Traditions of *tzedakah* and the directors' visions for the institution meant that the Jewish orphanage overcame many of the traditional liabilities associated with institutional life. Many Norwood alumni retained their ties to the orphanage – either seeking advice from the Headmaster or through reunions and the Old Scholars club.

I do not want to suggest that Norwood was an ideal place to spend one's childhood, but compared to other institutions, and the general treatment of the poor, Norwood was more child-centred, and tried to create a home-like atmosphere. We learn a great deal about Norwood by placing it in a comparative perspective with other British and Jewish institutions. During the period under consideration, charities such as Barnardo's and NCH viewed their charges with much greater concern about their souls and their potential for evil. Unlike Norwood, both NCH and Barnardo's moved away from congregate housing to a cottage system and many suggest this was a much more progressive approach to child rearing. Yet both orphanages provided less education, and placed even more emphasis on vocational training than did Norwood, and focused on salvation at the expense of the here and now.

Further comparison with Jewish orphanages in America suggests that individual personalities of volunteer and professional leaders and the level of orthodoxy of sponsors had a wide-ranging impact on the child rearing and educational policies of institutions and attention to these factors sets in relief the approach taken by Norwood's committee and staff. Congregate orphanages such as the Cleveland Jewish Orphanage also provide a comparative window on tensions between German and Russian Jews. Like Norwood, several American Jewish institutions sought to shield orphans and poor children from negative influences by shutting them off from the world into which they would enter at the tender age of 14. The Jewish Children's Home in Rochester, NY, though rather unresponsive to changes in childcare, placed its residents in public schools and allowed them some contact with neighbourhood children.[61]

Attention to such studies helps us understand what was distinctive about Norwood, and the impact of influences – Jewish and British – on the provision of care for Jewish children who could not depend on their biological families. Norwood, while far from the perfect replica of family life, which itself is often imperfect, provided many of its charges with a relatively stable 'home life'. Young adults left the home with a level of education that was comparable or better than most in the working class, remained dedicated to Judaism, and had benefited from a support system that, for its time, was quite successful in preparing them to enter a more independent existence.

ACKNOWLEDGEMENTS

The author gratefully acknowledges valuable assistance from Adrian Allan, Joseph Frazer, Tony Kushner, Karen Robson, Maureen Watry, and Chris Woolgar. She would like to thank Bowdoin College, the Hartley Institute (University of Southampton), the Indiana Centre on Philanthropy (Indiana University/Lilly Foundation), and the Lucius Littauer Foundation for their generous research support.

NOTES

1. On the Jewish Board of Guardians, see Laurie Magnus, *The Jewish Board of Guardians and the Men Who Made It* (London: Jewish Board of Guardians, 1909); V.D. Lipman, *A Century of Social Service, 1859–1959: The History of the Jewish Board of Guardians* (London: Routledge and Kegan Paul, 1959); Mordechai Rozin, *The Rich and the Poor: Jewish Philanthropy and Social Control in Nineteenth-Century London* (Brighton and Portland: Sussex Academic Press, 1999), pp.2–4. See also David Cesarani, 'Review' of *The Social Politics of Anglo-Jewry, 1880–1920* by Eugene C. Black and *A History of the Jews in Britain* by V.D. Lipman, *The English Historical Review*, 106 (July 1991), 676–8.
2. David Feldman, *Englishmen and Jews: Social Relations and Political Culture, 1840–1914* (New Haven, CT: Yale University Press, 1994); Todd Endelman, *The Jews of Britain, 1656 to 2000* (Berkeley, CA: University of California Press, 2002); Eugene Black, *The Social Politics of Anglo-Jewry, 1880–1920* (Oxford: Basil Blackwell, 1988).
3. Lara Marks, *Model Mothers: Jewish Mothers and Maternity Provision in East London, 1870–1939* (Oxford: Clarendon Press, 1994).
4. Rosalyn Livshin, 'The Acculturation of the Children of Immigrant Jews in Manchester, 1890-1930', in *The Making of Modern Anglo-Jewry* ed. by David Cesarani (Oxford: Basil Blackwell, 1990), pp.79–96; Suzanne Kirsch Greenberg, 'Compromise and Conflict: The Education of

Jewish Immigrant Children in London in the Aftermath of Emancipation, 1881–1905' (Ph.D. diss, Stanford University, Stanford, CA, 1981). In a comparison of nineteenth century Jewish and contemporary immigrant education, Geoffrey Short argued Jewish children succeeded because of teachers' expectations, English language acquisition, positive views of parents, willingness to meet needs of observant Jews, and the opportunity to avoid daily experiences of anti-Semitism by attending Jewish majority schools. Geoffrey Short, 'Accounting For Success: The Education of Jewish Children in Late 19th Century England', *British Journal of Educational Studies*, 41.3 (1993), 272–86.

5. Sharman Kadish, *'A good Jew and a good Englishman': the Jewish Lads' and Girls' Brigade, 1895–1995* (London: Vallentine Mitchell, 1995).

6. Susan L. Tananbaum, '"Ironing out the Ghetto Bend": Sports, Character and Acculturation among Jewish Immigrants in Britain', *Journal of Sport History*, 31.1 (2004), pp.53–75; idem, 'Biology and Community: The Duality of Jewish Mothering in East London', in *Mothering: Ideology Experience, and Agency* ed. by Evelyn N. Glenn, Grace Chang and Linda Forcey (New York: Routledge, 1994), pp.311–32; idem, 'Making Good Little English Children: Infant Welfare and Anglicisation in London, 1880–1939', *Immigrants and Minorities*, 12 (July 1993), 176–99. Lawrence Cohen's MA, the 'Impact of Norwood Judaism, Norwood Jewishness and Norwood Anglicisation on the Children' (University of Southampton, 2006) and his ongoing Ph.D. research will significantly add to our knowledge of childcare practices and policies.

7. Scholars discuss education, mothering, and associational networks in works such as: Carol Dyhouse, *Girls Growing up in Late Victorian and Edwardian England* (London: Routledge & Kegan Paul, 1981); Deborah Dwork, *War is Good for Babies and Other Young Children: a History of the Infant and Child Welfare Movement in England, 1898–1918* (London and New York: Tavistock Publications, 1987); Ellen Ross, *Love and Toil: Motherhood in Outcast London, 1870–1918* (New York: Oxford University Press, 1993).

For the classic study of Toynbee Hall, see Standish Meacham, *Toynbee Hall and Social Reform, 1880–1914: Search for Community* (New Haven, CT: Yale University Press, 1987). More recently, Seth Koven has analysed the motives of individuals who worked/lived in London's Slums, in *Slumming: Sexual and Social Politics in Victorian London* (Princeton, NJ: Princeton University Press, 2004).

For studies of American Jewish orphanages, see: Hyman Bogen, *The Luckiest Orphans: A History of the Hebrew Orphan Asylum of New York* (Urbana: University of Illinois Press, 1992); Reena Sigman Friedman, *These are our Children: Jewish Orphanages in the United States, 1880–1925* (Hanover: University of New England Press, 1994); Howard Goldstein, *The Home on Gorham Street and the Voices of its Children* (Tuscaloosa: University of Alabama Press, 1996); Gary Polster, *Inside Looking Out: The Cleveland Jewish Orphan Asylum, 1868–1924* (Kent, OH: Kent State University Press, 1990).

For an excellent study on American Jewish girls, see Melissa Klapper, *Jewish Girls Coming of Age in America, 1860–1920* (New York : New York University Press, 2005).

8. June Rose, *For the Sake of the Children: Inside Dr. Barnardo's, 120 Years of Caring for Children* (London: Hodder and Stoughton, 1987); Gillian Wagner, *Barnardo* (London: Weidenfeld and Nicolson, 1979). On Barnardo's use of photographs, see Seth Koven, 'Dr. Barnardo's "Artistic Fictions": Photography, Sexuality, and the Ragged Child in London', *Radical History Review*, 69 (1997), 7–45. On child emigration schemes see Joy Parr, *Labouring Children: British Immigrant Apprentices to Canada, 1869–1924* (Toronto: University of Toronto Press, 1994).

9. Lydia Murdoch, *Imagined Orphans: Poor Families, Child Welfare, and Contested Citizenship in London* (New Brunswick, NJ: Rutgers University Press, 2006).

10. Geoffrey Sherrington and Chris Jeffery, *Fairbridge: Empire and Child Migration* (London: Woburn Press, 1998).

11. Nigel Middleton, *When Family Failed* (London: Victor Gollancz, 1971), p.83, as cited by Harry Hendrick, *Child Welfare: England, 1872–1989* (London: Routledge, 1994), p.76. According to Jean Heywood, 69,030 came under poor law care in 1908, about one-third of whom were in workhouses or infirmaries. Jean Heywood, *Children in Care* (London: Routledge and Kegan Paul), p.90.

12. James Kincaid, *Child-Loving: The Erotic Child and Victorian Culture* (New York: Routledge, 1992), pp.88–9.

13. Stephenson, T.B. D.D. LL.D., Principal, 'General Survey', *The Twentieth Year of the Children's Home and Orphanage and Training School for Christian Workers and of the Missions and*

Agencies Connected therewith, being the year 1888–9, pp.3, 4. *For God and Country, Barnardo's Homes, 48th Annual Report*, 1913, p.3.

14. In 1795, Benjamin Goldsmid started a movement to found a Jews' Hospital. Jews' Hospital and Orphan Asylum (JHOA), *Annual Report*, 1894, p.20. On its 200th anniversary, Norwood and the London Museum of Jewish Life produced a book and exhibition on the Orphanage. See *What About the Children: 200 Years of Norwood Child Care, 1795–1995* (London: The Museum of Jewish Life and Norwood Child Care, 1995).
15. Dr Barnardo's, D239/ a3/17/28 'Environment', probably 1925, p.2.
16. Dr Barnardo's, *29th Annual Report of the Institutions known as Dr. Barnardo's Homes for Orphan and Waif Children*, 1894, pp.114–15.
17. C.S. Loch promoted this method for the COS, which was founded in 1869. See C.S. Loch, *Charity Organisation* (London: Swan Sonnenschein and Co., 1892).
18. Koven, 'Dr. Barnardo's "Artistic Fictions"' (see note 8), pp.15, 16. While 'scientific charities' sometimes responded from the heart – not the just the head, Barnardo himself reassured his readers that they investigated every candidate to eliminate, or at least minimise, deception. *The Nations' Waif Children, 39th Report of the National Incorporated Waifs' Association*, 1904, 9; D239/A3/1/20, *Annual Report of Dr. Barnardo's Homes (East End Juvenile Mission)*, 1887–88, p.11.
19. D239 A3/17/29, 'These 70 Years!' 1935, p.6.
20. See D.W. Bebbington, *Evangelicalism in Modern Britain: A History from the 1730s to the 1980s* (London: Unwin Hyman, 1989), see especially chapter 1, pp.1–19.
21. D239 A3/1/23, 'Dr. Barnardo's Homes' for Orphan and Destitute Children, *Annual Report for 1889*, pp.9–10.
22. Sisters of the Church, an Anglican Sisterhood, advertised their willing to accept illegitimate children. Accused of abuse by the COS, the orphanage came under Anglican supervision. Rene Kollar, OSB, 'Those Horrible Iron Cages: The Sisters of the Church and the Care of Orphans in Late Victorian England', *The American Benedictine Review*, 53.3 (2002), 264–84 (pp.270–71, 272, 284).
23. JHOA, *Annual Report*, 1895, p.23.
24. Book of Rules and Regulations of the Jews' Hospital, 1821 as cited by Edward Conway, 'The Origins of the Jewish Orphanage', *Transactions of the Jewish Historical Society of England*, 22 (1968–69), 55.
25. Ibid. p.57.
26. Riva Krut, Draft, History of Norwood, unpublished, 3; Todd Endelman, *The Jews of Georgian England, 1714–1830: Tradition and Change in a Liberal Society* (Philadelphia: JPS, 1979), pp.236, 237.
27. Conway (see note 24), p.56.
28. Ibid. p.59.
29. JH, *Annual Report*, 1868, p.5. According to Steven Singer, Jewish communal debates over curriculum centred on education for the middle and upper classes, not for the poor, since there was general consensus about working class education. Wealthier Jews typically received a limited Jewish education. Steven Singer, 'Jewish Education in the Mid-Nineteenth Century: A Study of the Early Victorian London Community', *The Jewish Quarterly Review*, 72.2–3 (1986–87), 163–78 (pp.163, 166–8).
30. Conway (see note 24), p.59.
31. JHOA, 1868, *Annual Report*, 1870, p.6.
32. D541/d1/1/4, NCH, Reports, Children's Home, 1888–92, The Twentieth Year of the Children's Home and Orphanage and Training School for Christian Workers and of the Missions and Agencies Connected therewith, being the year 1888–89, p.26.
33. *For God and Country, Dr. Barnardo's Homes, 57th Annual Report, 1922*, p.14.
34. *Jewish Chronicle*, 16 April 1869.
35. *Jewish Chronicle*, 13 January 1893, as cited by Conway (see note 24), p.64.
36. JHOA, *Annual Report*, 1895, p.15.
37. University of Southampton, AJ 19/B10, Visitors' Book, 9 March 1863–21 May 1939, 27 May 1897.
38. Polster (see note 7), pp.13–16, 28–32,
39. JHOA, *Annual Report*, 1867–68, p.7.
40. JH, *Annual Report*, 1873, p.7.

41. JHOA, *Annual Report*, 1885, p.15.
42. HOA, *Annual Report*, 1895, p.13
43. See for example: JHOA, *Annual Report*, 1911, pp.13, 20 and JHOA, *Annual Report*, 1923, pp.15, 17. For an insider's view of Norwood before and during World War II, see: David Golding, *Reminiscences of a Norwood Boy* (London: Laurie Stewart, 2005).
44. JHOA, *Annual Report*, 1910, pp.13–14.
45. *29th Annual Report of the Institutions known as Dr. Barnardo's Homes for Orphan and Waif Children*, 1894.
46. NCH, *The Twenty-Sixth Year of the Children's Home and Orphanage and Training School for Christian Workers*, 1894–95, p.25.
47. JHOA, *Annual Report*, 1903, p.12.
48. A rare reference in the 1925 *Annual Report* noted that 'The Committee is making a special effort to emigrate to the Colonies suitable lads who have no relations in this country able to offer them a home or financial support'. The orphanage received assistance from the Jewish Colonisation Association in placing ex-Norwood boys 'under purely Jewish auspices'. JHOA, *Annual Report*, 1925, p.21.
49. JHOA, *Annual Report*, 1895, p.15.
50. JHOA, *Annual Report*, 1907, p.12.
51. JHOA, *Annual Report*, 1910, pp.16, 17.
52. JHOA, *Annual Report*, 1911, pp.10, 11.
53. D239 A3/1/6, *Brief Report of the East-End Juvenile Mission, and Homes for Reclaiming Destitute Children of Both Sexes*, 1873–74, p.10. *Brief Report of the East-End Juvenile Mission, and Home for Working & Destitute Lads*, 1871–72, p.4.
54. D239/A3/1/20 *Annual Report of Dr. Barnardo's Homes (East End Juvenile Mission)*, 1887–88, p.19.
55. D239 A3/1/40, *These Forty Years, 40th Annual Report of Dr. Barnardo's Homes*, 1905, p.9.
56. D239/A3/1/44, *Seventy Thousand Rescues – Dr. Barnardo's Homes, National Incorporated Association*, 1909, p.8; *For God and Country, Barnardo's Homes, 48th Annual Report*, 1913, p.10.
57. Minutes of General Committee, 22 April 1926, as cited by Conway (see note 24), p.66.
58. For a discussion of assistance offered by the Salvation Army and Dr. Barnardo's Home, see Gertrude Himmelfarb, 'The Salvation Army and the Barnardo Homes', *Poverty and Compassion, the Moral Imagination of the Late Victorians* (New York: Knopf, 1991), pp.218–234.
59. James Kincaid, *Child-Loving: The Erotic Child and Victorian Culture* (New York: Routledge, 1992), pp.72, 78, 80, 81.
60. John Eekelaar, '"The Chief Glory": The Export of Children from the United Kingdom', *Journal of Law and Society*, 21.4 (December 1994), 487–504. Barry Coldrey, '"A Charity Which has Outlived its Usefulness": THE LAST Phase of Catholic Child Migration, 1947–56', *History of Education*, 25.4 (1996), 373–86.
61. According to Goldstein, unlike the Rochester orphanage sponsored by Reform Jews, who willingly adopted progressive reforms in child care, the commitment to Orthodox Judaism meant the Jewish Children's Home retained 'traditional practices'. Goldstein (see note 7), pp.46, 50. Between 1868 and 1878, Louis Aufrecht, for example of the Cleveland Jewish Orphan Asylum established a very regimented orphanage that utilised physical punishment and required silence at meals. His successor, Samuel Wolfenstein, replaced these methods with the more progressive approach of 'persuasion, kindness, and empathy'. Though Wolfenstein too, believed that the Asylum would better protect the children from turning to crime than if they lived with surviving family members or foster parents. Polster (see note 7), pp.11, 12, 28, 31 Friedman, who offers a comparison of three institutions, deepens our understanding of the interplay of local issues with trends in the Jewish community and mainstream society. Friedman (see note 7).

Counter-Institutionalism in Anglo-Jewry: The Norwood Rebellion

LAWRENCE COHEN

The research for this study relied on sources recorded by children who went to institutions, both Norwood and others – autobiographies, transcripts of interviews and articles in the Norwood Old Scholars Association's *Newsletter*. Without this source a history of counter-institutionalism and the Norwood Rebellion would not have been possible. The use of oral history is supplemented by reference to research on the role of myths in life stories as explored in Samuel and Thompson's *The Myths We Live By* and the psychology of memory as analysed in Sabbagh's *Remembering Our Childhood*. In Goffman's *Asylums* the authoritarian nature of the 'total institution' provides an insight in to the character of Norwood. Though there is little written on the counter-culture of institutions Humphries' *Hooligans or Rebels?* – a study of resistance by adolescents to agencies of control – provides a useful introduction. Information in official documentation – annual reports and minutes – are referred to but necessarily limited in extent.[1] Norwood was founded in 1876 as the Jews' Hospital and Orphan Asylum by the amalgamation of two older charities, the Jews' Hospital and Jews' Orphan Asylum. The conjoint institution provided in the one institution an asylum for destitute Jewish children. The institution was built in the barrack-style prevalent in its day and at its maximum housed over 400 children. It was split into the larger Main Building for boys and girls from the age of 8 to 14 and the smaller Gabriel Home for the infants aged from 5 to 8. Norwood provided an orphan home, religious and secular education and an after-care service when the children left. The organisational culture was characterised as a 'total institution' in which the children led an enclosed and disciplined life under the control of the Headmaster and a board of governors appointed from the Jewish community.

The institutional environment created three issues unanticipated when the asylum was established – an illiberal system of regimentation, a 'narrowing influence' that coloured institutional life with a monotonous grey existence and an 'emotional stunting' of the children deprived of personal attention. Over the course of the 85 years of the institution's existence, institutional disadvantages were countered by two countervailing forces. Externally, the social impact of advances in child development necessitated reforms at Norwood. Internally, the children adapted by creating a counter-culture. Officially condemned it nevertheless thrived and its history was excluded from official records. This essay examines the counter-culture and in particular the Norwood Rebellion of 1921.

Chronologically the rebellion took place several years after the First World War, which was a turning point in the institution's history. The pre-war period was a time of institutional optimism and expansion and the countervailing forces were incipient. The institution was proudly displayed as an example of Anglo-Jewish integrity caring for its own. The display took on a personal dimension when 'rosy-cheeked and healthy-looking orphans' were paraded at the annual public dinner. The community found it 'good enough' to make sentimental appeals as in the 'olden days' for its project of cultural assimilation, religious orthodoxy and training for employment but 'now higher standards had to be maintained'.[2] The inter-war period was a time when progress in child development forced the institution to recognise the 'evils of institutionalism'. Recognition came from the children most exceptionally by a revolt and from outside forces that called for liberal measures to temper the evils. What had previously had been good enough for the institution was no longer good enough for the children.

The inter-war institution at Norwood was humanised by liberal measures but good as they were, they proved not enough to counter the rising tide of social concern about the treatment of children in institutions. Activities such as field games, band-playing, lectures, trips and treats were 'unserious activities' which helped to lift the inmate out of himself making him oblivious for the time being to his actual situation. The activities were attempts to counter the 'narrowing influence' but their insufficiency left 'important deprivational effects of total institutions'.[3] There was the persistence of two other elements. Norwood remained unrestructured physically by retaining the congregate building and unrestructured ideologically by maintaining an authoritarian culture. The measure of its persistence was that style of living was still seen as acceptable after three-quarters of a century. On the eve of the Second World War the system of child dependency underwent a sudden and dramatic change – never to be the same again. Children who were used to living in an institution – insulated, isolated and knowing little of life in the outside world and religions other than Judaism – suddenly found themselves billeted in private homes in the wider community.[4]

The war changed attitudes and ideas about how to care for children. The way children were cared for, such as the discipline and punishment they were subjected to – the regimented routines that controlled every aspect of their lives, the food they ate that physically sustained them but left an 'institutional taste' that is well remembered in many scholars' recollections – are aspects of the unreconstructed ideology of institutional living examined in this study.

Institutionalism – Adaptation to Institutional Life

The style of management at Norwood was characteristic of the 'total institution'. It was a style where 'control and management is based on the principle that individual children must not step out of line and discipline is very strict and conformity is insisted on'.[5] Norwood was a total institution 'where a large number of like-situated individuals' were congregated in one place 'cut off from the wider society for an appreciable period of time'.[6] The total institution was seen as the most effective environment for training children and, according to this approach, in such an environment children were turned into 'sober, industrious citizens'. It was based on a social theory that the children contested through a counter-institutionalism that was a culture of deviance. The fact that it was unstructured and not focussed on any specific chronological moment has meant that 'deviance history' is often lost. It was not part of Norwood's official recorded history and traces of its recovery rely on the memories of scholars. Boris Cyrulnik states in his study of *Resilience* of children, 'if we attempt to understand this history ... we can associate memories that confer meaning with a disobedience to the past that encourages innovation'.[7] The approach adopted here is to discover the meaning of deviance culture as an innovatory response to the authoritarian regime.

The social theory in its conservative Christian form practised in Germany before the First World War 'maintained that by forcing the child to obey authority and habituating it to a moral way of life, the foundations for morality and for an autonomous ethical sense would be laid'.[8] Wilhelm Rhiel, an institution director in 1912, admitted much of the resistance within the reformatories was grounded in bitterness, since many of the children were very fond of their homes and parents and – wrongly – believed that they had suffered an injustice in being removed from them.[9]

The reaction of some educators was to see such resistance as 'a stubborn refusal to bow to legitimate authority and to face up to one's own sins and weaknesses – as the unreasoning revolt of anarchic egotism against the moral order of the universe'. It gave rise to an apparently increasing resort to corporal punishment as a disciplinary method.[10] Resistance by the inmates was seen as socially immoral whereas the inmates perceived resistance as a legitimate form of protest.

At Norwood, the 'Code of Discipline' was strict from the start and was inherited from the Jews' Hospital. Edward Conway, its former Principal and also its first major historian, has highlighted how the style had 'remained unchanged until the middle of the twentieth century' when he became Principal.[11] The code suggested for the Jews' Hospital and Orphan Asylum (JHOA) on amalgamation was that 'the discipline is not that rigid and ridiculous ... but a ready intelligent obedience to orders, and which seems to allow full play to individuality and yet restrains within proper bounds the undue exuberance of youthful spirits'.[12]

Conway's criticism and the experience of scholars suggested otherwise. The total institution operated in American Jewish orphanages resorted to

> dehumanising treatment which included admission procedures – referring to children by numbers, hair cropped short, ill-fitting uniforms which stripped them of their individuality with a dreary existence with sterile barrack-style dormitories, silent meals on long benches in great dining halls.[13]

Similarly, many Norwood scholars remember the trauma of admission. David Golding recalled: 'In just a few hours I had been taken away from my mother and family, my home, my people, and the world that I knew, handed over at the orphanage, stripped, bathed, given a number and the Gabrielite uniform.'[14] He underwent a process of personal and psychological dispossession and was made number 29. With the individual, 'a name identifies, denotes and signifies something, comes to be descriptive of it, and thus takes it out of the realm of the unknown or the amorphous'.[15] In the orphanage the new entrant became material 'to be shaped and coded into an object' acceptable to the Anglo-Jewish community. The child had to engage in activities that were incompatible with its conception of self, such as the artificiality of a daily regimented life.[16] Golding, who was at Norwood before the Second World War, recalled such a regime where children were 'forced to comply with strict discipline and having their freedom to walk in the outside world severely restricted for the duration of their childhood years'.[17]

The avowed objectives of the institution were straightforward, such as 'providing a home for maintaining, educating and apprenticing to industrial employment of poor children of the Jewish religion'.[18] However, each of the official goals 'lets loose a doctrine and within institutions there seems no natural check on the licence and easy interpretation that results'. The conclusion reached by an historian of American institutions is that 'a system of incarceration seems incapable of maintaining decency throughout all its sectors'.[19] In America superintendents of the major Jewish orphanages were committed to moral suasion rather than corporal punishment as the ideal method of disciplining. Despite an official ban on beatings for 'major offences' such as absconding, they still took place.[20] N26, who was at Norwood in the 1920s remembered that

> the greatest crime was to jump the 'wall' and run home because a child was homesick. The ultimate deterrent was a caning in front of all the boys, trousers down. It caused thick wheals on the buttocks. The boy was dressed in girl's clothes, boots and trousers confiscated.[21]

Against the licence of the authority, which one orphan described as based on the 'psychological use of power', the inmate was faced with the necessity of institutional adaptability.[22] It took on a number of forms ranging from acceptability to rejection. 'Colonisation' was where 'the inmate maximises his satisfactions from the system to provide a stable, relatively contented existence'.[23] Golding became colonised because

> Although in my early days I had hated the place so much, I had now become settled and contented. I had become 'orphanage wise', that is, acquired a second sense which enabled me to gauge just how far one could go with individual boys and masters. How to schmooz for things.[24]

The writer Leslie Thomas was sent to a Barnardo's Home called Dickies. After a few weeks there he felt a 'settled happiness'. He colonised Dickies where 'life was never dull – life was a constant adventure keeping one move ahead of the gaffer and all authority'.[25]

The ideal form of adaptation for the institution was 'conversion' where 'the inmate takes the official view and acts out the role of the perfect inmate'.[26] Such an ideal was fictionalised by J. Steinberg in an article entitled 'Memory Lane' in the Jewish Orphanage Magazine in which the boys showed 'great enthusiasm' for the regimented life, where there was 'never any reason to complain' and where they were 'never known to give trouble and always keep within bounds'.[27] T377 from his recollections was clearly a convert. On admission there were 'no tears or anything like that and I was quite happy to be looked after. In the Gabriel Home there was a lovely atmosphere. I had what I call a normal life'.[28] 'I know I settled in quite happily, was well cared for and enjoyed being spoilt by staff of the Gabriel Home.'[29] When he moved to the main building at 8 years of age he recalled

> I soon fell into the every day way of life – up at seven o'clock, wash, brush my teeth, say early morning prayers and then down to breakfast ... I know it sounds monotonous but it was routine we just took for granted. The same applied to the food we were given. I liked most of the food offered ... I was very happy in the main building.[30]

T377 identified with Norwood as he found, 'although an orphanage, it was a home for me'.[31] He summed up his experience using the word 'happy'. Similarly, Golding used 'contented'.[32]

Another scholar, N84, 'looking back on those Norwood days [was] reminded of the sadness and fear of the system'. He recalled that 'some of the children suffered psychologically and meeting them at reunions in later years, were still unable to speak of their life at Norwood. I was remembered apparently, by the staff as the child who didn't speak for a month'.[33] The trauma of psychological muteness was an extreme mode of 'situational withdrawal'.[34] His world was a far cry from the happy and contented worlds of others. He reflected 'when a person is sent to prison they know why they are there, but we little ones could never understand what we had done to deserve this experience'.[35] Alienated from his world and placed in an institution that merited his admission, N84 dismissed such meritoriousness as undeserving and saw himself as 'the sad little victim'.[36] The story is

something of a rarity in the pages of the *Newsletter* of the Norwood
Old Scholars Association (NOSA) as some scholars 'were unable to
speak of their life at Norwood'. Stories of 'the happiness that has been
brought into their lives, to the friendship and warmth' rather the sad
tales of the outcast were more forthcoming.[37]

The depths of psychological alienation were depersonalising for
Edward Dahlberg who was admitted to the Cleveland Jewish Orphan
Asylum in 1912. In his autobiography *Because I Was Flesh* he wrote,
'I have voided the use of "I" because I was obscure unto myself ...
Until my seventeenth year, when I left the orphan home, I was
suffering locality rather than a person'.[38] The person had become part
of 'a separate race of stunted children' and the locality, 'the asylum
grounds, its cinders, its junky buildings, were in their ruined infant
roots'.[39] 'He left the Jewish Orphan Asylum, but he was never to
obliterate its hymn because all experience is holy unto the heart which
feels.'[40] He did not suffer the obliteration with its loss of memory but
gave evidence of his lot through the autobiographical act of writing.

Maurice Levinson, who went to Norwood in 1917, found 'the
orphanage was no different from a prison'. The admission trauma was
an emotional stunting that denied the psychological release of crying.
'Crying was frowned upon and even forbidden' and on the first night
he was smacked for doing so.[41] On the second day he ran away back
to his mother but the threat of expulsion forced his return. It was an
individual act of rebellion and as an institutional adaptation the
'intransigent line' where the 'inmate challenges the system by not
cooperating with staff'.[42] Levinson was flogged in front of all the
children and the humiliation he felt made him swear 'I would get my
own back on the world'.[43]

The imposition of such punishment was not unusual at the time. In
the first decade of the century school 'sadism was considerable'. A
survey of recollections showed that 'at a rough guess, a good quarter
of Edwardian children left school to harbour resentments against
their teachers for the rest of their lives'.[44] Sheila Graham who went to
Norwood in 1911 thought 'the Headmaster was a sadist' after
witnessing how 'an absconded boy was caned in front of the whole
school'. He then had to wear girl's panties and made to stand on a
bench where all could see his disgrace.[45] The normality of such
treatment at the time could not diminish the impression it left on the
mind of a young girl to be remembered vividly over 60 years later.

Levinson retreated from his early intransigence to a mode of 'situational withdrawal' under the triple assaults of emotional neutralisation – 'in the end none of us really knew if we were happy or miserable'; physical deterrence – 'he developed a strong complex about Kaye for fear of being punished if he did something wrong'; and the indoctrination of gratitude – 'how lucky they were to be at the orphanage'.[46] 'He felt he was an outcast from society – unclean and below other people'.[47] When he left he reasserted his defiance and rejected the invitation by the Headmaster to write a letter of thanks, 'somehow I couldn't bring myself to write it'.[48]

His mode of adaptation was typical of 'a defensive response on the part of the inmate and finds his protective response to an assault upon self is collapsed in to the situation; he cannot defend himself by distancing himself from the mortifying situation'.[49] When defensive responses are made 'staff may penalise inmates for sullenness, insolence, sotto voce profaning asides etc. as grounds for further punishment'.[50] The register of Girls' Conduct at Norwood recorded the types of misconduct: 'Dirty, neglect of charges, disobedience, rudeness, calling names, impertinence, untruth, slapping charge, laziness, neglect of duty, striking little girl [in charge of], cleaning boots in dormitories, out of bounds, beating charge, shrieking.'[51] Such 'larking about' behaviour by the girls was 'acting as a multi-faceted means of resistance to institutional control'.[52]

Anti-social behaviour also included 'truancy, fighting, pilfering, mimicry, parodies, etc. It loosened bonds of deference and obedience and in the final analysis larking about was one of the most effective means of opposition available to resist authoritarian control'.[53] The most serious forms were 'participation in collective riots, absconding, bed wetting and fights'. The opposition they provided the children had a social function of limiting 'rigidities' in the system.[54] They acted as a safety valve for the various modes of adaptation and constituted a counter-culture to the total institution. Scholars' recollections provide a rich source of counter-cultural activities. A 'dormitory sub-culture' incubated acts of resistance such as the appropriation of food from the kitchen and the planning of illicit relationships. In the reformatory 'the most secretive and dramatic form of resistance within the subculture was the planning of escape attempts'.[55] The most dramatic and secretive act of resistance by the older boys in Norwood was outright rebellion and through the recollections of scholars the story of the Norwood Rebellion can be pieced together.

Counter-Institutionalism: The Norwood Rebellion

From the recollections of a number of Norwood scholars a specific rebellion by the boys took place about 1921. The evidence comes from the former children themselves and is imprecise in a number of ways. It is not clear just when the rebellion occurred. Indeed, there may have been several revolts by the children. It is also unclear who the leaders were as different names are mentioned. What the evidence does show is that the institutional regime was so unsatisfactory as to ignite outright opposition to the Norwood management. It illustrates in a very demonstrable way the feelings of some of the older boys towards a regime they had lived under for a number of years. The purpose of my study of Norwood history is to research the orphanage as an institution and the topic of children's rebellion is a small, obscure part of that history. It is history from below and can be linked to the world outside Norwood and to nineteenth and twentieth century institutionalism. Looking at strikes of children in schools elsewhere provides a comparison, although Norwood was unusual in that the rebellion took place in a closely controlled institution. The strike was an action undertaken by children and unusually demonstrated openly their feelings towards the institution that 'cared' for them.

Taylor – An Unconventional Approach
The revolt against the institution does not appear to be recorded in any of the archived documents. Officially it appears there was no such action. The only reference other than the ex-children's recollections is made by Sol Taylor, a teacher at Norwood who was appointed in 1918. In a recollection in 1968, couched in guarded language, he stated that Isidore Cohen led 'an unconventional approach to the Head and staff for improved "permissive conditions"'. Taylor admits 'in those days adults were not easily submissive, but we began to infuse into our work new trends in post-war academic and residential education'.

His personal chronology places the date of the incident in the year 1921.[56] 'The unconventional approach' was a revolt by the boys. Though Taylor admits conditions improved, he attributes the improvement to the education at the school, which seems an unlikely reason for a student uprising. His coded language states that the impact of the revolt changed the 'submissive' approach of the teachers towards the children and suggests discipline was a factor behind the discontent.

Taylor concluded that the boys' action had good moral reasons for it led to better education and a more permissive regime. After so many years and long after his retirement in 1945 Taylor was still very secretive on the strike and it makes it difficult to write a history of it from the perspective of the institution. Jean Peneff, an oral historian, found with such a 'cover up' 'You end up with complete misunderstandings and an inversion of the story. No story should be taken a priori to be an authentic account. You have to judge the degree of distortion. Our task consists in studying the largest number of cases'.[57] Fortunately it is possible to take up the task with the help of former children's accounts.

Kam's Rebellion

There are a number of cases of scholar recollections which are brief and contradictory. They are written from the perspective of the former children and provide additional important details. T40 in an interview in 1981 recalled what she called *Kam's Rebellion*.

> There was a rebellion because they weren't getting they THOUGHT enough food to eat, they were starving. They went on hunger strike for a few days. It was about 1923 or 1924. Kam led a group of boys who wanted more food. They wanted more bread, potatoes; they just wanted more to eat. They got what they wanted and it was all over. I personally, we, had plenty to eat. Perhaps the men were hungry, they wanted more. Never had anything like that on the girls' side.[58]

Though the dates and the name of the ring leader are not the same as in Taylor's reference it is clear the 'unconventional approach' was a rebellion. The nature of it, a hunger strike that lasted a few days, was exceptionally long when compared with accounts of other children's strikes – if it is to be believed.

In 1911 a wave of children's strikes took place all over the country and for a 'few hours freedom' the children, the newspapers of the time recorded, showed 'obvious signs of enjoyment'.[59] The strikes signified a sociological stage in the understanding of childhood. By the second half of the nineteenth century 'notable strides appear to have been made towards a more civilised treatment of children'. The social background was one of compulsory schooling and limitations on parental authority. It was increasingly realised that children pass through well-defined stages of development with different psychological characteristics.[60] 'By the 1890s the child had been discovered. It was defined in body and was beginning to be defined in mind'.[61] The wave of national strikes in 1911 provoked the first school strikes on anything like a national scale. The strikes were against corporal punishment and are said to have lasted three days in some places, having spread to over 60 towns. 'Children like adults were asserting their new status like the Labour Movement' and 'the enforcement of conformity and obedience through the cane crumbled when children felt caught up in a wider social excitement'.[62]

In Rosanna Basso's account of an Italian schoolchildren's strike in 1977 the whole period of the strike was compressed into a very short period of time which 'lasted just over half an hour' but it was sufficient to cause 'a total abandonment of school for the whole morning for a few pupils'.[63] Because of the ephemeral nature of the strike, 'once it is over it immediately disappears in to the past'. Such processes make 'it rare for a historian to be able to trace the stages of the strike'.[64]

> Because such strikes were a source of acute embarrassment to teachers and education authorities, they were conveniently forgotten and omitted from the pages of punishment books, committee minutes and official school histories, and it is only by listening to the reminiscences of people involved that we can discover the true nature and extent of this type of resistance.[65]

As with the Italian strike, it has been possible to retrace the past. When asked to define the word *strike* the Italian children related it to their own experience. The strike was 'fun', 'a complaint', 'opposing an order'. It took on various meanings. The term *rebellion*, however, defined as 'the open resistance to any authority', is the descriptive term used by the scholars who wrote of the Great Rebellion, the Kahn Rebellion and the Norwood Rebellion.[66] The expressions used are a memory device to encapsulate a far off event and in the process shape its meaning and in its recollected form became, for T40, Kam's Rebellion. The device becomes evidence and the recreated memory becomes the 'real-life' account. To elucidate the documentary value of the story can only result from 'the combined work of the narrator and the researcher'.[67]

This narrative is clear that the cause of the strike was insufficient food. The First World War brought hardship to Norwood. The Headmaster Marcus Kaye in March 1916 wrote in the *Jewish Chronicle*: 'The Jews' Orphanage has been almost engulfed in the wake of war' with diminished income and increased expenditure. His comments were part of an appeal for funds and concluded: 'Norwood wants to save them [the children] from suffering and want'.[68] In the following April, as part of the cutbacks, porridge was introduced for breakfast and this enabled a reduction in the quantity of bread eaten; 170 pounds of bread was saved by serving porridge twice a week.[69] The official record recorded the necessity for a change in part of the diet to save on costs and there are plenty of scholar recollections on the insufficiency of food. N25 remembered before the First World War:

> We at Norwood in those distant days were always hungry so fasting to us (on Yom Kippur) was a normal everyday practice. Breakfast was two small slices of bread and a smear of margarine, and a mug of lukewarm liquid watery milk called '2 bricks and whitewash' ... For 365 days, the meals were sparse and insufficient for growing children. We were always very hungry and without any hope of appeasement ... Many boys were caught pinching bread from the bins in the kitchens and scrumping apples from the trees, ravenously hungry. One took a risk of physical punishment to satisfy the pangs of young aching stomachs.[70]

The desperation of hunger drove him and others to individual acts of defiance – stealing food. N90, writing about her mother's experiences at Norwood before and during the First World War, found

> the worst thing was the constant hunger. She spent a great deal of time sneaking out whatever food she could get. She stored food in her knickers – even bread and butter. On one occasion a teacher discovered slices of bread and butter between the sheets. They were always hungry due to the shortage of food during the First World War. One girl stole two hot onions and hid them in her knickers. She had to be treated for burns on her bottom and the nurse could not understand how the girl had such blisters.[71]

She concluded of her mother, 'perhaps it was her way to rebel'; empty stomachs were a recipe for rebellious thoughts and the boys turned such thoughts into action, as T41 recalled.

> Boys went on a strike and locked themselves in the dormitories. Some ran home. Girls didn't go on strike but pinched what we could. We were very hungry during the war ... We were very undernourished as there was not enough food. The strikers flooded out the teachers' sitting room and demanded extra food.

The strike didn't last very long. They were promised two slices of bread and margarine and cocoa for tea.[72]

One of the features of the strike action was that the situation appeared intolerable and unjust to the children. They believed they had the right to protest and could succeed. The thought of revolt was transformed into the desire for revolt and then into actual revolt.[73] Girls did not go on strike but they found other ways to rebel. N27, who was at Norwood during the First World War, recalled that

> We were always hungry. I often think that credit for my survival in those days is due to apples (scrumping) and country air. On one occasion a group of us went in to sit and stare at the hanging fruit in the succah [hut specially erected for the festival]. A prank was played by someone turning out the electric light outside, and when that light went on again there was not one piece of fruit hanging in that succah.[74]

N25 agreed with N27 that 'the apples apparently helped our mutual survival'.[75] The succah with its pendulous ripe fruit triggered a 'fantastic development of consciousness' to bear fruit as a collective act of defiance by the children.[76] They audaciously opposed the system that had forced them into 'a single egalitarian community of fate' through the sacrilege of the succah.[77] The fruit became a fantasy of luxury, a feast of plenty when the spectre of 'mutual survival' was imagined.[78] In that imagination, the scholar recalled a story that gave credence to the strike.

The Great Rebellion

N15, who was at Norwood during and after the First World War, remembers what he calls *The Great Rebellion* staged by senior boys.

> They barricaded themselves in an upstairs dormitory and stocked piled enough bread and water to withstand a month's siege but a truce was arranged about midnight and only after a promise of no punishment. Why did we rebel? Wish I could remember.[79]

The title given to the revolt glorifies the event into something of major note. The details provided of the boys stockpiling food and water, barricading themselves in and planning a month's siege, adds a dimension of heroism and extravagance to the event to justify the name of the incident. The dormitory, albeit for less than a day, was transformed from a barrack of institutional control into a fortress of insurrection from which the institution was itself challenged. It was a battle which exemplified the boys' courage and strength to resist. The fragment of memory has a breathtaking quality when recalled almost half a century later.

On its own the fragment is too brief but in conjunction with the recollections of other witnesses it takes historical shape. The rebellion was most likely the same event as Kam's Rebellion. The author can be identified as the older brother of T40. His account shows the length of the revolt was not a few days but less than a day, though it is clear it was intended to last much longer. N15 could not remember the reason for the revolt but his sister well remembered the hunger that drove the boys to their action. He left Norwood in 1922 and T40 was admitted a year earlier in 1921 so it is possible from the scholar's evidence to pinpoint the rebellion to the year 1921 which ties in with Taylor's own chronology.[80]

An examination of the internal evidence suggests this recollection was what N15 was told about later rather than what he experienced himself. He did not say who the ringleader was, unlike the authors of the other recollections, which may account for using the glamorous title 'The Great Rebellion'. N15 admitted he did not know why the revolt took place, which might seem strange for someone who was there at the time and from whom a fuller account might have been expected. A piece of external evidence that gives credence to this reasoning is that a boy of the same name was admitted to the Gabriel Home on request from the Jewish Board of Guardians in 1911. The longest permitted stay was nine years, which meant this boy left before the revolt took place some ten years later.[81]

The terse cryptic reference mentioned by the teacher completely escapes the drama played out by the boys. Devoid of reference in official minutes and reports, the existence of the rebellion was denied by the authorities. It immediately disappeared into obscurity to remain a hidden yet significant piece of Norwood children's history until Taylor himself first mentioned it in a series of autobiographical sketches in the *Newsletter* in 1968. His article was the first revelation, but after him several scholars narrated their own recollections of the event in the hazy light of distant memories. The deviant behaviour of the boys has become accessible to the historian and only now can the rebellion be pieced together.[82]

The Kahn Rebellion

N26, who was at Norwood after the First World War, recalled his memory of the *Kahn Rebellion* with much detail.

> Some older boys who had apparently been reading too many comics and wishing to bring a little colour and excitement into the everyday humdrum life, in defiance of the masters, staged a little rebellion. We co-opted one of the kitchen staff in whom we confided our plan. She gave us the key to the pantry which we raided for food after hours, taking back sufficient loaves of bread to withstand a prolonged siege. Then we ate dry bread as unfortunately we forgot to take any margarine. During the siege one of the boys cut himself, one of the beds falling against him. The attempt to break down the barricades of beds and mattresses was defended with a water hose. But, as can be expected, the 'revolt' was squashed at 3am the following morning. The threat to expel the boy, Issy Khan, a most likeable and popular Head Boy, was withdrawn only when the boys threatened to march as in a squad, to and through the East End of London. It was not until some time later conditions in the Institution began to change but all the rebels had already left.[83]

This version of the strike is a more extensive account and fills out the practical details of how the boys obtained food through collusion with a member of the kitchen staff, if that is to be believed, and used the beds and mattresses to form the barricade. Forward planning went into their action with the prospect of a long siege under the leadership of the Head Boy. The respect of his position and his likeable character persuaded the other boys to follow him, no doubt to the consternation of staff now deserted by Kahn. A march through the East End, where most of the boys came from, would have horrified them, as a fundamental tenet of the moral teaching was never to bring the name of the institution into disrepute.

N26 remembered the name of the ringleader was Issy Kahn and clearly this is the same person as Sol Taylor's Isidore Cohen; Issy being a nickname for Isidore and Cohen an anglicised version of Kahn. During the First World War many English people with German sounding names anglicised them because of the possible link to the enemy. The Headmaster did just that and changed his name from Myer Kaiser to Marcus Kaye. It is most likely the name of the leader *Kam* T40 had in mind in her account of the rebellion is a corruption of Kahn. The ostensible reason given for the strike, to bring colour into the greyness of their lives, was an act of defiance and retaliation against the adults. For the boys the situation was reached where

> Habit appears not just a feature of everyday life but an existence in itself. This is the experience we call boredom, monotony, tedium and despair. On all sides there lies invitations to action ... new forms of behaviour, new locations, new partners.[84]

The revolt manifested the 'new forms of behaviour' – defiant action, the location of the barricaded dormitory and a partnership of the older boys. It mocked the humdrum, narrow institutional life. N49 who was at Norwood in the early 1920s, recalls

> Sunday was known as 'Starving Day' not because we had less food but because we had lots of time on our hands. On one occasion some boys played 'Follow my Leader' to go to the 'Upper Old', the boys' top dormitory. One boy fell off the fire escape and was then given six of the best and his name entered in the punishment book as a lesson to us all.[85]

The escapade had all the hallmarks of a trial run – the group, the leader, the place and the motives, starving boys and starving days. It was an invitation to action.

The Norwood Rebellion
N82 recollected the episode:

> In the early 1920s the boys stayed a rebellion. They felt they were not getting enough food and what they got was monotonous; the same fare was being served all the time. Levene wrote slogans such as WE WANT MORE FOOD on the walls. Several masters were cane-happy and enjoyed beating the boys which included the non-Jewish Mr Johnson. The rebellion was planned like a military operation and began one Sabbath morning after service. On this Sabbath some of the older boys started to fight with the masters as the column of children entered the long drive after being marched to Streatham Common. These boys then took over one of the dormitories and barricaded themselves inside. They had plenty of food and water.
>
> The next stage was placing other boys in charge of the kitchen. The uprising was partly about food. The younger boys who did not take part found there was very little food left and had

to share their beds as the older boys had commandeered their dormitory. A hosepipe was used to spray at any unauthorised people entering and someone was placed on the fire escape to prevent anyone gaining access. The rebellion was sparked by the Kayes being on holiday. By the time he returned some boys gave themselves up, became frightened and felt things had gone too far and others had tried to climb on to the roof ... But things did improve and Johnson left. Kaye made an example of the ringleaders to avoid a repetition by caning them including Hymie Zalkin, whose idea the rebellion had been and Louis Levene.[86]

Some of the details clearly contradict other accounts but this version adds further details and confirms other evidence. The opportunity for the uprising was the vacation of the headmaster and his wife, who was the matron at Norwood. On Saturday mornings the 'crocodile' march to Streatham Common was a regimented routine and on this rare occasion the crocodile, true to its real nature, snapped back at its keepers. Marching was a feature of orphanage life and this one occasion the march was the signal for revolt.[87] Levene's message has the fictional quality of Oliver Twist's plea. In the absence of an official memory, the corroboration relies on the other personal accounts and 'by extrapolation from such proven credibility' as the only good evidence from an undocumented, hidden world.[88]

N32, who went to Norwood in 1918, paints a grim picture of conditions in which the ingredients of hunger, time on their hands and the cane made an inflammatory combination:

The midday meal was stamped with the day of the week, the same dish on the same particular day – week by week, year by year. In all that time I never felt the need for a second helping of food ... My stomach grew disciplined to the amount of food I was given ... Sundays was a particularly bad day for us. There was nothing to do, except play football, quarrel among ourselves, or wander aimlessly about ... Hunger! One boy was caught with two kippers protruding from his pockets, probably stolen. 'But I was hungry, starving, Sir', he told the master. 'Hungry, you have no right to be starving', the master replied. Nevertheless, he was caned on the hand in front of the whole school in the quadrangle. Justice had to be done.[89]

But justice was on the side of the children or, in the words of T41's comment on Kam's Rebellion, 'the strikers were in the right'. It was legitimised by the bad conditions. The justice of the master was for the boys to dare question those conditions.

Another version of the strike was told by T377, who was admitted to Norwood in 1928. He says he spoke to members of the strike committee and in his account a strike took place in 1926:

> There was a great amount of strictness during the period 24 to 26 at the time of the General Strike. At that time the level of food was very, very low. During 1926 the boys went on strike, they had a little revolution of their own and they wanted better treatment. The outcome is that during 1927/8 things did improve. They barricaded themselves into some of the classrooms. It fizzled out after about a week ... There was an improvement in the food.[90]

The idea of a link between the General Strike and the Norwood strike on its own was plausible, although placing it in that year gives the narrative an even more heroic, radical context – as part of something even bigger. In the 1911 school strikes 'the children ... were consciously imitating – or learning from – their elders ... The children must have been listening at home to all the talk about strikes, all through the hot summer of 1911'.[91] Peneff advises 'no life story should be taken a priori to be an authentic account. You have to judge the degree of distortion. The scholar must give us the reasons why plausibility is attributed to one part of the history and doubt to another'.[92] The other accounts allow the plausibility of the Norwood Rebellion to have almost certainly happened but in the case of a brief mention of another strike by N83 who was at Norwood in the early 1930s, greater doubt must exist. He wrote: 'I also remember the rebellion when the masters were locked in a room and the brave leader was Solly Danziger'.[93] There is an absence of any mention by other scholars of this incident and his reference is extremely brief.

Counter-Institutionalism: Resistance to Corporal Punishment

The strike was an exceptional form of 'deviant' behaviour justified by the cause and necessarily arose from 'the social construction of reality' that provoked it. The total institution confronted the children with 'the reality of everyday life' that was 'paramount' and 'massive'. N24, who was at Norwood in the 1930s, thought

> depending on the period one was at Norwood the staff I presume and hope must have used all the latest knowledge and ideas to help

in their work. It is true that many years ago knowledge in this area was scanty and empirical. Probably the majority of staff must have reacted intuitively to their work. Thus were some kind, some harsh, some stern with strong discipline, some with weak discipline and our memories recall one or other of these attitudes and our reactions to the staff.[94]

The lack of uniformity of treatment by staff and their 'intuitive' conduct was conducive to the regimented style of living. At the Hebrew Orphan Asylum (HOA) in the 1920s and 1930 the children 'had more leisure time than previous generations as two free afternoons and weekends' but they were still regimented. 'No published rules existed, monitors and counsellors were free to make up their own and the punishments that went with them.'[95] Institutional size and arbitrary conduct were the structural realities against which forces of liberalisation had to contest.

At Norwood the orphanage had embarked on a programme of liberalisation under Kaye, yet its impact was limited by the persistence of the overwhelming reality of institutional life. It was beyond the resources of the children to change it and at most their impact could mitigate it. The revolt was the one form of collective action that contested the social structure of institutional life. It was the 'little revolution' as T377 described in his version, whereas 'larking about' behaviour constituted personal acts of defiance.[96] The defiant acts expressed the resentment of diffuse feelings of hate and hostility born of a sense of powerlessness against the system evoking them. The persistence of such acts as remembered by generations of scholars was the re-expressing of impotent hostility which left little change in values. Just once in a while the resentment became a source of genuine transvaluation when the frustration of institutional life led to 'full denunciation of previously prized values' and rebellion broke out.[97] From all the accounts the rebellion was treated as a serious affair drawing on a reservoir of resentful and discontented feelings. When the institutional system is a barrier to satisfaction of legitimate goals such as decent food and abolition of corporal punishment, the stage is set for rebellion as a legitimate response.

The abolition of corporal punishment was a contentious issue in institutions. At the HOA in 1934, the new dean Moses Shelesnyak planned to abolish it. Already in the previous two years its use had been on the decline, yet monitors and counsellors resisted the change as their absolute authority had been questioned. The institution was placed in a limbo of uncertainty in inculcating a new philosophy of discipline. The discipline and the injustices of it were hated by the boys yet its absence left a vacuum of control. It was a situation ripe for action and in the second oldest boys' dormitory action was triggered:

> About 6.30 before breakfast one boy was still in bed when the others were dressed. The counsellor was about to batter his head against an upturned bedpost when *an amazing revolt took place.* He felt a tap on his shoulder and turned round to find the entire dormitory gathered in the alcove – all 80 boys. Most were crowded around him and others were standing on beds and perched on lockers. 'Drop him' he was ordered by the boy who had tapped on the shoulder. For a moment the counsellor was stunned, not knowing what to do next. If he refused 80 boys stood ready to jump him and he knew he could not rely on the monitors to back him. At the moment the counsellor was literally saved by the bell. It gave him an excuse to get out of the crisis without loss of face. Dropping the boy, he ordered everybody to line up and march downstairs. He never struck another boy again nor did any other counsellor when the news got round.[98]

It marked the end of corporal punishment in the HOA and without any official proclamation. It had taken a revolt by the boys themselves to accomplish it.

The use of corporal punishment in Britain is a story of the contest between institutions and schools where it was liberally used and social reformers who wanted to restrict it. Boarding schools and class discipline relied heavily on corporal punishment and by 1906 when Britain was 'steadfastly retaining' flogging it had been abolished in America, France and Germany. 'Teachers ... were impelled to resort to it owing to pressure of class sizes and its indiscriminate and capricious use persisted in schools before 1914'.[99] The empiricism of size that necessitated its use and the arbitrariness marked by the lack of rules were features of the authoritarian institution. The JHOA, which inherited an authoritarian tradition of strong discipline on amalgamation, exemplified such features.

At Norwood, no punishment books are extant but there is a record of a complaint received by the Whitechapel Union in 1888 from the mother of a boy at the institution who had received '32 strokes with the birch' because of bed wetting. The child had been under treatment for 'incontinence' at the Hospital for Urinary Diseases. The mother said it was involuntary but the Headmaster, Reverend Harris claimed it 'a wilful and voluntary act'. An investigation by the Union found no entry in the punishment book. Henry Behrends, Norwood President, admitted 'that the punishment was severe' without amounting to cruelty though the Guardians defined the act as a cruel beating. Harris was instructed 'never to exceed 6 strokes with the cane or birch' and Norwood was chided by the Union 'for their obvious insensitivity in not considering that the boy had been punished for an involuntary illness'.[100] The resistance of the mother countered the arbitrary use of corporal punishment by Harris, who found himself challenged. A determined mother was not put off by a petulant 'I am Master here' when she wanted to see her other children. The response of the institution achieved a change in policy that mitigated the use of the birch and cane. Harris himself was forced to resign shortly after, which may have included his excessive discipline, of 'irregularities which have taken place into the conduct of the Institution'.[101]

In 1900 regulations were introduced that schools had to keep caning registers and from 1904 the Board of Education disapproved of the cane for infants and girls.[102] In the previous year the London School Board issued a revised code that 'emphasised all forms of punishment be kept to a minimum and corporal punishment not to be inflicted except for grave moral offences'.[103] However, the regulations were widely ignored by teachers and unofficial resort to corporal punishment with the hand, slipper or ruler was commonplace.[104] Norwood was no exception to the flouting of the regulations. In 1936 Matron's administration at the Gabriel Home was criticised as 'discipline too rigid'.[105] She subsequently resigned and in the interview for new staff at the Home 'it was laid down that corporal punishment must not be admitted by any member of Matron's staff. Punishment during school hours would, of course, be in accordance with the LCC regulations.'[106]

The tradition of using the cane was strong and N31, who was at Norwood in the 1930s, recalled 'the cane was in vogue at the time'.[107] It was claimed by Nathan Morris that 'in Jewish schools corporal punishment was almost universal'. In his lecture on Discipline and Punishment he argued that

punishment was seen as expiation of sins and also of eradicating evil habits and moral and intellectual reformation. Modern ideas on punishment were not the satisfaction of the ends of justice or protection of society but reformation of character. It is generally accepted the teacher must have undivided authority in school and discipline was the means to secure it.[108]

His view, which was circulated within the community in the pages of the *Jewish Chronicle,* gave support to Norwood's idea on discipline.

The Second World War was a watershed. 'It changed attitudes and ideas about how to care' for the children.[109] But that change did not affect corporal punishment and the vogue continued. N74 went to Norwood in 1946 and recalled on the occasion of her birthday they played the game of 'Dare, Truth or Promise'. She was to turn all 15 taps on in 15 sinks in the bathroom without spilling (letting the sinks overflow) a drop. She and the other girls were caught by the Headmaster, Alfred Lubrun who 'systematically caned all of us'.[110] Caning of girls had long been banned in schools but as the incident took place in a residential institution it did not apply and continued to be used. N83 recalled Lubrun's penchant when he had been given 'many canings including with a cricket stump occasionally on my backside'.[111]

The use of beatings within the JHOA that had been taking place under Harris still persisted 60 years later. It was an endemic problem of a large residential institution for children. The Curtis Committee set up by the government in 1945 to survey such institutions revealed for the first time the extent of their deficiencies. In the submission to the Committee it was admitted by Norwood that 'we have an extremely large number of very difficult children. I would rather not look back. I think one can see one's failures in the past. In the past it was a very large institution in every sense of the word'.[112] The evidence showed Norwood to be too large to cope with its 'difficult' children. It used largely untrained staff who operated intuitively and coped by using discipline as their means of control.[113]

Scholars' recollections and the evidence to the Curtis Committee contradicted the picture presented to the governors of an institution where 'there was relatively little delinquency' and where disciplinary treatment did not entail 'severe measures'.[114] The use of strong discipline endured right to the end of the orphanage's existence under the last superintendent, Jack Wagman. In his obituary, what NOSA remembered was the responsibility of 'a tremendous task having so many boys and girls, under one roof, so obviously there had to be house rules and discipline'.[115]

Counter-Institutionalism: Memory as a Historical Source

The Norwood Rebellion was a revolt by the older boys against the Norwood management in 1921 because of poor diet and harsh discipline. The source of the event is based on the recollections of six scholars written between 1969 and 2001 and in a passing reference by one teacher. They provide a version of events absent in any official document. The picture portrayed is based on memories five to eight decades after the event. The opportunity for bringing them to light was that the NOSA *Newsletter* started in 1967 to record past memories. The end of the old institution in the early 1960s created a discontinuity between the absence of its physical presence and the memories of it. The publication provided the means to memorise the past. The logo that appears at the top of the front page is the picture of the orphanage. 'Reinstating the environment in which an event has been experienced' for the *Newsletter* reader invites an entrance in to the memories it held.[116] The photograph picked by NOSA served to reinstate an *institutional* memory but for the individual scholar it was a *personal* invite.

Traditionally, the historian's research has been document-biased as voiced in the adage that 'the historian works with documents. There is no substitute, no history'.[117] Much of Norwood's history, including my own, is based on such contemporary material. What is left out is the evidence of the children, and for that reason it does not provide a total history. The corpus of available material is expanded from contemporary documentary material finite in the extent of its preservation by the inclusion of oral history, the scholars' recollections, open-ended as a living source. The importance of oral evidence is that it is a source of information not covered by the others – deviancy, counter-institutional culture, personal relationships, individual behaviour and revolts. Without the oral evidence the Norwood Rebellion would not have been known to have existed. Some scholars claimed 'the whole thing was hushed up' deliberately.[118] Its authenticity as a real event in the memory of scholars has determined the authenticity of personal recollections as a source in its own right, a source which refutes the adage and the historian's reverence of the document.

The various descriptions of the rebellion contain different accounts in which details of the event, the motives for rebelling, the boys who were involved and even when it took place are inconsistent and for that reason a precise account will never be known. What the historian has to judge is the degree of distortion and one way of dealing with it 'consists in studying the largest number of cases'.[119] Providing as much detail as possible in recollections may introduce 'the kind of sensory and perceptual associates' that can be taken as evidence that an event has been remembered rather than invented.[120] The seven accounts of the rebellion have been sufficient to construct a historical narrative. The documentary value of an event is an exercise in which the historian 'must provide us with the key which transforms the crude document into a historical source and must give us the reasons why plausibility is attributed to one part of the history and doubt to another'.[121] The key is the themes – the rebellion, larking about, deviance – and the placing of individual actions in a historical narrative. This essay places the one known strike within the wider realm of oral history. Its plausibility derives from the comparative evaluation of the recollected accounts and the wider context of counter-institutionalism.

Oral evidence, unlike archived documents, is the product of scholars' living memories. Psychological research shows 'all memory, whatever age it is laid down or recalled, is unreliable' and over time gets less accurate.[122] One way memory is unreliable is that it is not chronologically organised and this explains the different dates given for the revolt. Recognising the subjective in individual testimonies is a challenge to 'the accepted categories of history'.[123] The 'subjectivity in oral histories is certainly not to say that we are working with memories of a false past'. A high proportion of the detail in recollections remains objectively valid verified from other sources and 'by extrapolation from such proven credibility sometimes the only good evidence we have from an undocumented, hidden world'.[124] A lot of the details are consistent in scholars' accounts such as the canings mentioned in many of them; caning was part of the disciplinary regime. The main evidence for the rebellion is the scholars' accounts but a critical analysis of it has been utilised to demonstrate its authenticity.

The invitation by NOSA for scholars' recollections was also an act by the scholar as an adult to reflect where Norwood stood in his or her personal history. Marcus Kaye asked leavers to write a letter of thanks. Such letters were constrained in their criticism of the institution. The act of writing a letter implied an avowal of the life at Norwood. Levinson in his autobiography wrote he resisted writing a letter because in his personal history it denied him being a person.[125] The refusal to write a letter excluded the possibility of Kaye pasting it in his scrapbook as evidence of how good Norwood was for the children.[126] His autobiography, *A Woman from Bessarabia*, forms part of the life story of Norwood without which Levinson's side of the story would be untold.

An article appeared in the *Jewish Chronicle* in 1974 entitled 'They Asked for More and Got It', in which a number of scholars expressed criticism of Norwood. It was contradicted by a former teacher, Sol Taylor, and NOSA, claiming 'the article gave a very unfair picture of life at Norwood. It was a good Institution and made so by the people who administered it'.[127] The article's author replied: 'I gave a fair and undistorted account of what it was to be brought up in Norwood from the child's point of view.'[128] Taylor was criticised as showing only 'the teacher's side [which] left out the humanitarian part of school life which is just as vital as the educational side'.[129] The *JC* article opened up a dispute over what was the 'authentic version' of Norwood experience. There were two memories being fought over, one institutional and another by the individual scholars. At the level of an institution in historical imagery, a picture has been formed in which memory becomes part of the real life account and Norwood was a good institution.[130] But the historical narratives related by many scholars remember it was not 'good enough' for them.

The recollections rely on a remembered experience but for some scholars there was an absence of memory. N97, who went to Norwood in 1933, wrote that 'for a long time I preferred to block out the past'. It was meeting another Norwood boy that helped him to remember the forgotten years.[131] N71 wrote that 'he spent an unremarkable (to me) five years or so there and as far as I can remember nothing outstanding happened and I caused no ripples in the daily life there'.[132] Gerald Cohen, who went to Norwood in 1946, said that he remembered almost nothing of his Norwood time.[133] There may have been many scholars like them who thus have left no recollections.

The Newsons in their research on young children examined the importance of memory in the development of the young child. They found from their observations:

> The child relies on his parents' role as a memory bank to which he can refer for evidence of himself as an individual with a history. One of the means by which the ordinary child achieves a sense of personal identity is through his store of memories going back into

his own past, in which he himself and his close family play central roles. But the child does not maintain this store of memories on his own, but has them repaired, added to and embroidered upon in everyday conversation with his own family, the sharers of his memory. Recollecting past experiences between child and parent establishes him as person with a past that others know about and make real by their sharing of it. In contrast, the child who is deprived of parents may in fact have no single person who shares his own most basic and important memories, no one to confirm whether these memories are in fact correct or figments of the imagination, no one to polish up a fading memory before it is too late.[134]

They concluded: 'we are beginning to realise now what damage can be done to children in such environments by conditions which so diminish their private image of their own individuality'.[135] The research shows that the institutional environment can impede the social function of memory in the child and this deprivation for some scholars results in permanent memory loss.[136] Oral history extends the range of historical sources but even this source is not accessible for those scholars whose memory has been impeded by blocking out difficult elements of the past.

This study has examined the institution as it affected the children. It has largely relied on oral sources and the words of the children themselves. Their memories raise issues of authenticity – of oral evidence as a source, the content of oral evidence, 'inauthentic memory' and conflict over the 'true' memory. Despite limitations, they reveal a counter-culture of deviance and expose a piece of lost history – the Norwood Rebellion. The rebellion was a single event and affected only a few older boys. Yet what was persistent and affected many generations of children was the paramount reality of a total institution. The use of corporal punishment was based on the necessity of controlling a large number of children in an 'enormous' building. These structural constraints limited the liberalising impact of particular policies to make the life of the children better at Norwood. The Second World War was the catalyst that ended the total institution. Nothing, however, 'would ever be able to transform it from being a building of caves, tunnels, high echoes and cold comfort'.[137]

NOTES

1. Raphael Samuel and Paul Thompson, eds., *The Myths We Live By* (London: Routledge, 1990); Karl Sabbagh, *Remembering Our Childhood – How Memory Betrays Us* (Oxford: Oxford University Press, 2009); Irving Goffman, *Asylums – Essays on the Social Situation of Mental & Other Inmates* (London: Penguin, 1991); Stephen Humphries, *Hooligans or Rebels?* (Oxford: Basil Blackwell, 1981).
2. *JC*, 8 March 1911.
3. Goffman, *Asylums* (see note 1), pp.67–8.
4. Rickie Burman, ed., *What About the Children? 200 Years of Norwood Child Care 1795–1995* (London: London Jewish Museum & Norwood Child Care, 1995), p.45.
5. Juliet Berry, *Daily Experiences in Residential Life – a Study of Children and their Care-givers* (London: Routledge & Kegan Paul, 1975), p.100.
6. Reena Friedman, *These are Our Children: Jewish Orphanages in the United States, 1880–1925* (Hanover, NH: Brandeis University Press, 1994), p.34.
7. Boris Cyrulnik, *Resilience* (London: Penguin, 2009), p.186.
8. Edward Dickinson, *The Politics of German Child Welfare from the Empire to the Federal Republic* (London: Harvard University Press, 1996), p.102.
9. Ibid. p.102.
10. Ibid. p.103.
11. Edward Conway, 'The Institutional Care of Children, A Case History' (unpublished Ph.D. thesis, London University, 1957), p.90.
12. *JC*, 28 January 1874.
13. Friedman, *These are Our Children* (see note 6), p.38.
14. David Golding, *Reminiscences of a Norwood Boy* (London: L. Stewart, 2005), p.31. He was at Norwood 1935–43.
15. Max Adler, *Naming and Addressing – A Sociolinguistic Study* (Hamburg: Helmut Buske Verlag, 1978), pp.93–4.
16. Goffman, *Asylums* (see note 1), pp.26, 31.
17. Golding, *Reminiscences* (see note 14), p.7.
18. The mission statement of the Jews' Hospital and Orphan Asylum.
19. Goffman, *Asylums* (see note 1), pp.80–2; David Rothman, *Conscience and Convenience – The Asylum and its Alternatives in Progressive America* (Boston: Little Brown, 1980), p.420.
20. Friedman, *These are Our Children* (see note 6), p.46.
21. Norwood Old Scholars Association (NOSA), *Newsletter*, No.26, February 1972.
22. Friedman, *These are Our Children* (see note 6), pp.44–6.
23. Goffman, *Asylums* (see note 1), pp.61–5.
24. Golding, *Reminiscences* (see note 14), p.10.
25. Leslie Thomas, *This Time Next Year – Memoir of a Barnardo Boy* (London: Penguin, 1964), p.57.
26. Goffman, *Asylums* (see note 1), pp.61–5.
27. Jewish Orphanage Magazine, July 1936.
28. London Jewish Museum (LJM), Interview Transcript, tape 377, July 1994. He was at Norwood 1928–36.
29. NOSA *Newsletter*, No.78, April 1999.
30. Ibid.
31. NOSA, *Newsletter*, No.79, September 1999.
32. NOSA, *Newsletter*, No.78; Golding, *Reminiscences* (see note 14), p.10.
33. NOSA, *Newsletter*, No.84, September 2002. He was at Norwood 1929–35.
34. Goffman, *Asylums* (see note 1), pp.61–5.
35. NOSA, *Newsletter*, No.84.
36. Ibid.
37. NOSA, *Newsletter*, No.15, December 1969.
38. Edward Dahlberg, *Because I Was Flesh – The Autobiography of Edward Dahlberg* (London: Methuen, 1963), p.92.
39. Ibid. pp.73, 75–6.

40. Ibid. pp.90–91.
41. Maurice Levinson, *A Woman from Bessarabia* (London: Sacker & Warburg, 1964), p.48.
42. Goffman, *Asylums* (see note 1), pp.61–5.
43. Levinson, *A Woman* (see note 41), pp.52–3.
44. Paul Thompson, *The Edwardians –The Remaking of British Society* (London: Routledge, 1962), p.53.
45. Sheila Graham *The Late Lily Shiel* (London: W.H. Allen, 1979), pp.24–5.
46. Levinson, *A Woman* (see note 41), pp.57, 62.
47. Ibid. p.83.
48. Ibid. pp.62–4.
49. Goffman, *Asylums* (see note 1), p.41.
50. Ibid. p.41.
51. University of Southampton Archives (USA), Monthly Register of Girls' Conduct, C/8, July 1905–January 1915.
52. Humphries, *Hooligans or Rebels?* (see note 1), p.146.
53. Ibid. p.149.
54. Goffman, *Asylums* (see note 1), p.56.
55. Humphries, *Hooligans or Rebels?* (see note 1), pp.218–19.
56. NOSA, *Newsletter*, No.14, September 1969. Sol Taylor recalls his time at Norwood in the years 1918–28.
57. Jean Penoff, 'Myths in Life Stories', in *The Myths We Live By* (see note 1), p.42.
58. LJM, Interview Transcript, tape 40, 1981. She was at Norwood 1921–28.
59. D. Marson, *Children's Strikes in 1911* (Oxford: History Workshop Pamphlet, No.9, 1973), p.33.
60. Eric Hopkins, *Children Transformed – Working Class Children in Nineteenth Century England* (Manchester: Manchester University Press, 1994), p.315.
61. Harry Hendrick, *Child Welfare – Historical Dimensions, Contemporary Debate* (Bristol: The Polity Press, 2003), p.23.
62. Hopkins, *Children Transformed* (see note 60), p.321; Lionel Rose, *The Erosion of Childhood – Child Oppression in Britain 1860–1918* (London: Routledge, 1991), p.182.
63. Rosanno Basso, 'Myths in Contemporary Oral Transmission – A Children's Strike', in *The Myths We Live By* (see note 1), p.62.
64. Ibid. p.61.
65. Humphries, *Hooligans or Rebels?* (see note 1), p.91.
66. NOSA, *Newsletter*, 'The Great Rebellion', No.15; 'The Kahn Rebellion', No.26; 'The Norwood Rebellion', No.83.
67. Peneff, 'Myths in Life Stories' (see note 57), p.45.
68. USA, Headmaster's scrapbook, C/10, 3 March 1916.
69. USA, Headmaster's scrapbook, C/10, 26 April 1917.
70. NOSA, *Newsletter*, No.25, December 1971. He was at Norwood 1906–11.
71. NOSA, *Newsletter*, No.90, April 2005. Her mother was at Norwood 1909–17.
72. LJM, Interview Transcript, tape 41, 1981. She was at Norwood during and after the First World War. Her surname is the same as the daughter N90 (note 71) and is almost certainly the same person as her mother.
73. Basso, 'Myths' (see note 63), p.64.
74. NOSA, *Newsletter*, No.27, May 1972. She was at Norwood 1913–18.
75. NOSA, *Newsletter*, No.28, September 1972.
76. Basso, 'Myths' (see note 63), p.65.
77. Goffman, *Asylums* (see note 1), p.57.
78. Samuel and Thompson, *The Myths* (see note 1), p.13.
79. NOSA, *Newsletter*, No.15, December 1969.
80. Refer to notes 58 and 79. N15 was at Norwood 1914–22. He has the same surname as T40 and was most likely her older brother.
81. USA, House Committee minutes, C/7, 29 June 1911, 7 July 1911.
82. Paul Thompson, *The Voice of the Past* (Oxford: Oxford University Press, 2000), pp.154–5; Basso, 'Myths' (see note 63), p.61.

83. NOSA, *Newsletter*, No.26, February 1972. He was at Norwood 1918–25.
84. Stanley Cohen and Laurie Taylor, *Escape Attempts – The Theory and Practise of Resistance to Everyday Life* (London: Routledge, 1993), pp.42–4, 50–51.
85. NOSA, *Newsletter*, No.49, August 1982. He was at Norwood 1921–26; Golding, *Reminiscences* (see note 14), p.56.
86. NOSA, *Newsletter*, No.82, May 2001. The episode was authored by two scholars.
87. LJM, Interview Transcript, tape 376, p.8; Golding, *Reminiscences* (see note 14), p.62.
88. Samuel and Thompson, *The Myths* (see note 1), p.6.
89. NOSA, *Newsletter*, No.32, October 1973.
90. LJM, Interview Transcript, tape 377, 1994. He was at Norwood 1928–36.
91. Marson, *Children's Strikes* (see note 59), p.33.
92. Peneff, *Myths in Life Stories* (see note 67), p.45.
93. NOSA, *Newsletter*, No.83, September 2001. He was at Norwood 1932–33.
94. NOSA, *Newsletter*, No.24, August 1971.
95. Herman Bogen, *The Luckiest Orphans – A History of the Hebrew Orphan Asylum* (Chicago: University of Illinois Press, 1992), pp.199, 219.
96. LJM, Interview Transcript, tape 377.
97. Robert Merton, *Social Theory and Social Structure* (London: Collier-MacMillan, 1968), p.209.
98. Bogen, *The Luckiest Orphans* (see note 95), pp.229, 232–3.
99. Rose, *The Erosion of Childhood* (see note 62), pp.179–80.
100. William Fishman, *East End 1888* (London: Duckworth, 1988), pp.101–2.
101. USA, Minute Book, B/8, 29 January 1890.
102. Rose, *The Erosion of Childhood* (see note 62), pp.182–3.
103. The National Foundation for Educational Research in England and Wales, *A Survey of Rewards and Punishments in Schools* (London: Newnes Educational Publishing, 1952), pp.41–2.
104. Rose, *The Erosion of Childhood* (see note 62), pp.182–3.
105. USA, House Committee minutes, A3074, 2/2, 15 October 1936.
106. USA, House Committee minutes, A3075, 2/2, 15 August 1937.
107. NOSA, *Newsletter*, No.31, June 1973. He was at Norwood 1935–42.
108. *JC*, 15 October 1937.
109. Burman, *What About the Children?* (see note 4), p.47.
110. NOSA, *Newsletter*, No.74, April 1997. She was at Norwood 1946–51.
111. NOSA, *Newsletter*, No.83, September 2001. He was at Norwood 1946–52.
112. National Archives, MH102/1451, Paper C31, 27 August 1945.
113. NC, AR 1946.
114. NC, AR 1937.
115. NOSA, *Newsletter*, No.70, September 1995. Jack Wagman was superintendent 1958–61.
116. Alan Baddeley, *Essential of Human Memory* (Psychology Press, Hove, East Sussex, 2007), p.183.
117. Thompson, *The Voices of the Past* (see note 82), p.56.
118. NOSA, *Newsletter*, no 82, May 2001, The Norwood Rebellion.
119. Peneff, *Myths in Life Stories* (see note 67), p.41.
120. Baddeley, *Essentials of Human Memory* (see note 116), p.320.
121. Peneff, *Myths in Life Stories* (see note 67), p.45.
122. Sabbagh, *Remembering Our Childhood* (see note 1), p.194.
123. Samuel and Thompson, *The Myths* (see note 1), p.2.
124. Ibid. pp.5–6.
125. Levinson, *A Woman* (see note 41), p.62.
126. Two scrapbooks are in the archive at the University of Southampton.
127. *JC*, 22 November 1974, 'They Asked for More and Got it'; NOSA, *Newsletter*, No.36, January 1975.
128. NOSA, *Newsletter*, No.37, April 1975.
129. Ibid.
130. Peneff, *Myths in Life Stories* (see note 67), p.45.

131. NOSA, *Newsletter*, No.97, September 2008.
132. NOSA, *Newsletter*, No.71, January 1996. He was at Norwood 1948–53.
133. Gerald Cohen told the author.
134. John and Elizabeth Newson, *Seven Years Old in the Home Environment* (London: Pelican, 1978), p.444.
135. Ibid. p.139.
136. Sabbagh, *Remembering Our Childhood* (see note 1), passim.
137. Thomas, *This Time Next Year* (see note 25), p.136.

SECTION 2

CULTURE

British Jewish Literature and Culture:
An Introduction

NADIA VALMAN

How have Jews written and been written in British culture? Long a matter of almost total indifference, this now flourishing area of research was kick-started by the rumblings of discontent among Anglo-Jewish historians in the late 1980s, when the established historiography of British Jewry came under attack. As David Katz argued in 1994, the history of the Jews in Britain had been a 'Judaized version of "Whig History"; that is, the writing of ends-oriented history so that emphasis is placed on "precursors" and "pioneers" who have in some way "contributed" to a final event or institution'.[1] Historians for whom this 'end' was the integration and acculturation of the Jewish minority into British political, social and cultural life were replicating the 'apologetic' outlook of the mainstream Jewish leadership and institutions.[2] Instead of tracking the 'progress' of Anglo-Jewry, the work of historians like David Cesarani, Tony Kushner, Todd Endelman, David Feldman and Bill Williams focused on the tensions and conflicts of everyday experience.[3] Rather than showcasing the exemplary good citizenship and national loyalty of Jews, they looked at such issues as intra-communal conflict, non-conformity and antisocial behaviour, and argued that the Jewish presence in Britain was always contested. This approach paved the way for new historicised readings of literature focusing on texts as sites of conflict.

Research on Jews and British literature had until then been shaped by a similarly progressive narrative. Following the model of the first survey of its kind, Montague Frank Modder's *The Jew in the Literature of England* (1939), Linda Gertner Zatlin's *The Nineteenth-Century Anglo-Jewish Novel* (1981) claimed that novels by Jews registered increasing 'acculturation' over the course of the nineteenth century, and, concomitantly, that stereotyping in literature by non-Jews shifted from the 'conventional' to the 'complex' in response to writing by Jews.[4] Implicitly challenging this account, Bryan Cheyette's analysis of the post-emancipation Anglo-Jewish novel (1986) argued that late nineteenth-century Jewish literature was produced in response both to renewed anti-Semitism and to the conservative Anglo-Jewish self-image. Attention to the specific social and cultural contexts in which writers were publishing – such as the public response to large-scale Jewish immigration from eastern Europe – produced a more unpredictable, less obviously progressive story. The impact on Jews of what Cheyette calls the 'ambivalent Jewish stereotype', a rhetorical choice between the exemplary good citizen and the evil alien, formatively shaped Anglo-Jewish literature well into the twentieth century.[5]

Rather than continuing to consider the relationship between Jewish writers and the literary representation of Jews, however, scholarship in the following two decades has tended to split these two subjects apart. Efforts to rehabilitate forgotten Jewish authors originated in the 1990s, following increasing acknowledgement within the academy of the cultural importance of popular writers who addressed a niche readership or whose works provide a unique insight into the particularities of living in an ethnic or religious minority. As a result, we now know of Grace Aguilar, Hyman Hurwitz and Emma Lyons.[6] We also know of the previously unacknowledged significance of Jewish ancestry or experience in writers like Anita Brookner, Muriel Spark, Siegfried Sassoon or Mina Loy.[7] However there is no single approach to the study of Jewish literature in Britain. Some look for specifically Jewish theological or religious content in work by Jewish authors, focusing on Jewish textual forms such as the midrash,[8] Jewish appropriations or adaptations of Christian literary genres,[9] or Jewish uses of narrative from the Hebrew Bible.[10] Some have focused on the intertextual relationship between Jewish writers and those they perceived as precursors in a Jewish or Hebrew literary 'tradition'.[11] Others consider the Jewish writer as part of a 'subculture' in which communal concerns are expressed and contested through literature. Michael Galchinsky's work, for example, argues that fiction by early nineteenth-century Jewish women writers was designed to confront actively the control of education and religious institutions by Jewish men.[12] Another aspect of such scholarship focuses on Jewish writers' responses to representations of Jews in mainstream literary culture. In Cheyette's analysis, the attempt by Benjamin Farjeon to produce 'positive' versions of negative stereotypes, like the Jewish businessman, is an 'apologetic' stance; for Michael Ragussis, however, Grace Aguilar's conscious rewriting of the stereotype of the converted Jewess can be seen as an act of resistance against the dominant Christian culture.[13] Cheyette's work on twentieth-century literature, moreover, introduced a further set of terms for analysing Jewish writing, emphasising the 'diasporic images of in-betweenness, of simultaneously belonging and not belonging' prevalent in both modernist and post-war Anglo-Jewish literature.[14] In the 1980s and 1990s, then, new research cast writing by Jews as, in many different ways, challenging cherished notions of the English nation and English culture.

Even more prolific is scholarly work in the related field of representations of Jews in British literary and popular culture, or 'Semitic discourse'. Early studies tended to focus on stereotypes of Jews and to assume that such stereotypes persisted unaltered across the centuries.[15] However, this ahistorical approach was cast aside in *Constructions of 'the Jew' in English Literature and Society 1875–1945* (1993), which demonstrated that literary representations of Jews were not in fact fixed stereotypes but figures fissured by contradictions and repeatedly reshaped according to particular authors' social, political and aesthetic concerns.[16] The textual 'Jew' was now seen as a locus of ideological struggle. Cultural historians like Lisa Lampert and Anthony Bale read medieval representations of Jews as articulations of theological controversy; work on later centuries, like that of James Shapiro and Michelle Ephraim on Shakespeare, Marlowe and other early modern dramatists, and research by Michael Ragussis and myself on nineteenth-century novelists like Walter Scott, George Eliot and Anthony Trollope, considered literary 'Jews' as a product of debates about the nation.[17] More recently, the picture has been expanded to include popular culture: adventure writers like Rider Haggard and eighteenth-century stage performances (an indication of new areas for future research).[18] In their writing, these scholars sought to reconstruct the wider contexts in which Jewish figures appeared and to identify the ideological work they performed within larger national questions and debates. For example, James Shapiro reads Shylock's 'pound of flesh' in the post-Reformation context of the 'fascination and importance circumcision held for Elizabethans', who would have seen 'an occluded threat of circumcision' in Shylock's demand.[19] According to this approach, the figure of the 'Jew' – quite often unrelated to actual Jews – was seen as a crucial rhetorical device through which definitions of Protestant Englishness were focused. As dramatically articulated by Michael Ragussis, 'the Jewish question' can be located 'at the center of a profound crisis in … English national identity'.[20]

In contrast to this local perspective, another important strand in scholarship sought to describe a wider, pan-European discourse on Jews. In particular, the prolific work of Sander Gilman traced the representation of the deformed or diseased Jewish body across medical, sociological, linguistic, economic and political writings, as well as high and popular literatures in the nineteenth and twentieth centuries (and before and beyond). In *The Jew's Body* (1991) and numerous other studies, Gilman explored the myriad dimensions of cultural anti-Semitism and their impact on key Jewish thinkers such as Freud.[21] Others have extended this approach, looking especially at how the disciplines of medicine and sociology across Europe, the UK and America developed with reference to the notion of Jewish physical difference.[22] Gilman's work has also had a significant impact on research on Jews in British literature and culture, much of which followed his theoretical model in which the 'Jew' is understood as a figure of Otherness.[23] Throughout the 1990s his paradigm for reading the Jewish male body in fiction through the lens of theological or scientific anti-Semitism shaped numerous studies from the early modern period to high modernism.[24]

Gilman's European (albeit predominantly German) context for the study of representations of Jews, and Jewish responses, may have been too broad-brush to catch the unique local resonances and inflections that literary texts carry – whether that be George Eliot's complex philosophical response to the public debate about Disraeli's foreign policy in *Daniel Deronda* (1876) or Israel Zangwill's satire of Anglo-Jewish social climbing in *Children of the Ghetto* (1892). These texts draw on internationally recognised stereotypes of Jews, to be sure, but they do so within specifically *British* generic narrative conventions and invoke particular *national* histories. However, in another way Gilman's work looked forward to the more transnational approach that has provided a new source of interest for cultural studies in the twenty-first century. The nation is no longer the only framework for understanding the functions of publishing and reading; instead, new research is investigating the circulation and consumption of texts across national borders. My own work on nineteenth-century popular Jewish literature has taken this turn. With the other co-editors of *Nineteenth Century Jewish Literature: A Reader*, I have discovered that English, French and German Jewish literatures adapted and borrowed widely from each other, with similar themes – the 'ghetto', the Spanish Inquisition, the sacrificial

Jewess – appealing to readers in quite different national contexts.[25] Looking beyond our disciplinary boundaries has enabled us to examine more closely the construction of Jewish reading publics and their engagement with modernity.

In the years since the establishment of British Jewish literary studies the critical language through which scholars address key questions has become more complex. The literary stereotype, for example, is now not so readily understood as a form of cultural domination imposed upon Jews but a malleable form of rhetoric that can be deployed by Jews themselves and whose function is far from transparent. Debate continues to rage, for example, around the late nineteenth-century poet and novelist Amy Levy, who, for some critics, reproduces the racial discourse typical of her intellectual milieu and social class, and, for others, deploys techniques of irony or narratorial distancing in order to subject such discourse to critique.[26] Tracing imagery and rhetoric produces one reading; a narratological analysis produces another. Problematic again is the fact that Levy produced some very nasty caricatures of Jews in her personal correspondence, but adopted an indulgent, affectionate voice in the articles she wrote for the *Jewish Chronicle*. Such contradictions, or strategic stagings, suggest a version of Jewish identity that is not familiar or comfortable for the modern reader. The ambivalences displayed by writers for whom Jewishness was just one of many affiliations pose problems for critics who wish them to occupy clearer, more singular, more usable positions. An exclusive focus on what a Jewish writer is telling us about Jewishness, moreover, ignores the ways that texts bring together multiple influences; they speak to and are read by different readers and necessarily articulate conflicting identities. And it is these incoherences that are most challenging and illuminating about their texts.

Defining 'antisemitic discourse' has itself become more difficult in the wake of challenges like that of Daniel Boyarin's analysis of the self-loathing at the heart of Theodor Herzl's ideology of Zionism.[27] What might it mean to consider Herzl an anti-Semite? Meanwhile, literary representations of Jews long considered irredeemably anti-Semitic, like Anthony Trollope's fraudulent financier Augustus Melmotte in *The Way We Live Now* (1875), are now being reconsidered. In *The Temple of Culture: Assimilation and Anti-Semitism in Literary Anglo-America* (2000), Jonathan Freedman suggests that this exuberant and repellent figure is also a figure of desire – of philo-Semitism at the *same time* as anti-Semitism, of the thrills as well as the fears associated with rampant capitalism.[28] And the writers examined in Maren Tova Linett's *Modernism, Feminism and Jewishness* (2007) 'enlist a multifaceted vision of Jewishness to help them shape fictions that are thematically daring and formally experimental'.[29] However, this kind of argument – that cultural representations articulate complex or contradictory attitudes to Jews (or to what 'Jews' are imagined to represent) rather than simple hostility – is still not widely taken up.

In fact, it is striking that despite such important interventions, the old questions are still being asked. Anthony Julius's recent *Trials of the Diaspora: A History of Anti-Semitism in England* (2010), for example, eschews the tendency of most literary critics in the past two decades to view Semitic representations as metaphors for larger questions specific to time and place (indeed, he seems unaware of these scholarly developments). Julius seeks instead to reconstruct a repeating pattern of identifiable negative stereotypes in English culture through the centuries. Insofar as Julius reminds us that hostility, rather than increasing acceptance, has marked the history of Jews in England, his work continues the historiographical movement of the 1980s that refused a patriotic celebration of Jewish integration. But for Julius this approach is intended not to challenge the smugness of Judaised Whig history but to issue a warning about the more general dangers of the diaspora for Jews. His ultimate purpose in identifying the 'tropes' of anti-Semitic culture is to establish a continuity between them and contemporary expressions of anti-Zionism, which, he claims, 'now constitutes the greatest threat to Anglo-Jewish security and morale'.[30] This statement encapsulates how far the political landscape for British-Jewish studies has changed since the 1980s. In the context of the deteriorating political situation in Israel/Palestine, drawing attention to the persistence of anti-Semitic culture has become the characteristic gesture of the Anglo-Jewish establishment, rather than its critics.

Instead of a regression to old questions and methodologies, we need to build on the subtlest of the literary scholarship that has emerged in the last 20 years. We need more, not less, attention to the vast array of fantasies that the British literary imagination has projected onto Jews. We need to remember that Jewish writers themselves have participated in these discursive practices. We need a more developed theoretical understanding of the complex relationship between cultural texts – whether literature, art or modern media such as film and television – and popular attitudes, which does not simply assume that one can be read off from the other. Above all, we need to come to Jewish texts with questions, rather than expectations, about the meanings of Jewishness – with a view to how literary texts can open up the categories that critics, too often, would close down.

NOTES

1. David S. Katz, *The Jews in the History of England* (Oxford: Clarendon Press, 1994), p.vii.
2. David Cesarani, 'Dual Heritage or Duel of Heritages? Englishness and Jewishness in the Heritage Industry', in *The Jewish Heritage in British History: Englishness and Jewishness* ed. by Tony Kushner (London: Frank Cass, 1992), pp.29–41.
3. David Cesarani, ed., *The Making of Modern Anglo-Jewry* (Oxford: Blackwell, 1990); Kushner, *The Jewish Heritage in British History* (see note 2); Todd Endelman, *Radical Assimilation in English Jewish History, 1656–1945* (Bloomington: Indiana University Press, 1990); David Feldman, *Englishmen and Jews: Social Relations and Political Culture 1840–1914* (New Haven, CT: Yale University Press, 1994); Bill Williams, '"East and West": Class and Community in Manchester Jewry, 1850–1914', in *The Making of Modern Anglo-Jewry* (see note 3), pp.15–33.
4. Montagu Frank Modder, *The Jew in the Literature of England. To the End of the Nineteenth Century* (Philadelphia: Jewish Publication Society of America, 1960; first published 1939); Linda Gertner Zatlin, *The Nineteenth-Century Anglo-Jewish Novel* (Boston: Twayne, 1981), pp.122–3.
5. Bryan Cheyette, 'From Apology to Revolt: Benjamin Farjeon, Amy Levy and the Post-emancipation Anglo-Jewish Novel, 1880–1900', *Transactions of the Jewish Historical Society of England*, 24 (1982–86), 253–65 (p.264).
6. Michael Galchinsky, *The Origin of the Modern Jewish Woman Writer: Romance and Reform in Victorian England* (Detroit: Wayne State University Press, 1996); Cynthia Scheinberg, *Women's Poetry and Religion in Victorian England: Jewish Identity and Christian Culture* (Cambridge: Cambridge University Press, 2002); Judith W. Page, 'Hyman Hurwitz's *Hebrew Tales* (1826): Redeeming the Talmudic Garden', in *British Romanticism and the Jews: History, Culture, Literature* ed. by Sheila Spector (New York: Palgrave, 2002), pp.197–213; Michael Scrivener, 'Following the Muse: Inspiration, Prophecy and Defence in the Poetry of Emma Lyon (1788–1870), Anglo-Jewish Poet', in *The Jews and British Romanticism: Politics, Religion, Culture* ed. by Sheila Spector (New York: Palgrave, 2005), pp.105–26.
7. Louise Sylvester, 'Troping the Other: Anita Brookner's Jews', *English*, 50.196 (Spring 2001), 47–58; Bryan Cheyette, *Muriel Spark* (Plymouth: Northcote House, 2000); Peter Lawson, *Anglo-Jewish Poetry from Isaac Rosenberg to Elaine Feinstein* (London: Vallentine Mitchell, 2006); Alex Goody, '"Goy Israels" and the "Nomadic Embrace": Mina Loy Writing Race', in *'In the Open': Jewish Women Writers and British Culture* ed. by Claire M. Tylee (Newark: University of Delaware Press, 2006), pp.129–46.
8. Galchinsky, *Modern Jewish Woman Writer* (see note 6), pp.88–95.
9. See, for example, Karen Weisman, 'Mourning, Translation, Pastoral: Hyman Hurwitz and Literary Authority', in *Romanticism/Judaica: A Convergence of Cultures* ed. by Sheila Spector (Aldershot: Ashgate, forthcoming 2011).
10. Scheinberg, *Women's Poetry and Religion in Victorian England* (see note 6); Daniel Harris, 'Hagar in Christian Britain: Grace Aguilar's "The Wanderers"', *Victorian Literature and Culture*, 27 (1999), 143–69.
11. Lawson, *Anglo-Jewish Poetry* (see note 7).
12. Galchinsky, *Modern Jewish Woman Writer* (see note 6).

13. Cheyette, 'From Apology to Revolt' (see note 5); Michael Ragussis, 'Writing Spanish History: The Inquisition and "the Secret Race", chapter 4 in *Figures of Conversion: 'The Jewish Question' and English National Identity* (Durham, NC: Duke University Press, 1995), pp.127–73.
14. Bryan Cheyette, 'Introduction', *Contemporary Jewish Writing in Britain and Ireland: An Anthology* (London: Peter Halban, 1998), pp.xiii–lxxi (p.xxvi).
15. Edgar Rosenberg, *From Shylock to Svengali: Jewish Stereotypes in English Fiction* (London: Peter Owen, 1960).
16. Bryan Cheyette, *Constructions of 'the Jew' in English Literature and Society: Racial Representations 1875–1945* (Cambridge: Cambridge University Press, 1993).
17. Lisa Lampert, *Gender and Jewish Difference from Paul to Shakespeare* (Philadelphia: University of Pennsylvania Press, 2004); Anthony Bale, *The Jew in the Medieval Book: English Antisemitisms 1350–1500* (Cambridge: Cambridge University Press, 2006); James Shapiro, *Shakespeare and the Jews* (New York: Columbia University Press, 1996); Michelle Ephraim, *Reading the Jewish Woman on the Elizabethan Stage* (Aldershot: Ashgate, 2008); Ragussis, *Figures of Conversion* (see note 13); Nadia Valman, *The Jewess in Nineteenth-Century British Literary Culture* (Cambridge: Cambridge University Press, 2007).
18. Heidi Kaufman, *English Origins, Jewish Discourse, and the Nineteenth-Century British Novel: Reflections on a Nested Nation* (University Park: Pennsylvania State University Press, 2009); Michael Ragussis, *Theatrical Nation: Jews and Other Outlandish Englishmen in Georgian Britain* (Philadelphia: University of Pennsylvania Press, 2010).
19. Shapiro, *Shakespeare and the Jews* (see note 16), pp.114–15.
20. Ragussis, *Figures of Conversion* (see note 13), p.8.
21. Sander L. Gilman, *The Jew's Body* (New York and London: Routledge, 1991); idem, *Freud, Race and Gender* (Princeton, NJ: Princeton University Press, 1993). Also taking a pan-European approach are Daniel Pick, *Svengali's Web: The Alien Enchanter in Modern Culture* (New Haven, CT and London: Yale University Press, 2000); Bryan Cheyette and Laura Marcus, eds., *Modernity, Culture and 'the Jew'* (Cambridge: Polity Press, 1998); Bryan Cheyette and Nadia Valman, eds, *The Image of the Jew in European Liberal Culture 1789–1914* (London: Vallentine Mitchell, 2004).
22. John Efron, *Defenders of the Race: Jewish Doctors and Race Science in Fin-de-Siecle Europe* (New Haven, CT: Yale University Press, 1994); Mitchell B. Hart, *Social Science and the Politics of Modern Jewish Identity* (Stanford, CA: Stanford University Press, 2000); idem, *The Healthy Jew: The Symbiosis of Judaism and Modern Medicine* (New York: Cambridge University Press, 2007).
23. For example, Juliet Steyn, *The Jew: Assumptions of Identity* (London: Cassell, 1999).
24. Matthew Biberman, *Masculinity, Antisemitism and Early Modern English Literature: From the Satanic to the Effeminate Jew* (Aldershot: Ashgate, 2004); Carol Margaret Davison, *Anti-Semitism and British Gothic Literature* (Basingstoke and New York: Palgrave Macmillan, 2004); Neil R. Davison, *James Joyce, Ulysses, and the Construction of Jewish Identity* (Cambridge: Cambridge University Press, 1998); Marilyn Reizbaum, *James Joyce's Judaic Other* (Stanford, CA: Stanford University Press, 1999).
25. Jonathan Hess, Maurice Samuels and Nadia Valman, *Nineteenth-Century Jewish Literature: A Reader* (Stanford, CA: Stanford University Press, forthcoming).
26. See Naomi Hetherington and Nadia Valman, 'Introduction', in *Amy Levy: Critical Essays* ed. by Naomi Hetherington and Nadia Valman (Athens: Ohio University Press, 2010), pp.6–10.
27. Daniel Boyarin, *Unheroic Conduct: The Rise of Heterosexuality and the Invention of the Jewish Man* (Berkeley: University of California Press, 1997), pp.277–312.
28. Jonathan Freedman, *The Temple of Culture: Assimilation and Anti-Semitism in Literary Anglo-America* (Oxford: Oxford University Press, 2000). See also Phyllis Lassner and Lara Trubowitz, eds., *Antisemitism and Philosemitism in the Twentieth and Twenty-first Centuries: Representing Jews, Jewishness and Modern Culture* (Newark: University of Delaware Press, 2008).
29. Maren Tova Linett, *Modernism, Feminism and Jewishness* (Cambridge: Cambridge University Press, 2007), p.2.
30. Anthony Julius, *Trials of the Diaspora: A History of Anti-Semitism in England* (Oxford: Oxford University Press, 2010), p.xxxvii.

REPRESENTING THE ALIEN JEW

Blurring the Boundaries of Difference: *Dracula*, the Empire, and 'the Jew'

HANNAH EWENCE

The image of 'the Jew' in English literature has long proved to be a compelling topic for academic discussion, a topic through which a long narrative of anti-Semitic traditions has been mapped out and lamented over.[1] Yet recent discourse has sought to challenge interpretations of that image as 'a depressingly uniform and static phenomenon'.[2] Bryan Cheyette's path-breaking study, *Constructions of 'the Jew' in English Literature and Society: Racial Representations, 1875–1945* was at the forefront of this challenge, patiently demonstrating that far from being a fixed stereotype, the image of 'the Jew' in literature and society was, more precisely, a product of its time and of its creator. That is to say, so argued Cheyette, 'writers [did] not passively draw on eternal myths of 'the Jew' but actively construct[ed] them in relation to their own literary and political concerns'.[3]

Cheyette's insistence upon the significance of context was coupled with a critique of the discursive vocabulary formerly employed to categorise representations of 'the Jew'. The somewhat polemical terms 'anti-Semitism' and 'philo-Semitism', Cheyette has argued, did not adequately describe the multifarious and often ambiguous cultural images of 'the Jew'. Instead those labels loaded representations with quasi-political undertones, and allowed only that they indicated a 'positive' or 'negative' attitude. To address these issues, and to bring greater attention to the very ambivalence of representations of 'the Jew' in English literature, Cheyette suggested substituting these misleading labels with the umbrella term, 'semitic discourse'.[4]

This article, interpreting Bram Stoker's gothic masterpiece *Dracula* as a clear metaphor for the Jewish alien in *fin de siècle* Britain, constructs its analysis within this theoretical framework pioneered by Cheyette. However, whilst acknowledging the fluidity of representations of 'the Jew' and their dependence upon the discursive context, I also feel it is important to recognise that the image of 'the Jew' has remained constant in one regard – as a signifier of difference. Within an imperialist culture, narratives of racial 'difference' or 'otherness' as a means to define 'the self' operated throughout the empire. Yet, by the late nineteenth century, 'unlike the marginalized "colonial subjects" who were, for the most part, confined racially to the "colonies"', Jews were, by dint of their proximity to the 'motherland', the consummate 'other' within the British cultural imagination.[5] The growing presence of a Jewish immigrant population, complete with their 'foreign', even 'pre-modern' habits and customs, and an incomprehensible language, acted to further exaggerate the markers of racial and cultural difference.

Recent studies have become preoccupied with how 'the Jew', as a signifier of 'difference', has operated within a socio-political framework to reinforce, or to prompt a renegotiation of 'Britishness'. David Feldman has shown how the decision as to whether to extend constitutional rights to the Jews of Britain in the mid-nineteenth century was not simply a debate between liberalism and intolerance, or modernity and tradition, but brought into question the very relationship between state, nation, and religion.[6] Nadia Valman's recent accomplished study *The Jewess in Nineteenth-Century British Literary Culture* has followed Feldman's example by arguing that 'the figure of the Jewess marked out the axes of difference through which English Protestant identity was imagined'.[7] Importantly, however, Valman recognises that British writers did not go unchallenged in their appropriation of the literary image of 'the Jewess'. She shows how, across the century, 'the Jewess' was continually reclaimed by British-Jewish writers wishing to participate in the 'discursive battles' that were commonly refracted through Semitic representations. Yet Valman maintains that for British-Jewish writers to participate fully in those debates, they were frequently forced to adopt the literary forms and approaches of gentile writers. In this way, British-Jewish writers often found themselves complicit in the act of representing the 'other' even as they attempted to represent themselves. It was, however, this compliance which legitimised their literary voice, and made their work accessible for a wider audience. It is the central objective of this article to consider how a similar 'double bind' functioned in the late Victorian period when 'outsider' writers – of whom I shall argue that Bram Stoker was one – approached the Jewish immigrant 'other' in their fiction.[8]

Bram Stoker's gothic horror masterpiece, *Dracula*, might not immediately present itself as a text concerned with the Jewish immigrant, or indeed, with 'the Jew'. However, within academic discourse such a parallel has already been drawn, which references the Count's striking physiognomy, his distinctive racial 'otherness', perverse sexual appetite, effeminate characteristics and feminising power, and deviant capitalist tendencies.[9] Thus readings of Dracula as Jew evoked distinctly anti-Semitic rhetoric to forge the association. Certainly an analogy between vampire and Jew would also have been obvious to contemporary readers of Stoker's novel. Within Victorian discourse, linguistic signifiers of the gothic horror genre – 'vampires', 'blood-suckers', 'wolves' and 'vultures' – were commonly associated with the unscrupulous Jewish capitalist.[10] I shall suggest, however, that the analogy can be pushed a little further by grounding Stoker's vampire firmly within the era of its creation, and thus interpreting Dracula, and the threat his presence posed, not as a generic Jewish figure, but more precisely as a metaphor for the Eastern European immigrant Jew. At the time of the novel's publication in 1897, the influx of impoverished Jews into Britain was coming towards its peak. The growing presence of this visible racial and cultural 'other' in Britain spawned a debate which fed off the existing anxieties concerning sexual, racial, and moral degeneration. Indeed the association between the Jewish immigrant and fears of national degeneration became so ingrained within political as well as popular discourse, that Sir Charles Dilke, Liberal MP and supporter of the immigrants' cause, felt compelled to respond to the charges:

> Miserable as may be their [Russian Jews'] condition when they come here, they are not of a stock inferior to our own. They are of a stock which, when it mixes with our own in the course of years, goes rather to improve than to deteriorate the British race.[11]

With this context in mind, it seemed little stretch to imagine Dracula and the fear his presence invoked as a figurative exploration of the Jewish 'aliens question' in Britain. Certainly, the very label of 'alien', which became irrevocably indicative of the Eastern European Ashkenazi Jew by the 1890s, is itself evocative of the mysterious and threatening 'otherness', which is central to Dracula's menace. Anti-alienists of the era, the most outspoken of which was the social imperialist and writer Arnold White, further Gothicised the image of 'degenerate' urban dwellers – an explicit if unspoken reference to the alien Jew of the East End – speaking of their 'tainted constitutions', of their 'brains charged with a subtle mischief, and languishing or extinct morality', and of their intent to 'transmit a terrible inheritance of evil to the next generation' and to 'taint' a 'whole community'.[12] Dracula inspires all of these terrors, not least because he too is an immigrant in Britain, a self-professed 'stranger in a strange land'.[13] In this way, then, it seems feasible to associate Stoker's vampire specifically with the most visible 'other' of the time, the immigrant Jew, than with a more generalised and less identifiable 'other', or even the more familiar figure of the British Jew.

Superficially this interpretation appears sound. However, if Stoker was utilising anti-Semitic rhetoric, which typically defines Jew in rigid opposition to Gentile, he was not doing so in a straightforward manner. Throughout *Dracula*, normally converse positions do not remain so. The boundaries between 'vampire' and 'victim', 'foreign' and 'British', 'bad' and 'good', 'Jew' and 'Gentile', are repeatedly transgressed and confused. Our acquaintance with the Count in the first section of the novel places an emphasis not on his distinctive appearance but upon his aristocratic demeanour, his intellectualism, his disquieting familiarity. As Stephen Arata has remarked:

> Dracula is the most 'Western' character in the novel. No one is more rational, more intelligent, more organised, or even more punctual than the Count. No one plans more carefully or researches more thoroughly. No more is more learned within his own spheres of expertise or more receptive to new knowledge.[14]

The vampire assumes the traits presumed indicative of every Victorian gentleman. He is, in fact, 'more British than the British'. Dracula himself professes this intention to Jonathon Harker, the novel's protagonist. 'I am content if I am like the rest, so that no man stops if he sees me, or pause in his speaking if he hear my words, to say, "Ha, ha! A stranger!"'[15] In turn, Harker's encounter with the vampire quickly drains him of these idealised Victorian characteristics which Dracula so obviously possesses, leaving the Englishman weak, vulnerable, feminised – traits more typically associated with 'the Jew'.

Thus, we can see how the transgression of boundaries operates as 'two-way traffic'. The identity of both vampire and Englishman appear blurred and interchangeable. Therefore, throughout the novel, identity reversal occurs in multiple ways, many of which can be understood through what Stephen Arata terms 'a narrative of reverse colonization';

a scenario in which 'the colonizer finds himself in the position of the colonized, the exploiter becomes exploited, the victimizer victimized'.[16] Of course these types of fears were particularly pertinent for Britons, who, by the close of the nineteenth century, were increasingly conscious of their position as the imperial race, and of the dubious morality of certain imperial practices.[17] Within *Dracula* all of these fears are realised. British strength and dominance is undermined by an invading racial 'other' who inverts the balance of power from 'coloniser' to 'colonised'.

What is more, however, this fear of reverse colonisation can be understood not simply as a product of rational anxiety, but more accurately as a 'response to cultural guilt'. As Arata adds, 'In the marauding, invasive Other, British culture sees its own imperial practices mirrored back in monstrous form.'[18] This has its resonance most particularly in the British characters' fears of deracination – that Dracula's invasion and vampiric activity will eventually lead to the dissolution of the British race. Jonathan Harker fearfully contemplates this fate as he stands over Dracula's entombed and 'sleeping' body:

> This was the being I was helping to transfer to London, where, perhaps for centuries to come, he might, amongst its teeming millions, satiate his lust for blood, and create a new and ever-widening circle of semi-demons to batten on the helpless. The very thought drove me mad.[19]

Harker picks up a shovel in a fit of passion and raises it over his head to strike the vampire 'but as I did so the head turned, and the eyes fell full upon me with all their blaze of basilisk horror. The sight seemed to paralyse me'.[20] Emblazoned in full Gothicised imagery, the victim's helplessness, and by extension Britain's vulnerability in the face of the vampire threat, is starkly articulated.

This reverse colonisation narrative further intensifies as the plot progresses, and it becomes clear that Dracula intends to achieve his racial conquest of Britain through the sexual conquest of women's bodies. Virtuous Lucy Westernra is the first to fall under Dracula's power. In what is a thinly veiled metaphor, the Englishwoman invites the charming foreigner into her bedroom night after night, allowing him to remain until he is sated. The chilling parallel between Dracula's appropriation of the female body as a weapon of war, and this practice as a feature of imperialism is hard to overlook.[21] Here, Stoker's critique of imperialism is unmistakable.

Yet I would suggest that Bram Stoker not only ambiguously represents the 'other' in *Dracula* to facilitate a reverse colonisation narrative, but also as a strategy to offer a critique of late-Victorian race discourse. Indeed, as I shall show, the novelist's own ethnic origins, as well as his life experiences, were in fact central to such a strategy. As a Protestant growing up in predominantly Catholic Dublin, Stoker surely felt something of a social outsider from a young age. That the future novelist suffered from severe physical disabilities until the age of seven, which kept him largely isolated from the outside world, probably only accentuated such feelings. Neither did his adult life, the most part of which he spent as an Irish expatriate working as actor Sir Henry Irving's manager in London, serve to release him from his 'outsider' identity. His relationship with Irving was intense, and for Stoker all-consuming. The writer penned a lengthy and passionate monograph upon his friend's death in 1906, entitled *Reminisces of Henry Irving*, and named his only son after his long-time boss and friend.[22] Of course many have since speculated as to whether the relationship was a homosexual one, or if Stoker perhaps desired it to be such.[23] That topic is not one which this article has the remaining length, or indeed objective to discuss. What is clear, however, is that Stoker himself occupied a position of racial, spiritual, geographical, even sexual 'otherness', which I believe was central to his literary portrayal of the consummate outsider, Dracula.

Within the racialised discourse of the late nineteenth century, Stoker would no doubt have been sensitive to the turbulent nature of Anglo-Irish relations, and, more specifically, the often derogative references to the Irish as a 'primitive', 'dirty', 'violent' and 'criminal' race.[24] In this marginalisation, the Irish shared something with the Jews, who, as we have seen, were also feared in Britain for their pollutive, degenerate influence. Both groups were deemed 'primitive, premodern, and deeply superstitious' – representations which invoke the *Dracula* legend.[25] Moreover, both the Irish and the Jews were distinctive as migrant communities in Britain, visible examples of the 'other', known to populate, and thus largely define the cultural identity of London's impoverished East End in particular. Although Stoker was fortunate enough in his social standing not to have to inhabit the ghetto, his affinity with his fellow Irish seems likely. What is more, the novelist was in the habit of extending his sympathy for persecuted minorities beyond his fellow countrymen to the Jewish cause. In 1905 Stoker joined an artists' protest against the maltreatment of the Jews, which seemed the culmination of a slow growing respect and interest in the Jewish people throughout his career.[26] Against such evidence it seems increasingly difficult to conceive of Dracula as encoding an anti-Semitic rhetoric. Joseph Valente also reaches this conclusion, observing that,

> the close parallelism between Stoker's employment of prejudicial Jewish and Irish motifs ... in the construction of Dracula indicates that his monster is no more a piece of anti-Semitism than a racial attack on his own Anglo-Celtic bloodlines, but is rather a vehicle for destabilizing such racial typologies.[27]

This final statement is important. Throughout *Dracula*, Stoker represents the 'other' not as a means to participate in the anxious discourses of the era, but rather to challenge the very legitimacy of those discourses. And this is where my argument comes full circle. Dracula can *still* be understood as a metaphor for the immigrant Jew, and yet, contrary to the perceived atmosphere of the era, Stoker sketches 'the Jew' with a large degree of empathy. Dracula's very familiarity to the Victorian reader, as gentleman, as intellectual, as curious traveller, even as ambitious imperialist, are all qualities which seem to beg an identification, or, at the very least, self-recognition in the persona of the 'other'.

What is more, Stoker's seemingly sympathetic depiction of the immigrant Jew challenges perceptions of the era as charged with a pervading anti-Semitic atmosphere.[28] Instead this reading of *Dracula* draws attention to the existence of a counter discourse. Although it is difficult to establish with any confidence how far, and into which quarters of society philo-Semitic or pro-alien attitudes may have existed in *fin de siècle* Britain, that the Alien's Bill, which sought to control and prevent migration into Britain, faced considerable opposition certainly suggests pockets of support for the Jewish immigrant cause.[29] Even the social observer, Beatrice Potter, in her contribution to Charles Booth's 1889 publication *Life and Labour of the People of London*, was forced to concede:

> He [the Jewish immigrant] treats his wife with courtesy and tenderness, and they discuss constantly the future of the children. He is never to be seen at the public-house round the corner; but instead enjoys a quiet glass of 'rum and shrub' and a game of cards with a few friends on the Saturday or Sunday evening ... In short, he has become a law-abiding and self-respecting citizen of our great metropolis.[30]

Despite Potter's otherwise suspicious observations of her subject, she could not help but acknowledge the 'respectable' nature of the Jewish immigrants' behaviour. Here Cheyette's insistence upon employing the term 'semitic discourse' to define the often confused and ambivalent representations of 'the Jew' seems particularly pertinent. Stoker, however, certainly appeared committed to engaging a more positive image of 'the Jew'.

This conclusion seems naturally to beg the question, 'Can *Dracula*, therefore, be understood as propounding what a modern audience might define as "tolerant multiculturalism"?' To answer confidently in the affirmative might be a step too far, yet this close reading of Stoker's masterpiece does offer a substantial challenge to an interpretation of the novel as a simple confrontation between 'good' and 'evil'. The two sides seem to share too much in common. As we have seen, Dracula embraces this affinity from the outset. The Britons, however, finally acknowledge this affinity only in the vampire's final moment, noting 'in the face a look of peace, such as I never could have imagined might have rested there'.[31] Thus, in this final image all boundaries of difference seem to disintegrate, seemingly ridiculing the Britons' judgement of Dracula as inhuman, as 'alien', as a binary opposite to themselves – a judgement upon which their fears of the 'other' were ultimately based.

ACKNOWLEDGEMENTS

I would like to thank Tony Kushner, James Jordan and Diana Popescu for commenting upon earlier versions of this article, and the AHRC for making it possible for me to undertake this research.

NOTES

1. See, for example, David Philipson, *The Jew in English Fiction* (Cincinnati: Clark, 1889); Myer Jack Landa, *The Jew in Drama* (London: P.S. King, 1926); and Joshua Kunitz, *Russian Literature and the Jew* (New York: Columbia University Press, 1929). Lionel Trilling references all of these studies as 'all more or less engaged in vindicating the Jew' from 'misrepresentation' and 'slander', in his article 'The Changing Myth of the Jew' (1931) republished in *Commentary* (August 1978), 24–34 (p.24).
2. Edgar Rosenberg, *From Shylock to Svengali: Jewish Stereotypes in English Fiction* (Stanford, CA: Stanford University Press, 1960), p.297.
3. Bryan Cheyette, *Constructions of 'the Jew' in English Literature and Society: Racial Representations, 1875–1945* (Cambridge: Cambridge University Press, 1993), p.268.
4. Cheyette discusses this in the introduction to Ibid. pp.8–9.
5. Ibid. p.12.

6. David Feldman, *Englishmen and Jews: Social Relations and Political Culture, 1840–1914* (New Haven, CT: Yale University Press, 1994), p.28.

7. Nadia Valman, *The Jewess in Nineteenth Century British Literary Culture* (Cambridge: Cambridge University Press, 2007), p.2.

8. Bryan Cheyette has approached a similar question in his compelling essay 'The Other Self: Anglo-Jewish Fiction and the Representation of Jews in England, 1875–1905', in *The Making of Modern Anglo-Jewry* ed. by David Cesarani (Oxford: Basil Blackwell, 1990), pp.97–111.

9. See Judith Halberstam, 'Technologies of Monstrosity: Bram Stoker's *Dracula*, in *Cultural Politics at the Fin de Siècle* ed. by Sally Ledger and Scott McCracken (Cambridge: Cambridge University Press, 1995), pp.248–66; Howard L. Malchow, 'Vampire Gothic and Late-Victorian Identity', in *Gothic Images of Race in Nineteenth Century Britain* (Stanford, CA: Stanford University Press, 1996), pp.124–66; and Carol M. Davison, 'Britain, Vampire Empire: Fin-de-Siècle Fears and Bram Stoker's *Dracula*', in *Anti-semitism and British Gothic Literature* (Basingstoke: Palgrave Macmillan, 2004), pp.120–57.

10. Both Engles and Marx evoked Gothic imagery to describe 'the vampire property-holding class', whilst George Robb has pointed to the prevalence of the link forged between Capitalist Jew and the blood-sucking vampire in popular Victorian discourse, in his *White Collar Crime in Modern England: Financial Fraud and Business Morality, 1845–1929* (Cambridge: Cambridge University Press, 1992), p.97.

11. Charles Dilke, Parliamentary Debates (*Hansard*), House of Commons: Official papers, Vol.132, 29 March 1904, col.995.

12. Arnold White, *The Problems of a Great City* (London: Remington and Co Publishers, 1886), p.28. Although White seems to have been hesitant to name the object of his hostility directly in this publication of 1886, he had no reticence in doing so throughout numerous appearances as a witness for the parliamentary *Select Committee on Emigration and Immigration* (1888); *Select Committee on the Sweating System* (1889); *The Royal Commission on Alien Immigration* (1903), and in his numerous publications, most notably 'The Alien Immigrant', *Blackwood's Magazine* (1903), 132–41.

13. Bram Stoker, *Dracula* (Ware: Wordsworth Classics, 1993; first published 1897), p.19.

14. Stephen Arata, 'The Occidental Tourist: *Dracula* and the Anxiety of Reverse Colonization', *Victorian Studies*, 33.4 (Summer 1990), 621–45 (p.637).

15. Stoker, *Dracula* (see note 13), p.19.

16. Arata (see note 14), p.623.

17. See, for example, Eric Hobsbawm, *The Age of Empire, 1875–1914* (New York: Vintage, 1989), pp.82–3. Patrick Brantlinger, *Rules of Darkness: British Literature and Imperialism, 1830–1914* (Ithaca, NY: Cornell University Press, 1988) makes the important connection between an increase in social and political concerns about empire and imperial practice in the late-Victorian period, and the resurrection of the gothic novel.

18. Arata (see note 14), p.623.

19. Stoker, *Dracula* (see note 13), pp.44–5.

20. Ibid. p.45.

21. On this consult Ann Laura Stoler, 'Carnal Knowledge and Imperial Power: Gender, Race, and Morality in Colonial Asia', in *Gender and the Cross-Roads of Knowledge: Feminist Anthropology in the Postmodern Era* ed. by Micaela di Leonardo (Berkeley: University of California Press, 1991), pp.51–100; and Anne McClintock, *Imperial Leather: Race, Gender and Sexuality in the Colonial Contest* (New York: Routledge, 1995).

22. Numerous scholars interested in Bram Stoker reference the writer's relationship with Henry Irving as absolutely central to an understanding of the adult Stoker. See, for example, David Glover, *Vampires, Mummies, and Liberals: Bram Stoker and the Politics of Popular Fiction* (Durham, NC and London: Duke University Press, 1996), pp.2–21; and Malchow, (see note 9), pp.130–38.

23. See Talia Schaffer, '"A Wilde Desire Took Me": The Homoerotic History of *Dracula*', in *English Literary History*, 61 (Summer 1994), 381–425; Malchow, 'Vampire Gothic', pp.132–6.

24. For research in this area consult Roger Swift and Sheridan Gilley, eds., *The Irish in the Victorian City* (London: Croom Helm, 1985) and, more recently, the Special Issue 'Irish Identities in Victorian Britain', *Immigrants and Minorities*, 27.2–3 (July–November 2009).

25. See Joseph Valente, *Dracula's Crypt: Bram Stoker, Irishness and the Question of Blood* (Urbana and Chicago: University of Illinois Press, 2002), p.68 for a fuller discussion of this.
26. Cited in Bram Stoker, *The Essential Dracula: The Definitive Annotated Edition of Bram Stoker's Classic Novel* ed. by Leonard Wolf (New York: Penguin, 1993), p.413, n.17. It has also been pointed out that Bram Stoker's full name – Abraham Stoker – probably meant that the writer was frequently mistaken for being Jewish – another clue which might help account for the complete absence of anti-Semitism in any of Stoker's publications. See Malchow, (see note 9), p.155.
27. Valente (see note 25), p.69.
28. Colin Holmes, *Anti-Semitism in British Society, 1876–1939* (London: Edward Arnold, 1979).
29. The most persuasive of which borrowed from the liberal tradition which pitted the agenda of the restrictionists against the image of Britain as a nation with a 'long' and 'honourable' tradition of granting asylum to those in need of it. David Feldman, 'The Importance of being English: Jewish Immigration and the Decay of Liberal England', in *Metropolis – London: Histories and Representations since 1800* ed. by David Feldman and Gareth Stedman Jones (London and New York: Routledge, 1989), pp.56–84, has defined the passage of the Aliens Act (1905) as 'one of the turning points in the decline of liberal England'.
30. Beatrice Potter, 'The Jewish Community', in *Life and Labour of the People of London* ed. by Charles Booth (London: Williams and Norgate, 1889–91), pp.566–90 (p.584).
31. Stoker, *Dracula* (see note 13), p.314.

Wandering Lonely Jews in the English Countryside

TONY KUSHNER

[M]ajority, mainstream versions of the Heritage should revise their own self-conceptions and rewrite the margins into the centre, the outside into the inside.

(Stuart Hall, 1999)[1]

In 1945 and 1946 732 children, survivors of the Holocaust, were flown to Britain to recuperate.[2] Compared to the *Kindertransport*, through which close to 10,000 refugee children came to Britain in the last ten months of peace, the story of the 732, misleadingly referred to as 'The Boys' (over 10 per cent were female), has hardly been remembered even though they shared some of the same organisational structure.[3] Whilst both of these movements have yet to achieve a critical and sustained academic historiography, the *Kindertransport* has, at a popular level since the late twentieth century, become part of the national commemorative landscape in Britain. Moreover, the *Kindertransport* scheme is now recognised internationally as one of the major acts of rescue during the Nazi era.[4] But for the children who came after the Second World War, the near absence of memory is as true in the places where they were originally looked after as it is at a national level in the UK and more globally within Holocaust commemoration.

The reason for this amnesia, especially in relation to the *Kinder*, is not accidental. These children do not 'fit' easily into wider narratives, whether Jewish or non-Jewish, or whether local, national or global. It will be argued here that it is the children's 'otherness' to so many concepts – including those relating to place, experience, nationality, class and religion – which explains their obscurity. Such inconspicuousness exists in spite of the intense efforts that were made to help them at the time and the remarkable and multi-layered experiences of the children themselves.

In the analysis which follows, two particular contexts relating to place and identity will be emphasised to explore the processes of othering and inclusion in relation to the children. The methodology will be transdiciplinary: it is an attempt to bridge the existing literature on refugees from Nazism. Studies so far have been dominated firstly by historical and sociological-historical studies and secondly by literary/cultural approaches, with little dialogue between the two.[5] In this particular case, insights into the responses to the 732 child survivors will be gathered especially through the mythical figure of the 'Wandering Jew' and its place in Christian and Jewish discourse. Using this powerful and perennial image makes an exploration of both history and culture essential.[6] In addition, the work of historical geographers and anthropologists will also be drawn upon. Such trespassing of disciplinary boundaries is, perhaps, not always appropriate in the study of British Jewry, or rather it is only made possible once certain foundations have been laid by those working in specific academic traditions. Nevertheless, in many areas transdisciplinarity enables the complexity of the subject matter to be understood, as is beginning to happen with regard to responses to the arrival of east European Jews in Britain at the fin de siècle.[7] It also provides a means by which the multi-layered experiences of this minority group can be confronted. Moreover, as the analysis which follows covers both 'now' and 'then', it will tease out the relationship between history and memory and between individual and collective constructions of the past and present. In so doing, it will confront the tensions generated by the intriguing meeting of the 'there' of the Holocaust and the 'here' of post-war Britain.

The starting point of this study is William Wordsworth, the English Romantic poet who has come to symbolise and dominate the identity of the Lake District. He was not the first to write about Lakeland and to give it a distinct identity, but as Melvyn Bragg notes, 'Wordsworth immortalised it'.[8] Since then, the Lake District has been advertised in the heritage industry as 'Wordsworth country' – a national park of some 900 square miles 'Described by many as the most beautiful area in England'.[9] Physically, the Lake District is located in the relatively new (1974) county of Cumbria (previously Cumberland, Westmorland and parts of Lancashire), or, as has been quipped with less administrative preciseness, 'Wordsworthshire'.[10]

It was to the Lake District that the largest group of these children – roughly 300 – were initially settled. They had been grouped together after the war at Theresienstadt and were flown from Prague to Crosby-on-Eden, near Carlisle in the north of England. A second group were flown from Munich to Stonycross in the New Forest in the south of England.[11] Those in the north were bussed to Calgarth near Windermere and those in the south to a large stately home in Hampshire – Wintershill Hall in Durley. Even within the limited recognition of this refugee movement, it is the Windermere camp that is remembered whereas the experiences in Wintershill Hall have been largely concealed. It is true that the numbers in the Hampshire reception camp were approximately half those of Windermere.[12] Yet it is, perhaps, not so much size as the wider fame of the Lake District itself that has prompted the northern reception centre to be remembered at the cost of the southern.

Recent commemorative work, much of it prompted by the Heritage Lottery funded project, 'From Auschwitz to Ambleside', has focused on Windermere. This remarkable project has begun to re-awaken local memories even though none of the original site where the children were housed survives.[13] Wintershill Hall, in contrast, having been a family home for many generations, including that of a branch of the prominent Anglo-Jewish (Sebag-)Montefiores from 1937 to 1946, now functions as private offices and is in a fine state of repair.[14] The absence of physical remains was one of a variety of factors hindering memory work in Windermere – the story of the children has been hidden within what has become 'The Lost Village of Calgarth'.[15] Contrarily, its clear presence in Durley, Hampshire – admittedly in what William Cobbett in his *Rural Rides* in 1823 described as 'one of the most obscure villages in this whole kingdom' – has not acted as a prompt to rediscover the narratives of the child survivors who were present there.[16] It suggests that other, more important, factors are at work in the Lake District when explaining the lacunae relating to the Windermere children. As Doreen Massey notes, 'The identity of places is very much bound up with the *histories* which are told of them, *how* those stories are told, and which memory turns out to be dominant'.[17] Put bluntly, Wordsworth and the 'Lake poets' have, not surprisingly, dominated the memory and identity of the district at the expense of alternative histories. It is, as a recent photographic essay of the landscape makes clear in terms of ownership, '*Wordsworth's* Lake District'.[18]

The attention given to the Romantic writers in the Lake District explains superficially why the story of the child survivors has been forgotten at a local level. Yet the work of Wordsworth, especially his poem 'The Wandering Jew', as well as the writings of the other Romantics and their complex construction and reconstruction of this figure, also facilitates a way of confronting the experiences of the children.[19] It enables an analysis of the 'othering' process that has left these survivors, in the words of anthropologist Mary Douglas and her work on the concepts of pollution and taboo, as 'matter out of place'. It reflects a wider tendency with regard to refugees who, as Liisa Malkki reminds us, are 'liminal in the categorical order of nation-states'.[20]

Wordsworth's poem, written and published in 1800 when he had recently settled into the remote, beautiful and primitive Dove Cottage in Grasmere,[21] reveals classic Romantic ambivalence towards the figure of 'the Jew'.[22] Within some Romantic writing, the figure of the 'Wandering Jew' was presented in all its hideous, unambiguous medieval and even pre-medieval form – as a grotesque male Christ-killer, his monstrosity given an additional gothic twist of criminality and alienness. In 1856, the American Romanticist, Nathaniel Hawthorne, in his *English Notebooks*, described a Lord Mayor's banquet in London's Mansion House where he confronted

> the very Jew of Jews; the distilled essence of all the Jews that have been born since Jacob's time; he was Judas Iscariot; he was the Wandering Jew; he was the worst, and at the same time, the truest type of his race, and contained within himself ... every old prophet and every old clothesman, that ever the tribes produced; and he must have been circumcised as much [as] ten times over.[23]

In fact, the man was a distinguished gentleman, the brother of David Salomons, the Lord Mayor and pioneer for Jewish emancipation in Britain.[24] In spite of this reality, Hawthorne's prejudiced mind delighted in the sight of this man who justified 'the repugnance I have always felt towards his race'. His journal entry was, however, classically bifurcated, with Hawthorne extolling the dark, mysterious beauty of this 'Shylock's' female partner.[25]

With Wordsworth, however, as with Hawthorne's fellow American Romanticist, Herman Melville,[26] there is an *identification* with the 'Wandering Jew' and the attraction of him as *a part of* nature, but also *apart from* the local landscape. The very idea of alienation, of belonging, and not belonging, and the necessity of movement is at the heart of Wordsworth's poem. It begins with the harmony between motion and home achieved by nature:

> Through the torrents from their fountains
> Roar down many a craggy steep,
> Yet they find among the mountains
> Resting-places calm and deep...

The poem closes with the tension caused by the failure of man to replicate this relationship and, from this, Wordsworth's identification with the figure of the legendary tormented Jew:

> Day and night my toils redouble,
> Never nearer the goal;
> Night and day, I feel the trouble
> Of the Wanderer in my soul.[27]

There is, as Judith Page suggests, poetic sympathy for the 'Wanderer'. Nevertheless, as she adds, 'the figure is an almost pure idealization – there is no physical description of person or place – just a state of mind'.[28]

Wordsworth is now remembered as being essential to understanding the Lake District. He was at the forefront of the movement to preserve its 'true' character through his opposition to the railway spur that ends at Windermere but which he feared would extend as far as his beloved Grasmere. Yet Wordsworth was also an agent for change. His guidebooks and poetry inspired a popular interest in the Lake District. Their very success promoted a desire to visit the area, including from the poor whom he believed would spoil its calm and tranquillity for the educated classes.[29] As one of his biographers notes, Wordsworth was not against railways per se: 'he had written a poem about them and used them with pleasure'. Nevertheless, he 'feared all the common people from Lancashire would come into his vale and ruin it'.[30] To Wordsworth, and later to the artist and critic John Ruskin, it has been suggested (again utilising the work of Mary Douglas) 'To facilitate working-class entry into the inner sanctum of ... Lakeland would be to condone "matter out of place"'.[31] Even so, 'he later bought shares in the railway company which proved very profitable, and his objections were forgotten'.[32] This 'twoness' towards newcomers and change is evident also in the story of the child survivors in Windermere.

The children were sent to Calgarth, an industrial estate on the shores of the Lake. It is of major significance that this site was already regarded as alien to Windermere. During the war the estate had been constructed to build flying boats. The Calgarth 'village' consisted of the factory itself and temporary accommodation huts for its workers – over 1,500 at its peak.[33] As over half the workers recruited for the factory were 'outsiders' it was given the local nickname of 'Chinatown'.[34] None of the workers were Chinese or indeed of immediate immigrant background. Nevertheless, their origins from the major industrial cities of the north-west of England made them alien and the moniker Chinatown literally orientalised their presence: the reference point, presumably, was the Pitt Street area of Liverpool, the Chinese quarter of the port since the late nineteenth century and perhaps the most 'exotic' place that local imagination could conjure up.[35]

In 1948, the Conservative travel writer S.P.B. Mais re-visited the Lake District as part of his survey of the surviving heritage of England following the destruction of the war. Mais had been one of the key writers and broadcasters in the inter-war years, popularising the English countryside and the physical evidence of the country's past.[36] He was now anxious to discover what damage had been done not only by enemy bombing but also through the needs of the war economy. When visiting Windermere he noted that the only change since the war was the addition of the flying boat factory. Mais stated that the 'locals' could not wait for the Calgarth estate to be demolished. As a true heir of Wordsworth, Meir claimed that 'The people of Windermere are rightly jealous of their land, and any attempt to spoil the fair face of their lake or its shores by any factory or hutment erection is hotly resented'.[37]

Mais was confident that demolition of this 'alien' estate would soon follow. To him, Windermere and the Lake District more generally had a greater significance and therefore restoration to the pre-war period was essential: 'Here if anywhere in England we can still recover that sense of freedom which has been lost in almost every other district.' To this place of 'harmony and serenity' which Wordsworth had 'perfectly' described, 'discriminating visitors' would always be welcome – like the poet and his opposition to the railway extension, the key was to ensure that newcomers appreciated the unchanging heritage of the Lake District. In this Mais was not alone.

During the Second World War, Jewish visitors were often perceived as unwelcome and undeserving of its tranquillity and peace. The famous Mass-Observation diarist Nella Last, who lived on the edge of the Lake District, was bemused to find her son bemoaning that Bowness, the major town next to Lake Windermere, was 'stiff with Jews', townsfolk from Manchester whom he regarded as 'parasitic people'.[38] For Last's son, as for Mais, those coming in must not in any way undermine its traditions or landscape. The urban Jews of the world's first industrial city had no place through reasons of class, race and region in Lake Windermere and its surrounds.[39] And it was within the temporary estate of Calgarth, within a place/space so culturally loaded – yet still functioning as a factory – that the War Office located billets for the child survivors in autumn 1945. As the Jewish organisers of the scheme noted: 'The hostel is unfortunately not a self-contained unit but is part of a bungalow camp. Some of the work people still live in some of the other houses.'[40]

But there was an even deeper pre-history in local memory with regard to Calgarth. In legend, repeated in many guides to and histories of Windermere and the Lake District, the story of the 'two skulls' and the 'world of shadows' was repeated:

> To Calgarth Hall in the midnight cold
> Two headless skeletons cross'd the fold. ...
> The skeletons two rushed through the yard,
> They pushed the door they left unbarr'd,
> Laid by their skulls in the niched wall,
> And flew like the wind from Calgarth Hall.[41]

In folk memory, the skulls of the 'wicked squire'd victims always come back' – it is a classic story of Gothic horror located in a decaying Elizabethan manor house and estate. If the estate was no more, memories of it still existed when the factory at Calgarth had been erected.[42] It is with the two images of the ultimate alien presence of 'Chinatown' and that of the 'living dead', alongside a deep sympathy connected to their experiences, that contemporaries – Jewish and non-Jewish – would confront the presence of the children. Not surprisingly, given this heady mix of emotional baggage attached to the place and to the newcomers, it would take some time for those around them to adjust to both the normality and abnormality of the 732.

In the National Archives files relating to the scheme – clumsily, but revealingly, named the Committee for the Care of Children from the Concentration Camps, the struggle of Home Office officials to 'place' the children is neatly illustrated. Initially labelled 'Proposed scheme for bringing Jewish children from Bergen-Belsen Concentration Camp to UK for rehabilitation', the words 'Jewish' and 'Bergen-

Belsen' were crossed out by Home Office officials.[43] For Britain and within British culture in 1945 especially, Belsen was *the* place of Nazi crimes and instantly connected to the horror images of the newsreels, radio broadcasts, newspaper reports and exhibitions.[44]

Even months after their arrival in Windermere, newspapers referred to the 'Children from Belsen'.[45] The same was true in Wintershill Hall in Hampshire. The local newspaper reported their arrival with the headline 'From Belsen to [the] New Forest',[46] and the *Jewish Chronicle* summarised their double vulnerability with the title 'Belsen Orphans in England'.[47] Dr Oscar Friedmann, a former refugee from Nazism himself who had run Jewish children's institutes in Berlin, was in charge of Wintershill Hall. He told Mollie Panter-Downes, the English journalist and writer, in an interview reproduced in the *New Yorker*:

> You know, it's funny, the English press has called these children who have come over here Belsen children, but many have never been to that camp. Belsen and Buchenwald have taken all the limelight, but there were others far worse, far more horrible, which no one seems to know about. Many of our boys have been in four or five camps, and if you ask them, they say Treblinka, in Poland, was the worst.[48]

Such a realisation would be a long time in coming in British society, and it was Belsen which was for many years the byword for Nazi crimes against humanity. But if Belsen was 'proof positive' of Nazi atrocities,[49] the metaphors used to describe the sights and smells that confronted the liberators were other worldly and essentially theological. Belsen was a hell 'camp' and it was especially 'Dante's inferno' that was evoked to describe the indescribable.[50] In short, a Christian construction of 'hell' was used to represent the place of Jewish suffering, a discourse that was so deeply entrenched that it was also to be found in Jewish descriptions of Belsen.[51]

Contemporaries contested two prisms within which to construct narratives of the children's experiences: first, truth versus atrocity propaganda, and second, the worldly versus the demonic. The tensions within both these tendencies made it difficult to understand the backgrounds of these children and the problems they were now facing. Thus the official report of the Westmorland County Council noted that 'They have become less and less inclined to talk of the past, and the tendency to exaggerate their adventures is dying down', a well-meaning but revealing example of early British inability to confront the scale and horror of the Holocaust.[52] Elsewhere, the same report produced statements from three boys about their persecution during the war. They were, it noted, 'the sons of educated parents and [therefore] able to give a reasonably dispassionate account of their experiences'.[53] Such patronising comments were reproduced in the first English-language account of the Holocaust. Gerald Reitlinger's *The Final Solution* (1953) diminished the importance of survivors' testimony as they were 'seldom educated men'.[54]

The reverse tendency of seeing the children as if they came from another planet – that of Belsen – also simplified their varied war experiences. In reality, as Friedmann highlighted, only a minority had been in Belsen and some had survived outside the complex Nazi camp system in hiding. It is even possible that a small number, the very youngest, were of semi-privileged *Mischlinge* background.[55] The varied experiences of these children catapulted through ghettos, slave labour camps, in hiding, on the run, and in death camps,[56] reflected the nature of the Holocaust but it was not one that fitted the simplistic understanding of early post-war Britain.[57] Moreover, their very survival made them atypical. Deborah Dwork, the leading authority on children and the Holocaust, suggests that 'only 11 percent of Jewish children alive at the beginning of the war survived its conclusion', totalling roughly 170,000.[58]

It should be noted, however, that it was partly the harsh limitations imposed by the Home Office, again based on a narrow reading of what typified Jewish suffering during the war, that explains why only 732 and not the full quota of 1,000 children could be found to meet the regulations. This process began with the well-meaning intervention of British Jewish refugee workers. In early May 1945, Otto Schiff of the Jewish Refugee Committee wrote to Sir Alexander Maxwell, Permanent Under-Secretary at the Home Office. Schiff submitted a request to help some orphans from Leonard Montefiore, a leading British Jewish philanthropist, who was in Paris. A year later, Montefiore explained what had motivated his intervention: 'I saw some of the first arrivals brought by air direct from the camps. I have never seen anything so ghastly in my life. The people I saw were like corpses that walked. I shall never quite forget the impression they made.'[59]

Montefiore wanted something done, arguing 'for the temporary admission to this country of about 1,000 Jewish orphan children from the camps in Buchenwald and Belsen'.[60] In later May 1945, Montefiore visited the Home Office himself. Here he was explicit about why the children should come from these particular camps. It was, he argued 'right that England should do something to show sympathy, and also because ... there is no better way of impressing on the British people the horrors of the concentration camps than by bringing some of the actual victims to this country'.[61] Maxwell was in agreement but clear in his response that it must not be extended:

> It must, of course, be understood that this is an exceptional arrangement made for dealing with the specially pitiful condition of children found in concentration camps, and must not be taken as a precedent for requests to bring to this country other children or young persons, or older persons, who are in a distressed condition on the Continent.[62]

Slowly, once the scheme was under way, it was extended to include those from other concentration camps, especially those from the east – initially it was limited to those from Germany alone.[63] Nevertheless, what constituted proof of persecution remained a problem and the regulation of who was eligible still focused on those who had been within the Nazi concentration camp structure. It is telling with regard to the power of the imagery associated with Belsen and Buchenwald that the organisation set up to deal with the scheme shortened its title simply to that of the 'Committee for the Care of Children from the Camps' (CCCC), lacking any geographic or historic precision.[64] Hesitantly, by January 1946 Schiff and other refugee workers asked for the scheme to include 'orphan or homeless children who have not necessarily been in a camp'. The Home Office civil servant noted that 'ex hypothesi' such children could not be brought under the 'Distressed Relatives' scheme which stipulated that those under its umbrella should have suffered in the Nazi camps. Nevertheless, they agreed to the extension because the numbers coming under the children's scheme had been so limited.[65] The reasons for this were partly the strict conditions and focus on the camps but also the desire of the children to go to other destinations, especially Palestine and North America. Such decisions were not apolitical. As an exasperated Schiff told Maxwell, there was

> little prospect of more children coming from Germany because the leaders of the camps ... are fanatical Zionists, who refuse to contemplate the possibility of children going anywhere except to

Palestine. They would rather let them remain in the poor conditions obtaining in the camps ... than let them come to this country.[66]

It is these factors, rather than the absence of other child survivors as has been claimed in popular histories of the scheme, that explains the low figure of those who came under its auspices.[67] Moreover, as early as March 1946 the Jewish Refugee Committee proposed to limit the scheme to a ceiling of 800 'for financial reasons'.[68] Neither the refugee organisations nor the government wished to extend the scheme too broadly for both economic and political reasons. A scheme to bring surviving relatives from the western camps to Britain was severely curtailed as, according to Alexander Maxwell:

> to admit for indefinite periods all 'relatives' who have had a bad time in a camp – brothers, sisters, brothers-in-law, sisters-in-law, uncles, aunts, nephews, nieces, and in some cases their minor children – would involve a substantial addition to our alien population at a time when there is a shortage of housing, food and supplies generally.[69]

It has already been noted that contemporary estimates put the number of Jewish child survivors at some 170,000 (out of 1.7 million before the Holocaust). Moreover, it seems likely that it was the strict criteria imposed by the Home Office in conjunction with the refugee organisations that accounts for the smaller number of girls who came under this movement. Aside from those in the camps for 'privileged' Jews in Belsen and Theresienstadt, where families might survive together, at least initially, the majority of girl survivors would have been in hiding throughout the war.[70] Some girls were also sent to Sweden to recuperate after the war and were thus not available for the scheme.[71]

The *Kindertransport*, to which some of the personnel and much of the structure of the 1945/46 scheme owed so much, was interpreted very differently. The pre-war child refugees were seen, ultimately, as rescuable in body and soul, and the discourse that accompanied them was in many ways Christian. The children were to be 'saved' and ever greater attention has been paid to one of the rescuers, Nicholas Winton, almost automatically now described as 'Britain's Schindler'. Of part Jewish origin, Winton was not practising and was happy for the children he helped bring over to be sent to be looked after by the Barbican Mission to the Jews.[72]

In contrast, the children on the 1945/46 scheme were seen by many as beyond redemption. The beauty and quiet of the Lake District would hopefully bring back physical health, but there was a sense that they could never recover sufficiently to be part of the nation. It was emphasised that the children, already checked to be free of infectious diseases, were *only* here to recuperate. They thus did not even have the temporary transmigrant status initially given to the *Kindertransport* – their legal position was even more marginal. It was, the senior Home Official advised his Secretary of State, on the strict 'understanding that it is the responsibility of the refugee organisations to make arrangements for their emigration as soon as emigration becomes practicable'. Some, he added, 'might go to Palestine, some to Australia and some to the United States'.[73]

Their perceived rootlessness and un-Englishness was internalised also by those in the CCCC who came largely from the liberal Jewish and liberal Christian worlds. The leading force was Leonard Montefiore, a gentle person who in many ways became a father figure to the Windermore boys and girls. To him a sense of Englishness was ingrained and essential to his identity. He was a classic nineteenth century figure like his father before him, the founder of Liberal Judaism, Claude Montefiore, who described himself as 'an Englishman of the Hebrew persuasion'.[74] In 1936 Leonard Montefiore related how whenever he visited Woburn House, which then housed many of the major British Jewish organisations, 'and pass the door of the Jewish Museum, I wonder whether my appropriate place is not there rather than anywhere else in the building'.[75] At that stage the collecting policy of the Museum was not to accept items that were not at least 100 years old and elite in nature. He was a man out of time and place and yet drawn to help those who had suffered the worst of twentieth century barbarity.

In 1946, whilst addressing Jewish students at his old university, Cambridge, Leonard Montefiore gave an impassioned speech about the children. He referred to them in relation to his own congregation, the West London Synagogue, the oldest reform community in Britain and still its leading place of worship and religious authority. Without any sense of malice, Montefiore remarked that 'By no stretch of the imagination is it conceivable that any of these children will become a member of [this] Synagogue'.[76] Ironically, one of these children, Hugo Gryn, became the best known and respected of West London's rabbis and the voice of moral authority in late twentieth century Britain.[77]

Indeed, it was Montefiore who persuaded Gryn to come under the scheme.[78] So why was it that Leonard Montefiore, such a friend to the children, could not envisage them even becoming a member let alone a leader of his synagogue?

Montefiore's roots were ultimately foreign but they were to be found in the early years of the readmission of the Jews to England and to the elite Sephardi and western European Ashkenazi communities. 'Two of the most distinguished of the old-established Anglo-Jewish families were united in his ancestry' – the Montefiores and the Goldsmids.[79] The child survivors in England were largely east European Jews from the small towns and industrial cities of Poland especially. They were thus separated from Montefiore by class, politics, nationality and religious practice. They were not only defined by him as victims of persecution but as *ostjuden*; they were, to him, of the same type of those who came to Britain before 1914 in their hundreds of thousands and transformed Anglo-Jewry. 'The boys and girls who arrived at the aerodromes', Montefiore wrote in 1947, 'were remarkably similar in appearance to those who stepped off some immigrant ship from Libau or Riga way back in 1907 or thereabouts.'[80] 'If one could visualise their homes', he wrote in an internal memorandum in October 1945, 'it is most likely one would see an orthodox home, in the strictest and narrowest sense, orthodox in the sense that U.S. orthodoxy would seem a very wishy washy sort of orthodoxy.'[81] It is no accident that alongside their allotted place in the religious sphere being located as outside the ultra-anglicised and elite reform movement, they were also perceived by Montefiore as potential workers and artisans in the economic realm.

When told by the children that they wanted to train to become doctors or musicians, Leonard was firm in response: 'Think of something else.'[82] Apprenticeships in the workshops of Manchester and London working for those of east European Jewish origin was indeed the path of many. To the elite of British Jewry, the child survivors of the Lake District and Hampshire countryside were too 'other', too placeless, too radical, and too orthodox in origin to be fully anglicized. The hope was that they would quickly re-emigrate, thereby fulfilling the pledge to the British government that their stay would be temporary. If there *was* to be a place for them it was to be industrial towns of Britain alongside their fellow *ostjuden*. Again, Montefiore was clear in the 'tough love' philosophy of Victorian philanthropy and in cutting down 'unrealistic' expectations:

No doubt there have been certain disappointments. They thought England was a very rich country where all the things they had missed for so many years would be provided by the incredible number of incredibly rich Jews who lived here. They had not the faintest conception of economic conditions prevailing in this country.[83]

The children, he noted in early 1947, had to be told it was 'high time [they] should consider how to earn a living ... [T]hey are apt to consider any small talent they possess as the proof of their genius. They are disinclined to accept the fact that much seeming drudgery accompanies the first steps in any trade or occupation'.[84]

Stereotypical assumptions, reflecting wider societal expectations, similarly conditioned the training the girl survivors received from the CCCC. In Surrey two neighbouring hostels were created for a number of the children once they had left Windermere and Wintershill Hall. The very young children, including some who were babies, were looked after in Bulldogs Bank where Anna Freud played a prominent role.[85] The older ones, including a high percentage of girls, were located in Wier Courtney, Lingfield, in the house of Jewish entrepreneur, Sir Benjamin Drage. The possibility of bringing some of the youngest from Bulldogs Bank to Wier Courtney so that the older girls could 'learn mothercraft' was raised several times by the CCCC.[86] The girls from Wier Courtney were trained as secretaries, hairdressers, sales girls and typists with only one noted as 'working for [a] higher school certificate'.[87] The aim was to be 'realistic' for the children's/young adults' futures and also to justify and limit the amount spent on them through instilling independence. By 1950 the CCCC scheme had cost over £400,000.[88]

But what of these 'Wandering Jews' themselves? The mythology of the movement, on a much smaller scale, replicates some aspects of the internal stories of the *Kindertransport*. Britain proved redemptive and they recovered from their experiences and went on to have successful lives and rebuild families in that country. None of this narrative, part of the official storyline as presented by Martin Gilbert's *The Boys*, whose subtitle, *Triumph over Adversity*, exemplifies such an approach, is without foundation.[89] But just as the experience of the 100 girls has been airbrushed from this picture,[90] reflecting the wider marginality of women in Holocaust historiography,[91] so have the less palatable aspects of their years of reception and recovery in Britain. These lacunae reflect a wider tendency in the still limited study of children in the Holocaust in which critical perspectives have, understandably, been lost sight of through the tendency towards sentimentality and a happy ending. This is neither surprising, nor necessarily to be criticised given the overpowering loss created by the murder of one and a half million Jewish children.[92]

So how did the youngsters view Windermere, a place they experienced initially in the glories of late summer? In the 'official' version Windermere has been described as 'paradise' – a biblical illusion to the Garden of Eden if through a Christian or at least a non-Jewish discourse.[93] It was similarly referred to as 'heaven'.[94] Michael Perlmutter is even more Christological in his description: 'I was reborn in Windermere in 1945. The promise of England was a dream to a teenage boy who no longer believed he could believe in dreams. But it happened.'[95] Such memories, recalled over 60 years later, at a basic level reflect the changing fortunes of the children from persecution and brutal anonymity to rehabilitation and individual care. Yet the discourse used to describe that transformation also reveals the shaping of identities thereafter. The contemporaries confronting the children had to deal with the realities of the children and the problems they faced. As a leaflet produced to raise money for '700 Concentration Camp orphans' acknowledged,

> If, at the age of 12 or 13, you had suddenly been flung into prison and came out again five or six years later, what would you want most? You would want to catch up with the time you had missed or thought you had missed. If then you had suddenly been flown to a foreign country and had to learn a foreign language, would it be odd if you felt a bit bewildered and thought that, after all, freedom did not bring the Paradise you had expected?[96]

Subsequent memories of Windermere, to meet the desire for a 'rebirth', have tended to smooth away the tensions and difficulties that inevitably affected the children's initial months in England given the traumas they had experienced and the challenges they now faced to rebuild their lives.

The hope of the organisers was that the English countryside itself would act as a restorative aid to their physical and mental recovery. 'We are rightly', Montefiore noted in October 1945, 'parking the children in country districts.'[97] By 1947, Montefiore himself acknowledged the sentimental naivety of the organisers, including himself, in this respect: 'We expected children, we had talked about children, and written about children. We had pictured under sixteens who could be sent to school or nursed back to health in the peace of an English countryside.'[98] Contemporary reporting of their arrival similarly emphasised the redemptive quality of the English pastoral and the pathos of the children. The London *Evening Standard* noted that 'The most pathetic of all victims of Nazi cruelty have arrived in this country to be helped back to health and hope.' These 'tragic' children would, it added, 'learn to live again in freedom amid the lovely scenery of the Lake District'. To reassure its readers (and no doubt under guidance from the Aliens Department of the Home Office) it concluded that this was to be a temporary stay 'while plans for their emigration are being completed'.[99] The article shared S.P.B. Mais' belief that the countryside and especially the Lake District represented the essential characteristic of Englishness – freedom. But Mais had also insisted that only 'discriminating visitors' would be welcome in the Lake District. Like the industrial estate of Calgarth itself, the 300 children were visiting only temporarily. By 1948, when Mais re-visited the shores of Lake Windermere, there was literally no trace left of the children.[100]

The local newspaper, the *Westmorland Gazette*, reporting their 'Arrival in Lakeland', highlighted how the children had 'escaped death from gas and burning and have now been removed to ideal surroundings for rest and recuperation'.[101] The landscape was truly inspiring, nature at its most intensely beautiful, combining England's longest lake and some of its highest mountains. Yet although through Wordsworth it was seen as quintessentially English it was also regarded as somehow foreign because of its extremes of natural formation. It was too wild and dangerous, evoking to some the continent of Europe and especially the Alps.[102]

The child survivors too regarded it ambivalently. They had been brought to the countryside to recuperate – to walk and climb, eat and sleep, and to regain their strength and a sense of liberty. Nevertheless, they were accommodated and schooled in the middle of a small industrial estate. They appreciated its beauty and the chance to explore the local landscape. As Mayer Hersh recalls, 'we were walking around ... whole areas, the Lake District and Bowness and Windermere and other places. We went for long walks and we really enjoyed it'.[103] Roman Halter regained strength through swimming in the lake and later took part in international events in the sport.[104] Even more spectacularly, Ben Helfgott, later leader of the '45 Aid

Society (Holocaust Survivors) organisation represented England in the Olympic Games as a weightlifter during the 1950s. He recalls the many games of football, volley ball and hiking in the Lakes, part of what he refers to as the three month 'dream' of being at Windermere.[105] In Wintershill Hall, Magda Bloom, who had survived Auschwitz and Belsen, and her friend Marta saw the house and its surrounding countryside as 'fairyland. It was a mild autumn. The trees were still green and there were roses everywhere ... we just revelled in being free'.[106]

The children were, however, also mourning for a world that had been destroyed and were deeply unsettled about their uncertain future. Rest and recuperation soon gave way to a sense of frustration and boredom in the remoteness of the places they had been sent. Their physical recovery – at least in terms of weight – had largely occurred *before* they were flown to England – they were not the skeleton-like figures that many locals anticipated and now mistakenly re-remember.[107] There was little to do, other than visit the local cinemas, and there was none of the excitement of the big city that had been briefly offered and sampled in Prague. Recent oral history suggests amongst the older boys a desire to assert their manhood even if this meant resorting to the unlikely fleshpots of Kendal, hardly the metropolis.[108] As Montefiore noted as early as October 1945, aside from smoking, 'I should be greatly surprised if they had not formed other and far less innocent habits'.[109] The official local report covering their experiences noted that there was 'some evidence of homosexuality' and that the boys 'have been pestered by young English girls'.[110] It is more than possible that such pestering was not simply one way and some local tensions undoubtedly existed over such matters.[111] No wonder then, given the quiet nature of the Lake District and the Hampshire countryside, that most left for Manchester and London, or in the case of Magda Bloom, Birmingham, as soon as they were able and allowed to do so.[112] All these cities provided not just economic opportunities but also thriving Jewish communities of east European origin within which the children could rebuild their lives.

Within Anglo-Jewry the children were an oddity – they were, as Montefiore noted, closer to those of east European origin than the more recent arrivals from central Europe in the 1930s, but still distanced from the former by their scarring experiences during the war. Indeed, it was a few exceptional German Jewish refugees, such as Oscar Friedman, who helped take care of the children in the two reception camps. The cultural and experiential distance was illustrated by Perec Zylberberg, who was at Windermere having survived the Lodz ghetto and a variety of Nazi concentration camps. Several years after Windermere, a club was set up for the children and Perec's suggestion of naming it the Klepfish Club, in honour of the young Bundist fighter of the Warsaw ghetto, Michal Klepfish, was rejected by the British Jewish organisers. What sort of fish, they wondered, was a klepfish? It was eventually named the Primrose Club, far more English in its associations, though ironically popularised by Benjamin Disraeli, another Jewish outsider in British society.[113]

Only with the belated recognition of the Holocaust from the 1990s onwards would some of these young survivors gain recognition inside and outside the Jewish community. Even then, those that never fully recovered have been forgotten by all but those in the small survivor community, a net itself that is far from inclusive especially in relation to gender and place. In clinical fashion, Leonard Montefiore reported to Anthony de Rothschild, one of the biggest supporters of the Central British Fund for Jewish Relief (the umbrella organisation for the CCCC), that by 1950 57 of the children still required financial support. This included 'twenty invalids', some of whom were in his eyes 'hopeless'.[114] Yet the domestication of the Holocaust in late twentieth and early twenty-first century Britain has, to some extent, help bring home and naturalise these 'Wandering Jews' who came after the war. Some, indeed, have been honoured, allowing a life story of one of the survivors to be described as one 'from the depths of humanity to the pinnacles of success, from Belsen to Buckingham Palace'.[115]

There are still elements of their stories that there is a reluctance to accept – one largely relating to how 'other' they were regarded at the time. First, there is little or no recognition of the limitations imposed on their entry confined by stay and numbers. Numbers were to be kept low partly for financial reasons – this was a scheme sponsored not by government but privately by British Jewry – hence the decision after a few months to cut the absolute ceiling by 20 per cent. It was also for political reasons – the government feared anti-Semitism and did not see Jewish refugees, including child survivors, as racially desirable. In 1945, even post-Belsen, the 'Jew' was still perceived as 'other' to British or more specifically English national identity.[116]

Second, the children themselves were sometimes and not surprisingly more difficult than the ideal of innocent but suffering victims that contemporaries desired. It is a wider expectation, Christological in inspiration, that expects nobility through suffering, even and perhaps especially through the Holocaust. It is worth remembering as a corrective that in Britain its most notorious and violent landlord, Peter Rachman, was a survivor, as was the gangster Maurits de Vries, who helped run the red light district of Amsterdam after the war.[117] If none of the Windermere or other children gained such infamy, the cases of Rachman, de Vries and others show that not all survivors had the warmth, humanity and vision of Hugo Gryn. Leonard Montefiore wrote in 1950 lamenting the 'hard core' cases of the children under his care: 'we have half a dozen tough guys who have no great enthusiasm for work in any shape'. Another aged 15 'has all the makings of a delinquent. A typical case for Basil's [Henriques] Juvenile Court'.[118]

To conclude, the forgotten 'Wandering Jews' of Windermere found themselves, like the literary mythic figure confronted by the Romantics, subject to fascination and sympathy, fear and rejection. They came to England on a wave of repulsion following the concentration camp revelations, which created intense horror but also misunderstandings about the complexity and range of the Nazi genocidal machine. As figures escaping from the furnace of hell, they were expected to find and often genuinely regarded the English countryside and especially the Lake District as its opposite – paradise. But if this sublime example of English nature was meant to help the youngsters to recuperate, the experience showed that Englishness itself was far from porous. West London Synagogue, for example, was a place where resources might be found for the children, but it was never perceived as somewhere they might worship.

Told not to exaggerate, or to keep quiet, it is not surprising that after the initial efforts to help them and the genuine kindness that was shown to the children in their first settlement at Windermere and Hampshire, thereafter their greatest strength was within the group itself. But rather than gain, as Wordsworth and other Romantics had fantasised, from perpetual wandering and the freedom that allegedly brought, most of the former children settled in particular places – in Britain, Israel, America and elsewhere – and attempted where possible to rebuild families around them, and to re-establish a 'place called home'.[119] Yet if they became rooted to cities such as Manchester and

London, increasingly those who were originally flown to the north of England have returned to visit Windermere. In so doing, they have provided memories which might still form a more inclusive history of Windermere and the stories the Lake District tells of itself.

Black photographer Ingrid Pollard was born in Guyana in 1953 and came to Britain three years later. Her exhibition *Pastoral Interludes* (1984) explores the English countryside and 'feeling I don't belong'. Evoking Wordsworth especially, the texts accompanying her photographs question the nature of Englishness and exclusion. Her first image in this exhibition has Pollard alone resting against a dry stone wall. The accompanying text reveals her ambiguity towards the beauty of the landscape and her place within it:

> it's as if the black experience is only lived within an urban environment. I thought I liked the LAKE DISTRICT, where I wandered lonely as a Black face in a sea of white. A visit to the countryside is always accompanied by a feeling of unease, dread...[120]

The cultural anthropologist Wendy Joy Darby, exploring the Lake District during the 1990s by taking part in rambler groups, queried the absence of ethnic minorities within them. It was explained to her that 'their particular absence in the Lake District [was because] this was not a place that held "their" history ... Blacks and Asians were seen to be urban'.[121] Ingrid Pollard's *Pastoral Interludes* and John Kippin's photograph 'Muslims at Lake Windermere' (1991), showing Muslim men praying in a corner of a field near the Lake with the women and children around them, are thus political interventions challenging notions of English exclusivity within the landscape. As John Taylor suggests in *A Dream of England* (1994), with these photographs 'the meaning of the countryside is in transition'.[122]

Since the early 1990s, the desire to open up heritage within major national organisations to people of all backgrounds has indeed intensified. In 2003, for example, it was stated that 'English Heritage seeks to understand the diversity of this country's heritage and promote a more inclusive past ... [It] values the heritage of the different cultures that have been woven into our shared history over hundreds of years'.[123] Nevertheless, exclusion based on narrow definitions of Englishness, past and present, has far from disappeared.[124] Whilst roughly 10 per cent of the English population is non-white, just 1 per cent of visitors to the national parks of

England are people of colour. This imbalance is part of what Trevor Philips, head of Britain's Equality Commission, provocatively refers to as the 'passive apartheid' of the English countryside.[125]

Yet if the Lakes and their poet laureate, Wordsworth, remain 'quintessentially English',[126] his evocation of the 'Wandering Jew' enables a connection to be made between Ambleside and Auschwitz. Moreover, Wordsworth's 'tenderness towards his children' was articulated through 'some of his finest poems [which] pre-emptively record early death and the sorrow of losing a child'.[127] It was thus no coincidence that Liza Shleimowitz, whose parents had been brutally murdered by anti-Semites in the Ukraine during the early 1920s, and who with her siblings was left in a transit camp, Atlantic Park (near Southampton), after their rejection in Ellis Island through racist American immigration policies, should identify with Wordsworth's poetry, and especially the 'Lucy' poems and their enigmatic portrayal of loss. Her school notebooks, which she took with her to South Africa where she was eventually found a home, include a lovingly transcribed verse from the poem, the only writing that is in English:

> She dwelt among the untrodden ways
> Beside the Springs of Dove,
> A maid whom these were none to praise
> And very few to love. ...
> She lived unknow[n] and few could know
> When Lucy ceased to be;
> But she is in her grave, and, oh,
> The difference to me![128]

The Lake District, as the rest of the English countryside, has many different histories and even those that dominate, such as the narratives relating to William Wordsworth, enable plural readings. Whether the story of the child survivors, whether in Windermere or Wintershill Hall, will remain marginal as 'matter out of place ... not [to] be included if a pattern is to be maintained',[129] or, alternatively, to become integrated, is unclear. Through the English Romantics, notes Wendy Joy Darby, 'The Lake District was made into an icon, a window through which a greater reality or truth could be perceived, be it of God or England – although the two were not necessarily different from one another.'[130] Thereafter, the Lake District has continued to be made and re-made. Arthur Ransome's novels, starting with *Swallows and Amazons* (1930) have, for example, become 'identified with a particular vision of England: a pastoral, old-fashioned utopia set in the Lake District sometime between the wars, with its roots in the Edwardian heyday of the British Empire'.[131] This is not far removed from Darby's 'Wordsworthshire', 'compounded of drifts of daffodils, lakeside strolls, the ever-hovering presence of the National Trust's long-ago comforting world of Peter Rabbit and Mrs Tiggy Winkle, and high teas taken in gleaming dark wood interiors set with chintz and lustreware'.[132]

It is hard to imagine that the story of the Holocaust survivor children would fit into such versions of Wordsworth's Lake District. Nor, for that matter, would that of Liza Shleimowitz who had witnessed the rape and murder of her mother in the Ukraine after the First World War and who took consolation in Wordsworth's poetry in an English transmigrant camp. The same has been true of the Dadaist, Kurt Schwitters, who left Nazi Germany in 1937 to escape arrest as a 'degenerate artist'. He settled in Ambleside next to Lake Windermere at the end of the war and remained in the area until his death in 1948. It has been noted that now 'there are no signs of his ever having been [in the Lake District]. Whilst there is a plethora of shops and cafes bearing the names of the Lake Poets and Beatrix Potter's rabbits, you will find none bearing his name'.[133] But such heritage struggles are part of a bigger battle over national identity at both a political and cultural level in which exclusion in the early years of the twenty-first century still remains the dominant force. This, however, may not always be the case. To return to Doreen Massey's theoretical contribution on places and their pasts:

> The description, definition and identification of a place is ... always inevitably an intervention not only into geography but also ... into the re(telling) of the historical constitution of the present. It is another move in the continuing struggle over the delineation and characterisation of space-time.[134]

Progress *has* been made in this most important of English localities, such as Ingrid Pollard's 'witty series of pictures that put black people into the frame of Wordsworth's Lake District',[135] and the work of Another Space's 'From Auschwitz to Ambleside' project on the survivor children themselves. This study began with the thoughts of cultural critic Stuart Hall, and his vision for a more inclusive heritage which would 'rewrite the margins into the centre, the outside into the inside'. This is not special pleading, as Hall makes clear, but the necessity of representing more adequately the degree to which 'their' history entails and has always implicated 'us', across the centuries, and vice versa. The African presence in Britain since the sixteenth century, the Asian since the seventeenth century and the Chinese, Jewish and Irish in the nineteenth have long required to be made into a much more 'global' version of 'our island story'.[136]

With this in mind, embracing the local, national and global as well as the particular and the universal, I will close with two of these children and how they have taken their experiences and wider Jewish narratives to make messages for all humankind. They are ones that expose the danger of being other and the vulnerability the process of othering causes more generally.

Ben Helfgott has done more than anyone to keep these 'children' together in Britain and beyond. He has helped create a world of mutual support but one which reaches out beyond the confines of this small community: 'I believe our story is "pour encourager les autres" because every day there is someone who feels helpless, feels a need for support, especially the young with specific difficulties.'[137] One of these was Vesna Maric, who came to Britain in 1992 as a teenager fleeing persecution in Bosnia-Herzegovina. She relates how when she arrived in England the expectation was 'something a little more like "proper" refugees: people suffering, hardship visible on their faces, clothes torn and wrinkled, children's eyes crusted with tears'. Instead, there was a determination 'not [to] advertise our misery'. Vesna and her party were taken to the Lake District to recuperate where they were treated with kindness but also with some fear and patronisation. As she concludes, 'It's not easy suddenly becoming a refugee'.[138] And Vesna's story brings us finally to Auschwitz survivor Hugo Gryn, who came over in the last major flight of children in February 1946 and became lifelong friends with Ben Helfgott. In his last speech in 1996, referring to asylum seekers, those contemporary 'Wandering Jews' without the safety of the concept of home either through time or place, Hugo stated: 'It seems to me that true religion begins with the law about protecting and shielding the alien and the stranger ... There are so many scars that need mending and healing it seems to me that it is imperative that we proclaim that asylum issues are an index of our spiritual and moral civilisation.' As he concluded, 'How you are with the one to whom you owe nothing, that is a grave test and not only as an index of our tragic past'.[139]

ACKNOWLEDGEMENTS

I would like to thank Trevor Avery of Another Space for his help and generosity in working on this project. It is part of a wider project working towards a cultural history of the Holocaust survivor children being carried out with Dr Aimée Bunting.

NOTES

1. Stuart Hall, speech at national conference, 'Whose Heritage? The Impact of Cultural Diversity on Britain's Living Heritage', G-Mex, Manchester, 2 November 1999, reproduced in Jo Littler and Roshi Naidoo, eds., *The Politics of Heritage: The Legacies of 'Racw'* (London: Routledge, 2005), p.34.
2. The first, brief, historisation of this movement was provided by Norman Bentwich, *They Found Refuge: An Account of British Jewry's Work for Victims of Nazi Oppression* (London: Cresset Press, 1956), pp.74–7. Sarah Moskovitz, *Love Despite Hate: Child Survivors of the Holocaust and their Adult Lives* (New York: Schocken Books, 1983) was the first detailed study, focusing on the children who were sent to Weir Courtenay, a large house near Lingfield, Surrey after the initial reception camps. The only detailed history of the movement is by Martin Gilbert, *The Boys: Triumph over Adversity* (London: Weidenfeld & Nicolson, 1996).
3. See, for example, the narrative provided by Bentwich, *They Found Refuge* (see note 2), chapter 5 which presents the later scheme as a brief afterword (pp.74–7).
4. See Tony Kushner, *Remembering Refugees: Then and Now* (Manchester: Manchester University Press, 2006), chapter 4 for an analysis of memory work associated with the *Kindertransport* in Britain and beyond.
5. The best historical work on refugees from Nazism has been focused on state responses to their entry. See especially Louise London, *Whitehall and the Jews 1933–1948: British Immigration Policy and the Holocaust* (Cambridge: Cambridge University Press, 2000). The literary cultural approach is dominant within the *Yearbook of the Research Centre for German and Austrian Exile Studies* vol.1 (1999) onwards.
6. See Joseph Gaer, *The Legend of the Wandering Jew* (New York: Mentor Books, 1961); and Galit Hasan-Rokem and Alan Dundes, eds., *The Wandering Jew: Essays in the Interpretation of a Christian Legend* (Bloomington: Indiana University Press, 1986).
7. See, for example, Eitan Bar-Yosef and Nadia Valman, eds., *'The Jew' in Late-Victorian and Edwardian Culture: Between the East End and East Africa* (Basingstoke: Palgrave Macmillan, 2009); and Hannah Ewence's contribution to this volume.
8. Melvyn Bragg, *Land of the Lakes* (London: Secker & Warburg, 1983), p.198.
9. See, for example, 'What is Wordsworth Country?', in http://www.wordsworthcountry.com/whatisit.htm (accessed 15 June 2010).
10. W. Darby, *Landscape and Identity: Geographies of Nation and Class in England* (Oxford: Berg, 2000), pp.211–12. See also Dave Russell, *Looking North: Northern England and the national imagination* (Manchester: Manchester University Press, 2004), p.54.
11. For the details of all the flights, see HO 213/1797 in National Archives, Kew.
12. For Wintershill Hall see Mollie Panter-Downes, 'A Quiet Life in Hampshire', *New Yorker*, 2 March 1946; and Tony Kushner and Katharine Knox, *Refugees in an Age of Genocide: Global, National and Local Perspectives during the Twentieth Century* (London: Frank Cass, 1999), pp.210–11.
13. Trevor Avery, ed., *From Auschwitz to Ambleside* (Sedbergh: Another Space, 2008). Supported by the Big Lottery Fund 'Their Past Your Future', this project has led to exhibitions, school packs, and a website, http://www.anotherspace.org.uk/a2a/index. htm (accessed 29 June 2010). It also prompted the television documentary, 'The Orphans Who Survived the Concentration Camps', BBC 1, 5 April 2010. Author site visit with Trevor Avery, 18 August 2009. There has been a basic archaeological mapping of the site to reveal the foundations of some of the major buildings.
14. Hilda Stowell, *Wintershill Hall Hampshire from the Period of Roman Occupation to 1972* (Chichester: Chichester Press, 1972), p.12. On the offer from James Sebag-Montefiore to

provide his home, see Central British Fund council minutes, 22 October 1945, in CBF archives, File 9/179, microfilm collection, University of Southampton.

15. Trevor Avery and Rosemary Smith, eds., *The Lost Village of Calgarth* (Sedbergh: Another Space, 2009).

16. G.D.H. and Margaret Cole, eds., *William Cobbett: Rural Rides* (London: Peter Davies, 1930), p.175, entry 6 August 1823 describing the parish of Durley.

17. Doreen Massey, 'Places and their Pasts', *History Workshop Journal*, 39 (Spring 1995), 182–92 (p.186).

18. Alex Black and Hazel Gatford, *Wordsworth's Lake District: The Landscape and Its Writers* (Sevenoaks: Salmon, 2001); emphasis added.

19. Sheila Spector, ed., *British Romanticism and the Jews: History, Culture, Literature* (New York: Palgrave, 2002); Judith Page, *Imperfect Sympathies: Jews and Judaism in British Romantic Literature and Culture* (New York: Palgrave Macmillan, 2004).

20. Mary Douglas, *Purity and Danger: An Analysis of the Concepts of Pollution and Taboo* (London: Routledge, 1996 [1966]), p.41; Liisa Malkki, 'National Geographic: The Rooting of Peoples and the Territorialization of National Identity among Scholars and Refugees', *Cultural Anthropology*, 7.1 (1992), 24–44 (p.34). See William Knight, ed., *Journals of Dorothy Wordsworth* (London: Macmillan, 1930), chapters 3–6, on Grasmere, 1800 to 1803; Jonathan Wordsworth, *William and Dorothy Wordsworth: The Dove Cottage Years* (Grasmere: Wordsworth Trust, 2008).

22. William Wordsworth, 'Song for the Wandering Jew', in *The Poetical Works of William Wordsworth* ed. by E. de Selincourt (Oxford: Clarendon Press, 1952), pp.158–9; Page, *Imperfect Sympathies* (see note 19), pp.175–6.

23. Randall Stewart, ed., *The English Notebooks by Nathaniel Hawthorne* (New York: Oxford University Press, 1941), p.321. See Regine Rosenthal, 'Inventing the Other: Ambivalent Constructions of the Wandering Jew/ess in Nineteenth Century American Literature', in *Representations of Jews Through the Ages*, eds., Leonard Greenspoon and Bryan Le Beau (Omaha: Creighton University Press, 1996), p.177 for a careful analysis of Hawthorne's gendered bifurcated representation of Jews.

24. Todd Endelman, *The Jews of Britain 1656 to 2000* (Berkeley: University of California Press, 2002), pp.106–7.

25. Stewart, *The English Notebooks* (see note 23), p.321.

26. See Rosenthal, 'Inventing the Other' (see note 23), pp.181–4 for Melville.

27. *The Poetical Works* (see note 22), pp.158–9.

28. Page, *Imperfect Sympathies* (see note 19), pp.175–6.

29. See his letters to the *Morning Post* in 1844 concerning the Kendal and Windermere Railway reproduced in William Wordsworth, *Guide to the Lakes* (London: Frances Lincoln, 2004), pp.135–48. See also Hunter Davies, *A Walk Around the Lakes: A Visit to Britain's Lake District* (London: Frances Lincoln, 2009), pp.130–31 for acerbic comment on Wordsworth's hypocrisy in his attitudes to the masses.

30. Hunter Davies, *William Wordsworth: A Biography* (London: Weidenfeld and Nicolson, 1980), pp.322–3.

31. Darby, *Landscape and Identity* (see note 10), pp.155–6.

32. 'Explore the history around Kendal Railway Station', Kendal Station, site visit, 8 July 2010.

33. Allan King, *Wings on Windermere: The History of the Lake District's Forgotten Flying Boat Factory* (Sandomierz: Stratus, 2008); Liz Rice, ed., *Flying Boats and Fellow Travellers* (Sedbergh: Another Space, 2008).

34. Rice, *Flying Boats* (see note 33), pp.4, 5.

35. On the history of the Chinese community in Liverpool, see Colin Holmes, *John Bull's Island: Immigration and British Society, 1871–1971* (Basingstoke: Macmillan, 1988), pp.32–3, 78–9.

36. Darby, *Landscape and Identity* (see note 10), pp.173–4.

37. S.P.B. Mais, *The English Scene Today* (London: Rockliff, 1948), p.257.

38. Richard Broad and Suzie Fleming, eds., *Nella Last's War: A Mother's Diary 1939–45* (Bristol: Falling Wall Press, 1981), p.83, entry for 3 November 1940.

39. Ibid. p.269.

40. Central British Fund council minutes, 22 August 1945, File 9/145, CBF microfilm archives, University of Southampton.

41. 'The Armboth Banquet', reproduced in John Page White, *Lays and Legends of the English Lake District* (London: John Russell Smith, 1873), pp.170–73.

42. W.G. Collingwood, *The Lake Counties* (London: Frederick Warne, 1932), p.27. See also Peter Nock, *Tales and Legends of Windermere* (Windermere: Orinoco Press, 1989), pp.5–7.

43. Cover of file HO 213/1797 GEN 323/6/11.

44. See Joanne Reilly, *Belsen: The Liberation of a Concentration Camp* (London: Routledge, 1998); Joanne Reilly *et al.*, eds., *Belsen in History and Memory* (London: Frank Cass, 1997); David Cesarani and Suzanne Bardgett, eds., *Belsen 1945: New Historical Perspectives* (London: Vallentine Mitchell, 2006).

45. Frank Davey, 'Children from Belsen have London Feast', *News Chronicle*, 6 December 1945.

46. *Southern Daily Echo*, 31 October 1945.

47. *Jewish Chronicle*, 2 November 1945.

48. Mollie Panter-Downes, 'A Quiet Life in Hampshire', *New Yorker*, 2 March 1946.

49. This was the title of the Paramount News newsreel of Belsen. See Nicholas Pronay, 'Defeated Germany in British Newsreels: 1944–45', in *Hitler's Fall: The Newsreel Witness* (London: Croom Helm, 1988), pp.42–4.

50. See Reilly, *Belsen: Liberation of a Concentration Camp* (note 44), passim.

51. Ibid.

52. J. Dow and M. Brown, *Evacuation to Westmorland from Home and Europe 1939–1945* (Kendal: Westmorland Gazette, 1946), p.58.

53. Ibid. p.52.

54. Gerald Reitlinger, *The Final Solution* (London: Vallentine, Mitchell, 1953), p.581.

55. Aimée Bunting and Tony Kushner, discussions with Trevor Avery, Windermere, 11 December 2009.

56. Deborah Dwork, *Children with a Star: Jewish Youth in Nazi Europe* (New Haven, CT: Yale University Press, 1991), provides all these subheadings.

57. More generally, see Tony Kushner, *The Holocaust and the Liberal Imagination: A Social and Cultural History* (Oxford: Blackwell, 1994), chapter 7.

58. Dwork, *Children with a Star* (see note 56), pp.xxxiii, 274 (n.27).

59. Leonard Montefiore, 'Address given to the Cambridge University Jewish Society, 18 October 1946' (Parkes Library, University of Southampton.

60. Schiff to Maxwell, 4 May 1945 in National Archives, HO 213/1793.

61. Alexander Maxwell, 24 May 1945, minutes of meeting with Leonard Montefiore in National Archives, HO 213/1797.

62. Maxwell to Schiff, 1 June 1945, in National Archives, HO 213/1797.

63. W. Lyon memorandum, 25 February 1946, on 'Existing and proposed schemes for bringing children to the UK', in National Archives, HO 213/782.

64. See the minutes of this committee from 1945 to 1950 in file 198, Central British Fund microfilm archives, University of Southampton.

65. Prestige to Lyons, 12 January 1946 in National Archives, HO 213/1797.

66. Maxwell to Prestige, 10 January 1946 in National Archives, HO 213/1797.

67. Anton Gill, *The Journey Back from Hell: Conversations with Concentration Camp Survivors* (London: Grafton, 1988), p.165.

68. Lyons memorandum, 25 March 1946, National Archives, HO 213/782.

69. Quoted in H.H.C. Prestige memorandum, 21 September 1945 in National Archives, HO 213/618 E409.

70. Gilbert, *The Boys* (see note 2), p.2, states that the 'reason there were so few girls among the youngsters brought from Prague is that it was much harder for girls to survive'. Whilst this was true for the extermination and slave labour camps, it must be suggested that it was easier for reasons of disguise for girls to survive in hiding.

71. See also Carole Bell Ford, *After the Girls Club: How Teenaged Holocaust Survivors Built New Lives in America* (Lanham, MD: Lexington Books, 2010).

72. See Kushner, *Remembering Refugees* (note 4), chapter 4.

73. Sir Alexander Maxwell to the Home Secretary, 12 May 1945, HO 213/1797.

74. Daniel Langton, *Claude Montefiore: His Life and Thought* (London: Vallentine Mitchell, 2002).

75. Leonard Stein, 'Memoir', in *Leonard Montefiore 1889–1961: In Memoriam* ed. by Leonard Stein and C.C. Aronsfeld (London: Vallentine Mitchell, 1964), p.13.

76. Montefiore, 'Address given to the Cambridge University Jewish Society' (see note 59), p.10.
77. Hugo Gryn with Naomi Gryn, *Chasing Shadows* (London: Penguin Books, 2001).
78. Gill, *The Journey Back from Hell* (see note 67), p.165.
79. Stein, 'Memoir' (see note 75), p.3.
80. Leonard Montefiore, 'Our Children', *Jewish Monthly*, 1.1 (April 1947), 19.
81. Leonard Montefiore, memorandum 15 October 1945 in Central British Funds committee minutes, file 9/169, CBF microfilm archives, University of Southampton.
82. Montefiore, 'Address given to the Cambridge University Jewish Society' (see note 59), p.5.
83. Ibid. p.8.
84. Montefiore, 'Our Children' (see note 80), pp.20–21.
85. See Moskovitz, *Love Despite Hate* (see note 2), passim.
86. CCCC minutes, 2 January 1946, file 198/18, CBF microfilm archives, University of Southampton.
87. In 1948 the children from Wier Courtney were transferred to Lingfield House, Isleworth. For examples of their occupations, see 'A Statement about Lingfield House', (1958?), file 200/72 in CBF microfilm archives, University of Southampton.
88. Stephany to Montefiore, 8 February 1950, provides year by year figures, file 202/151 CBF microfilm archives, University of Southampton.
89. Gilbert, *The Boys* (see note 2).
90. *The Journal of the Holocaust Survivors '45 Society*, No.34 (2010) reveals the inclusion and exclusion that occurs at a general level. It includes an article by Zdenka Oppenheimer, 'Where the Daffodils Grow' (p.58) which includes her experiences at Windermere and then Weir Courtney, Lingfield, Surrey. It also has on its last page (p.102) a photograph 'The Boys' in Windermere Autumn 1945, which contains 20 individual photographs, none of them girls.
91. See, in contrast, Dalia Offer and Lenore Weitzmann, eds., *Women in the Holocaust* (New Haven, CT: Yale University Press, 1998).
92. Dwork, *Children With a Star* (see note 56), p.256.
93. Rice, *Flying Boats* (see note 33), p.6; 'The Orphans Who Survived the Concentration Camps', BBC 1, 5 April 2010 for the use of the word 'paradise'.
94. David Hirszfeld quoted in Avery, *From Auschwitz to Ambleside* (see note 13), no page.
95. Michael Perlmutter, 'The Bonds of Windermere', *Journal of the '45 Aid Society*, 18 (December 1994), 8.
96. Central British Fund, *This is Rehabilitation* (London: Central British Fund for Jewish Relief and Rehabilitation, 1946), no page. Pamphlet located in Parkes Library, University of Southampton.
97. Montefiore memorandum, 15 October 1945 in Central British Fund council minutes, file 9/169, in CBF microfilm archives, University of Southampton.
98. Montefiore, 'Our Children' (see note 80), p.19.
99. '300 of the Nazis' Youngest Victims Here for Health: Windermere Home', *Evening Standard*, 20 August 1945. This newspaper article was filed by the Home Office. See National Archives, HO 213/1793.
100. Mais, *The English Scene Today* (see note 37), p.257.
101. *Westmorland Gazette*, 18 August 1945.
102. Davies, *A Walk Around the Lakes* (see note 29), p.123; Russell, *Looking North* (see note 10), p.54.
103. Quoted in Avery, *From Auschwitz to Ambleside* (see note 13), no page.
104. Gilbert, *The Boys* (see note 2), p.296.
105. Ben Helfgott, interview with Trevor Avery and Chris Atkins, 23 June 2008. I am very grateful to Trevor for sending me a copy of the transcript of this interview.
106. Zoe Josephs, *Survivors: Jewish Refugees in Birmingham 1933–45* (Birmingham: Meridian Books, 1988), p.179.
107. See local testimony in Avery, *From Auschwitz to Ambleside* (see note 13), no page.
108. Information related to the author by Trevor Avery.
109. Montefiore memorandum, 15 October 1945 in Central British Fund committee minutes, file 9/169 CBF microfilm archives, University of Southampton.
110. Dow and Brown, *Evacuation to Westmorland* (see note 52), p.59.
111. Tony Kushner and Aimee Bunting, conversation with Trevor Avery, 8 July 2010.

112. Joseph, *Survivors* (see note 106), p.179.
113. Perec Zylberberg, 'Recollections', diary entry 21 October 1993, copy in the possession of Tony Kushner.
114. Montefiore to Rothschild, 13 December 1950 in file 112/49, CBF microfilm archives, University of Southampton.
115. Paul Oppenheimer, *From Belsen to Buckingham Palace* (Laxton: Beth Shalom, 1996), p.191.
116. See Kushner, *The Holocaust and the Liberal Imagination* (see note 57), pp.234–5.
117. Shirley Green, *Rachman* (London: Michael Joseph, 1979). There are various Dutch documentaries on de Vries.
118. Montefiore to Anthony de Rothschild, 13 December 1950, file 112/49-50, CBF microfilm archives, University of Southampton.
119. See, for example, the reminiscences and life stories presented in the *Journal of the '45 Aid Society*.
120. Phil Kinsman, 'Landscape, Race and National Identity: The Photography of Ingrid Pollard', *Area*, 4.27 (1995), 301–2.
121. Darby, *Landscape and Identity* (see note 10), p.245.
122. John Taylor, *A Dream of England: Landscape, Photography and the Tourist's Imagination* (Manchester: Manchester University Press, 1994), p.258 and colour plates 16, 23.
123. English Heritage, 'England's Heritage – Your Heritage' (2003).
124. See the comments of Jo Little, 'Introduction: British Heritage and the Legacies of "Race"', in *The Politics of Heritage* (see note 1), pp.1–19.
125. Homa Khaleeli, 'Why Don't Black People Camp?', *Guardian*, 9 July 2010.
126. Ibid. p.29.
127. Margaret Drabble, 'Foreword', in *The Romantic Poets: William Wordsworth* (London: Guardian, 2009), p.6.
128. School notebooks in possession of Cyril Orolowitz, Cape Town, the son of Liza.
129. Douglas, *Purity and Danger* (see note 20), p.41.
130. Darby, *Landscape and Identity* (see note 10), p.87.
131. Roland Chambers, *The Last Englishman: The Double Life of Arthur Ransome* (London: Faber and Faber, 2009), p.3.
132. Darby, *Landscape and Identity* (see note 10), pp.211–12.
133. Russell Mills, introduction to Barbara Crossley, *The Triumph of Kurt Schwitters* (Ambleside: Armitt Trust, 2005), p.6. His Ambleside collage the Elterwater Merzbarn, was moved to Newcastle in 1963 and in 1970 his body was taken from Ambleside churchyard to his birth town of Hanover.
134. Massey, 'Place and their Pasts' (see note 17), p.190.
135. Naseem Khan, 'Taking Root in Britain: The Process of Shaping Heritage', in *The Politics of Heritage* (see note 1), p.134.
136. Hall, 'Whose Heritage' (see note 1), p.31.
137. Ben Helfgott, letter to Trevor Avery, 2008, in the Another Space project, 'Avenue of Exile'.
138. Vesna Maric, *Bluebird: A Memoir* (London: Granta, 2010), p.29 and passim.
139. Hugo Gryn, *A Moral and Spiritual Index* (London: Refugee Council, 1996).

SELF-REPRESENTATIONS

Assimilated, Integrated, Other: An Introduction to Jews and British Television, 1946–55

JAMES JORDAN

In an article in the *Jewish Chronicle* in March 2006, David Herman described how there had been a significant Jewish contribution to the so-called 'golden age of British television from the 1960s to the 1980s, not just in the boardroom but at every level, from behind-the-screen executives to writers, producers and actors'. Moreover, he continued, it was 'on TV, the real national theatre of post-war Britain, that Jews found their voice in British culture'.[1] While it is true that the influential writers, actors, producers and presenters named by Herman – a roll-call of figures who are now part of the British television canon including Mike Leigh, Jack Rosenthal, Arnold Wesker and Tom Stoppard – were all at the forefront of their profession in this period, it is also true that there had been a considerable Jewish presence in, influence on and contribution to post-war British television before the 1960s.[2] Indeed in the immediate post-war years Jews could be seen – although not necessarily seen as Jews by either themselves or the medium – in various shows and roles, many of which helped define British television and with it, to a degree, post-war Britain. This included people as different as band leaders Geraldo and Oscar Rabin; artistic performers ranging from Alicia Markova to Gertrude Holt and Alma Cogan; variety entertainers and comedians Cilli Wang, Harry Green and Vic Wise; and actors including Abraham Sofaer, Miriam Karlin, David Kossoff, Sid James, Yvonne Mitchell and Sydney Tafler. There were also prominent roles behind the camera for individuals such as Heads of Light Entertainment Ronald Waldman and Brian Tesler, ground-breaking drama producer Rudolph Cartier, and writers Wolf Mankowitz, Sid Colin and Dennis Norden. Finally, but no less importantly, and certainly with no less variety, there were roles for

Jewish actors playing Jewish and non-Jewish parts, and different portrayals of Jews and Jewish characters played by Jewish and non-Jewish actors.

It is perhaps surprising, therefore, that while there has been much written on the role and representation of Jews in American television and film, and on the prevailing notion of the relationship between Jews and the media more widely, there has been little academic work looking specifically at the issue of Jews in British television (and, indeed, film) more generally, either in terms of how Jews have been represented on-screen, or on the wider cultural contribution and impact of off-screen writers, producers and directors. Similarly while there have been analyses of race, gender and religion in respect of British television, these have tended to engage with the Jewish case only briefly or tangentially (if at all), and usually as part of a comparative framework. That is, while there have been many excellent studies involving Jews who have made an important contribution to television in various capacities, there has been no sustained analysis of the overall impact and depiction of Jews in British television which is comparable to the work on America such as Jonathan and Judith Pearl's *The Chosen Image: Television's Portrayal of Jewish Themes and Characters* (1998), David Zurawik's *The Jews of Prime Time* (2003), or Jeffrey Shandler's evaluation of the Holocaust on the small screen *While America Watches* (1999).[3]

This article, intended as no more than a prolegomenon, uses documentary sources to provide an overview to the variety of on-screen images of Jews and Jewish life in the first ten years of post-war television in Britain, including an introduction to television's initial engagement with the Nazi persecution of the Jews of Europe. It considers, therefore, the output of the BBC during its period of monopoly from the resumption of the Television service in June 1946, to the start of commercial broadcasting in September 1955. This was a significant period for television in Britain, a time which saw it grow from being of minority interest only – transmitted from Alexandra Palace for an average of 28 hours weekly to a potential audience of 12 million, but with, in reality, fewer than 8,000 combined sound and television licence holders – to having nationwide prominence and appeal with 50 hours of programmes per week, coverage across 95 per cent of a population of approximately 50 million, and over five million licences issued.[4] Frustratingly, this analysis of television's images seldom involves the images themselves.

As is well documented, the majority of the BBC's television programmes of this period were broadcast live and never recorded, or if they were recorded then they have long since been destroyed or wiped. But although the images themselves are now lost, from the surviving documentation it is possible to make what appear to be reasonable assumptions as to the diversity of the depictions seen across those ten years. They included images of assimilated Jews whose Jewish identity could remain unreferenced, alongside programmes which highlighted Jewishness, challenged prejudice and celebrated integration as well as programmes which appear to have replicated the anti-Semitic stereotypes and image of 'the Jew' seen in cinema, stage and literature.

In the absence of the images, the methodology employed in this introductory piece is largely one of archaeology, uncovering and reconstructing the broadcast programmes from the documents held at the BBC's Written Archives Centre (WAC) in Caversham.[5] These documents include scripts, policy papers, personnel files and individual production folders for separate programmes, as well as correspondence, newspaper clippings and the BBC's own internal Viewer (later Audience) Research Reports, all of which provide additional information about those now lost programmes, their institutional context and reception. When considered alone, some of the more complete production files give a sense of the various ways in which characters were to be depicted and how decisions were reached; when used in conjunction with press cuttings, audience research and the BBC's own correspondence with both individuals and representative bodies of Anglo-Jewry such as the Anglo-Jewish Association or the Board of Deputies of British Jews, they provide a snapshot of the racial, religious and cultural tensions which could exist in post-war Britain.

In producing even this basic summary of BBC television's images of Jews and Jewish life, one is confronted with the question of definitions. As Gavin Schaffer's and Didi Herman's contributions to this collection make clear, the answer to the question of what makes someone a Jew or Jewish remains contentious, and for some unresolved. In order to circumvent this question, this article takes as its starting point the BBC's Central Registry index cards held at the WAC. The record cards catalogue chronologically by theme and period the output of both radio and television. For the years 1946–55 they record nine television programmes on the subject of 'Jews':

JEWS

10.12.50	For the Children: 'Chanukah' – A re-enaction of the Jewish Festival of Dedication.
17.12.52	Film: Tomorrow is a Wonderful Day.
17.9.53	For the Children: The Fish and the Angel. (Vivian Milroy) Play covers quite a long period of Jewish history.
26.9.53	David Kossoff: A programme of Jewish Folk Humour.
23.11.53	Programme for Deaf Children: Fr. the Residential School for Jewish Deaf Children.
6.5.54	About the Home. Jewish Cookery. Evelyn Rose showed how to make cheese blintzes.
19.8.54	About the Home: Evelyn Rose demonstrated the way to make Holishkes and Lokshen pudding.
12.1.55	Panorama, no.7. Sholom Aleichem. Two excerpts from one of the Jewish plays from the Embassy.
18.1.55	Lies my Father told me. About Jews.[6]

These nine programmes – four made by the Talks Department, three for Children's Television, one an imported film from Israel, and one a Drama production about Canadian Jewry – demonstrate both the diversity of the BBC's programmes and the versatility of the taxonomy of 'Jews'. For example, although both programmes were produced by the Talks Department, Evelyn Rose's demonstrations of Jewish cookery for *About the Home* (tx. 6 May and 19 August 1954), were markedly different in content and form to actor David Kossoff's performance the previous year (tx. 26 September 1953), in which he had delivered a 15-minute monologue of Jewish folk humour in the guise of an old Jewish tailor. And both would appear to have little in common with the other Talks programme listed above, an episode of the current affairs programme *Panorama* (tx. 12 January 1955), which included a live performance of excerpts from Wolf Mankowitz's *The World of Sholom Aleichem*.[7] Yet beyond the obvious differences, all three, indeed all nine programmes in the list, were engaging television's predominantly non-Jewish audience with Jewish life, traditions and culture, giving some, as *The Jewish Chronicle* noted in respect of Kossoff's one-man show, 'their first taste of the richness, warmth and simplicity of Jewish folk humour'.[8]

A similar comparison can be made between the two programmes broadcast as part of the afternoon slot *For the Children*. In the first of these, 'Chanukah' (tx. 10 December 1950), Jewish life in Britain was again the focus, this time through the 're-enaction of the Jewish

Festival of Dedication' as demonstrated by three generations of the Goldbloom family. Led by the Reverend J.K. Goldbloom, the founder of the Redman's Road Talmud Torah and noted Zionist, the programme concluded, according to the production file, with the grandchildren singing *Hatikvah*.[9] By contrast, the second programme, 'The Fish and the Angel' (tx. 17 September 1953), was a Biblical play which told the story of 'the journey and marriage of Tobias ... [as] taken directly from The Apocrypha'.[10] Although this did indeed cover 'quite a long period of Jewish history', it was not seen in the production files as a programme about Jews, but rather about Christian scripture, so much so that instructions were issued for it to be recorded for use in case of 'a national emergency, such as national mourning'.[11] Differences between the two programmes were also evident in the BBC's Audience Research Reports. First set up in January 1950, the BBC's Audience Research section compiled reports on programmes which were based on the findings of a panel of viewers who 'kept records of the extent to which their sets were used and expressed their opinions of the programmes they watched'.[12] According to the reports for these two programmes, 'The Fish and the Angel' was 'very enjoyable and absorbing', with the report noting that parents in particular 'approved the Biblical theme, and said that television was an excellent medium for the teaching of scripture to young children'.[13] 'Chanukah', however, was less successful:

> [This programme was] beyond the comprehension of children and heavy going for adults ... there was so much Yiddish spoken that it was difficult to understand and most [viewers] appeared to feel that the programme's potential interest was really limited to Jewish viewers and that, for others, it was merely tedious and boring.[14]

A more detailed look at the BBC's Research Reports for the other programmes on the list (where reports exist) suggests that such a response was not unusual for programmes which engaged with the Jewish faith or included the use of Yiddish or Hebrew. There was, for example, an evident dissatisfaction with *Lies My Father Told Me* (tx. 18 January 1955), Ted Allan's play about religious/secular tensions across three generations of a Montreal Jewish family. While this was admittedly in part because the production was poor (even the supportive *Jewish Chronicle* called it 'a slow-moving, rambling piece'[15]), the majority of viewers who 'actively disliked' the production did so because they 'were inclined to dismiss the play as "something deep about spiritual training" that ... carried neither interest nor conviction. Lack of sympathy for Jewish problems – particularly religious ones – was the main reason for this dissatisfaction'.[16]

The paucity of television broadcasts on the BBC's index cards, a dearth especially notable when compared with the wealth of radio material, is not an indication of a lack of interest in 'Jews', but rather a reflection of the limits of television and the BBC's own indexing.[17] By that I mean that the other documents at the WAC show that Evelyn Rose appeared in *About the Home* on more than two occasions, and similarly there was more than one broadcast of Programmes for Deaf Children which came from the Wandsworth Residential School for Jewish Deaf Children.[18] In fact an examination of the *Radio Times* and the *Jewish Chronicle* reveals that television produced many more programmes '[a]bout Jews'. There were, for example, programmes which featured prominent British Jews, including Basil Henriques in *The Course of Justice* (tx. 1950 and 1953), introducing the work of the Juvenile Court, the Magistrate's Court and the Assizes; Lord Samuel being interviewed by David Butler on the life of a cabinet minister for *Men of Authority* (tx. 29 November 1950); and *Bless 'Em All* (tx. 9 May 1955), a celebration of the tenth anniversary of VE day, in which Lady Henriques and members of various children's clubs portrayed life in an air-raid shelter.

There were also a number of Drama productions which, the surviving documentation suggests, featured Jews in ways both positive and negative. It is widely recognised that early television drama tended to produce for the small screen plays which had already been successful on the stage. It is perhaps no surprise therefore that television retold stories which appear to have contained familiar images of 'the Jew' such as the Jewish pawnbroker/antique dealer (*The Shop on Sly Corner* (tx. 8 April 1948 and 22 November 1953), *The Angel who Pawned her Harp* (tx. 26 November 1951), or *The Brown Man's Servant* (tx. 3 August 1953)), or turned to Shylock in *The Merchant of Venice* (tx. 1 July 1947 and 13 May 1955), or the legendary figure of *The Wandering Jew* in Michael Barry's version of the play by E. Temple Thurston (tx. 30 January 1947).[19] Of course in the absence of recordings of the programmes themselves, it is impossible to be certain as to what they showed, but in some cases it is possible to make reasonable judgements based upon how these programmes were received by the audience. Some, for example, generated a good deal of correspondence between the BBC and Anglo-Jewry as represented by either the Anglo-Jewish Association or the Board of Deputies of British Jews. One such programme was broadcast on the evening of 7 March 1949, when in an episode of Robert Barr's documentary series *London After Dark* (a series which demonstrated how Scotland Yard combated crime), two men were seen plotting to steal from a hosiery warehouse. According to a letter of complaint sent a few days later to the BBC by Sidney Solomon, the Board of Deputies' Executive and Press Officer, both of these men were 'made up to have a Semitic appearance'. Moreover they

> break into a warehouse owned by a Mr Mendel, again a completely unnecessary Jewish name, kill the night watchman and steal the stockings. The description given out by the Yard of the wanted men is that of having long noses, dark hair and pale complexions.
>
> The Jewish community has had to tolerate a good deal of ill-informed and prejudiced allegations as to the part its members are supposed to play in the black market. These allegations have been shown time after time to be grossly exaggerated, but nobody has yet dared to suggest that in crimes of violence Jews play anything but an infinitesimal part. The impression given by this programme was, obviously, that here we have Jewish criminals, committing the crime of murder, stealing from a Jewish warehouse and monopolising the time of the police, not only in pursuing Jewish criminals but in guarding Jewish property.

It was, Salomon concluded, 'a stupid and vicious piece of anti-Semitic propaganda'.[20]

The BBC's reply confirmed to Salomon that, as far as they were concerned, 'there was absolutely no anti-Semitic slant to the programme', the actors playing the roles of the criminals were Londoners, neither were Jews, and there was 'no question of their being made up to have a Semitic appearance'.[21] 'As I have assured you on previous occasions', concluded M.G. Farquharson, director of the BBC secretariat, 'any such intention would be repugnant to the BBC.'[22] At the same time as replying to Salomon, Farquharson, possibly aware of the sensitivity of the issue, copied his reply to Norman Collins, the Controller of Television. 'Although [Salomon] writes in violent terms', begins Farquharson in his covering letter,

I know that this is because he is pushed on from behind by people who are in a very sensitive state of mind, and who get very worked up indeed by any appearance of anti-Semitism in our programmes. ... Mr Salomon is a very sensible man and I think it is important that he should remain satisfied that people in positions of control here would genuinely dislike and reject any forms of anti-Semitism.[23]

Although there were regular complaints from Anglo-Jewish bodies about such depictions, in some respects the more problematic plays were in fact the annual Passion plays which could portray Jews collectively as a bloodthirsty mob, and individually as manipulative and untrustworthy schemers. 'How can inter-faith relations be advanced', asked the *Jewish Chronicle* in response to the 1954 version of *Caesar's Friend* (tx. 11 April 1954), 'when millions of viewers see Caiaphas and other Jewish priests depicted as bigoted, sinister, gloating plotters who blackmail Pilate.'[24] Less problematic were the historical dramas which presented other, often more nuanced examples of Jewish life and Jewish/non-Jewish relations, including W.P. Lipscomb's *The Man with a Cloak Full of Holes* (tx. 20 August 1946) in which Abraham Sofaer portrayed Luis Santangel, Chancellor of the Court of Aragon and a baptised Jew; and *Portrait of Rembrandt* (tx. 22 April 1952), a re-telling of the artist's life featuring the Jewish quarter of seventeenth century Amsterdam and starred Martin Miller as Rabbi Manasseh ben Israel with Maurice Bannister as 'a rather Cockney street trader'.[25] There were also a number of modern plays written by Jewish authors that looked to the future rather than the past. Plays such as Sylvia Regan's *The Golden Door* (tx. 3 April 1951) in which American and Jewish life converged in the story of the Feldermans, an immigrant family learning to adjust to their new life in New York; or the extremely popular first post-war version of Elmer Rice's *Counsellor at Law* (tx. 4 February 1951), the story of George Simon (again played by Abraham Sofaer), the Jewish boy from the East Side who fights his way up to become one of New York's leading lawyers.[26] There were also dramas set in the East End such as *The Same Sky* (tx. 10 August 1952), Yvonne Mitchell's take on the tragedy of Romeo and Juliet which confronted Jewish and non-Jewish prejudice in a play which proved popular with all audiences, even if a 'few [viewers] were embarrassed by the choice of such a controversial subject – the racial antagonism between Gentile and Jew'.[27]

Less popular but no less significant was Wolf Mankowitz's ghost-story *The Bespoke Overcoat* (tx. 17 February 1954, remade the following year as a film by Jack Clayton), one of the most striking of post-war dramas starring Alfie Bass and David Kossoff as the two friends Fender and Morry.[28] Jewish tradition and culture were depicted in another story with a ghostly theme in one of the most remarkable BBC plays of the period, an English language version of Ansky's *The Dybbuk* (tx. 21 October 1952). This was the first post-war production to bring nineteenth century *shtetl* life to the British television screen. Using a predominantly Jewish cast and where possible authentic costume, the play was both criticised and praised in equal measure by the mainstream press, with one viewer for the BBC's internal Audience Research Report being clear in their dislike of this production:

> This might have had some significance for members of the Jewish communities but I am sure for the ordinary viewer it was pointless and afforded no relaxation in a dreary evening's television. There are surely plenty of good English dramatists without resorting to this type of hocus-pocus![29]

The Dybbuk's producer, the Austrian-Jewish émigré Rudolph Cartier, was one of the key figures of post-war British drama. He had arrived in the UK in 1935 having left Germany soon after the rise of Hitler and was a staff producer at the BBC from 1952 until his retirement in 1969. Across this long career he regularly produced programmes which confronted totalitarianism, often making reference to the Nazi persecution of the Jews of Europe. He was not alone in this. Analysis of Britain's post-war cultural relationship with the Holocaust seldom looks to television, and when it does the incorrect assumption tends to be that 1945–61 saw no engagement with the subject. This is because of several factors: an ignorance of television's output, in part because of the lack of surviving copies of the programmes themselves; a paradoxical reluctance on behalf of British scholars of the Holocaust to consider television as a serious medium even though it is often cited as being responsible for key moments in the furthering of interest in the Holocaust through such productions as *The Warsaw Ghetto* (BBC, tx. 18 November 1965) and the mini-series *Holocaust* (BBC 1, tx. 3–6 September 1978); and finally because of the prevailing notion held more widely that the 1940s and 1950s more generally was a period in which the Holocaust was absent from academic and cultural discussions. For example,

David Cesarani, in his book *Justice Delayed* (1992) writes of a 'silence ... [which] descended over the history of the genocidal campaign against the Jews of Europe' in Britain in the immediate post-war years.[30] Similarly, in his section on Great Britain in David Wyman's collection of essays, *The World Reacts to the Holocaust*, Cesarani describes how the Holocaust 'only began to register in British novels, poetry and drama in the 1980s. ... Theatre, film and television turned to the Holocaust as a subject somewhat later'.[31] However, as Cesarani's own article in this collection attests, it has been increasingly recognised that this blanket assessment does not stand up to scrutiny, and that while the concept of 'the Holocaust' did not exist in the 1940s–50s, the Nazis' treatment of the Jews was far from ignored. It may not have been understood or recognised, but it was there. In respect of British television, and television drama in particular, it had in fact been present, albeit mainly allegorically, as early as May 1949 when the BBC produced a version of Irwin Shaw's *The Gentle People* (tx. 17 May 1949).[32] This reunited the 1940 London cast of Abraham Sofaer and Ernest Jay as the two old friends, Jonah Goodman and Philip Anagnos, whose peaceful lives are threatened by the actions of a local gangster, Harold Goff (Robert Ayres). What should they do? Act or accept their fate? The dilemma of the play was, as Lionel Hale summarised in the *Radio Times*, the dilemma of the two men: 'Jonah is for action, Philip for submission. To appease or not to appease?' In the play's denouement, in a move which was originally intended as a warning against acquiescence to Hitler, but had added resonance by 1949, the two friends kill Goff. As Hale concluded, the play's message remained clear for a post-war audience: 'the meek shall inherit the earth – but only if they know when to abandon their meekness'.[33]

Over the next six years a succession of plays dealt with the murder of European Jewry in a number of different ways. These included Jan de Hartog's *Skipper Next to God* (tx. 7 October 1951), the story of one man's efforts to land safely in America his 'cargo' of 146 German Jewish refugees in the last years of the 1930s; and *Almost Glory* (tx. 3 May 1953), which focused on a Polish Jew's experiences as a slave labourer, including being forced by the Nazis to build roads using Jewish gravestones.[34] Tackling issues closer to home and depicting what life could be like for a Jewish refugee living in Britain, Wynyard Browne's *Dark Summer* (tx. 4 September 1951) tackled British anti-Jewish prejudice in its tale of an Austrian-Jewish refugee from Hitler who acted as a nursemaid for a British officer blinded by the war.[35] A few years afterwards *Stolen Waters* (tx. 21 March 1954) involved the convoluted tale of a Jewish man 'masquerading, even to his wife, as an English Gentile' who stands to inherit a fortune as long as he makes public the fact that 'he was born a Jew'.[36] The play ended with the revelation that the promised inheritance had already been used to assist Jewish victims of the Nazis.[37]

Less directly, traces of the Holocaust could also be detected in documentaries and docudramas which examined the plight of displaced persons across Europe: Norman Swallow's *I Was a Stranger* (tx. 12 September 1951); *Special Enquiry. No.1: Refugees* (tx. 31 July 1953); and *The World is Ours. No. 4: The Waiting People* (tx. 8 October 1954). The plight of the Jews of Europe was also referenced in some more unusual ways, such as the episode of *Designed for Women* (tx. 8 March 1951), in which, amid discussions of spring hats, gardening and shopping, Joan Gilbert interviewed Ida and Louise Cook who recounted their 'unusual personal adventure story', telling how they had 'used their interest in continental opera productions to cloak their work for getting refugees out of the power of the Nazis'.[38] Similarly, an episode of the popular *Saturday-Night Story*, entitled 'The Long Road' (tx. 23 February 1952), featured regular host and noted story-teller John Slater recounting his search for the daughter of a friend who had been killed by the Nazis. He spoke of his friend's disappearance, of visiting 'Haifa [and] struggling up the slopes of Mount Carmel', and finally of how he 'could hear [his friend and the other dead] in the autumn rustle of bones in Belsen, see them in the trodden grey ash round the furnaces, feel them in the dead air – but they were gone'.[39]

Belsen was also present in documentary films and serials which made use of the images of liberation, most notably two seminal serials (one American and one British) which commemorated the war: NBC's celebration of the American Navy *Victory at Sea* (Episode 26, 'Design for Peace' (tx. 4 May 1953)), and the BBC's *War in the Air* (Episode 12, 'The Cold Dawn' (tx. 24 January 1955)), a survey of the RAF which was commissioned as a direct response to *Victory at Sea*.[40] In the latter, the still powerful and fresh images of liberation were accompanied by a narration from Richard Dimbleby, a man deeply associated with Belsen in popular British memory: 'Every man keeps a private memory of war and mine is this – the concentration camp at Belsen; the proud criminal of a man called Kramer. Belsen, a place of agony with the stench of death.'[41]

Furthermore early television could also provoke engagement with the murder of the Jews of Europe even when not directly addressing the subject on-screen. An episode of the discussion programme *Viewfinder* (tx. 10 November 1954) saw Aidan Crawley interviewing Field Marshal Albert Kesselring, a decision which was condemned by Willi Frischauer writing in *Reynolds News* four days later:

> The campaign for the complete rehabilitation of the old Wehrmacht, including Himmler's SS men, is only just beginning. German history is being hurriedly re-written and the result reads remarkably like one of the late Dr Goebbels's more audacious efforts. There was, it is now said, nothing really wrong with the Nazis. They may have gone a little too far on the Jewish question. Otherwise they were simply premature anti-Communists. ... They were efficient! Why, one single SS extermination unit in the Ukraine managed to kill and bury 96000 Ukrainians and Jews smoothly and without a hitch in less than a month. ... Kesselring, most honoured war criminal, is allowed to spit on the graves of six million people who were murdered by the SS, and probably thinks that they would have won the war in the West if they had not been so busy exterminating in the East.

Finally, the legacy of liberation and the Holocaust were also being referenced in a number of broadcasts which focused on Israel, including one of the most controversial of all productions of this period, *The Prisoner* (tx. 19 February 1952). Written by actor Andrew Cruickshank, *The Prisoner* was a one-off drama about the Arab–Israeli conflict and the first television play to be set in the modern state of Israel. It depicted the story of the Israeli army's pursuit of Helga Baumer (Elizabeth Sellars), a fugitive suspected of murdering the Israeli security minister, Spiegelmann (who is never seen on-screen). In a complicated plot told in retrospect, it transpires that Spiegelmann had been a Nazi in pre-war Germany until being forced to flee after once it was discovered that his mother was Jewish. This was but one of many contentious plot issues which led to the *Jewish Chronicle* calling it a production 'likely to arouse much anti-semitic feeling' and to give an impression of Israelis as 'a cruel, ultra-nationalist people with expansionist ideas'.[42] The BBC's documents record the subsequent complaints and efforts to resolve the controversy, ending with a meeting between Michael Barry, telvision's Head of Drama, and Michael Arnon, the Israeli Legation's Press Attaché in London. To resolve the dispute Arnon requested that 'a more constructive view of his people and their endeavours ... be shown to counter-act' the damage done by *The Prisoner*. Although there is no direct evidence to this effect, it seems reasonable to conclude that this was one of the reasons behind the screening later that year of *Tomorrow's a Wonderful Day* (aka *Adamah*, Israel, dir. Helmar Lerski, 1948; tx. 17 December 1952), one of the nine programmes on the BBC's index cards, and the first showing in Britain of a film produced in Israel.[43] Images of Israel were used in a more complex way in episode three of *Men Seeking God* (tx. 10 May 1954), a six part series which explored 'other men's faiths ... through the eyes of a devout believer'. In this programme, MP Christopher Mayhew presented a view of Judaism through the eyes of a believer in Israel (Rabbi Jacob Herzog, son of the Chief Rabbi in Jerusalem) and Britain (Rev. Isaac Levy, Senior Jewish Chaplain to HM Forces and minister of Hampstead Synagogue). A live studio interview with Levy was complemented with a number of pre-filmed sequences which showed Jewish life and religious practice in London and Israel. Those pre-filmed montages – the only parts of the programme to survive in the BBC's archives – included images of Levy's home and Hampstead Synagogue, footage of Jewish refugees arriving for the first time in the new state of Israel, and the Ghetto Fighters House Museum in Israel. For the latter, a panning shot of the museum's interior showed a camp uniform displayed as an artefact, a survivor walking across the museum's floor, and an information board which gave a breakdown of the number of Jewish dead and a total figure of 6,246,500.[44] The closing shot focused on the museum's founder Miriam Novitch as she displayed to the camera a selection of musical instruments which had been made by the Germans out of scrolls.

There was, therefore, a wide variety of Jewish identities to be found in post-war British television, and in fact from 1946 to 1955 the BBC produced far more programmes about 'Jews' than the nine listed in the WAC's index cards. Indeed there are far more than those given above and this is in no way meant as a complete list. Rather it is intended as an introduction to the number of different ways in which Jews were seen on British television in the post-war period, and to illustrate the richness of both television and the BBC's archives for scholars of British Jewish studies. It demonstrates the need for a more detailed survey of the BBC's output in this largely forgotten period of broadcasting, one which will seek to place the cultural meaning within a wider context. Such a project holds many challenges. Should, for example, the Jewish case be understood in isolation? If not, then should this analysis compare the British case with that seen in America, across Europe, or in other parts of the world where the BBC was operating? Should the discussion of television be traced first back through the BBC's radio output? Or should comparisons be drawn not with different media or different countries, but rather in the experiences of other minority groups in Britain? Or perhaps, adding further complications still, a larger study should begin by making a comparison within television itself. From 1946 to 1955 Television changed beyond recognition, moving from the minority to the mainstream. Did this change bring with it a change in the types of programmes being shown? Is television in the immediate post-war period in fact far more sympathetic to Jewish issues than it would be in later years precisely because in that early period television was only of esoteric interest?

ACKNOWLEDGEMENT

I am grateful to Hannah Ewence and Tony Kushner for their comments on earlier drafts of this paper.

NOTES

1. David Herman, 'Great Channel Swimmers', *Jewish Chronicle*, 3 March 2006, p.27.
2. In fact one could argue that this influence went back as far as 1936 and the opening day of the BBC's regular television when Hyam 'Bumps' Greenbaum conducted the BBC Television Orchestra. For one of the few summaries of the importance of Jews to the early BBC, see Martin Jolles, 'Jews and the BBC (1922–1953)', *JHSE Newsletter*, 10 (May 2004), 3–4.
3. Jonathan Pearl and Judith Pearl, *The Chosen Image: Television's Portrayal of Jewish Themes and Characters* (Jefferson, NC: McFarland, 1998); David Zurawik, *The Jews of Prime Time* (Hanover, NH: Brandeis University Press, 2003); or Jeffrey Shandler's evaluation of the Holocaust, *While America Watches: Televising the Holocaust* (Oxford: Oxford University Press, 1999).
4. For a breakdown of licence figures and transmission coverage see *BBC Annual Report 1946–1947* (London: HMSO, 1947) to *BBC Annual Report 1955–1956* (London: HMSO, 1956), passim. The definitive guide to the BBC's introduction of television remains Asa Briggs, *The History of Broadcasting in the United Kingdom. Volume IV: Sound and Vision* (Oxford: Oxford University Press, 1979).
5. The documents are extensive, but not complete and for that reason some of the programmes discussed do not have BBC WAC production folders or references. For an excellent introduction to the challenges of researching early television see Jason Jacobs, *The Intimate Screen: Early British Television Drama* (Oxford: Oxford University Press, 2000), pp.1–24 *passim*. For a more general introduction to the lost programmes see Dick Fiddy, *Missing, Believed Wiped: Searching for the Lost Treasures of British Television* (London:

British Film Institute, 2001).

6. The production file references (where kept) for these programmes are BBC WAC T2/29 *Children's TV: Chanukah*; BBC WAC T6/55 *TV Films: Youth Aliyah Movement*; BBC WAC T2/48 *Children's TV: The Fish and the Angel*; BBC WAC T32/122 *TV Talks: David Kossoff*; BBC WAC T2/37 *Children's TV: Programmes for the Deaf*; BBC WAC T32/1 *TV Talks: About the Home*; and BBC WAC T32/266 *TV Talks: Panorama* and BBC WAC T32/1193 *TV Talks: Panorama*, January 1955. There are also entries in the index cards for 'Religion – Jewish', 'Religion – Hebrew', 'Israel' and 'Palestine', but these are not cross-referenced with the entries for 'Jews'.

7. This featured an excerpt from the play's third part, 'The High School'. Introduced by David Kossoff, the small cast consisted of Miriam Karlin, Meier Tzelniker, David and Jeremy Spenser. As Head of Drama Michael Barry wrote to *Panorama* editor Michael Barsley, 6 December 1954, '[*Sholom Aleichem*] is a most unusual play that has had overwhelming success in New York and is by way of being a Jewish classic. ... It will be a theatrical event worth commenting upon'. BBC WAC T32/266 *TVTalks: Panorama*.

8. *Jewish Chronicle*, 2 October 1953, p.23.

9. Undated press release prepared by Cecil Madden, Acting Head of Children's Television, BBC WAC T2/29 Children's Programmes: *Chanukah*.

10. Writer Vivian Milroy to Assistant Head of Copyright, 24 August 1953, BBC WAC T2/48 Children's TV: *The Fish and the Angel*. The story of Tobias was familiar to adult viewers through the pre- and post-war versions of James Bridie's play *Tobias and the Angel* (tx. 1 May 1938, rpt. 6 May 1938, and 28 September 1947). For more on these productions see BBC WAC T5/533 TV Drama: *Tobias and the Angel*.

11. Memo R.G. Walford, Assistant Head of Copyright, to Milroy, 26 August 1953, BBC WAC T2/48.

12. *BBC Annual Report 1950–1951* (London: HMSO, 1951), p.29. See also Robert Silvey, *Who's Listening? The Story of BBC Audience Research* (London: Allen & Unwin, 1974).

13. BBC WAC VR/53/468 'The Fish and the Angel'.

14. BBC WAC VR/50/511: 'Chanukah'. It seems unlikely that the programme contained the wide use of Yiddish (as opposed to Hebrew) as is claimed here. Such comments are in themselves a reflection of the distance between the Jewish and non-Jewish audiences and illustrate the interesting material which the WAC can provide.

15. *Jewish Chronicle*, 21 January 1955, p.28.

16. See report BBC WAC VR/55/33 *Lies My Father Told Me* in BBC WAC R9/7/13 Audience Research Reports, January–February 1955.

17. The records for radio consist of 12 cards referencing 76 programmes, including such interesting items as Martin Buber speaking in 1947 on 'The Special Way: Study of the Jewish mystic sect Chassidim' (Third Programme, 10 August 1947), Godfrey Talbot's series of reports from Hamburg a month later which told of the arrival at the German port of the *Exodus 1947* (Home Service, 8–9 September 1947), and Christopher Sykes' 1951 programme 'Spes Israelis – A Study of Cromwell's Readmission of the Jews in 1655' (Third Programme, 9 September 1951).

18. Evelyn Rose was also scheduled to appear on 3 June 1954 and 9 December 1954 demonstrating how to make butter sponge, potato latkes and potato kegel. For the recipe for the latter see *Radio Times*, 3 December 1954, p.38.

19. See BBC WAC T5/465 *The Shop at Sly Corner* and BBC WAC T5/328 *The Merchant of Venice*.

20. Sidney Salomon to M.G. Farquharson, 10 March 1949 in BBC WAC R41/19/2 Programme Correspondence Section: Board of Deputies, 1949–54.

21. Kathleen Haacke to DS (M.G. Farquharson, Director of Secretariat), 15 March 1949, BBC WAC R41/19/2.

22. Farquharson to Salomon, 17 March 1949, BBC WAC R41/19/2.

23. Farquharson to CTel (Norman Collins), 18 March 1949, BBC WAC R41/19/2.

24. *Jewish Chronicle*, 23 April 1954. Other Easter programmes included *Good Friday* (tx. 26 March 1948 and 7 April 1950), *A Man's House* (tx. 15 April 1949; see BBC WAC T5/309), *Spark in Judea* (tx. 5 April 1953; BBC WAC T5/486) and *Family Portrait* (tx. 10 April 1955). For more on *Caesar's Friend* see BBC WAC T5/74.

25. *Jewish Chronicle*, 25 April 1952, p.22.

26. The 1951 version earned an outstanding reaction index of 91 (out of 100) on the Audience Reaction Report and was considered 'the ideal type of play, superb in every respect' and 'the best we have ever seen on Television'. See BBC WAC VR/51/53 Counsellor at Law.

27. BBC WAC VR/52/355 *The Same Sky* in BBC WAC T5/488 TV Drama: *The Same Sky*.

28. *Bespoke Overcoat* was largely unpopular because it was considered slow-moving and depressing rather than because of any explicit anti-Jewish displeasure.

29. BBC WAC Audience Research VR/52/474: *The Dybbuk*. See James Jordan, '"What we have gained is more than that small loss": Rudolph Cartier and *The Dybbuk*', *Jewish Culture and History*, 11.1–2 (2009), 156–172.

30. David Cesarani, *Justice Delayed* (London: Mandarin, 1992), p.177.

31. David Cesarani, 'Great Britain', in *The World Reacts to the Holocaust* ed. by David Wyman (Baltimore: The Johns Hopkins University Press, 1996), pp.599–641 (p.627).

32. See BBC WAC T5/205 TV Drama: *The Gentle People*.

33. Lionel Hale, *Radio Times*, 13 May 1949, p.29.

34. BBC WAC T5/475 TV Drama: *Skipper Next to God*.

35. *Jewish Chronicle*, 7 September 1951, p.22.

36. *Daily Telegraph*, 22 March 1954.

37. *Jewish Chronicle*, 26 March 1954, p.26.

38. *Birmingham Post*, 15 March 1951. See Ida Cook, *Safe Passage* (London: MIRA, 2008). First published as *We Followed Our Stars* (London: Mills and Boon, 1950).

39. BBC WAC T32/125 TV Talks *Designed for Women*; and T32/301 TV Talks *Saturday Night-Story*. For a draft copy of Slater's script see BBC WAC TVArt1 John Slater, 1946–56.

40. American films shown on television also featured the liberation of the camps. *The True Glory* (USA, dir. Carol Reed and Garson Kanin, 1945; tx. 17 December 1950 and 3 September 1954), the winner of the 1946 Academy Award for best documentary, used these images partly to represent Nazi depravity, but primarily as a symbol of victory and freedom, linking liberation with the return home of American troops. In *Three, Two, One – Zero!* (tx. 11 November 1954), an NBC produced documentary which warned of the potential dangers of atomic power, comparisons were made between the depravity of the camps and the horrors of Hiroshima and Nagasaki.

41. BBC WAC T6/295 TV Films *War in the Air*.

42. *Jewish Chronicle*, 22 February 1952, p.16. BBC WAC VR/52/70: *The Prisoner*, 7 March 1952. For the production details see BBC WAC T5/TV Drama: *The Prisoner*. There were also 41 criticisms made directly to the BBC complaining that the play was 'anti-Semitic'. See BBC WAC R41/211 Programme Correspondence Section: TV Memos, 1952–54.

43. This moving film celebrated the Youth Aliyah movement through the fictional story of the teenager Benjamin, a former concentration camp inmate making his new home in Israel. For a summary see http://www.cine-holocaust.de/cgi-bin/gdq?efw00fbw 000299.gd. The film itself can be viewed online at http://www.youtube. com/watch?v=9iXkhML3MHk courtesy of the Spielberg Jewish Film Archive. For more on the BBC's screening see BBC WAC T6/55 TV Films: *Children and the Youth Aliyah Committee*.

44. The total figure is illegible on screen but is given in BBC WAC T32/253/10 *Men Seeking God: Judaism*.

Displaced, Dysfunctional and Divided: British-Jewish Writing Today

RUTH GILBERT

I was an English Jew – that was my dysfunction.[1]

In 2003 Bryan Cheyette noted that 'there exists a commonplace perception, despite a good deal of evidence to the contrary, that Jewish writers in Britain do not exist'.[2] But the situation is changing. Jewish writing has long been a powerful strand of British cultural life and, in recent years, I would argue, it has gained a new momentum. In fiction, memoirs and journalism, writers are addressing increasingly challenging questions about what it means to be both British and Jewish in the twenty-first century. This article will explore the ways in which these questions are debated within a range of contemporary Jewish literature.

British-Jewish writers today are shaking off a culture of reticence and self-censorship born of anxiety and embarrassment, which arguably inhibited previous generations of Anglo-Jewry. From Jeremy Gavron's experimental literary fiction to more popular texts such as Giles Coren's *Winkler* or Charlotte Mendleson's *When We Were Bad* which was shortlisted for the Orange Prize in 2008, British-Jewishness is being represented in diverse ways in contemporary writing.[3] Indeed, Donald Weber has recently suggested that this current wave of new Jewish writing in Britain might represent the 'flowering' of 'an Anglo-Jewish literary "revival"'.[4] He argued that 'Anglo-Jewish writers … are getting mouthy, raising their Jewish voices unabashedly – and in public'. Weber cites as further evidence of this 'revival' cultural events such as Jewish Book Week, The Jewish Film Festival and the high profile given to new writers such as Naomi Alderman (winner of the Orange Prize in 2006).[5]

Moreover, established writers who have not previously foregrounded their Jewishness, such as Mike Leigh, are now engaging more explicitly with Jewish themes. Commenting on a 'new world in which we [Jews] are another ethnic, cultural faction', Leigh notes that, 'some of us are old enough to remember what it was like when you didn't say you were Jewish'.[6] His play about the complexities of contemporary Jewish family life, *Two Thousand Years*, sold out within days at the National Theatre in 2005. Linda Grant, writing about the play, coins the term 'shouty Jews' to describe both the play and some of the responses she witnessed to it.[7]

However, there is another side to this, as Weber terms it, 'stunning burst of productivity' in British-Jewish literature. Perhaps it is a little premature to hail a new wave of British-Jewish writing based on the emergence of a handful of potentially invigorating writers. In autumn 2006, David Herman, writing in *The Jewish Chronicle*, bemoaned the 'apparent absence of Jewish novelists in the highest echelons of contemporary fiction'.[8] His complaint focused on the dearth of British-Jewish writers included in short-lists of major literary prizes and in particular a poll in *The Observer* Sunday newspaper charting the most significant novels of the last 25 years. This kind of article in many ways perpetuates a tone of debate that is familiar and not entirely helpful; that is, Jews are endlessly marginalised. But it signals a need for caution: whilst celebrating the vibrancy of British-Jewish culture at present, we might also have to acknowledge the ambivalent attitudes towards Jewishness which are deeply engrained within British culture.

On the one hand we have what seems to be a glittering explosion in British-Jewish writing, a new confidence; but, on the other hand, a lingering sense of exclusion from the mainstream of British life. Certainly, the situation today is complicated. Whilst Jews have for a number of years been viewed as providing a model for successful assimilation into British life it is also true that anti-Semitism still surfaces in some more or less subtle ways and that anti-Semitic attacks are reportedly rising.[9] Clearly world politics, and most notably the Israel–Palestine situation, significantly impact on attitudes towards Jews in Britain. Moreover, given the fraught debates about religious and ethnic identities that are so unsettling Britain at the moment, representations of Jewishness are more charged than they have been for a number of years. But this seemingly contradictory picture is not necessarily an inhibiting or creatively constricting issue. Central to the work of contemporary British-Jewish writers is the profound ambiguity about Jews that can be traced back throughout the history of Anglo-Jewry. It produces a rich generative tension that is not always comfortable or easy to digest. And this is the point. It is what gives this writing edge.

This paradox is perhaps best exemplified in discussions about the status given to the work of Manchester born Jewish novelist, Howard Jacobson. Jacobson's widely reviewed and highly publicised novel *Kalooki Nights* won the 2007 *Jewish Quarterly* Wingate Literary Prize but failed to make the Man Booker shortlist. Jacobson's novel presents an uncompromising, robust and deliberately challenging exploration of Jewishness. He has described it himself with characteristic understatement as, 'the most Jewish novel that has ever been written by anybody, anywhere'.[10] And, this is not a Jewishness located at a distance in a far away time or place. It is set in 1950s Manchester and present day London and presents a head-on confrontation of what it means to be a British Jew of the post-war generation. *Kalooki Nights* is both funny and disturbing, audacious and bitter. It expresses an insecurity and rage at the heart of Anglo-Jewry. It is not a comfortable read. So, does this, what we might term *hyper-Jewishness*, account for Jacobson's exclusion from the Booker? Not really. We could argue that he has missed out on the prize for another reason entirely: that is, because he writes within the comic novel genre, a form that has simply never been popular with Booker juries. But of course he won it in 2010 for *The Finkler Question*.

In the following discussion, I want also to question this emphasis on ambiguity and tension. I think that a subtle shift is taking place: British-Jewish writers today are becoming increasingly interrogative about notions of exclusion in Jewish identity and are perhaps more alert to the pleasures and possibilities of diverse and diffuse forms of identification. And this shift might make a Jacobson style head-on confrontation with displacement, dysfunction and division (however ironically charged) begin to seem somewhat dated.

British-Jewish Literature: Coming From Behind?

David Brauner, in his 2001 study *Post-War Jewish Fiction*, detects a shift in the state of the field from his period of researching the subject as a doctoral student in the 1990s to the publication of his book at the turn of the millennium. His study looks at both British and American texts. Like Cheyette, Brauner recounts that he had been met with a repeated sense of disbelief that such a thing as British-Jewish fiction even existed. 'Over the last few years', he notes, 'whenever I have mentioned the subject of my work in progress to friends and colleagues, their first response has been to ask, with various degrees of flippancy, whether there is any British-Jewish fiction.'[11] And, yet, when the book was published in 2001 his concern was that 'conversely ... this book might be drowned in the flood of new studies of Jewish literature'.[12] Although interest in British-Jewish literature has developed at quite a rate over recent years, I do not think that Brauner's trepidation has yet been realised. Some significant and exciting work in this field is being produced but this remains a relatively under-populated and unconsolidated area of study.[13]

Until quite recently there has been a pervading sense that American writing has somewhat dominated the literary and cultural agenda. As a result, current studies are increasingly recognising the need to untangle the British experience from the American and the wider European perspectives and focus on the *particularity* of the Anglo-Jewish context. As Cheyette asked in 2003, 'What is it about Britishness that is so deforming?'[14] This is a question that has been addressed by historians as well as literary critics. In 1994 David Cesarani argued that British-Jewish culture has been characterised by 'a tradition of self-deprecation and a lack of collective self-esteem'.[15] Cesarani and Tony Kushner have provided vital insights about the ways in which ideas of Jewishness have been constructed in British culture.[16] In fact, many recent developments in British-Jewish studies could not have progressed without such careful historical contextualisation. Literary critics, cultural commentators and writers are now far more prepared to explore the complexities of what it means to be a British Jew, including the difficulties of the past, than they might have been 20 years ago.

In a lecture given in 2006 to commemorate the readmission of the Jews to England in 1656, Howard Jacobson, on particularly bullish form, confronted some of these issues. He argued that English Jews (there is a real slippage between ideas of Britishness and Englishness throughout these debates) have historically been mired by self-consciousness and in order to avoid accusations of 'introversion' and parochialism have deliberately avoided writing explicitly about their own experiences.[17] He claims that the aggressive confidence of American Jewish writers such as Saul Bellow and Philip Roth has not been repeated in the English context because Jews have only been 'welcomed' to this country with a degree of caution. English Jews have not reshaped 'what is meant by Englishness' because it is only recently that Britain has acknowledged that it is very much a culture under construction.[18] Unlike Americans, British Jews have been absorbed into the existing fabric of British life rather than redefining the weave itself.

So, we have, for example, in the title of Anthony Blond's memoir, *Jew Made in England* (2004), a rather astute recognition of the thoroughly integrated yet fundamentally distinct relationship between Jew and country.[19]

For Jacobson, Jews have been inhibited by the 'tranquillity', the lack of crisis, of British life. Ultimately he suggests that we need to find ways to be Jewish that are not based on denial, apology, weak imitation of the American model, or 'the anguished spirit of the Eastern European shtetl'.[20] Instead, he concludes that:

> We have been in this country a while now. The story of our finely tuned accommodations to English culture is a fascinating one, sometimes tragic, often heroic, always funny, and never less than urgent beneath a quiescent surface. It is time we told it. We should be more interested in ourselves as English Jews. ENGLISH ... JEWS.[21]

So, whereas for Cheyette some writers, such as Harold Pinter and Anita Brookner, have chosen to efface or codify their Jewishness, and others, such as Clive Sinclair and Elaine Feinstein, have succeeded by 'transcending and transfiguring their Britishness', Jacobson has arguably set the tone for a new generation of writers by confronting the interface between Jewishness and Englishness/Britishness in his work.[22] But is confrontation really what is required?

In the next section, I am going to look at a few examples from recent memoirs to think about these questions of perceived exclusion and British Jewish identity. Some of these examples point to painful moments of marginalisation and these are important. However, are we always displaced, dysfunctional and divided by our encounters with difference? Or is it that we are in many respects formed rather than deformed by this tension?

British-Jewish Memoirs: 'A Category Error'

Linda Grant has recently described herself as 'a category error'. Drawing implicitly again on the notion of 'shouty Jews', she notes that 'everyone knows that the British are tactful, decorous, well-mannered, prudent, prone to meaningful silences, and Jews are – well, the opposite'.[23] This ironic but nonetheless seemingly impossible contradiction in British-Jewish identity is a recurring theme in many recent memoirs and novels. There is a prevailing tone of disconnection running through many of these texts. As Jacobson put it in *Roots Schmoots*, recalling his own childhood sense of split identity whilst growing up in 1950s Manchester: 'we faced in opposite directions, we were our own antithesis'.[24] Sometimes this sense of dislocation is expressed as a yearning for wholeness. But, the uncertainties associated with being a 'category error' are also productive – as the awareness of in-betweenness, of not quite belonging, generates a productive spirit of self-reflexive enquiry.

In *Jacob's Gift: a Journey into the Heart of Belonging* (2006), a family memoir and thoughtful exploration of what it means to be both British and Jewish, Jonathan Freedland recounts a story that exemplifies a typical experience for many British Jews who descend from immigrants. 'Once', he writes of his early schooldays, 'there was a family tree project':

> Each of us had to trace our ancestors back as far as we could. Boys with names like Lowe, Sutherland and Blyth returned with hefty, parchment-style scrolls – unfurling forebears whose lives were etched on church records stored since medieval times in villages in Suffolk or Cornwall. One boy had gone all the way back to 1066; his scroll touched the floor. I held a single sheet of A4 paper bearing the names of my great-grandparents and the – estimated – date of 1880. That was as far back as I could go.[25]

This memory sums up a recognition of what it means to be a child, grandchild or even great grandchild of immigrants in a country that has traditionally valued continuity and longevity in lineage. This lack of rootedness, the flimsy connection to the British past, symbolised by Freeland's undersized family tree, is a recurring theme in other second and third generation Jewish memoirs. As many theorists have observed, diasporic Jews have, inevitably, to rely on memory rather than place in order to make and renew identities. Grant, writing about her mother's disintegrating memory makes the point that:

> If you lose your memory in Yorkshire, Yorkshire is all around you. You can go to the parish church and there are the records of births and marriages and deaths. That's not to say your experiences are commonplace, it's just that they are easier to replicate ... But what was particular in my mother's case was that in her brain resided the very last links with her generation. And what a generation it was – those children of immigrants who had in their heads two worlds, the one they lived in and a partial, incomplete place that their parents had handed on to them.[26]

In some ways this typifies the immigrant experience in general. But for many British Jews of Eastern European heritage, this is further complicated by the fact that places of Jewish history and memory were brutally annihilated in the Holocaust. The rupture from the past is in this respect deeply traumatic and unnaturally abrupt.

Grant recounts in *Remind Me Who I am Again* how her parents lived in post-war Britain 'with divided hearts'. They were in many respects British patriots, but they also supported the terrorist action that would drive the British out of Palestine and lead to the establishment of Israel in 1948. For Grant this apparent contradiction was formative. 'While slavishly trying to imitate *them*, – the English', she recalls, 'I also became self-divided.'[27] Reflecting on memories of her loud, generous and, to her teenage eyes, excruciatingly embarrassing father, Grant observes that she took for granted the 'vulgar luxuries' that he could provide yet she also longed for 'a dry, mild, laconic father with a name like James or Charles or Timothy and a distinguished war record'.[28]

This sense of marginalisation from the mainstream can, of course, evoke a desire for the other that is pleasurably charged as well as potentially alienating. Freedland describes this effect when he recalls his schoolboy awareness of the fundamental difference between 'the bright, bespectacled Jewish young women, their talk full of ideas, their hair full of dark curls', and 'the others, the Kates, Katherines and Sophies who were unmistakably *other*. Their very ordinariness', he remembers, 'the straightness of their hair, the button brevity of their noses, made them irresistibly exotic. They were so *English*'.[29] The erotic charge of this frisson has been exploited to outrageously comic effect by Jacobson among others. His fiction is populated by a series of hapless Jewish men who suffer repeated romantic and sexual humiliations at the hands of the heartless Aryan women whom they find unbearably cruel and magnetically irresistible.[30]

So, self-mocking and entertaining as it may be, the theme of self-division runs deep. For many contemporary British Jews this sense of being split between different worlds, the past and the present, the old world and new, Jewishness and Britishness, is highlighted by tensions that are evoked in reconciling sometimes ambivalent feelings about the State of Israel to their everyday identities as British Jews. Freedland eloquently articulates his own sense of split loyalties, describing himself as occupying 'a curious double role', whilst working as a journalist for the resolutely anti-Zionist newspaper, the

Guardian, and also feeling a long-standing deep connection to Israel, the country in which his mother was born.[31] The point of *Jacob's Gift* is to face this tension which Freedland sees as more than just a personal dilemma. Reflecting on how this predicament erupted for him in 2002 he argues that British Jews, as a whole, were in the midst of 'an identity crisis'.[32] Like Grant he detects 'a category error' at the heart of this crisis. His memoir is finely tuned to the nuances of identification as he explores moving stories about how earlier generations of his family responded in very different ways to these questions of connection and allegiance.

Half-Jewish: Hyphenated Identities

These issues of identification are complex and ongoing and are articulated across a range of contemporary British-Jewish writing. The memoirs that have been discussed so far have been by writers of the immediate post-war generation, the so-called 'baby boomers' born in the late 1940s and 1950s. I want now, in the next section of this discussion, to focus in part on a younger generation of British Jews (born mostly in the 1960s and 1970s), a generation for whom connections to their Jewish identities have become, in many cases, increasingly diluted.

Rodinsky's Room (1999) written by Rachel Lichtenstein with Iain Sinclair is a key example of the seemingly troubled relationship with Jewishness that this generation has expressed.[33] Grant and Freedland question the complexities inherent in categorising British-Jewish identity, but seem nevertheless to have a workable notion of what Jewishness is and how they place themselves within this identification. Whereas Lichtenstein has, perhaps more typically of her generation, a far more secure connection to an English or British identity but a far less secure sense of her own Jewishness; her text exemplifies a tendency to rue the loss of an imagined Jewish past. Like many Jews of her generation Lichtenstein is the grandchild of the ghetto but the child of affluent suburbs, in her case the far reaches of Essex. In her text Lichtenstein narrates a quest to discover the story of David Rodinsky, a mysterious figure who had inexplicably disappeared from his room above the Princelet Street synagogue in the 1960s. In tracing his story Lichtenstein struggles to resolve her own Jewish identity. It emerges almost half way through the book that her mother is not in fact Jewish. In many ways the underlying impetus of the text is to reconcile this somewhat repressed aspect of her identity. To reject the blandness of a thoroughly assimilated English existence (summed up by the flatness of the Essex landscape) in order to appropriate a rather more textured identity based in nostalgic ideas of a Jewish East End.

The book undoubtedly speaks to a shared experience for many British Jews who feel displaced from their collective past and mourn the loss of ethnic and cultural distinctiveness that Jewishness seems to bestow. In this respect, *Rodinsky's Room* seems to articulate insecurity. But it is a deceptively confident story. It narrates a tension in Jewish identity and recognises, implicitly, that there is, perhaps, an exhilaration or at least kind of pleasure to be found in the friction that is generated by not quite fitting in.

I want to use this example from *Rodinsky's Room* to move on to the next part of my discussion which focuses not so much on what it means to be Jewish and therefore not quite British (a theme that has preoccupied much Jewish writing); but on what it means to be perhaps thoroughly British but actually not quite Jewish. In other words, many British Jews today feel that they are British, but they might be far less certain about how they define themselves in relation to Jewishness.

In a 2005 *Jewish Quarterly* article titled 'On Not Being Jewish Enough' the artist Jonathan Leaman articulates a hesitant identification with Jewishness.[34] His mother was Jewish (she was born into a long established line of English Jews) and his father was non-Jewish. Although Leaman is clear that in different circumstances the Nazis would have certainly considered him to be Jewish he begins his reflection on how Jewishness has informed his artistic practice with the somewhat mischievous claim, 'I am not Jewish, and this is a line or two on the kind of Jew I am not'.[35]

Leaman avoids the nostalgic tone that infused Lichtenstein's search for identity but, like Lichtenstein, Jewishness is for him also located in the past not the present. 'Jews were archival notes', he says 'and nothing seemed further from myself.' He explains that his mother's Jewishness was 'an enlightened, liberal and watered-down Judaism, the more so for not sharing the motifs of exile, transit and extinction', the very motifs that Lichtenstein pursues in searching for her own Jewish identity.[36] Leaman recognises that the effect that this rather mild form of Jewishness had on him was of a nebulous and diffuse nature:

Jewish boys were let off assembly – I wasn't Jewish enough for that. We ate matzos and hot-cross buns, cold fried fish and sausages – Jewishness was a distant echo of smoked cod's roe, winks and disembodied shadows happening through other people's half-open doors.[37]

It is an evocative description. The Jewish writer today often inherits such a legacy, whilst not necessarily having any really immediate connection to what seem to be authentic Jewish experiences. And in many ways Leaman's 'not-Jewishness' is the cooler flip-side to Lichtenstein's more overwrought journey of self-discovery. Both accounts underscore the point that the Jewish past, for third, fourth and fifth generation British Jews, is often made up of echoes, winks and shadows. It is, like the lingering smell of yesterday's chicken soup, both enticing and unsettling. And it pervades in subtle ways.

This is not say that all Jews today feel entirely connected to their Britishness or entirely disconnected from their Jewishness. Clearly this is not the case. What I am suggesting is that whilst some sense of exclusion might still exist, it is increasingly likely to be developed in response to and alongside a range of other differences. The novelist and short story writer Tamar Yellin provides an interesting example. She has written recently about her Jewishness and her relationship to Englishness. In particular she has reflected on her experience of reading within the traditions of English literature and her intense identification with the novels and landscape of the Brontës. Yellin was born in Northern England and has made her home in Yorkshire today. But in an article for the *Jewish Quarterly* in 2007 Yellin describes an awareness that, as the Jewish daughter of a Polish immigrant and a third generation Jerusalemite, she was also in some ways excluded from the traditions of what she terms Brontëland.

She recounts a conversation she had with her Polish born mother on a visit to the Yorkshire Moors as a teenager. 'I sat gazing at the moors', she writes, 'and turning to my mother, cried: "isn't it beautiful!" and my mother, the Zionist, mournfully replied, "but it isn't ours".'

Her words ran me through the heart. It was intensely painful to be denied a sense of belonging in the countryside I loved. At worst I was a traitor; at best an oddity. In that moment I realised that to be a Jew in the English landscape was no less anomalous than to be a Jewish writer in the landscape of English literature. Yet it was

in that moment that I began to find myself.
      To be a writer is to be an outsider.[38]

So, whilst Jacobson had quite savagely satirised the Jewish alienation
from the English pastoral tradition in an early novel, *Peeping Tom*
(1984), for Yellin her anomalous connection to the English landscape
brings about a moment of creative tension, a moment of self-
discovery.[39] Although she romanticises the position of the artist and
the Jew (both cast as eternal outsiders) her identity is reformed rather
than deformed in this anecdote of dispossession.

Yellin explores these themes in her story 'Kafka in Brontëland', a
tale in which a Jewish woman living alone in a Yorkshire village
becomes fascinated by an enigmatic stranger of uncertain origins
whom the locals call Kafka. 'Kafka the outcast, Kafka the Jew', the
narrator comments.[40] By the end of the story she has found a way to
belong. From the Irish backgrounds of some village families, to the
half-Jewish shop owner and the south-east Asians who live down the
valley, this is, Yellin suggests a landscape populated by Kafkas. The
fact is that the Brontëland that Yellin has fetishised is itself nostalgic,
an idea that does not reflect the diversity of contemporary Yorkshire,
or the possibilities of living as a Jew within the social, cultural and
literary topographies of England today. So, in her mythologisation of
place and history Yellin initially constructed her own exclusion, only
to resignify her identity within an ever changing landscape.

Towards the end of her *Jewish Quarterly* article Yellin notes that her
sense of her own Jewishness had been further complicated by the recent
discovery that her great-grandmother was in fact an Irish Catholic. So
what we see here is that it is not just that the Yorkshire community is
ethnically and culturally mixed but that plurality exists within the
genealogy of most identities, including Jewishness. Many Jews in
contemporary Britain have ethnically and religiously mixed backgrounds
and increasingly they will create more diverse new families. How
Jewishness evolves within such a context is yet to be seen. But for some
writers Jewishness is connected to identity and creativity in ways that are
figurative as well as literal and embodied. Jewishness is in this way a
trope, signifying a collective history that has been marked by
dispossession and suffering, but also a more contemporary sense of
identities that are provisional, partial and performative.

In the same 2007 edition of the *Jewish Quarterly* that Yellin had
contributed to, Adam Thirlwell wrote a piece titled 'On Writing Half-
Jewishly'.[41] In this, Thirlwell takes up the idea of Jewishness as a

trope. He reflects on Jewishness 'as a motif for placelessness', and argues, like Yellin, in what is really a modernist gesture, that exile is the root of literary writing. Thirlwell goes on to explain on a more personal level why this is particularly meaningful to him: 'Perhaps this is a belief of mine which is intimately related to the fact that, although my mother is Jewish, I still feel half-Jewish. I can be sensitive, therefore, to overly stringent demarcations.'[42] One can detect here a certain defensiveness about identification. Unlike Lichtenstein's angst ridden journey into the Jewish past, or Leaman who seems to rather enjoy exploring 'not being Jewish enough', or even Yellin's realisation that cultures are not fixed in windswept moments from nineteenth century novels, Thirlwell resolves his own sensitivities by pronouncing that, 'like me, the Jewish is always half-Jewish'.[43]

This idea that 'Jewish is always half Jewish' is provocative. Whilst themes of not belonging are clearly central to much Jewish writing, Thirlwell's claim effectively dismisses the idea that there could ever be a wholly Jewish identity. To the extent that all identities are provisional, constructed and contingent this might be the case; and I have certainly suggested that partial identifications with Jewishness characterise much contemporary British-Jewish writing. But there is a danger that Thirlwell's contention threatens to dispose of any meaningful sense of what it is to be Jewish. The implications of such a manoeuvre are explored explicitly in Andrew Sanger's recent novel, *The J-Word*, which reflects explicitly on the problematic potential of 'the whole being less than the sum of the parts'.[44]

In the following edition of the *Jewish Quarterly* Cynthia Ozick responded to Thirlwell's article with outrage. Interestingly, Ozick attacked Thirlwell for what she perceived as particularly *British* brand of Jewish self-consciousness which resulted in what she termed, the 'ahistorical lukewarmness' of his essay. 'The ... hallmark of Jewishness', she argues, 'lies precisely in its distinction-making: the knowledge, the bold assertion ..., that one thing is not another thing ... that people are born wholes, not halves. And that the purpose of seeing distinction is to make choices.'[45] Partly this is a clash between a US and British perspective, a matter again of confidence in asserting the existence of what could be termed a 'Jewish sensibility', or as Ozick puts it elsewhere, a '*substratum* that is recognizably Jewish'.[46] So an American writer such as Nessa Rapoport can talk about 'the possibility of a literature whose spine and sinews would not be simply Jewish experience, but Jewish materials and Jewish dreams', and another

American writer, Robert Lasson, can define himself as 'a gastrointestinal Jew'.[47] These are explicit, definite and gutsy identifications against which Thirlwell's 'half-Jewishness' might well look irresponsibly timid.

But also perhaps this conflict signifies a generational shift in perception. Put simply, Ozick, born in New York to immigrant parents in 1928, and Thirlwell, who was born in North London in 1978 in comfortable and privileged circumstances, have distinctly different experiences of Jewishness. Thirlwell's approach to identity is perhaps inevitably formed by a postmodern sense of subjectivity in flux. One could argue that perhaps his generation is actually far more comfortable with not quite belonging to any identity in particular. Yet Thirlwell's discussion is not entirely playful; what Ozick sees as flippancy and half-heartedness can also be read as a more troubled reflection on lack of distinctiveness in identification.[48]

Recent reflections on Jewish identity circle round these issues of distinctiveness and definition. In her 2002 novel, *The Autograph Man*, Zadie Smith's hero is Alex-Li Tandem, a Chinese-Jewish hero born and bred in North London. Following Lenny Bruce, Tandem compiles an endless compendium that sets out to divide the world into that which is deemed to be Jewish and that which is (in these terms) 'Goyish'. So, for example, in the category of office items: the stapler is clearly Jewish whilst the paper-clip and mouse-mat are Goyish.[49] Tandem is of course, as his name suggests, the embodiment of hybridised, multiple, postmodern subjectivity, and his list points to the ludicrous and futile nature of trying to fix and itemise identities. And yet, however risible the project is, it is also somehow compelling. Whilst in many ways celebrating the dissolution of certainties we also seem to crave distinction. Peculiarity is appealing. As readers we might be left wondering, despite our better judgement, if there is after all something more Jewish about a stapler than a paper-clip.

In twenty-first century Britain, Jewishness is one difference among many. But many contemporary British-Jewish writers highlight the desire to identify the particularity of their difference, whilst acknowledging that that difference is neither fixed nor final, but always open to change, re-signification and re-interpretation. The question is not if Britishness and Jewishness are attached, but perhaps instead *how* they are attached. Much writing today is driven by an interest in hyphenated identities. Underlying this, then, we may ask, is it a staple or paper-clip that holds such identities together?

NOTES

1. Howard Jacobson, *Kalooki Nights* (London: Jonathan Cape, 2007), p.56.
2. Bryan Cheyette, 'British-Jewish Literature', *Jewish Writers of the Twentieth Century* ed. by Sorrel Kerbel (New York: Fitzroy Dearbon, 2003), pp.7–10 (p.7).
3. See Jeremy Gavron, *The Book of Israel* (London: Scribner, 2003); idem, *An Acre of Barren Ground* (London: Scribner, 2005); Giles Coren, *Winkler* (London: Vintage, 2006); Charlotte Mendleson, *When We Were Bad* (London: Picador, 2007).
4. Donald Weber, 'Anglo-Jewish Literature Raises Its Voice', *JBooks.com*, 12 July 2007, http://www.jbooks.com/interviews/index/IP_Weber_English.htm.
5. Naomi Alderman, *Disobedience* (London: Viking, 2006).
6. Mike Leigh, 'Mike Leigh Comes Out', Interview with Golda Zafer Smith, *Jewish Renaissance* (October 2005), 6–8 (p.8).
7. Mike Leigh, *Two Thousand Years* (London: Faber and Faber, 2006); Linda Grant, 'It's Kosher', *Guardian*, 20 September 2005, http://www.guardian.co.uk/religion/Story/0,2763,1573997,00.html.
8. David Herman, 'Where Are the Novelists?', *Jewish Chronicle*, 20 October 2006, p.43.
9. See for example, Mark Townsend, 'Rise in Antisemitic Attacks "the Worst Recorded in Britain in Decades"', *Observer*, 8 February 2009, http://www.guardian.co.uk/world/ 2009/feb/08/police-patrols-antisemitism-jewish-community; *Report of the All-Party Parliamentary Inquiry into Antisemitism*, 7 September 2006, http://www.thepcaa.org/ report.html; *Community Security Trust Report*, 2008, http://www.thecst.org.uk/docs/ Incidents_Report_08.pdf.
10. Howard Jacobson, 'Howard Jacobson Talking', 21 January 2006, interview by Cara Wides, http://www.somethingjewish.co.uk/articles/1730_howard_jacobson_talk.htm.
11. David Brauner, *Post-War Jewish Fiction: Ambivalence, Self-Explanation and Transatlantic Connections* (Basingstoke: Palgrave, 2001), p.x.
12. Ibid. p.ix.
13. Bryan Cheyette's *Diasporas of the Mind* (forthcoming) is likely to make a significant contribution to the field.
14. Cheyette, 'British-Jewish Literature' (see note 2), p.8.
15. David Cesarani, *The Jewish Chronicle and Anglo-Jewry* (Cambridge: Cambridge University Press, 1994), p.2.
16. See for example Tony Kushner, *The Jewish Heritage in British History: Englishness and Jewishness* (London: Frank Cass, 1992); idem, *Anglo-Jewry since 1066* (Manchester: Manchester University Press, 2009); and Todd Endelman, *The Jews of Britain 1656 to 2000* (Berkeley: University of California Press, 2002).
17. Howard Jacobson, 'Now We are 350', *Jewish Quarterly*, 20 (2006), 41–6 (p.45).
18. Ibid. p.44.
19. Similarly the title of Barnet Litvinoff's memoir, *A Very British Subject* (London: Vallentine Mitchell, 1996), signals a somewhat ironic relationship to British identity.
20. Jacobson, 'Now We are 350' (see note 17), p.46.
21. Ibid. p.46.
22. Bryan Cheyette, 'British-Jewish Literature' (see note 2), p.10.
23. Linda Grant, *The People on the Street: a Writer's View of Israel* (London: Virago, 2006), p.5.
24. Howard Jacobson, *Roots Schmoots: Journeys Among Jews* (London: Penguin, 1993), p.3.
25. Jonathan Freedland, *Jacob's Gift: A Journey into the Heart of Belonging* (London: Penguin, 2006), p.14.
26. Linda Grant, *Remind Me Who I Am Again* (London: Granta, 1998), p.31.
27. Ibid. p.71.
28. Ibid. pp.71–2.
29. Freedland (see note 25), p.15.
30. See for other examples Howard Jacobson, *Coming From Behind* (London: Black Swan, 1984); idem, *Peeping Tom* (London: Black Swan, 1985); idem, *The Mighty Walzer* (London: Vintage, 2000).
31. Freedland (see note 25), p.25.
32. Ibid. p.29.
33. Rachel Lichtenstein and Iain Sinclair. *Rodinsky's Room* (London: Granta, 1999).
34. Jonathan Leaman, 'On Not Being Jewish Enough', *Jewish Quarterly*, 196 (Winter 2004/5), 49–51.

35. Ibid. p.49.
36. Ibid. p.50.
37. Ibid. p.51.
38. Tamar Yellin, 'A Jew in Brontëland', *Jewish Quarterly*, 208 (Winter 2007), 68–9 (p.69).
39. For an analysis of the 'Jewish anti-pastoral' see Brauner, *Post-War Jewish Fiction* (see note 11), chapter 3.
40. Tamar Yellin, 'Kafka in Brontëland', in *Kafka in Brontëland and Other Stories* (London: The Toby Press, 2006), pp.11–22 (p.14).
41. Adam Thirlwell, 'On Writing Half-Jewishly', *Jewish Quarterly*, 208 (Winter 2007), 4–5.
42. Ibid. p.4.
43. Ibid. p.4.
44. Andrew Sanger, *The J-Word* (London: Snowbooks, 2009), p.246. For a full discussion of Sanger's novel see Ruth Gilbert, *Writing Jewish: Contemporary British-Jewish Literature* (Houndmills: Palgrave, forthcoming).
45. Cynthia Ozick, 'Responsa', *Jewish Quarterly*, 209 (Spring 2008), 5.
46. Ozick, cited in 'Forward', *The Slow Mirror and Other Stories: New Fiction by Jewish Writers* ed. by Sonja Lyndon and Sylvia Paskin (Nottingham: Five Leaves, 1996), p.3.
47. Nessa Rapoport and Robert Lasson, cited in 'Forward' (see note 46), p.2.
48. The debate was developed further by Gabriel Josipovici who framed it in terms of a contest between realism and postmodernity. Gabriel Josipovici, 'Boxing Clever', *Jewish Quarterly*, 210 (Summer 2008), 70–72. These issues are still ongoing and formed the basis of the recent Jewish Book Week discussion, 'A Beginner's Guide to Jews on the Edge', between Thirlwell and Will Self (28 February 2010).
49. Zadie Smith, *The Autograph Man* (London: Penguin, 2003), p.90.

OUT OF THE GHETTO

Negotiating Jewish Identity through the Display of Art

KATHRIN PIEREN

An important focus of museum studies in the last 20 years has been to deconstruct the symbolic power of museums and art galleries. The role such institutions can play in constructing and reinforcing identities has been explored for various populations.[1] Studying exhibitions and museums therefore helps us to understand the social dynamics of specific collectivities. As the opening up of the princely collections to a mass public coincided with the birth of the nation state in Europe, it is of little surprise that the function of museums to construct national identities has been a particularly fruitful area of study. However, it has been shown that regional and local museums as well as museums established by cultural, ethnic, social or religious groups have similar roles. Moira Simpson's broad study shows that culturally specific (she calls them 'community-focused') museums frequently have at least a double purpose: to preserve cultural heritage and pass knowledge and skills to the in-group in an attempt to keep its identity vital on one hand, and to present its culture to the general public on the other, often in order to counter misconceptions held by the majority population and correct distortions in the way the minority is represented by mainstream institutions.[2] Among other roles, such duality of purpose has also been observed for Jewish museums in the diaspora.[3]

The two exhibitions that are going to be discussed in this paper, the Anglo-Jewish Historical Exhibition of 1887 and the Exhibition of Jewish Art and Antiquities of 1906, have attracted considerable scholarly interest. Past research has clearly shown that they had an important political and cultural function. To place Anglo-Jewry firmly within English society for fear of, and as a response to, anti-Semitism and marginalisation by the Gentile majority was shown as being a major driving force for the Anglo-Jewish establishment involved in both exhibitions.[4]

The present paper builds on this knowledge, but will look at the exhibitions from a slightly different angle. Comparing two seemingly very similar exhibitions and their reception by the press, I seek to show how the meaning of displays changes over time and what factors can influence museum representation. This will give an indication of the potential of museum studies research for the study of culture while at the same time highlighting the need for caution when drawing conclusions about socio-cultural dynamics from museum representations. In order to do that, I will briefly sketch how museum studies have approached the polysemy of museum exhibits.

Some Thoughts on Methodology

Undoubtedly, museums are made for public consumption, which makes their exhibits open for interpretation. Nevertheless, studies that critically examine the power of museums have often ignored audiences or implied that they read exhibitions in the way intended by their makers; this can be said for some of the above-mentioned studies.[5] Conversely, the present case study is based on the more recently acknowledged role of museum visitors as 'active interpreters and performers of meaning-making practices'.[6] In this approach, which is supported by education and communication theory and builds on media and literary studies, meaning in museums is

> not fixed within objects, images, historical resources, or cultural sites, but ... produced out of the combination of the object/the image/the site itself, the mode of presentation, what is known about its history and production, and visitor interaction.[7]

The negotiation of meaning depends on a variety of factors. From the visitors' point of view, for instance, it may hinge on their socio-cultural background, expectations and foreknowledge or the sequence in which they visit a display. What has been explored in recent visitor research studies has also been shown for displays in the past.[8] Kate Hill's research on municipal museums in the second half of the nineteenth century suggests that, although members of the working class did attend museums, they did not necessarily adopt the 'civilised' behaviour that these institutions aimed to inculcate.[9] Moreover, Seth Koven found testimonies about working class visits to the picture exhibitions at St Jude's parish school, the precursor of the Whitechapel Art Gallery, which imply that these visitors interpreted the pictures in their own terms, at times challenging the ideological underpinnings of the philanthropic endeavour.[10] Assuming an active visitor role, however, does not imply a complete randomness of possible responses as meaning making takes place within specific socio-cultural contexts that make certain readings more likely than others. Furthermore, the relationship between the institutions that shape the exhibits and the visitors that interpret them is one of unequal power. This means that a display is never completely open to interpretation.[11]

To look at newspaper reviews in order to investigate perceptions and possible divergences from the intended exhibition narratives, as is suggested here, is clearly a poor substitute for personal accounts. Yet, in the absence of such testimonies, and if one abandons the idea that the press is representative of public opinion, they can be useful in two ways. If newspapers do not necessarily reflect their readers' opinions, exhibition reviews can nevertheless be expected to influence the readers' ways of perceiving an exhibition (which is their primary function). Maybe even more importantly, they provide an indicator of the range of possible readings beyond those preferred by the exhibition makers. Thereby they render the picture about the consumption of these displays more complete than if it were just assumed that the consumption of the exhibits exactly mirrored the intentions of their producers.

Starting from the actual exhibit and regarding its meaning as a negotiation process is part of an approach that treats museum displays as texts that can not only be read in multiple ways, but which also produce unintentional, ambivalent and contradictory meanings.[12] A central element that is only going to be touched upon in this article but which is crucially influencing the meaning produced by a display is, of course, the collection itself and how it came into existence. A variety of contemporaneous and even conflicting motives, such as nostalgia, local or national pride, and economic interest, inform the nature of collections and sometimes they reflect the interests of only a handful of people, even if they are eventually used to represent a collectivity.[13] This implies that exhibitions do not necessarily (fully) reflect the values and attitudes of those who curate them. The curators might, on the other hand, have aims that are not reflected by the displays themselves and which risk being ignored by a textual approach. Whilst it could be argued that they are irrelevant for the response a display evokes, these 'unrealised' intentions are a key to understanding the motivation of those segments of a population who have the power to represent it in public in the first place.

The focus of the following case study will be on the change in the representation and consumption of art which is part of the Jewish art discourse that had started in the nineteenth century and was characterised by lively debates in the first quarter of the twentieth century in various national contexts.[14] The significance of these two exhibitions for this discourse and for the development of Jewish museums in Europe has been acknowledged by Richard Cohen and Dominique Jarrassé.[15] The scale and public dimension of the 1887 exhibition made it stand out in the history of Jewish collecting and museums, while the inclusion of Jewish contemporary artists in the 1906 event introduced the notion of a specific Jewish fine art which became an object of debate. Whilst Cohen and Jarrassé come to their conclusions from the wider perspective of international developments, I suggest going back to the displays in their local contexts to investigate how this change was effected through the interaction of objects, place and visitors. Knowledge of the local context within which these exhibitions were produced and consumed not only helps to understand that specific situation, but also provides a basis for effective comparison. Similar motivations and motifs were at work in the staging of exhibitions and the foundation of other Jewish museums in Europe; local, national and transnational approaches are therefore complementing, rather than competing with, each other. Insofar as London would for years to come remain the only British city with significant temporary and permanent displays of Jewish art and history which, however, claimed to be representative of British Jewry and were widely presented as such by the press, their significance in fact went well beyond the local context.

The 1887 Anglo-Jewish Historical Exhibition

Isidore Spielmann, an engineer who would later become a major art impresario in Britain's international exhibitions, initiated the Anglo-Jewish Historical Exhibition at the Royal Albert Hall in honour of Queen Victoria's Golden Jubilee. Whilst being part of a longer-term

strategy to counter growing anti-alienism and anti-Semitism[16] that
had started to bubble up once more with the arrival of large numbers
of Eastern European immigrants,[17] the organisers also attempted to
reclaim and popularise Anglo-Jewish history in view of a perceived
diminution in community cohesion.[18] The legacy of the exhibition
was the Jewish Historical Society of England set up by the core
members of the organising team in 1893.[19]

The exhibition was realised with the help of an over 100-people
strong exhibition committee and it was complemented by
exhibitions at the South Kensington Museum, the British Museum
and the Public Record Office. The over 2,500 objects on display
encompassed: historic relics and records; Jewish ceremonial art;
antiquities; coins and medals; and portraits of Anglo-Jewish
personalities.[20] The narrative put weight on the political history of
the Jews in Britain and their longstanding and successful integration
into the majority society. Only very few references were made to
poor Jews living in the East End of London, and conflicts within the
Jewish population or between them and non-Jews were located in
the distant past.[21] Parallel to this patriotic account, the prominent
exhibition of antiquities told a story of the spiritual and historical
connectedness of Anglo-Jewry with the ancient world and thus,
indirectly, with the diaspora. Not all of this was the result of a
clearly defined strategy, notably Spielmann had at first not intended
to include any religious or archaeological items.[22] There is also
evidence to show that the various personalities involved had their
own agendas for this exhibition, some more interested in
professionalising Anglo-Jewish history, others more concerned with
decorum and the good reputation of British Jewry in the eyes of the
Gentiles.[23]

Most popular with the public was the art on display. The term
does not refer to the portraits of rabbis, boxers and communal
leaders, which were considered part of the historical exhibits, but to
religious objects. The Torah scrolls, menorahs, Kiddush cups, spice
boxes, and other ceremonial items offered themselves for two
readings. Divided up in three departments according to the place of
worship ('synagogue', 'home' and 'personal'), the layout of the
objects and the description of their religious use in the catalogue
integrated them in their ritual context. However, in the introductory
chapter the catalogue referred to them explicitly as ('ecclesiastical')
art.[24] Furthermore, the objects were exhibited in a highly

aestheticised manner (in the display the classification was partly broken up and the precious metal objects were exhibited against a dark background, often arranged to form a symmetrical pattern[25]) which emphasised their artistic qualities. The absence of text in the exhibition space (it all had to be looked up in the catalogue which not every visitor possessed) made the aesthetic reading of the exhibit rather more probable than the religious one, although this must have been different for Jewish and Gentile audiences. The *Jewish World*, for instance, acknowledged the power of the exhibition to instil pride and evoke personal memories in Jewish visitors.[26]

The focus on art was not accidental, but a strategy to attract visitors who were expected to be charmed by the 'artistic beauty' of these objects in a predominantly historical display that was not considered sufficiently appealing on its own.[27] Importantly, the press replicated the aesthetic interpretation of the objects. The *Times*, for example, praised 'the richly embroidered mantles, crowned with nests of tinkling silver bells' and referred to the religious appurtenances as 'the art collection'.[28] The *Jewish Chronicle*, moreover, stated that '[i]t will come, we fancy, as a surprise, and to most as a pleasant surprise, to find that the Exhibition is in so large a degree an art exhibition'.[29] The successful display of all those art objects even brought the chairman of the committee to express his hope that the exhibition had stimulated the development of Jewish ritual art.[30] Whilst the show itself demonstrated the existence and beauty of Jewish art, belying the prejudice that Jews could not be creative (purported in the nineteenth century by people such as Richard Wagner in *Das Judenthum in der Musik*[31]), the catalogue text delivered an apology for the assumed lack of a *specifically Jewish* art, stressing that these objects were produced in the style of the countries Jews lived in. The Judaica therefore added the double story of a community unified by common religious traditions and distinguished by its artistic achievements; the framework of reference was the nation.

With over 12,000 visitors (most likely members of the middle and upper classes although four free Saturdays and subsidised school visits from Jewish schools also targeted poorer audiences) the paying exhibition was considered a success.[32] It was well received by the Jewish and mainstream press which mostly shared the interpretations of the organisers, emphasising the elegance of the opening event, praising the interest of the objects and their great appeal to various audiences.[33] Nevertheless, some mainstream newspapers assumed Jewish difference on the basis of the ancient origins of Judaism when they referred to Jews as 'the Chosen People',[34] 'the Old Testament'[35] and 'the Hebrew race'.[36] This was even more explicit in the reviews of the *Daily Telegraph*[37] and the *Pall Mall Gazette*, for whose authors the representation of Jews as English, while having a connection with the Holy Land, seems to have worked as a marker of difference. In an orientalising manner and despite the fact that the vast majority of the exhibits referred to *Anglo*-Jewish history, the *Pall Mall Gazette* located Jewish culture in a space outside the national context when suggesting that the exhibition would be particularly instructive and interesting 'to those interested in Oriental customs, art, races and religion'.[38] Clearly the identity discourse underlying this judgement did not accommodate the complex identity presented in the exhibition; rather, the display of 'exotic' objects seems to have turned the subject of the exhibition, Anglo-Jewry, into 'exotica' themselves.

The 1906 Exhibition of Jewish Art and Antiquities

Several of the organisers of the 1887 exhibition were involved in the 1906 Exhibition of Jewish Art and Antiquities at the Whitechapel Art Gallery. It was modelled upon the earlier display and initiated by a member of the former exhibition committee, Canon Samuel Barnett, the founder of the university settlement 'Toynbee Hall' in the East End of London.[39] Barnett was an early honorary member of the Maccabaeans, a club of Jewish professionals who aimed to promote a Jewish secular culture, and when he and his wife had founded the gallery in 1901 he had received the financial and moral support of the Anglo-Jewish establishment.[40]

In the moralising tradition of the gallery,[41] the lofty goal of the 1906 event was to uplift the spirits of the poor and Barnett was also convinced that it would create 'a link between the East and the West, between Jews and Gentiles'.[42] This was timely as the Jewish immigrants that had been settling from the 1880s onwards in increasing numbers in the notoriously poor and overcrowded Jewish East End had become the object of growing hostility from the local population, eventually leading up to the 1905 Aliens Act.[43] Whilst countering Gentile prejudices[44] had already been an aim in the 1887 exhibition, this time the *Jewish World* commented that

East joins West, in more senses than one. For not only do all sections of the community, from the highest to the humblest, meet, as it were, upon a common platform where all are of equal standing, but the art of the Orient is wedded to that of our Western surroundings.[45]

Although displaying the same object categories, the exhibition was more modest than the earlier one. It also focused less on emancipation history, a central story in the previous display, and presented fewer archaeological artefacts.[46] Instead, the choice of objects and the way they were shown in a mass display (probably the result of spatial constraints), scarcely commented upon in the catalogue and lacking an easy to distinguish display logic which neglected provenance or function, stressed the commonality of Jewish experience in Britain and beyond. For example, one case contained, inter alia, a German *Memorbuch*, an Egyptian prayer book, an Italian doctor's prescription book and the Romance of Nizami in Hebrew-Persian.[47] This was partly the effect of the eclectic book collections on loan from private collectors that were displayed under the lenders' names rather than thematically. English history was still a strong element in the exhibition, but the accent of the narrative had shifted from 'Anglo-Jewish' to 'Jewish', as the title implied.

This was reinforced by the most important innovation of the exhibition, the display of works by British and foreign artists. Whilst in 1887 it had been up to the ceremonial art to demonstrate Jewish artistic achievement, this function was now transferred onto the works by contemporary artists and artists from the recent past such as Solomon J. Solomon, Max Liebermann, Simeon Solomon and Jozef Israëls. The catalogue's text on Jewish art was published not under 'ecclesiastical art', but under the new title of 'Jewish art'.[48] The religious appurtenances, on the other hand, were restored to their ritual interpretation in the catalogue (where they were still termed 'ecclesiastical art') and by a more religiously contextualised display (as the few available pictures seem to indicate). By exhibiting the works of different styles, media, subject matter and provenance under the common heading of 'Jewish art', the exhibition presented visitors with the concept of Jewish art as art produced by Jews. However, this ethnic dimension was contested even in the interpretation of the exhibition itself as well as in the reception by the press. The author of the catalogue, prominent art critic and brother of Isidore Spielmann, Marion Harry Spielmann, who also reviewed the exhibition in the *Jewish World* and *The Graphic*, presented Jewish art again in the national context of its production, arguing that, although some artists might choose to paint Jewish subjects with a particular passion, their art was no different from the art of the countries they lived in.[49] To contribute to the glory of the English school, he was convinced, was the natural course and aim of the Jewish artistic production in Britain, thereby aspiring to aesthetic assimilation. Conversely, for *Haham* Moses Gaster, another member of the exhibition committee in 1887 and in 1906 and an early Zionist, Jewish and English art were not mutually exclusive categories as each indicated a specific 'spirit' added to an assembly of traditions inherited from various places and times. To him, the exhibition clearly showed the 'unity of the Jewish race'.[50]

The *Jewish Chronicle* held yet another concept of Jewish art, basing it on iconography. While discussing foreign and English artists separately, it focused on the difference between 'Jewish pictures' and pictures 'of no Jewish interest' according to subject matter, identifying the emergence of a 'new Jewish school' in Britain whose works it regarded as revealing the Jewish soul. This school would encompass representations of 'the alien at worship and study' and possibly scenes of persecution and suffering.[51] By including in its definition of Jewish art paintings from artists such as Moses Maimon and Leopold Pilichowski, which were inspired by contemporary events in Russia and Eastern Europe, the paper reinforced the idea of a common Jewish identity beyond the religious sphere.[52]

Other newspapers picked up the narrative of the exhibition makers, not discussing Spielmann's concept of Jewish art, but acknowledging the achievements of Jews in the arts.[53] With over 150,000 visitors and more than 20,000 catalogues sold, the free exhibition was the best attended six-week exhibition since the gallery had first opened.[54] Whilst the local people were enthusiastic visitors,[55] they also 'rub[bed] shoulders with Gentile pilgrims from the West'.[56] Mainstream papers praised religious objects as well as fine art for their aesthetic qualities, but distinguished between ancient and modern Jewry. For the *Daily News* the ancient origins of Jewish traditions and their continuing relevance in the present held a particular fascination and they might have been the reason for its perception of mystery pervading the East End; the history of the 'ancient race' contrasted with the 'versatility of the modern Jew' who was seen as producing mostly art with no distinctive Jewish character.[57] Spielmann argued along the same lines, but was more explicit in establishing a direct link between Jewish communities and specific art forms. He identified contemporary fine art with universal values and modernity while associating 'art *objects*', the Judaica – 'important beyond all to the Jewish denizens of the East End' – with parochialism and pre-modernity.[58] It seems that by trying to bridge the gaps between the various Jewish and Gentile communities, the exhibition suggested an idea of Jewish ethnic identity that provoked new constructions of difference. While this appears to be indicative of the prejudices and ambivalences towards Jewish immigrants held in middle and upper class circles, it also points towards the tensions that can potentially arise for minority groups in exhibitions between representing themselves positively as a coherent group to a mainstream audience and reflecting the group's diversity and inner divisions to its members.[59]

Juliet Steyn has rightly observed that the exhibition invited the local immigrant population 'to become spectators of a culture already complete', the Western European culture, despite the fact that various notions of Jewish identity were competing with each other.[60] Indeed, an article on '*Di kulturele entwiklung fun di yiden in england*' ('The cultural development of the Jews in England'), published a few days after the exhibition's opening, in *Der yidisher ekspres*, illustrates that some immigrants had a rather different outlook on these issues.[61] Unlike Spielmann, the author did not regard specific Jewish culture as antiquated, but as something generally lively and thriving. Not so in Britain, however, where he could not identify any culture with a lasting value which also bore '*dem yidishen shtempel*' ('the Jewish stamp'), such as literature in Yiddish. The author blamed this on the fragmentation of the Jewish population: in the struggle for survival recent and more settled immigrants had no time to dedicate themselves to the arts, and native Jews ('*geshefts-leyt un aristokraten*' – 'businesspeople' and 'aristocrats'), because of their liberty and comfortable life in England, '*lieben alzding wos es is english, [un] sey hasen, oder sey seynen wenigstens gleychgiltig zu ales wos es is yidish*' ('love everything English [and] hate, or are at least indifferent, towards anything Jewish'). Although his was the voice from a disempowered segment of the Jewish population, it is doubtful whether this journalist was passively enduring the educational zeal of the likes of Canon Barnett and Marion Harry Spielmann.

Conclusions

With regard to the Jewish communities of London and, by implication, Britain the start of two interrelated shifts can be discerned in the representation of Jewish art between the two displays of 1887 and 1906: the first shift goes from religious and decorative to profane and fine art. This happens at a time when the production of works of fine art by Jews becomes more visible and its specific character is publicly debated. It ties in with what Dominique Jarrassé formulated for the Jewish art discourse in Europe in the late nineteenth and early twentieth century: the gradual change from a religious to an ethnic conception of Jewish art. But while he suggests that, albeit the Exhibition of Jewish Art and Antiquities marks a turning point, the actual change takes place only in the Zionist context in Berlin where an 'Exhibition of Jewish Artists' was shown the year after,[62] I would argue that in the London context the shift in *focus* is clearly discernible between the two events even though the concept of Jewish art as ethnic was socially still contested. What the case study shows well is the gradual change in the interpretation of exhibits and the negotiated character of museum representation between various stakeholders.

The change in the art discourse relates to the second shift in the representation of Jews from a community characterised by common religious traditions, a spiritual connection with Ancient Israel and a strong attachment to England towards their representation as a transnational ethnic group (that shares inter alia a common religion). However, this does not necessarily reflect a cultural shift from a predominantly religious concept of Jewishness to an exclusively ethnic consciousness, let alone a consensus of a common culture among British Jewry. Indeed, the narratives produced by the artistic displays were influenced by museum-specific factors such as the availability of collections, spatial constraints and target audiences. Had the Anglo-Jewish Historical Exhibition not included archaeological or ritual objects, as originally planned, for example, it would have conveyed a rather different idea of Jewish identity. Furthermore, the intentions expressed by the organisers and the articles in the press in 1906 contain references to the well-known social and cultural divide between recent immigrants and the British Jewish middle and upper classes, and testify to the ambivalence of the latter between communal solidarity and differentiation with the immigrant population. While reviewing the displays and discussing art, these texts reproduce the claims over the definition of Jewish culture from exponents of various segments of the Jewish population who used stereotyped attributes to exclude each other from cultural entitlement, thereby reinforcing the cultural divide.

Interesting is the frequent use by organisers and stakeholders of the shorthand 'East' and 'West End' to indicate all kinds of socio-cultural difference. If the stereotypical representation of the East End was common in late nineteenth and early twentieth century London, in the reception of the Whitechapel exhibition the East–West metaphor was entangled with the nineteenth century Hellenism–Hebraism debate and references to the oriental origins of Judaism. Particularly in the Anglo-Jewish Historical Exhibition the reference to antiquity and the bible held an appeal to Gentile visitors (something the *Jewish Chronicle* was aware of and the organisers might well have been), but the mainstream press equally used it as the marker of Jewish difference in the present.[63] Whilst in 1887 some papers had opposed Jewishness to Gentile Englishness, in 1906 the 'other' was the Jewish immigrant who was seen as representing Jewish tradition and, in its negative conception, backwardness as opposed to modern European Jewry.

With regard to the representation of Jewish identity through the display of art in London exhibitions, it will take the passage of time, the strengthening of the immigrant communities, the establishment of Zionism, and changes in the general art discourse and production to consolidate the above changes, but we can already spot the beginnings of a diversification in the negotiation of Jewish identity in the public sphere.

I hope this brief case study has provided an idea of the different factors that inform material culture displays and demonstrated that they do not necessarily reflect a clear strategy of the curators. To capture underlying, contradictory and implicit messages and to include reception can help an understanding of the complexity of meanings produced by exhibitions and to place them in their broader cultural context. Yet it would be wrong to think that 'anything goes'. As the sources in this particular case illustrate, the press generally reproduced the narratives fostered by the displays in largely similar ways, although there are a series of significant contestations that testify to the breadth of possible responses and illustrate the negotiated character of museum representations.

For the purpose of demonstrating the use of museum studies for the understanding of social relations and the construction of identity within the public sphere I have focused exclusively on the way art was represented and received in two temporary exhibitions. The limitations of this approach are obvious and need not be expanded upon. It is understood that these events were part of a wider cultural field and a set of competing and overlapping discourses on identity, art, citizenship etc. However, the pioneering character of these displays and their strong presence in the press gave them a visibility beyond London and had a lasting impact on subsequent Jewish self-representations in Britain and elsewhere. The changes in the displays and the discussions that ensued are therefore more important than the cases themselves might initially indicate.

ACKNOWLEDGEMENTS

The research for this article was made possible thanks to a Collaborative Doctoral Award granted by the Arts and Humanities Research Council, as well as the support of the Institute of Historical Research and the Museum of London. I would like to thank the following friends and colleagues whose comments have helped me improve my text: John Clifford, Hannah Ewence, Lily Kahn, Derek Keene, Ed Marshall, Rhiannon Mason, James Moore, Andrew Newman.

NOTES

1. To mention a few well-known landmark studies: Ivan Karp and Steven D. Lavine, eds., *Exhibiting Cultures: The Poetics and Politics of Museum Display* (Washington and London: Smithsonian Institution Press, 1991); Ivan Karp *et al.*, eds., *Museums and Communities: The Politics of Public Culture* (Washington and London: Smithsonian Institution Press, 1992); Tony Bennett, *The Birth of the Museum: History, Theory, Politics* (London: Routledge, 1995); Carol Duncan, *Civilizing Rituals: Inside Public Art Museums* (London and New York: Routledge, 1995); Sharon Macdonald and Gordon Fyfe, eds., *Theorizing Museums: Representing Identity and Diversity in a Changing World* (Oxford: Blackwell; Cambridge, MA: Sociological Review, 1996). While the present article focuses on museums, the same trend can be observed in the study of cultural heritage in general: *The Ashgate Research Companion to Heritage and Identity* ed. by Brian Graham and Peter Howard (Aldershot: Ashgate, 2008).
2. Moira G. Simpson, *Making Representations: Museums in the Post-Colonial Era* (London and New York: Routledge, 1996).
3. Among the more recent publications that discuss the specific functions of Jewish museums and their relation to Jewish identity discourses in various time periods and places are: David Clark, 'Jewish Museums and Jewish Renewal', in *New Voices in Jewish Thought* ed. by Keith Harris, Vol.2 (London: Limmud Publications, 1999), pp.70–91; Rickie Burman, 'Presenting Judaism', in *Godly Things: Museums, Objects and Religion* ed. by Crispin Paine (London and New York: Leicester University Press, 2000), pp.132–42; Katharina Rauschenberger, *Jüdische Tradition im Kaiserreich und in der Weimarer Republik, Zur Geschichte des jüdischen Museumswesens in Deutschland* (Hannover: Verlag Hahnsche

Buchhandlung, 2002); Klaus Hödl, 'The Turning to History of Viennese Jews: Jewish Identity and the Jewish Museum', *Journal of Modern Jewish Studies*, 3.1 (March 2004), 17–32.

4. For the 1887 exhibition see David Cesarani, 'Dual Heritage or Duel of Heritages? Englishness and Jewishness in the Heritage Industry', in *The Jewish Heritage in British History: Englishness and Jewishness* ed. by Tony Kushner (London/Portland, OR: Frank Cass, 1992), pp.29-41 and in the same collection Tony Kushner, 'The End of the "Anglo-Jewish Progress Show": Representations of the Jewish East End, 1887–1987', pp.78–105; Jeffrey David Feldman, 'Exhibiting Judaica or Jewish Exhibitionism: A Comparison of Two Nineteenth-Century Exhibitions' (unpublished M.Phil. thesis, St Cross College, Oxford University, 1993. MS. M.Phil. c.1510); Michael E. Keen, 'Die "Anglo-Jewish Historical Exhibition" und die Judaicasammlung des Victoria & Albert Museums', in *Wiener Jahrbuch für Jüdische Geschichte Kultur & Museumswesen* Band 1 1994/1995 (Wien: Verlag Christian Brandstätter), pp.71–87; Peter Stansky, 'Anglo-Jew or English/British? Some Dilemmas of Anglo-Jewish History', *Jewish Social Studies*, 2.1 (Fall 1995), 159–78; Barbara Kirshenblatt-Gimblett, 'Exhibiting Jews', in *Destination Culture: Tourism, Museums and Heritage* (Berkeley and London: University of California Press, 1998; first published in 1992 under the title 'From Cult to Culture: Jews on Display at World's Fairs'), pp.79–128. For the 1906 exhibition see Juliet Steyn, 'The Complexities of Assimilation in the 1906 Whitechapel Art Gallery Exhibition "Jewish Art and Antiquities"', *Oxford Art Journal*, 13.2 (1990), 44–50. Richard Cohen and Dominique Jarrassé included both exhibitions in their international surveys. Richard I. Cohen, *Jewish Icons: Art and Society in Modern Europe* (Berkeley and London: University of California Press, 1998); Dominique Jarrassé, *Existe-t-il un art juif?* (Paris: Biro éditeur, 2006). To be fair, the more recent studies have taken a wider stance on these exhibitions, pointing out that the Englishness represented coincided with references to transnational Jewish identities in the 1887 exhibition and suggesting that the 1906 exhibition was more inclusive towards the immigrant communities than had previously been thought. However, there is a basic consensus concerning the role of the exhibition for the construction of Englishness in a situation of exclusion. Peter Gross, 'Representations of Jews and Jewishness in English Painting, 1887–1914' (unpublished PhD Thesis, University of Leeds 2004. BL Theses GRO); Tobias Metzler, 'Jewish History in the Showcase', *Museological Review*, 12 (2007), pp.101–11; Irit Miller, 'Anglo-Jewish Exhibitions at the Turn of the 20th Century: Integration and Separatism', *Iyunim Bitkumat Israel: Studies in Zionism, the Yishuv and the State of Israel*, Vol.18 (Sede Boqer: Ben-Gurion Research Institute, 2008), pp.389–416 (Hebrew).

5. Rhiannon Mason makes a similar point about 'cultural theory-inspired museum critiques'. Rhiannon Mason, 'Cultural Theory and Museum Studies', in *A Companion to Museum Studies* ed. by Sharon Macdonald (Malden, MA and Oxford: Blackwell Publishing, 2006), pp.17–32 (pp.25–6).

6. Eilean Hooper-Greenhill, 'Studying Visitors', in *A Companion to Museum Studies* (see note 5), pp.362–76 (p.362).

7. Rhiannon Mason, 'Museums, Galleries and Heritage: Sites of Meaning-Making and Communication', in *Heritage, Museums and Galleries: An Introductory Reader* ed. by Gerard Corsane (London and New York: Routledge, 2005), pp.200–214 (p.203). An illustrative example is Diana L. Linden's study about the display of Ben Shahn's late work at the Jewish Museum in New York and at the Detroit Institute of Arts in which she demonstrates that audience expectations and the museological context in which the artwork was shown impacted radically on its perception as being primarily the expression of a 'Jewish' rather than a 'modern American' artist in spite of the Jewish Museum's original intentions. Diana L. Linden, 'Modern? American? Jew? Museums and Exhibitions of Ben Shahn's Late Paintings', in *The Art of Being Jewish in Modern Times* ed. by Barbara Kirshenblatt-Gimblett and Jonathan Karp (Philadelphia: University of Pennsylvania Press, 2008), pp.197–207.

8. Studies that explore the variety of possible readings of museum displays using various methodologies are, for instance: Bella Dicks, *Heritage, Place and Community* (Cardiff:

University of Wales Press, 2000); Gaynor Bagnall, 'Performance and Performativity at Heritage Sites', *Museum and Society*, 1.2 (2003), 87–103, http://www.le.ac.uk/ms/museumsociety.html (accessed 15 January 2008); Richard Sandell, *Museums, Prejudice and the Reframing of Difference* (London and New York: Routledge, 2007). With regard to a Jewish museum, see Kathrin Pieren, '"Being Jewish Is More than the Holocaust Experience": What Visitors See at the Jewish Museum Berlin', *Social History in Museums*, 29 (2004), 79–86.

9. Kate Hill, *Culture and Class in English Public Museums, 1850–1914* (Aldershot: Ashgate, 2005), chapter 7, pp.125–42.

10. Seth Koven, 'The Whitechapel Picture Exhibitions and the Politics of Seeing', in *Museum Culture: Histories, Discourses, Spectacles* ed. by Daniel J. Sherman and Irit Rogoff (London: Routledge, 1994), pp.22–48.

11. For a discussion on the changing notions of the power balance between the media on one side and consumers on the other, on which I base this observation, see David Morley, 'Theories of Consumption in Media Studies', in *Acknowledging Consumption: A Review of New Studies* ed. by David Miller (London and New York: Routledge, 1995), pp.296–328.

12. Mason (see note 5), pp.26–9.

13. An example of a public museum whose early collecting policy was mainly informed by the cultural and political interests of one person against the aesthetic trends of the time was the Harris Library, Museum and Art Gallery in Preston. James R. Moore, 'Periclean Preston, Public Art and the Classical Tradition in Late-Nineteenth-Century Lancashire', *Northern History*, XL.2 (September 2003), 299–323.

14. Jarrassé (see note 4).

15. Cohen (see note 4), pp.197–8; Jarrassé (see note 4), pp.48–50.

16. Cesarani (see note 4).

17. Geoffrey Alderman, *Modern British Jewry* (Oxford: Clarendon Press, 1998), pp.110–32.

18. Cohen (see note 4), pp.193–4. On the importance of Anglo-Jewish history for community-building see: *Jewish World*, 8 April 1887, pp.5–6 (which refers to the exhibition); *Jewish Chronicle*, 17 June 1887, pp.6–7; Lucien Wolf, 'A Plea for Anglo-Jewish History', Presidential Address, 11 November 1893, *Transactions of the Jewish Historical Society of England*, 1 (1893–94), 1–7 (p.7); Sir Isidore Spielmann, 'Presidential Address to the Jewish Historical Society of England', 9 February 1903, *Transactions of the Jewish Historical Society of England*, 5 (1902–5), 43–56 (pp.55–6).

19. Lucien Wolf, 'Origins of the Jewish Historical Society of England', Presidential Address, 15 January 1912, *Transactions of the Jewish Historical Society of England*, 7 (1911–14), 206–15.

20. *Catalogue of the Anglo-Jewish Historical Exhibition, Royal Albert Hall, London, 1887*, compiled by Joseph Jacobs and Lucien Wolf, illustrated by Frank Haes, Publications of the Exhibition Committee No.IV (London: F. Haes, 1888).

21. With its Whiggish outlook on history, sanitised picture of British tolerance and the emphasis on Jewish decorum, the exhibition has been seen as part of an apologetic tradition in Anglo-Jewish historiography that continued far into the twentieth century. Cesarani (see note 4); Kushner (see note 4); Stansky (see note 4).

22. *Catalogue of the Anglo-Jewish Historical Exhibition* (see note 20), p.xxv.

23. My Ph.D. thesis contains a detailed account of the Anglo-Jewish Historical Exhibition and the early history of the Jewish Historical Society of England.

24. *Catalogue of the Anglo-Jewish Historical Exhibition* (see note 20), p.83.

25. I am grateful to Dr Eva Frojmovic for pointing this out to me.

26. *Jewish World*, 8 April 1887, p.5.

27. Frederic David Mocatta, 'Report to the Members of the General Committee', *Catalogue of the Anglo-Jewish Historical Exhibition* (see note 20), p.207.

28. *Times*, 6 April, 1887, p.4.

29. *Jewish Chronicle*, 1 April 1887, p.8.

30. Mocatta (see note 27), p.213.

31. Jarrassé (see note 4), pp.60–61.

32. Mocatta (see note 27), p.210–11.

33. The following newspapers were included in the analysis: *Der arbeter fraynd, The Builder, Times, Pall Mall Gazette, Daily News, Daily Telegraph, East End News, East London Observer, Evening News, Evening Standard, The Graphic, Illustrated London News, Jewish Chronicle, Jewish World, Life, Lloyd's Weekly Newspaper, Manchester Guardian, Morning Post, Museums Journal, News of the World, Penny Illustrated Paper, Punch, People, Pictorial World, Tribune, Westminster and Lambeth Gazette*. The majority of these papers did refer to the exhibition, although some with only a few lines or just advertising the event.

34. *The Graphic*, 9 April 1887, p.375.

35. Apparently a remark overheard by the journalist during the opening event. *The People*, 10 April 1887, p.13.

36. *Daily News*, 4 April 1887, p.4.

37. *Daily Telegraph*, 4 April 1887, p.3.

38. *Pall Mall Gazette*, 5 May 1887, p.11.

39. In a letter to Solomon J. Solomon dated 23 May [1905], Canon Barnett had suggested an exhibition 'illustrating Jewish history, life and art' to be held in the Whitechapel Art Gallery. *Minutes of the meeting of the Jewish Exhibition Committee*, 22 October 1905. Archive of the Whitechapel Art Gallery. I am grateful to Rachel Dickson for providing me with a copy of this document.

40. *Jewish Chronicle*, 15 March 1901, p.14.

41. Koven (see note 10); Steyn (see note 4), p.44.

42. Quoted in *Supplement to the Jewish Chronicle*, 9 November 1906, p.ii.

43. According to Geoffrey Alderman, London's Jewish population had grown from about 46,000 on the eve of the Russian pogroms to about 135,000 in 1900. It was estimated in 1899 that roughly 120,000 Jews lived in the East End. Alderman (see note 17), pp.117–18.

44. To counter anti-alien prejudice, the exhibition committee initially suggested that the industrial and commercial contribution of the immigrants to the British economy should be shown by displaying handiwork or statistics. This idea does not appear to have been realised for reasons unknown to the present author. *Minutes of the Meeting of the Jewish Exhibition Committee* (see note 39), 22 October 1905 and 5 March 1906.

45. *Jewish World*, 9 November 1906, p.560.

46. Whitechapel Art Gallery, *Exhibition of Jewish Art and Antiquities*, 7 November to 12 December 1906, Noon to 10 p.m. Apart from displaying fewer relevant objects, the catalogue did not contain anything like the several pages-long text on the history of British Jewry contained in the catalogue of 1887. *Catalogue of the Anglo-Jewish Historical Exhibition* (see note 20), pp.1–7. The strong presence of archaeological artefacts in 1887 had been due to the involvement of representatives of prominent archaeological societies on the exhibition committee.

47. Whitechapel Art Gallery (see note 46), pp.33–4.

48. Ibid. pp.84–5; *Catalogue of the Anglo-Jewish Historical Exhibition* (see note 20), 83–4.

49. Whitechapel Art Gallery (see note 46), p.85; *Jewish World*, 7 December 1906, pp.650–51.

50. *Jewish World*, 7 December 1906, p.647.

51. *Supplement to the Jewish Chronicle*, 9 November 1906, pp.iii–v (p.iv).

52. Cohen (see note 4), chapter 6.

53. The following newspapers were included in the analysis: *Der arbeter fraynd, Daily News, Daily Telegraph, Dibre hayomim, East End News and London Shipping Chronicle, East London Observer, Jewish Chronicle, Jewish World, The Graphic, Der yidisher zhournal, Der yidisher wechentlicher zhournal, Illustrated London News, Museums Journal, Pall Mall Gazette, Times, Der yidisher ekspres*. Ten of these 16 papers reported on the exhibition. Exceptions were *Pall Mall Gazette, Illustrated London News* and the Yiddish papers other than *Der yidisher zhournal*.

54. University College London, Special Collections, Mocatta Boxed Pamphlets BA 6WHI. *Whitechapel Art Gallery Report*, 1906, p.9.

55. C. Campbell Ross quoted in *Jewish World*, 7 December 1906, p.647.

56. Marion Harry Spielmann in *The Graphic*, 24 November 1906, p.692.

57. *Daily News*, 7 November 1906, p.12.

58. *The Graphic*, 24 November 1906, p. 692 (emphasis added).

59. On the basis of the double function of many minority museums discussed above I apply here to those museums in general what Rickie Burman has observed for museums established by religious minority groups (see note 3), p.136.
60. Steyn (note 4), p.50.
61. *Der yidisher ekspres*, 14 November 1906, p.3 (translation K.P.).
62. Jarrassé (see note 4), p.50.
63. '"For the great mass of men and women in this country anything biblical has a charm which nothing can lessen or destroy": *Supplement to the Jewish Chronicle*', 8 April 1887, p.2.

From Bola d'Amour to the Ultimate Cheesecake: 150 Years of Anglo-Jewish Cookery Writing

JANE GERSON

In July 2004 the *Jewish Chronicle* (*JC*) asked readers for their favourite chicken soup recipes. Flooded with responses, the *JC* concluded: 'It seems that only two chicken soup ingredients are sacred – the chicken and the onion. Everything else is up for spirited debate.'[1] The precise relationship between text and practice in cookery writing is hard to determine. It is difficult to identify which recipes disseminated in books and cookery columns are made and who makes them. Even, or maybe especially, when a particular dish is highly popular and strongly identified with a specific community, recipes for its preparation are invariably disputed. In Jewish circles arguments about the merits of different recipes for chicken soup are legendary. While cookery books may not reveal in a direct way what food people prepare in the privacy of their homes, they do yield valuable information. They encode messages about the desirable eating habits of the communities they address, incorporating their aspirations into manuals for eating in everyday life. As much as their overt role of providing instructions to prepare food, cookery books are 'a malleable medium for expressing subtle distinctions of class, religious orientation and cultural identification'.[2]

Nevertheless food writing has received scant attention from academics. As Nicola Humble, a historian of British cookery books, observes, food writing is 'among the most commercial of literary forms, yet what we might call its textuality – the way it addresses its readers, the form and genesis of its recipes, its tone of voice – remains essentially unregarded'.[3] In terms of Anglo-Jewish historiography this is a notably under-researched area. Despite the enormous fascination of the Jewish press with ideas of Jewish food and the explosion in publications about food in recent years there has been little professional historical research into the subject. In 1975 the former editor of the *JC*, John Shaftesley, published an engaging, discursive essay called 'Culinary Aspects of

Anglo-Jewry'.[4] The essay provided many leads for further research, many of which remain to be explored. Nevertheless the essay sparked interest in some neglected Anglo-Jewish cookery books and with the growth of food history in the 1980s a number of these books were reprinted.

The publication in 1983 of a facsimile edition of the first Anglo-Jewish cookery book, *The Jewish Manual or Practical Information in Jewish & Modern Cookery with a Collection of Valuable Recipes & Hints Relating to the Toilette*, published anonymously by 'A Lady' in 1846, caused a flurry of excitement in the Jewish press.[5] Later attributed to Judith Montefiore, the wife of the celebrated Jewish philanthropist, Moses Montefiore, *The Jewish Manual* aimed to make available 'the receipts peculiar to the Jewish people', addressing both the 'Jewish housekeeper' and also 'those ladies who are not of the Hebrew persuasion'.[6] The 'discovery' of the first Anglo-Jewish cookery book made good copy, but as Barbara Kirshenblatt-Gimblett has revealed, this 'discovery' had been made on at least six previous occasions from 1903 to 1975 and the fact it was treated as a revelation in 1983 tells its own story of selective public memory.[7]

Despite renewed enthusiasm for Judith Montefiore's work, reactions to the recipes in *The Jewish Manual* reveal an anachronistic perception of what can be identified as 'Jewish food', at odds with Montefiore's original intention. Ironically the first self-defined attempt by an Anglo-Jewish woman to distinguish an identity for Jewish cookery in Britain has largely been regarded as 'not Jewish enough' by twentieth century commentators. John Shaftesley definitively established this opinion in his 1975 essay, although it had already been expressed in Jewish journalism since the 1950s. Writing for the *JC* in 1951, Rachael Beth-Zion observed: 'The recipes do not strike the modern reader as being particularly Jewish.'[8] Shaftesley spelt out the obvious subtext to this, writing: 'Lady Montefiore, giving mainly general and Sephardi recipes, is singularly oblivious of Yiddish and East European dishes.'[9]

This view has persisted despite developments in Jewish food history and the publication in Britain of Claudia Roden's *Book of Jewish Food* in 1997, which in its global reach definitively constructs a Jewish food identity beyond the parameters of Ashkenazi cookery.[10] Yet this did not deter the journalist Adam Raphael from writing in 1998 that *The Jewish Manual* 'set out a number of "receipts" consistent with the religion, but few that you'd recognize as Jewish food today. Plenty of French or English recipes, lots from Spain or Portugal. Few from Eastern Europe

... there is no gefilte fish'.[11] The omission of gefilte fish, the iconic Ashkenazi Sabbath dish, was clearly problematic for Raphael and indicates how culinary identity is subject to historical processes. Ideas of what food can be deemed to represent Jewish identity raise questions as to the precise relationship between particular dishes and their identification as 'Jewish'. There is clearly a dissonance between the historical practice of Anglo-Jewish food identity, and the way that identity is practised in contemporary Britain. This survey of the work of three leading Anglo-Jewish cookery writers, Judith Montefiore, Florence Greenberg and Evelyn Rose, spanning a century and a half of Anglo-Jewish cookery writing, reveals the extent to which what is regarded as distinctively 'Jewish' cookery depends on historically and culturally determined values.

'Receipts Peculiar to the Jewish People'

The publication of *The Jewish Manual* in 1846 marked a watershed in Anglo-Jewish food history, demonstrating a founding act of Jewish culinary distinctiveness. In the preface to her book, Judith Montefiore (1784–1862) announced:

> Our collection will be found to contain all the best receipts, hitherto bequeathed only by memory or manuscript, from one generation to another of the Jewish nation, as well as those which come under the denomination of plain English dishes, and also such French ones as are now in general use at refined modern tables.[12]

This pronouncement augured nothing less than the establishment of an Anglo-Jewish cuisine bringing together Spanish and Portuguese Sephardi and German Ashkenazi recipes with select French and English dishes. As Kirshenblatt-Gimblett observes, Montefiore 'affirmed the existence of a distinctive Jewish cuisine while presenting it as a cosmopolitanizing influence'.[13]

The Jewish Manual was published in June 1846 in London, Edinburgh and Dublin for the steep price of five shillings. (Fifteen years later the complete bound volume of *Mrs Beeton's Book of Household Management* cost seven shillings and sixpence). The book ran to 244 pages divided between 'practical information in Jewish and modern cookery' and 'valuable recipes and hints relating to the toilette'. The cookery section contained chapters on soups, sauces and forcemeat, fish, meats and poultry, vegetables, pastry, sweet dishes, preserves, pickling and 'receipts for invalids'. There was also a glossary that gave an interesting combination of French and Spanish cooking terminology. The choice of recipes accurately reflected Judith Montefiore's background and cultural influences. She was born into an Ashkenazi family who had emigrated from Holland during the 1770s. In 1812 her marriage to Moses Montefiore joined her to a distinguished Sephardi family who were members of Bevis Marks Synagogue in London; a congregation that Judith joined after her marriage.[14]

Despite the synthesis of cuisines from different countries, Sephardi dishes are a dominant influence in the book, with many ingredients and recipes deriving from Spain and Portugal. The glossary of unfamiliar terms includes 'chorissa', described as 'a sausage peculiar to the Jewish kitchen of delicate and *piquante* flavour'. Another Sephardi term in the glossary is 'salmis', described as 'a hash, only a superior kind, being more delicately seasoned, and usually made of cold poultry'.[15] Savoury Sephardi recipes included 'a superior white soup' called *almondegos* soup; *escobeche*, a fried fish dish marinated in ginger, allspice and cayenne pepper; *impanada*, another spicy fish dish; and 'fowls stewed with rice and *chorisa*'.[16] Illustrating an example of Judith Montefiore's fusion style of cookery, a recipe for *kugel and commean* mixes Sephardi, Ashkenazi and English influences.[17] *Commean* derives from the Sephardi Sabbath dish *hamin*, made with beef, Spanish peas and beans, while *kugel* is an Ashkenazi pudding. Kirshenblatt-Gimblett observes: 'In Lady Montefiore's version, the *kugel* is a sweet English pudding made of suet, bread crumbs and brown sugar, seasoned with nutmeg, ginger, cloves and allspice.' She notes that this conjunction offers 'a quintessential synthesis' of Sephardi and Ashkenazi cuisine: 'This one dish thus combines terminology from two Jewish languages (Anglo-Sephardic vernacular and Yiddish) and culinary principles from two cultures (Jewish and British).'[18]

Given the historical importance of *The Jewish Manual*, its reception in the *JC* was surprisingly muted. The *JC*'s reviewer rather condescendingly wrote:

> This useful little book reminds us how comparatively useless are the ordinary cookery books in the Jewish kitchen; and it certainly supplies a desideratum of which not merely the good housekeeper, in the complimentary sense of the term, but the accomplished hostess who desires to give an hospitable and agreeable entertainment, will not be slow to avail herself.[19]

One is left to speculate what the uncomplimentary sense of 'the good housekeeper' might be, but the tone of the review clearly reveals that the book was being marketed for the 'accomplished hostess' of the superior Anglo-Jewish household, or at least the aspiring accomplished hostess. Reflecting the values of her period, Judith Montefiore is wary of the ability of servants, warning that if the mistress of the household found household management too 'humble' a pursuit, she would be 'incompetent to direct her servant, upon whose inferior judgment and taste she is obliged to depend'. Such dependency would inevitably lead to social failure, with the hostess:

> continually subjected to impositions from her ignorance of what is required for the dishes she selects, while a lavish extravagance or parsimonious monotony betrays her utter inexperience in all the minute yet indispensable details of elegant hospitality.[20]

The descriptive words of approval – superior, elegant, fine, refined, judicious, graceful; and those of disapproval – inferior, hackneyed, vulgar, common place, crude – used repeatedly throughout *The Jewish Manual* drum in the ideological message of the work.

The transformation of one of the few dishes still commonplace in the late twentieth century Jewish kitchen, *lokshen* pudding (a sweet, spicy pudding made with noodles), into an elegant and superior confection is representative of the general approach. The anglicised Yiddish title 'a luction' is given the alternative name 'a Rachael' and French terminology is introduced with the first instruction being to 'make a thin *nouilles* paste'; finally the pudding is rendered superior at the table: 'When turned out pour over a fine custard, or cream, flavored with brandy, and sweetened to taste.'[21] The discovery of a familiar Jewish dish led the reviewer of *The Jewish Manual* in the *JC* in 1951, to exclaim under a caption 'Alias Lokshen!' that it proved 'on closer inspection to be no more or less than our old friend – a lokshen pudding!' She went on to query 'does a pudding under another name smell just as sweet?'[22]

The judicious renaming of a common Jewish dish and subtle use of a language suffused with significance for class and status deliberately constructs a Jewish culinary identity as superior, keen to disguise any vulgar origins. In this Judith Montefiore was adopting a ploy common to cookery book writing since ancient times; the aristocratic purloining and embellishment with status ingredients of common, peasant dishes. The medieval historian of food, Massimo Montanari, describes, for example, how a common dish of turnips in a fourteenth century Tuscan cookery book was ennobled by the addition of socially superior spices: 'The logic of the discourse is clear: once spiced, any food whatsoever becomes worthy of the master's table.'[23] *The Jewish Manual* represents an act of culinary ennoblement, conferring Jewish food identity with the attributes necessary to be esteemed in well-to-do Victorian society. It cautions aspiring Jewish households to eschew vulgar and coarse practices at the table while asserting a discreet culinary superiority, derived from continental influences, to command respect in non-Jewish society.[24]

The ultimate status recipe in *The Jewish Manual* was bola d'amour. Bola d'amour was a well-established Sephardi sweet, the most luxurious of a range of 'bolas' from the Iberian Peninsula. (Bola is a generic name and remains a common term for a wide range of Sephardi cakes and pastries.) Claudia Roden explains that it is very like the Italian confection, *Monte Sinai con Uova Filate*, which is still made in Livorno to celebrate Purim. Roden draws a connection between Moses Montefiore's Livorno origins and the inclusion of bola d'amour in the *Jewish Manual*.[25] In a British context the recipe was clearly marked out as exotic and superior, deriving added charisma from its romantic name. Bola d'amour was a fabulous concoction requiring twenty eggs spun into threads with white sugar and shaped into a pyramid with layers of marzipan and citron. Judith Montefiore described it as an 'exquisite confection' and, assuming a readership with wealth equivalent to her own, stated in a throwaway last line that it was 'generally ornamented with myrtle and gold and silver leaf'.[26]

Roland Barthes, in his essay on 'ornamental cookery', describes a 'dreamlike cookery, presented not to be cooked ... but to be marvelled at'.[27] We are increasingly familiar with this phenomenon but according to Massimo Montanari this appears to have been a function of cookery books from their inception and the inclusion of recipes that were designed for fantasy rather than cooking was a well-developed phenomenon in Victorian England. Nicola Humble cites Mrs Beeton's inclusion of a recipe for turtle soup in her *Book of Household Management*, 'a dish so expensive and complicated that it ... was quite beyond the scope of a domestic kitchen': 'The point of such rarefied inclusions is to give the upwardly mobile reader something to aspire to and to establish Household Management as an arbiter of elegant living.'[28] Unlike Mrs Beeton, who certainly never had the means or social standing to make real turtle soup, the Montefiores were more than able to realise the most extravagant of dishes in the *Jewish Manual* and bola d'amour was no doubt a special occasion spectacle for the Montefiore household's elegant table. But it was clearly only a confection for the most elite and wealthy Jewish households, leaving the aspirational Jewish middle classes to dream about such glamorous feasts when reading the cookery book.

The distinctive thread of Anglo-Jewish culinary tradition established by Judith Montefiore did not definitively emerge again until the twentieth century. Even after mass immigration from Eastern Europe in the late nineteenth century, the typical East European food that proliferated in sites such as London's East End did not initially influence the character of Anglo-Jewish cuisine.[29] On the contrary, the mission of indigenous Jews was to anglicise and integrate Jewish immigrants from Eastern Europe, including an effort to teach them English cookery. This project was manifested by the publication of a spate of cookery books for the Jewish working class offering an education in cheap English dishes supplemented by cursory descriptions of Jewish dietary law and a section on Passover cooking.[30]

It was not until 1934 that an Anglo-Jewish cookery book of comparable importance to *The Jewish Manual* was published. The *Jewish Chronicle Cookery Book* by Florence Greenberg provided British Jews with a comprehensive collection of recipes for all aspects of food provision appropriate to the twentieth century Jewish household.[31] This was followed in 1947 by the publication of *Florence Greenberg's Cookery Book*, a landmark in Anglo-Jewish culinary history, which became the definitive Anglo-Jewish cookery book in the post-war period, re-printed in many revised editions and an essential item in most Anglo-Jewish households.[32]

An 'Unwholesome' Tradition

The career of Florence Greenberg (1882–1980) as the authoritative Jewish cookery writer in twentieth century Britain began by chance. In May 1920 Leopold Greenberg, then editor of the *JC*, married his second wife, Florence Oppenheimer.[33] Enthused by her excellent cooking skills, and despite her protests that she had 'no literary ability', Greenberg encouraged his new wife to write a cookery column for the *JC* and in September 1920 the 'Jewish Cookery' column was launched.[34] Florence Greenberg continued to write the column for the next 42 years, retiring at the age of 80 in 1962.

Florence Greenberg was the product of a Jewish home, which she described as 'a typical, middle-class Victorian household'.[35] Her father, Alexander Oppenheimer, was from Germany and her mother, Eliza Pool, was from a Dutch background. Her maternal grandfather, Salomon Pool, born in Holland, became Parnassim of the Sephardim Synagogue in London, although 'belonging originally to the German section of his coreligionists'.[36] The synthesis of Ashkenazi, Sephardi and Victorian culture shaped the sensibility of Florence Greenberg just as it had shaped that of Judith Montefiore, but her life experience was very different. Florence Greenberg's early aspiration to become a nurse was obstructed by her father's strict Victorian attitudes and she did not realise her ambition until she was 29. She became a nursing sister in the First World War, going to Gallipoli, Egypt and Palestine, where she served with such distinction she was mentioned in dispatches.[37]

Florence Greenberg's training as a nurse was an important influence in her approach to cookery, which was orientated by a concern with health. While her background had features in common with those of Judith Montefiore, the historical conditions that Greenberg contended with make a stark contrast with the preoccupations of her aristocratic forebear. The straitened conditions of middle-class life in Britain after the First World War, with households coping with a scarcity of many staple food products and a drastic decline in domestic service, transformed attitudes to domestic life. It was in this environment that Florence Greenberg's first 'Jewish Cookery' column appeared without a credit or editorial comment on 10 September 1920.[38] While working within the established Anglo-Jewish culinary tradition, Florence Greenberg's approach was inclusive and sensitive to economic limitations. From the outset the column provided modest, carefully presented recipes appropriate for a wide range of households. It was addressed directly to housewives cooking for their families themselves and was full of sensible, economic advice. An early column on casserole cooking, for instance, advised the purchase of a safe boiling mat to place underneath the casserole, which 'cost only 6d at ironmongers'.[39] In another early column recipes for cakes and biscuits were given because they were 'all simple and quite economical. Most are made without eggs – a great consideration in these days'.[40] The cakes were typical Anglo-Jewish fare and included Dutch butter cakes, gingerbread and coconut pyramids.

The Jewish cookery column proved extremely popular with readers and there was soon demand for an up-to-date cookery book. After

Leopold Greenberg's death in 1931, Florence Greenberg approached the new editor of the *JC*, her stepson Ivan Greenberg, with a proposal for such a book. In March 1934 the *Jewish Chronicle Cookery Book*, 'edited by Mrs L.J. Greenberg', was published at a cost of 3/6d and was promoted in the *JC* with the tag 'a Long-Felt Want Supplied'.[41] The book's 308 pages provided a comprehensive collection of recipes for all aspects of family food provision. There were chapters on hors d'oeuvres, soups, fish, vegetables, luncheon and supper dishes, meat dishes, poultry and game, sauces, and salads. No fewer than six chapters were devoted to sweets and pastries and a further four to cakes, biscuits, bread, jams and confectionary. There were also special sections on savouries, egg dishes, casserole and invalid cooking as well as sandwiches and beverages. In the opening pages there was information about 'The Modern Kitchen', 'Food Values', 'Feeding of Children 2–6', and an innovatory section on 'a Slimming Diet'. There was also a short entry on how 'to Kasher Meat and Poultry'.[42]

Despite the trappings of a conventional and comprehensive cookery book in the style of nineteenth century manuals, the work marked quite a bold break with tradition, and an attempt to influence modern Jewish dietary habits. The preface stated:

> Through the marvels of modern inventions, elaborations in cookery have become easily possible. But the nutritive value of food may be seriously altered by these elaborations – e.g. the essential vitamins may be completely destroyed. The fact that certain culinary processes alter the nutritive value of food is one important reason why I have omitted from this book some of the traditional Jewish recipes. A secondary reason for their exclusion is that there is little time for the modern woman to spare in preparing such things, even if they were wholesome.[43]

This modernising agenda resulted in the omission of a significant number of traditional Jewish dishes. Prominent amongst these were *cholent* (Sabbath stew typically made with meat and dried beans), potato *latkes* (potato pancakes), *tzimmas* (sweet beef brisket and carrot casserole), chopped liver, salt beef, *blintzes* (East European yeast pancake), and bagels. Nor were there any recipes for apple *strudel*, coffee *kuchen* (yeast cake) or cheesecake with cheese in it. 'Cheese' in the medieval period referred to curds in general and by the eighteenth century milk curds were rarely used to make cakes. Lemon or almonds were the common flavourings for 'cheesecakes' in the Victorian period (lemon, almond and Seville orange were suggested as flavourings for cheesecake in *The Jewish Manual*).[44] By including recipes for lemon and almond 'cheesecake' in the 1934 book, Florence Greenberg revealed her Victorian rather than Ashkenazi heritage.[45] Similarly, Ashkenazi chicken soup received remarkably little attention. Only 'Chicken Soup *a la Francaise*' was included in the chapter on soup, with the familiar 'chicken broth' only making an appearance in the chapter on 'invalid cookery'.[46] The traditional recipes that were included were mostly given with English, not Yiddish names, (for example beetroot soup and honey cake, but not *borsht* and *lekach*). Yiddish was used very sparingly, notably for 'Gefieltte Fish' (given in quotation marks) and *lockschen* pudding.[47]

Whilst not admitting many traditional Ashkenazi dishes, particularly those from Eastern Europe, the book retained a range of Sephardi dishes that were present in *The Jewish Manual*. The book, for instance, included recipes for bola cake and other Sephardi classics such as fish in egg and lemon sauce as well as the *Marranos* inspired Dutch cakes, butter cake and the unusually named 'stuffed monkey' (a sweet pastry with a spicy filling). Florence Greenberg also employed Spanish terminology, like '*panada*' (to describe the basic constituent for soufflés), a term also used by Judith Montefiore who appears to have been an influence. Indeed it is known that Greenberg had a copy of *The Jewish Manual* amongst her extensive collection of cookery books.[48]

Instead of highlighting traditional and festival food as the cornerstone of Jewish cookery as is usual in contemporary Jewish cookery books, Florence Greenberg's mission was to promote healthy eating. 'More and more we realise and appreciate the dietary value of fresh, uncooked fruit and vegetables', she wrote in her introduction to salads, 'foods which were hitherto only edible in a cooked state are now relished raw'.[49] She advised that potatoes 'should never really be peeled before they are cooked' because 'so much nourishment lies immediately underneath the skin'.[50] Educating children in good eating habits was a stated priority and 'feeding of young children' was regarded as forming 'the most important section of the housewife's duties'.[51] When it came to sweets, she recognised that they were 'essential for the majority of children under modern nervous conditions' but their consumption should be limited.[52] For 'would-be slimmers' she advised, 'light wholesome food with a very large proportion of fruit and green vegetables'.[53]

The promotion of health at the expense of tradition contained an unstated subtext, which was implicitly critical of the eating habits of East European immigrants. As an English-born, middle-class woman and a trained nurse, Florence Greenberg absorbed the attitudes of the nutritional experts of her day that were critical of Jewish immigrant food culture. In promoting their advice she sought to exclude the supposed ill-effects of the heavy, greasy food of much Jewish immigrant cookery. In the process she also excluded a significant aspect of the culture and, to some extent, religious practice that was bound up with traditional dishes. In excluding *cholent* from her cookery book, for instance, she also denied the religious injunctions concerning Sabbath food. The issue was not only one of health, but also of anglicisation and class differences in the Jewish community. The promotional extracts from reviews in the *JC* stressed the book was 'equally applicable to cooking for non-Jewish tables' and 'suitable for all kitchens'.[54] High regard for the *Jewish Chronicle Cookery Book* was largely due to its impeccably 'English' credentials. These credentials enabled her to gain work from the Ministry of Food during the Second World War, giving talks across the country and for the BBC's daily government sponsored food programme *The Kitchen Front*. Through these appearances Florence Greenberg became a familiar name to housewives in Britain. However, although a famous cookery writer within Anglo-Jewish circles, Greenberg never referred openly to her Jewish identity and its influence on her cookery in her radio broadcasts.

Florence Greenberg's Cookery Book

After the war the *JC* prepared for the publication of a new cookery book by Florence Greenberg tailored to the culinary demands of post-war society. The advertisements that appeared in December 1947 editions of the *JC* described the book as offering 'Recipes for austerity combined with recipes for the days of plenty. Compiled in conformity with the Jewish dietary laws'.[55] Ambrose Heath, a well-known English cookery writer and broadcaster of the period, wrote a glowing review for the *JC*. He particularly admired 'the large number of recipes that show touches of inventiveness and initiative … where the genius of the Continental cook has touched and illuminated the dullest of ordinary dishes'.[56] The twin themes of the 'continental' (rather than Jewish) nature of the recipes and their accessibility to non-Jewish users were strong elements in marketing the book. However this did not mean that the book reached a non-Jewish market. When Penguin Books became interested in buying rights for a paperback edition in 1965, the *JC* acknowledged that Penguin sales would not infringe theirs, as the market was quite different.[57] The *JC* publication was wholly aimed at newly married Jewish women who required instruction in how to cook for a modern Jewish household. The appeal therefore was to a Jewish user who felt reassured by the idea that the recipes were not locked into a Jewish culinary ghetto.

Ambrose Heath's review underlined this attitude and as a revered English (non-Jewish) cookery expert himself, his verdict was highly influential. He predicted that Florence Greenberg's cookery book would prove to be 'the standard work' not just for the austerity present, but for 'cookery in general'. For Jewish households in the following years, this is precisely what the book became. The imagined alliance with a British tradition is clearly demonstrated in what became the copywriters' favourite epithet for Florence Greenberg – 'the Jewish Mrs Beeton'.

It is interesting to compare the differences and similarities between the 1934 and the 1947 book, which, despite the change of name and post-war re-launch, would be more accurately described as a revised and enlarged new edition than as a new work. While the structure of the book remained essentially the same, there were some significant changes in the content. Firstly, the bold attempt to sweep aside much traditional food as indigestible and laborious was curbed. The introduction no longer made reference to the omission of traditional Jewish recipes. Nor was there any longer a reference to the modern woman having 'no time to spare' to make them. Instead there was a new emphasis on the exotic flavour of the dishes which would help 'vary and enliven' the meals of the general public. Traditional Jewish dishes (described as 'Continental') were presented to meet this objective:

> I refer particularly to some of the fish dishes, sauces, and puddings: 'gefillte' fish for instance, a delicious mixture of stewed fish, vegetables, and ground almonds; sweet and sour sauce, a universal favourite made with stock, vinegar, and syrup; almond pudding, and apple *steffon* flavoured with cinnamon.[58]

The suggestion was that some Jewish housewives might have lost knowledge and attachment to these traditional recipes. In general the 1947 volume began to signal a greater tolerance for Ashkenazi dishes and even an attempt to acquaint middle-class Anglo-Jewry with their East European heritage.

There were a number of traditional, East European dishes in the 1947 edition that had not made an appearance in 1934. Carrot *tzimmas*, potato *latkes*, boiled salt beef, *blintzes*, Purim fritters, *haman taschen* (Purim pastries), apple strudel, cheese cake (with cheese in it), *rothe gruetze* (a type of red berry fool), coffee *kuchen*, and pickled gherkins all made a first appearance in the post-war book.[59] There was also a greater use of Yiddish terminology. Beetroot soup, for instance, was now called '*bortsch*' in a sub-heading.[60] As Florence Greenberg responded to public demand in her revisions, it is likely that these recipes were included by popular request. The remarkable relegation of chicken soup in 1934 was also addressed in 1947, when chicken broth was rescued from the Invalid cookery chapter and instated with the main soups.[61] The culinary influence of late nineteenth and twentieth century immigration, so evident in the diverse fare offered by Jewish bakers and confectioners, delicatessens, butchers and fishmongers in areas of immigrant settlement, had been almost wholly excluded from the 1934 *JC Cookery Book*. In 1947, the inclusion of a growing number of traditional Ashkenazi dishes indicated that immigrant food was now being admitted into the established Anglo-Jewish culinary canon, as mediated by Florence Greenberg and the *JC* readership which she represented.

The move from being the *JC* book to being Florence Greenberg's book signalled its new status as a national resource, written by a cookery expert recognised by the British establishment. *Florence Greenberg's Cookery Book* marked an assertion of cultural identity that announced the legitimate existence of an Anglo-Jewish culinary tradition. The book, which was marketed on a much larger scale than the 1934 publication, did not take a marginal role, either as an elite manual for the upper classes, or as an 'educative' tool for working-class Jewish immigrants. It announced that Jewish cookery was a mainstream, authoritative practice of equal value to the English canon. The new confidence was not, as it was in a later period, an affirmation of ethnic diversity, but rather a claim to a British Jewish identity.

Although Florence Greenberg's reputation continued to rise in the post-war period, the style and content of her book had been forged in the inter-war and wartime periods, and derived, ultimately, from her middle-class, Anglo-Jewish, Victorian upbringing. Despite making some concessions to the growing nostalgia for traditional East European fare and Yiddish terminology in the post-Holocaust era, she did not wholly adapt to the new climate. Florence Greenberg belonged firmly to an earlier tradition with the emphasis on 'anglo' rather than 'ethnic' food. She did not represent the Ashkenazi wave of delicatessen food – the bagels, lox, pastrami, cheesecake and strudels, which were popularised in post-war Britain largely influenced by trends in America. Nevertheless, aiming to capitalise on the trend for 'ethnic' cuisine, Penguin Books approached the *JC* in 1965 with a view to publishing *Florence Greenberg's Cookery Book*. The *JC* quickly agreed and the Penguin paperback, *Jewish Cookery*, was published in 1967. The Penguin book was an exact reproduction of the 1963 edition of *Florence Greenberg's Cookery Book*, but it was packaged to appeal to a generation who identified Jewish food with American style *haimishe* cooking. It featured colour photographs of apple strudels on the front cover and a pastrami and pickle roll on the back – iconic images of Ashkenazi 'deli' food, rather than representative of Florence Greenberg's recipes. There is no record of readers' responses to the Penguin paperback, but it proved very successful and after many editions it finally went out of print in 1997.

Reinventing Tradition

Despite the dominant reputation of Florence Greenberg, it was the Manchester born cookery writer Evelyn Rose (1925–2003) who can be credited with the most concerted effort to develop a modern, post-war identity for Anglo-Jewish cookery. Unlike Florence Greenberg, who confined herself to testing and writing recipes without literary pretensions, Evelyn Rose was a food writer and prolific journalist. Paul Levy, in his obituary of Rose, asserted that she 'was probably the first professional Jewish cookery writer, at least in Britain', noting that Florence Greenberg, as the wife of the editor of the *JC*, 'for many years contributed her recipes for nothing, even signing over to the paper the royalties from her books'.[62] Florence Greenberg produced a single definitive cookery book that only required periodic updating, while Evelyn Rose, competing with a growing number of Jewish cookery writers, published new books every few years.

Nevertheless Evelyn Rose did produce a comprehensive cookery book to rival Florence Greenberg. In 1976 *The Complete International Jewish Cookbook* was published, aspiring to provide a manual for the Jewish household in the late twentieth century. The book comprised almost 700 pages – more than twice the length of *Florence Greenberg's Cookery Book*. In addition to the chapters on starters, fish, meat, vegetables, desserts, baking, and preserves there was a chapter on entertaining and an extensive section on Jewish festival food running to nearly 100 pages. The book was reprinted in several editions and in 1992 a revised *New Complete International Jewish Cookbook*, including the innovation of a section on vegetarian food, was published. Evelyn Rose always endeavoured to ally traditional Jewish cookery with an innovative approach. Indeed the opening sentence of Rose's introduction to the *International Jewish Cookbook*, which suggests that even the biblical Rebecca experimented in the kitchen, was clearly an attempt to reassure her public that innovation was an ancient Jewish tradition:

> One can almost pinpoint the exact occasion, in the second millennium BCE, when the art of Jewish cookery was born. On that day the course of world history was changed when the matriarch Rebecca, by the judicious use of herbs and spices, gave the savour of wild venison to the insipid flesh of a young kid, and established a culinary philosophy of 'taste with economy' that has been followed by her descendants ever since.[63]

While Evelyn Rose's cookery writing attempted to break the mould of Anglo-Jewish cookery writing, she also sought to establish new connections with Jewish food history.[64]

Early in her career, in 1954, she presented a cookery segment on a BBC programme called *About the Home*. In marked contrast with Florence Greenberg's suppression of her Jewish identity in the British media, Rose produced a series on Jewish cookery for the programme in which Ashkenazi food and Yiddish names were featured prominently. She showed her audience how to make cheese *blintzes*, *plava* (sponge cake), *holishkes* (stuffed cabbage), *lokshen* pudding, potato *latkes* and potato *kugel* while the *Radio Times* published recipes for these dishes alongside notes about their Jewish context.[65] In 1958 Rose became the cookery editor for Manchester's *Jewish Gazette* for which she wrote a weekly column. From 1959 she started writing for the *JC* alongside Florence Greenberg and in 1963 she became the *JC*'s cookery editor after Florence Greenberg's retirement – a position she retained until her death in 2003.

Although a career woman herself, Evelyn Rose's journalism presented a strong family oriented image with the housewife placed firmly in the kitchen. Rose's early recipes have been described as being for women 'with three hours to spare to prepare a mid-week supper'.[66]

Directors of Vallentine Mitchell and *JC* Publications showed their concern at her more leisured approach and expensive tastes in comparison with Florence Greenberg, when they described the manuscript of Rose's first book, *The Jewish Home*, as 'too obviously aimed at the upper-middle-class'.[67] Rose strongly promoted the idea that new technology and convenience food could reconcile the opposing pressures on women between going out to work and fulfilling their traditional role within the family, including the preparation of traditional fare. This was a compromise in comparison with Florence Greenberg's initial, radical objective outlined in 1934 to simply exclude traditional food when 'there is little time for the modern woman to spare in preparing such things'.[68]

In another clear break with Florence Greenberg's style, Evelyn Rose was keen to promote once frowned upon East European dishes, adapted for modern housewives in their new suburban kitchens. According to one obituary she made '*haimishe* recipes with a modern take' her distinctive style.[69] She not only adapted traditional dishes to a modern, but also to an affluent setting. The middle-class fashion for promoting *haimishe* food skirted over any reference to the poverty and hardship that permeated Jewish immigrant memoirs.

While retaining a foothold in *haimishe* tradition, recipes were adapted to meet the requirements of new technology in the kitchen and new ingredients. In an article titled 'Tradition up to date', for instance, Rose gave recipes for blender *borscht* and refrigerator *kuchen*, asserting that modern kitchen appliances could create a 'contemporary version of the old traditions, giving a "*haimishe*" quality to our food'.[70] Her innovative recipes for cheesecake illustrate the process. By the time Evelyn Rose took over the *JC*'s cookery column cheesecake was already becoming widely available with readymade varieties on sale in grocery stores and the new supermarkets. Evelyn Rose soon adopted the American approach to making cheesecake, modernising the *haimishe* recipe. For *Shavuot* in 1965 Rose declared a break with 'the traditional Russian and Polish version', which was deemed to be 'a simple affair', and gave a recipe for what she regarded as the 'ultimate cheesecake' – a 'velvet cheesecake', which became a favourite with *JC* readers.[71] Having broken the bounds of the traditional East European recipe, innovative cheesecake recipes began to proliferate in Rose's cookery column, ranging from low calorie, refrigerated versions made with cottage cheese, a biscuit base and fruit toppings, to four inch deep cakes baked with double cream and chocolate. Such innovations were quickly assimilated into Jewish culinary tradition, and when the *JC* conducted a survey of 'the nation's favourite fress' in 2002, cheesecake entered the top ten at number nine.[72]

No less important than the reinvention of traditional Ashkenazi food was a new promotion of Sephardi food. Complementing her advocacy of traditional East European Jewish dishes, Evelyn Rose also embraced modern Sephardi cookery. This was not a rediscovery of the old Spanish and Portuguese recipes from *The Jewish Manual*, which were still partly represented in Florence Greenberg's work. Rather it reflected the availability in Britain of new produce from the Mediterranean as well as the stimulus of new recipes brought by post-war Jewish immigrants from the Middle East. The cultural exchange of cooking practices in the Sephardi and Ashkenazi kitchens became a theme of Rose's cookery articles early in her career. One article asked 'Have you ever tried Sephardi cooking?' and asserted:

> In Manchester we have a very strong Sephardi community some of whose traditional dishes are relished by Ashkenazi-born members of the community who are fortunate enough to have friends and relatives with the Sephardi know-how, or to be invited as guests to Sephardi functions.[73]

According to a report about a luncheon where 'Sephardi dishes took their place among the pickled meat and salads', there were such high levels of appreciation of the Sephardi dishes that it 'could very well augur Sephardi cuisines for many husbands and children in Ashkenazi homes'.[74] A 1960 article entitled 'A new Jewish cuisine?' elaborated the idea of connections between the different Jewish cultures:

> The Ashkenazi Jew will think of potatoes as a staple food whilst the Sephardi cannot imagine life without rice, though both may eat the same chicken. The Russian Jew will enjoy a stuffed cabbage leaf with mincemeat, the Syrian a stuffed green pepper. The Austrian Jew will dream of mother's apfel strudel, rich with raisins and spice; the Turkish Jew will only long for 'baklava', made with an almost identical pastry but with a filling of even greater richness.[75]

When Evelyn Rose began writing for the *JC* on a weekly basis in 1963, promotion of Sephardi food was a prominent feature of her column. An early series of articles 'For the New Housewife' introduced *JC* readers to 'Cooking with Exotic Vegetables'. Rose recommended introducing green peppers, aubergines and pimentos into the housewife's 'culinary repertoire' and gave introductory descriptions of each of these unfamiliar products.[76] Later she gave recipes to incorporate them into meat dishes. In 'Sephardi ways with mincemeat' she wrote: 'Pimento, pepper and sweet mixed spice, pine kernels and sesame seeds ... these provide the characteristic tang and texture of Sephardi meat cookery.'[77] In the context of Jewish culinary culture 'the practice of mixed origins' was indicated by the growing tendency to mix elements of Ashkenazi and Sephardi cuisine. The pressure to produce innovative cooking, supplying the demands of an increasingly global marketplace, propelled the trend.

Although tradition was continually evoked, creative adaptation and proliferation of different recipes for the same dish became standard practice. In this context the categories of Ashkenazi and Sephardi food were rendered ever more malleable. By the 1980s the practice of hybridity was being extended to mixing Ashkenazi and Sephardi elements in the same recipe. In 1988 a recipe for traditional Ashkenazi *haman taschen* used a 'meltingly tender short pastry' that was 'borrowed from Sephardi cooks, who use it to make wonderful moulded biscuits like *Mamoules*' (Middle Eastern date or nut-filled pastries). To complete the fusion approach, Rose recommended stuffing them with 'a traditional Ashkenazi filling such as spiced apples and raisins or poppy seeds'.[78] There is more than an echo here of Judith Montefiore's synthesis of diverse culinary cultures in her recipe for *Kugel and Commean* published nearly 150 years earlier.

Evelyn Rose's approach was indicative of contemporary culinary developments influenced by globalisation, yet it also connected with the practice of Jewish food identity so elegantly expressed by Judith Montefiore in *The Jewish Manual*. The Victorian era gave rise to a unique Anglo-Jewish cuisine, rooted in the British experience and specific to it. In their cross-fertilisation of Sephardi, Ashkenazi and English elements, Anglo-Jewry delineated a culinary identity that found its clearest expression in Judith Montefiore's *Jewish Manual*. This provided the foundations for Florence Greenberg's mid-twentieth century output, which she updated and adapted but did not fundamentally change. Ironically, Florence Greenberg's radical effort to jettison some traditions in the interests of nutrition has not been acknowledged by subsequent generations, despite her becoming a revered figure, central to Anglo-Jewish food heritage.

In the post-war period new expectations were invested in food. Divergent pressures required Jewish food to be traditional, abundant and 'ethnic', but also convenient, slimming and mass-produced. Jewish cookery began to embody the identity crises and fractures of post-war Anglo-Jewish society. Evelyn Rose tried to draw together competing tendencies that were threatening to fragment the Jewish community in Britain, in an effort to create culinary harmony from apparent conflict – tradition and innovation; the 'woman of worth' in the Jewish home and modern careerism; unfamiliar Sephardi ingredients and flavours with traditional Ashkenazi dishes. She attempted to negotiate this conflicted arena aiming to achieve reconciliation in the kitchen.

The operation of Anglo-Jewish memory in relation to food reflects that of historical memory in general – the act of remembrance is continually counterbalanced by a process of forgetting and omission and what we now construct as 'Jewish' food does not necessarily correspond with historical records of what past Jewish communities ate. Judith Montefiore's refined construction of Anglo-Jewish cuisine no longer resonates as Jewish with a contemporary readership. The cuisine represented social attitudes about gender and class, signifying values and behaviour that were intended for an elite and have become part of culinary history. It is now hard to imagine that the Sephardi cakes called bolas, so prominent in *The Jewish Manual*, were once an integral part of Anglo-Jewish food culture. Yet Henry Mayhew described how 'Jew boys' sold 'the cakes known as "boolers"' in the East End streets[79] and one correspondent to the *JC*, anxious about sugar rationing during the First World War, announced that 'in the opinion of the East End' bolas 'fall into the category of being an indispensable food'.[80] Anglo-Jewish food writing gives us a unique insight into the connections between past and present in the making of what we perceive to be 'indispensable' to Jewish food identity, even if it will never resolve the argument about the best recipe for chicken soup.

NOTES

1. *JC*, 30 July 2004, p.32.
2. Barbara Kirshenblatt-Gimblett, 'The Kosher Gourmet in the Nineteenth-Century Kitchen: Three Jewish Cookbooks in Historical Perspective', *The Journal of Gastronomy*, 2 (Winter 1986–87). 51–89 (p.82).
3. Nicola Humble, *Culinary Pleasures: Cookbooks and the Transformation of British Food* (London: Faber & Faber, 2005), p.9.
4. John Shaftesley, 'Culinary Aspects of Anglo-Jewry', in *Studies in the Cultural Life of the Jews in England* ed. by Dov Noy and Issachar Ben-Ami (Jerusalem: Magnes Press, 1975), pp.367–99.
5. Judith Montefiore, *The Jewish Manual or Practical Information in Jewish & Modern Cookery*

with a Collection of Valuable Recipes & Hints Relating to the Toilette (London: Sidwick & Jackson, 1985; 1st edn 1846).

6. Ibid. pp.i–v.
7. Kirshenblatt-Gimblett (see note 2), p.80.
8. Rachael Beth-Zion, 'An Old Cookery Book', *JC*, 8 June 1951, p.18.
9. Shaftesley, 'Culinary Aspects of Anglo-Jewry' (see note 4), p.395.
10. Claudia Roden, *The Book of Jewish Food: An Odyssey from Samarkand to Vilna to the Present Day* (London: Viking, 1997; 1st edn 1996).
11. Adam Raphael, 'What About a Happy New Diet?', *JC*, 18 January 1998, p.39.
12. Montefiore, *Jewish Manual* (see note 5), p.ii.
13. Kirshenblatt-Gimblett (see note 2), p.54.
14. Ibid.
15. Montefiore, *Jewish Manual* (see note 5), pp.xiii, xv.
16. Ibid. pp.11, 39, 45, 83.
17. Ibid. p.55.
18. Kirshenblatt-Gimblett (see note 2), p.59.
19. *JC*, 3 July 1846, p.164.
20. Montefiore, *Jewish Manual* (see note 5), p.iv.
21. Ibid. p.118.
22. Rachael Beth-Zion, 'An Old Cookery Book', *JC*, 8 June 1951, p.18.
23. Massimo Montanari, *Food Is Culture* (New York: Columbia University Press, 2004), p.38.
24. Montefiore, *Jewish Manual* (see note 5), pp.i, v.
25. Roden, *Book of Jewish Food* (see note 10), pp.496–7.
26. Montefiore, *Jewish Manual* (see note 5), pp.114–15.
27. Cited in Humble, *Culinary Pleasures* (see note 3), p.151.
28. Ibid. p.247.
29. A number of cookery books published in Britain did represent East European Jewish cookery, some in Yiddish, but these did not gain influence in acculturated Anglo-Jewish society.
30. See *Aunt Sarah's Cookery Book for a Jewish Kitchen* (Liverpool: Yates and Hess, 1872); May Henry and Edith B. Cohen, *The Economical Cook: A Modern Jewish Recipe Book for Housekeepers* (London: Wertheimer, Lea and Co., 1889); Miss M.A.S. Tattersall, *Jewish Cookery Book* (London: Wertheimer, Lea and Co, 1895).
31. Mrs L.J. Greenberg, ed., *The Jewish Chronicle Cookery Book* (London: JC Publications, 1934).
32. Florence Greenberg, *Florence Greenberg's Cookery Book* (London, JC Publications, 1947; revised 2nd edn 1949; revised 3rd edn 1951; revised 4th edn 1953; revised 5th edn 1955; 6th edn 1958; revised 7th edn 1963; 8th edn 1968).
33. Announcement of marriage, *JC*, 7 May 1920.
34. Judy Miller, 'Mrs Beeton Jewish Style', *JC Colour Supplement*, 21 March 1980, p.28.
35. Maurice Jay, 'From Gallipoli in World War I to the Kitchen Front in 1939', *West London Synagogue Review*, 39/40 (March/April 1971), p.5.
36. Doreen Berger, transcribed and ed., *The Jewish Victorian: Genealogical Information from the Jewish Newspapers 1871–1880* (Witney: Robert Boyd, 1999), p.462.
37. Judy Miller, 'Mrs Beeton Jewish Style', *JC Colour Supplement*, 21 March 1980, p.26; Jay, 'From Gallipoli' (see note 35), p.5.
38. 'Some Dinner Hints', *JC*, 10 September 1920, p.15.
39. 'Casserole Cooking', *JC*, 17 September 1920, p.15.
40. 'Cakes and Biscuits', *JC*, 24 September 1920, p.20.
41. *JC*, 9 March 1934, p.25.
42. Greenberg, *JC Cookery Book* (see note 31), pp.9–20.
43. Ibid. p.5.
44. Montefiore, *Jewish Manual* (see note 5), p.108; Mrs Beeton recommends '4 dozen cheesecakes' in her bill of fare for a picnic for 40 persons.
45. Greenberg, *JC Cookery Book* (see note 32), pp.179, 183.
46. Ibid. pp.32, 219.
47. Ibid. pp.49, 167.
48. 'Florence Greenberg re-views a 120-year old Anglo-Jewish cook-book', *JC Food and Wine Supplement*, 15 July 1966, p.xii.
49. Greenberg, *JC Cookery Book* (see note 31), p.149.

50. Ibid. p.79.
51. Ibid. p.15.
52. Ibid. p.16.
53. Ibid. p.18.
54. *JC*, 22 June 34, p.8.
55. *JC*, 5 December 1947, p.6; *JC*, 26 December 1947, p.16.
56. Ambrose Heath, 'Good Cooking – Help for Every Housewife', *JC*, 2 January 1948, p.13.
57. Minute, VM & JC Publications, 23 September 65, 5/12, SUA.
58. Greenberg, *FG's Cookery Book* (see note 32), p.6.
59. Ibid. pp. 91, 123, 150, 236, 242, 371, 252, 254, 288, 345, 412.
60. Ibid. p.36.
61. bid. p.37.
62. Paul Levy, Obituary of Evelyn Rose, *Independent*, 24 May 2003.
63. Evelyn Rose, *The New Complete International Jewish Cookbook* (London: Robson, 2000, 1st edn 1997), p.xiii.
64. Ibid. p.xvii.
65. *RT*, 30 April 1954, p.38; *RT*, 28 May 1954, p.38; *RT*, 13 August 1954, p.38; *RT*, 3 December 1954, p.38.
66. Jan Shure, 'The Icing on our Cake', *JC*, 23 May 2003, p.25.
67. Minutes VM & JC Publications, 30 September 1965, item 5, 5/12, MS 225, SUA.
68. Greenberg, *JC Cookery Book* (see note 31), p.5.
69. Jan Shure, 'The Icing on our Cake', Obituary of Evelyn Rose, *JC*, 23 May 2003, p.25.
70. Evelyn Rose, 'Tradition up to Date', *JC* Kashrut Supplement, 2 November 1962, p.xi.
71. 'Sweet and Savoury for *Shavuot*', *JC*, 28 May 1965, p.23.
72. 'The Nation's Favourite Fress', *JC*, 22 November 2002, p.45.
73. 'Have You Ever Tried Sephardi Cooking?', *MJG*, Food and Wine Supplement, 22 June 1962, p.ii.
74. *MJG*, 6 July 1962, p.3.
75. 'A New Jewish Cuisine?', *MJG*, 4 March 1960, p.4.
76. 'For the New Housewife', *JC*, 14 December 1962, p. 29.
77. 'Sephardi Ways with Mincemeat', *JC*, 15 March 1963, p.41.
78. 'Melting Moments at Purim', *JC*, 26 February 1988, p.30.
79. Henry Mayhew, *Mayhew's London: Being Selections from London Labour and the London Poor* (London: Pilot Press, 1949, 1st edn 1851–52), p.286.
80. *JC*, 27 April 1917, p.27.

From *Mon Pays*, the *Shtetl* and the *Desh* to London's East End:[1] A Rationale for Comparative Migrant Studies

ANNE KERSHEN

It was not until the early 1970s that studies of the nuts and bolts of immigrant settlement became an accepted facet of academe, following on the late E.P. Thompson's seminal work *The Making of the English Working Class*, which was published at the end of the 1960s – Thompson describing his protagonists as the 'losers of history'.[2] At this time, in America and Britain, others were undertaking research on Jewish immigration in England, the outcome of which would be published in the 1960s and 1970s.[3] It had taken almost a century for 'warts and all' accounts of the arrival of Eastern European migrants to become part of the academic world.[4] By comparison there was far less temporal separation between the arrival of Bangladeshi immigrants and research and publication which recorded the experience and impact of their settlement. That wave of incomers to Britain (as Pakistanis[5]) began in the late 1950s; one of the earliest researchers into the Bangladeshi community in London being John Eade, whose book on the political and social structure of the East London community appeared in 1989.[6]

It was in that same year that I took up the post of senior research fellow at Queen Mary, the London University College located in the heartland of the traditional first point of settlement for immigrants to London. As a facet of my previous research had been the tailoring trade in East London,[7] it seemed only rational to select the area and its history as the focus of my next study. It did not take long for me to recognise the necessity and validity of moving from the singular (Eastern European Jews) to the plural (Huguenots, Jews and Bangladeshis). Though still highlighting the former, the research hypothesis I sought to test was that the Eastern European Jews' experience of settlement in London's East End was fashioned more by the aspirations common to all immigrants and by location and tradition of place than by the character of the specific ethnic community. I sought to argue that the Jewish East End was part of a continuum that had begun with 'petty France' in the eighteenth century, carried through with the 'little Jerusalem' of the late nineteenth century and on into Banglatown at the end of the twentieth century. By so doing I looked to move out of the cul-de-sac that British Jewish history had become and take my work into the burgeoning field of migration studies.

Comparative study was not new to me as my earlier work had examined, and compared, Jewish and English trade unions in the nineteenth and first half of the twentieth century. In this I had deconstructed the general into particular categories under headings which included; English/immigrant; male/female; capital city/regional city; skilled/unskilled – each with Thompson's 'losers of history' as the leading actors. The binary approach enabled me to see the Jewish experience within a broader framework, one which encouraged the conceptualisation of the organisation of labour under the headings of gender and place as well as ethnic minority.

By the end of the 1980s, as the Berlin Wall came down, the 'Jewish East End' was disintegrating. A new immigrant community was on the rise. Bangladeshis were living and working in buildings once inhabited by the Eastern European Jews and praying in mosques once used as places of prayer by Jews and, before them, by Calvinist refugees from seventeenth century France.

In order to test my hypothesis I put the three East End migrant groups under the microscope. By so doing, both in time and place, I was embracing three very different sending societies; Huguenots from Western Europe in the seventeenth and eighteenth centuries, Jews from Eastern Europe in the late nineteenth and early twentieth centuries and Bengalis from the South Asian sub-Continent in the second half of the twentieth century. I then selected a range of themes by which to measure the migrant experience.[8] Acknowledging the limitations of space for this paper I will report on only three of these, namely religion; language and economic activity; arguably three of the most important pillars of immigrant life.

Religion

Religion played a central role in the early stages of migration and settlement for all three groups: for the Huguenots it was the *raison d'être* for leaving France; for Jews, the perennial outsiders and wanderers, it was the root of their alienation and as such the major push factor for departure from the Pale and, following arrival in London, a focal point for the new community. For the first generation of Bengalis, though initially of little importance in terms of a catalyst for departure, Islam was to take on a defining role as the bachelor enclaves transformed into communities and the first generation English born came to terms with their place – and displacement – in British society. All three groups, irrespective of religious requirements, looked to worship close to home. Thus it was no surprise to discover a continuity of spatial location; the Huguenot chapel becoming the synagogue, and then the mosque. The prime example of this is the building which stands on the corner of Brick Lane and Fournier Street, build in 1743 by the Huguenots to accommodate those who could no longer fit into the French Church in Threadneedle Street.[9] All three groups used their places of worship as conduits for community interaction, welfare and news. For Jews and Huguenots they acted as central distribution and control points for communal charities and as bases of communal control. In the case of all three religions, women had no clerical role and, until the opening of the East London mosque in Whitechapel Road in the mid-1980s, Muslim females rarely, if at all, entered the house of prayer, unlike their Jewish counterparts, who sat in airless galleries or behind curtained partitions. In the home, females played a pivotal role, particularly Muslim and Jewish women who were responsible for the provision of food that conformed to religious dietary requirements.

For all three groups, religion provided a code for living: for Jews and Muslims the code extended to diet and regularised daily prayer attendance. Religion provided a bridge between sending and receiving societies – a familiar physical and psychological landmark in an alien landscape; acting as a figurative as well as real centre of community and welfare. Irrespective of the 'who', or the 'where from', in the case of all three minority 'outsider' groups, religion played a welcoming, accommodating and controlling element of the migrant experience.

Language

Language facilitates entry into mainstream society as well as promoting exclusion. Those who cannot – or will not – speak the language of the receiving society are restricted to linguistic ghettoes; those who can, not only gain entry but, in addition, access to British citizenship.[10] The three migrant groups – and their mother tongues – under the microscope here provide contrasting subjects for examination. Although the language of the Huguenots and those that spoke it were subject to xenophobic forms of criticism – 'damned sound of French' and the 'croaking of frogs'[11] – French was, and for many still is, perceived as a manifestation of gentility and learning. By contrast, Yiddish and Sylheti[12] were stigmatised as dialects of the lower class.

For the Huguenots, French created job opportunities and entrée (as tutors) into aristocratic families; though rarely as equals! Almost all the refugees from France recognised the need to learn English and adopt it as their 'mother tongue'. The few that chose not to did so because they believed their absence from home would be short. They saw no necessity to learn an alien language – in the event the period of exile for French Calvinists was 102 years.[13] Yiddish was the lingua franca of Ashkenazim[14] in the diaspora. Working and living within a Jewish migrant environment (or ghetto) some had no time for, and saw no need to attend, the English classes that Jewish trade unions and the established community mounted to enable the replacement of 'a miserable jargon which is no language at all'.[15] However, there were some men who, eager to learn and better themselves, became regular attendees. There was no choice for the children, those attending the Jews' Free School were forbidden to speak the *mommaluschen*,[16] whilst pupils at Christ's Church School in Brick Lane were only allowed Yiddish as a bridge to English – their teachers learning the language in order to communicate with their pupils, some of whom had never heard English till they went to school. One hundred years on teachers at the same school had to learn yet another foreign language, Bengali/Sylheti, in order to communicate with the new wave of immigrant pupils. In spite of the cultural face of Yiddish literature, press and theatre, the language remained the badge of the immigrant and for those keen to iron out the ghetto bends, one to be eschewed as soon as possible.

Sylheti is a language of place, born out of the region of Sylhet. It is the mother tongue of 95 per cent of Bangladeshis living in the London Borough of Tower Hamlets. Apart from limited religious usage it has no written history. The combination of a very poor level of education and rural background has resulted in a very high level of illiteracy amongst first generation Bangladeshi immigrants. Paradoxically, the nation-state of Bangladesh was born out of a civil war with Pakistan, one of the main issues in the fight for nationhood being the retention of the Bengali language. Thus, in contrast with the other two groups, particularly the Eastern European immigrants, it was respect for, and the learning of, their mother tongue language that became the priority for the first generation English born Bengalis. By the 1970s, it was recognised that literacy in mother tongue was a vital teaching tool in the progression to fluency of the language of mainstream society. Mother tongue classes became a part of Bangladeshi life in East London. Initially run privately, they are now subsidised by local government, which recognises the part it plays in immigrant life. As one of my students explained, 'I need to learn Bengali in order to write letters home and deal with official documents for my parents'. The learning of English has a gendered dimension, for while some of the first generation males have learned to read and write in English, their wives have not. And whilst some have just not bothered, prepared to live their lives in the linguistic ghetto and have their children and husbands act as interpreters, others have been actively discouraged, as another student told me, 'my mother used to speak English but she doesn't any more'.

Economic Activity

As highlighted at the outset of this paper, Huguenots, Jews and Bangladeshis migrated for a variety of reasons. Yet for economic reasons all, including the Huguenot refugees, chose East London as the initial place of settlement.[17] Weber argued that the Judeo-Christian tradition encouraged and honoured commercial success, whilst within Islam rational capitalism is impossible, it being an occidental phenomenon. I would counter this by saying that in each case – *including* that of the Bangladeshis – material/economic mobility has proven to be an underlying theme of the migrant experience. Evidence also counters the commonly held views that all Huguenots were successful. In reality, whilst some of the Huguenots developed dynastic businesses – Bresson, Selincourt, Dollond, Ogiers, Courtauld, de Lamerie – others suffered extreme poverty and hardship, often resorting to wage undercutting with the resultant reciprocal xenophobic outbursts.

Though on the surface the Eastern European Jews bore little resemblance to the Huguenots, they imported the same willingness to work long and hard in order to achieve economic security and mobility in their newly designated homeland. Unlike their French predecessors, few of the immigrants from Russia and Russia/Poland were skilled. For most, employment was to be found in dark and unhealthy sub-divisional sweatshops in which jackets and trousers, caps and sticks, sideboards and tables were produced in a multiplicity of processes by unskilled and low skilled workers suffering the worst conditions, the longest hours and the lowest wages – the archetypal sweated labour. Only the ruthless few made it out of the ghetto. One such was Morris Cohen, an emigrant from Imperial Russia who recognised the potential of producing women's tailored garments 'wholesale' and supplying these to merchants who had previously imported ladies jackets and skirts from Germany and France. Within 20 years Cohen had built up an impressive ladies wholesale tailoring empire and retired to Brighton.[18] For the most part however, it was the children and grandchildren of the immigrants that made the transition from tailors, machiners and pressers to pharmacists and doctors, from bakers and cabinet makers to barristers and accountants. In many ways those first generation immigrants can be compared to the children in the desert, they saw the promised land but did not enjoy its fruits.

In an analysis of the 1991 census it was suggested that, in economic terms, Bangladeshis were analogous with the Irish immigrants and, unlike the Jew, destined to be blue collar workers. It is always dangerous to analyse the nature of a migrant group before it has been established for at least two generations. The Bengalis have proved no exception. As in the case of the Jews and Huguenots, there were some early success stories: Shirazul Huque became a millionaire as owner of the restaurant *Shampan* on the corner of Brick Land and Hanbury Street, and was a motivating force behind the creation of Banglatown. Others have grown rich as travel agents – organising the regular extended return visits to Bangladesh – some as property owners or leather garment manufacturers. But the majority of the first generation remained stuck in the *bedesh*,[19] sending remittances back home while maintaining their families over here, never having acquired quite enough money to fulfil the migrant dream and return home as 'rich men of high status'. Yet things are changing, especially amongst the younger generation. The number of Bengali graduates increases annually, as does the volume of Bangladeshi professionals and entrepreneurs. Some of the latter took advantage of the Thatcherite 'right to buy' policy by purchasing the council properties of their parents, subsequently letting to the new wave of Eastern European immigrants, themselves moving out to the suburbs once occupied by the earlier migrants from the East End.[20]

Conclusion

There is no doubt that an exploration of the process of settlement is an important element in the study of the migrant experience. Grass-roots level examinations of the strategies employed to facilitate the integration process can at times produce results which are unexpected and which contradict conventionally accepted patterns. For example, evidence shows that not all Jewish incomers sought to learn the language of their new homeland, even though they had no intention of returning to the *heim* (home). However, it takes research into other minority settlers to discover that this situation was not unique to the Eastern European Jews; some Huguenots and Bangladeshis were resistant to linguistic assimilation whilst others were denied the opportunity.

Religious practices and patterns are telling in that they too can be compared and contrasted. For example, whilst second and third generation Huguenots and Jews moved from the temples and *chevras* of 'home' into Anglicised synagogues and English churches, young Bengalis are manifesting a more intense religiosity and entering mosques which openly pronounce their adherence to the *umma* as opposed to a rootedness in Britain.

As has been illustrated above, contrary to perceived tradition and recent expectation, all three minority groups produced both affluent entrepreneurs and struggling workers. Immigrants are regularly placed under the microscope and judged by their successes and failures; though there are those who believe that all the Huguenots were 'profitable strangers' and that 'all Jews are rich'. What comparative immigrant research demonstrates is that, using Thompson's terminology, all communities have their winners and losers and that the migrant has to struggle harder in order to succeed. The journey to success may take generations or decades and is measured in different ways. What is success for one may be deemed failure for another. It is only by regularly updating research, unearthing new facts and reassessing what we have in the light of what we find, that we can begin to comprehend the migrant experience and, within that, the place of the Jewish immigrant in relation to others.

What does the above suggest for current and future studies of British Jewish history? In my introductory paragraph I referred to the researching and writing of the Jewish immigrant experience as becoming lodged in a cul-de-sac and, though I would support the view that there has been, and will continue to be, a need for in-depth, mono-ethnic/spatial research, I would argue that if the intellectual discourses between those engaged in past, present and future migrant studies are to have vibrancy and relevance, they have to be situated on a broadly informed, and informative, landscape. This is not to suggest that British Jewish studies no longer have a *raison d'être*, but rather that those engaged must be a part of the bigger picture.

NOTES

1. *Mon Pays* – my land is what many Huguenots referred to when they talked about 'home'. John Kleir's definition of the *shtetl*, 'any settlement inhabited by Jews'. For emigrants from the Pale, the physical reality became a myth to be packaged, taken overseas, and reconstructed in a different spatial context; thus taking on a different form – for some becoming a conduit for hybridity. It is important to remember, as Kleir stressed, that, wherever located in Europe, Jewish settlement was never isolated from 'the rest', there were inevitable points of interaction, as in the case of all minority communities. *Desh* is the Bengali word for home or homeland, it too has become mythologised by those who left it in order to go to the *bidesh* (abroad, elsewhere) and earn enough money to return home as 'rich men of high status'. The inability of the majority to accumulate sufficient wealth to achieve their ambition resulted in what is commonly referred to today as the myth of return.

   For a detailed and comparative account of the three groups see Anne Kershen, *Strangers, Aliens and Asians: Huguenots, Jews and Bangladeshis in Spitalfields 1660–2000* (London: Routledge, 2005). The main published works on the Huguenots are: R. Gwynn, *Huguenot Heritage: The History and Contribution of the Huguenots in Britain* (Brighton: Sussex Academic Press, 2001); and R. Vigne and C. Littleton, *From Strangers to Citizens* (Brighton: Sussex Academic Press, 2001).

2. See E.P. Thompson, *The Making of the English Working Class* (London: Penguin, 1968).

3. Lloyd Gartner's, *The Jewish Immigrant in England 1870–1914* (London: George Allen

and Unwin, 1960); William J. Fishman's *East End Jewish Radicals 1875–1914* (Duckworth, London, 1975).

4. Exceptions to this were the survey carried out in 1900 by Charles Russell and Harry Lewis, *The Jew in London: A Study of Racial Character and Present-day Conditions* (London: Fisher Unwin, 1900) and Vivien Lipman's survey, *A Social History of the Jews in England 1850–1950* (London: Watts & Co., 1954). The celebratory *A History of the Jews in England*, (Oxford: Clarendon Press, 1941) by Cecil Roth, devoted virtually no space to the 'losers', concentrating instead on the history of the Anglo-Jewish establishment.

5. With partition in 1947 the region of north-eastern India which had a predominantly Muslim population was ceded to Pakistan. In 1971, after a bloody civil war, it became Bangladesh. Thus many of those who had arrived as immigrant Pakistanis in reality became Bangladeshis.

6. J. Eade, *The Politics of Community* (Aldershot: Avebury, 1989).

7. This appeared in print as Anne Kershen, *Uniting the Tailors* (London: Frank Cass, 1995).

8. See Kershen, *Strangers, Aliens and Asians* (note 3).

9. By the early nineteenth century the building had become a missionary for the conversion of Jews and then a Methodist Chapel, by the end of the century it was the synagogue of the *Mazichke Hadath*. In 1974 it was sold to the local Bangladeshi community for conversion into a mosque.

10. Under the British Nationality Act of 1981 it became a perquisite of British citizenship that the applicant have 'a sufficient knowledge of the English, Welsh or Scottish Gaelic language'.

11. See Kershen, *Strangers, Aliens and Asians* (note 3), p.197.

12. Yiddish is the Hebraic German language of Askenazi Jews from Central and Eastern Europe; Sylheti is the dialect spoken by some 95 per cent of the Bangladeshi immigrants in Spitalfields. Though at one time it did have a written form, this has long since ended and currently it is solely a spoken dialect of those from Sylhet.

13. Freedom of worship was granted to the Calvinists in 1787, two years before the French Revolution.

14. Jews from Central and Eastern Europe.

15. *Jewish Chronicle*, 4 May 1883.

16. mother tongue.

17. Though the Huguenots were escaping from the harsh regime of Catholic France, they still had a choice to make in the sense of where they sought refuge – they could have gone to the Low Countries, Germany or even North America. However, with its nascent silk industry and growing consumer society, London offered the silk weavers, merchants, silversmiths and goldsmiths the opportunity of economic entrepreneurship and mobility.

18. For more on Cohen see, Kershen, *Uniting the Tailors* (note 9), p.102.

19. The Bengali word for over there, or abroad.

20. For a more detailed account of the economic activities of Huguenots, Jews and Bangladeshis see Kershen, *Strangers, Aliens and Asians* (note 3), chapter 7.

CONCLUSION

An Accidental Jewish Historian

BILL WILLIAMS

It may be that I am unique amongst the contributors to this collection in that Anglo-Jewish history provided a late and accidental side door into the discipline of academic history. Before 1971, when I was commissioned by a retired businessman to write a history of Manchester's Jewish community, I confess to knowing next to nothing about either Judaism or Jewish history.

My view of Jews, in so far as I had one, was as those for whose conversion we prayed at my Jesuit school, and as the target of my father's visceral Socialist anti-Semitism. It was not the capitalists who were exploiting the working people, but the 'Jewboys', with their worldwide conspiratorial intent. I grew up with an anti-Semitism which I could almost taste.

Before I reached Manchester, I had only one close relationship with a person of Jewish origin, a gentle, soft-spoken Londoner called Ben Simmons, a middle-aged lecturer in English at what was then the Malayan Teaching Training College in Penang. One memory of him is of his walks with his wife, Celia, to a nearby village of desperately poor and exploited Tamil rubber-tappers, whom he befriended and who came to look upon him as their mediator with what was then the distant British colonial administration. Another is of him as a learner-driver stuck diagonally within a box of four traffic lights. Although he was in many ways my guide as a teacher of teachers, we rarely, if ever, talked about things Jewish. I knew only that he ate kosher. In 1961 a gang of Malay burglars broke into his house and murdered him for no better reason that he was the only one of us in a compound of perhaps 20 houses to put grills around his windows and a strong metal gate across his front door (surely, the thieves reasoned, he was guarding things of value).

Could this awkward man, with his inability to drive his car through traffic lights be part of any international conspiracy that was ever likely to work? Had the securing of his house anything to do with his anxieties as a Jew? The first Jewish ritual I attended was his burial in Penang.

I returned to Manchester (my birthplace) in 1967 with an interest in what might vaguely (and I was vague) be seen as 'minority experience'. I had once led my Chinese, Indian and Malay teacher-trainees on a satisfying project to identify and record the mosques and Muslim shrines in the rural districts of Penang Island, where I obtained some acquaintance with Islam and its differing sects. In what was then Malaya, I was increasingly confronted with the tensions that existed between the urban-living Chinese and the Malay peasantry, and with the policies of 'Malayisation' which were attempting to advance the participation of Malays in the economy and politics at the expense of the Chinese. I got to know of government contracts made, in reality, by Chinese businessmen, but fronted by Malays to render them legal. Malayisation included the introduction of legislation which gave preference to Malay applicants for entry to the college in which I worked.

All this tuned in with my own family's sense of being part of several 'minorities'. My mother's Lancashire ancestors had survived in Elizabethan England as Papist recusants; my Welsh-speaking father had been refused the right to speak Welsh in an English-controlled school. We were for many years a Catholic family, with Socialist inclinations, in a small North Wales town, Llangollen, in which nonconformist Christianity and Liberal politics dominated. My father was a tee-total publican.

Which explains why, when I was approached by the retired Jewish businessman (he had owned a chain of low-level clothing stores) in Manchester to write the history of a minority community, I found the idea more than congenial. Since I was working from scratch and, although they didn't know it, with the emotions of anti-Semitism still at work, a group of advisors, all of them men, was brought together called 'The Committee for the Publication of a History of Manchester Jewry'. Its chairman was a solicitor, Walter Wolfson, its vice-chairman a local playwright and poet, Hymie Gouldman, both of them members of what I came to understand were middle-of-the road synagogues; an insurance agent who, if I had known the word, I would have described as *haredi*; and three elderly men who had fallen out of love with Judaism and opted for apathy or, in one case, Marxism. They became my advisers and, more importantly, my mediators with the Jewish community.

These were unfortunately the days before oral history had been properly invented, so all I have to record my first contacts are hand-written scribble. It took me some time to recognise just how large and historically important the Jewish community was and how I was already in personal touch with people who had played important roles within it: the commissioning businessman had been a key figure on the Jewish Refugee Committee of the 1930s; the solicitor a former pillar of the Manchester *Yeshivah* and in 1936 the (unsuccessful) candidate for a seat (in the Labour interest) on Salford City Council; the poet a graduate of the Jewish Literary Society movement and the writer of a popular play 'From Cheetham Hill to Cheadle', which spanned the gap between the Yiddish speaking, slum-dwelling immigrants of the late nineteenth century and the anglicised Jewish families of the Manchester suburbs; the insurance agent an important activist in the creation in the 1920s of *Machzikei Hadas*, the seedbed of Manchester's present important and growing *haredi kehillah*; of the two 'secular' members, one had taken the lead in 1939 in the formation of a Manchester *Hachsharah*, the other as a shop steward in the largely Jewish Upholsters Union. All this I only gradually came to know and, even more gradually, to understand.

These were no more likely participants in world conspiracy than Ben Simmons. The third non-religious Jew on the committee was a hairdresser with a salon (which I came to use) on Piccadilly Station. Whatever the committee meant to its Jewish members, who were exceptionally kind and gentle with this beginner, to me it was the beginning of a train of thought which led in time to my own response to anti-Semitism: 'the ordinariness of being Jewish'. By now, for reasons personal and rational, totally un-, even anti-religious, I was introduced to Judaism by Gabriel Brodie, a Czech refugee of the 1930s who had become rabbi of the 'Great and New Synagogue' (a coming together of what had once been warring congregations) and secretary of the Manchester *Yeshivah*, of which he had been a student.

As a supposed historian, one immediate discovery was the chaotic nature of Manchester's Jewish heritage – buildings, artefacts and documents – as the community had moved between the late 1920s and the early 1960s from Cheetham Hill chiefly northwards towards the middle-class jungles of semi-detacheds in Crumpsall and Prestwich. No one had thought to take any measures to preserve what was seriously at risk during this period of transition, when homes, synagogues and factories were serially abandoned. The bulk of Zionist records had been lost when, in 1967, the room in which they were kept was turned into the headquarters of a fund-raising drive during the Six Day War: symbolic of the way in which history itself could trample on its own past. Other records, of Jewish clubs, charities, youth organisations and the many lesser synagogues of Cheetham, Hightown and Strangeways, if they had survived at all, survived by chance; in some notorious cases they had been buried in the debris of their demolished buildings. It was a loss which was compounded by the much earlier disappearance of trade union and *chevra* records perhaps taken in Yiddish in disposable (or, at any rate, disposed of) exercise books. It soon became clear that the writing of any Jewish community brought with it the moral imperative of recording and preserving the Jewish heritage and deploying oral history (brought into fashion in the early 1970s, particularly by the historians Paul Thompson and Raphael Samuel). It became clear, too (and this reinforced my Marxist family heritage), that there was a 'people's history' of Manchester Jewry, for which there were few written records, but which had to be produced alongside the institutional history of which remnants still existed.

Fortunately for me, the *shamash* at the Great Synagogue, Jacob Schwalbe, had failed to destroy (rather than preserved) its records, dating from the 1820s, without which a history of the Jewish community could not have been written. They lay, damp and frayed in a synagogal basement which had once been a hub of social and political activity; all that otherwise remained in it was a ruined *mikvah*, a deserted caretaker's flat and photographs of Jewish worthies, including Nathan Rothschild, who had once lived in Manchester, and Nathan Laski, the great dictator of Manchester Jewry between the 1920s and his death in 1942. My first research was conducted in this basement; it then proceeded to the boardroom of a building (now selling bathrooms) which was then still the headquarters of the Manchester Jewish Board of Guardians. The result, in 1976 was the publication of what for me, whatever anyone else thinks of it, was an 'apprentice piece', *The Making of Manchester Jewry*, which took local Jewish history from 1740 up to 1875.

Writing it, and seeking to interpret events, was a learning process that passed through several stages, some of them unproductive. It quickly became clear (and this was also part of the Marxist legacy) that Jewish history could not be written in terms of its internal mechanisms of change, whether these were perceived in local, national or international terms. Jewish history did not have Jewish causes, or, at any rate, not *only* Jewish causes. The Manchester Jews School was not created in 1840 only out of a supposed love of the

Jewish people for education per se, or as a way of 'proving' the Jewish community worthy of emancipation, although those were clearly amongst the motives of its (largely merchant) creators. It needs to be set equally in the context of the strong (and effective) movement in Manchester for the setting up of schools for the working classes, and, still more, within the social context of a Jewish elite of cotton merchants seeking a place within a liberal bourgeoisie then developing in Manchester as a dominant social, political and cultural force. The Jews School was, in part at least, an emerging Jewish bourgeoisie in philanthropic mode.

So too was the Manchester Jewish Board of Guardians, founded in 1867 in the face of an increasing influx of Jews from Eastern Europe (a phenomenon which begins in Manchester not with the assassination of Czar Alexander in 1881 but with the opening of Manchester's Victoria Station in 1844). The strategies of the Board had little to do with Talmudic teachings on the priority of charity, and were based much more obviously on the selective and deterrent methods enshrined in the New Poor Law. These methods, it might be argued, were only tweaked by a communal belief in the new immigrants as potential workers rather than as irrecoverable paupers. The same is true of many later institutions of communal philanthropy created by a Jewish social elite. The Jewish Working Men's Club (1889) was modelled on the wider working men's club movement but set within a framework of Jewish observance and adapted for specific Jewish purposes, particularly for the anglicisation (and de-politicisation) of the Jewish working man. The first Manchester battalion of the Jewish Lads Brigade (1899) was created to pass on to Jewish youth the grim social morality and even grimmer patriotic inclinations with which British youth were being sadly inculcated by the Church Lads Brigades. The Manchester Jewish Ladies Visiting Association (1884) was a Jewish child of middle-class women inspired by the philanthropic aims of their Christian sisters.

The Visiting Association's records also revealed the crucial role played by Jewish women of the middle classes, not only in Jewish, but in civic history. Amongst the figures to emerge were some whom Anglo-Jewish history had overlooked. One was Abigail Behrens, the daughter of the Jewish cotton merchant, Philip Lucas, who led the local movement for Jewish emancipation and was (in 1851) Manchester's first Jewish city councillor, and the wife of Edward Behrens, one of Manchester's leading cotton manufacturer-merchants.

She was not only a leading figure in civic and Jewish philanthropy, but one of the founders of the Manchester High School for Girls, founded to promote the entry of women to the professions. There was something to learn too from the fact that in 1881 she and her husband employed 19 servants (not one of them Jewish) to minister to the needs of a family of six. The only household of similar size in Manchester in 1881 was a ramshackle house in Red Bank, with three families, four lodgers and various hangers-on, all arrived recently from the Russian Empire.

It may be that these rather obvious 'insights', however since problematised, have now become part of the general currency of research into the Anglo-Jewish experience, but they were not obvious to me or to my Jewish advisers, who were rather anxious that I should lay some stress on qualities seen as quintessentially Jewish (compassion for the poor, loyalty to the city and the nation, love for the British Royal family) and tone down my record of such 'obviously non-Jewish activities' as crime, radical political dissent, republicanism and conscientious objection.

It also soon became evident that divisions within the community attributed to religious difference, differences in national origin or, *in extremis*, Jewish querulousness, had a base in social change, as Jewish immigrants at every economic level were overtaken by the ambitions and expectations embedded in the English class structure. It was not that difference on matters of belief and ritual were unimportant; it was that they happened in a community divided not only in terms of class, but in terms also of the finer distinctions between the 'rough' and the 'respectable' within the Jewish working-class districts. New synagogues emerged to satisfy the social gradations, and personal ambitions, even within a single street.

The Making of Manchester Jewry was written, without apology, against a background of social and economic change. The pressure for religious change is often generated by groups with some form of inner social cohesion; the degree of that cohesion often determines the degree of its success. Even the founders of as distinctive a religious body as *Machzikei Hadas*, which owed much to the kind of international trends to which Todd Endelman has drawn attention, were held together by their commonality as inter-marrying families of entrepreneurs in the Manchester trade in cotton fents. More importantly, the cultural, political and social consequences of mass immigration were worked out by a 'new middle class' of an (at first) mildly successful nouveaux riches: small-scale industrialists in the cotton industry, pawnbrokers, moneylenders, warehousemen and shopkeepers. It was they, it might be argued, who superimposed on an institutional structure reflecting the interests of a Jewish cottonocracy, formations more in keeping with the traditions of Eastern Europe. They provided the backbone of such new, immigrant-inspired institutions as Jewish Benevolent Societies (shorn of the expectations of the Jewish Board of Guardians), the Manchester Jewish Hospital (1904) and the first Manchester organisations inspired by Herzlian Zionism.

At the time I began working on this later period, in the late 1970s, it was still possible to speak to surviving *alrightniks*, or, at worst, to their children. This became an essential preparatory strategy for later (and still to be written) Manchester Jewish history. My advisers, already irritated because I had asked them to pick out Jewish names from the local trade directories, now asked what reason I had to listen to 'old men's tales', and particularly to old men who the late lamented Raphael Samuel in particular (he now became and remains my mentor) advised me to listen to: ordinary men (and women) who were far from the *macharite* stars of modern Jewish history, but who had spent most of their lives slaving in the immigrant trades, supporting the (now supposedly lost) Marxist cause, opposing the Zionist mission and in other ways making themselves thoroughly unpopular with the suburbanising core of the community. The long-term result of Raph's unruly legacy is my recent decision to supervise a doctoral student funded jointly by the University of Manchester and the Manchester Jewish Museum, commencing work this coming October and using as her research base the museum's substantial holding of recorded interviews, on 'nonconformity' (of whatever variety) within the Manchester Jewish community. This was inspired, too, by the paper read at the 'Whatever Happened to British Jewish Studies?' conference by Mark Levene and his revised contribution to this volume.

Oral history provides the means of reaching parts of the Jewish experience, as the advert goes, that other methodologies cannot reach: the inner working of the family, the role of women in the economy, the experience of the neighbourhood, the realities of life on the shop floor. One eye-opening combination of working-class archives retrieved from destruction and oral evidence provided information on a Jewish 'newsagent' in Manchester's nineteenth century Jewish Quarter who sold English and Yiddish newspapers and ritual artefacts, rented his top floor to the Jewish Machinists, Tailors and Pressers Trade Union, encouraged its customers to play chess at the back of the shop and carried a small and cheap lending library of booklets in Yiddish. The booklets, with the newsagent's name stamped on them, were retrieved from a sack in the possession of friendly scrap dealers: they turned out to be weekly parts of Yiddish penny dreadfuls printed in New York, with titles like *Life amongst the Cannibals* and *Maria and Murder in the Red Barn*.

More seriously, although that shop is serious enough when placed in the context of a Jewish neighbourhood network, there is oral testimony which recounts, amongst many other things, gang warfare in the Jewish Quarter (including a Jewish gang named, if I remember correctly, 'Shaun Spudah' after a winner of the Derby), the beginning of Jewish left-wing formations, instances of anti-Jewish feeling at street level, and the experience of itinerant occupations, like market-trading and Scotch drapery, rarely documented. A researcher using the museum's tapes recently was surprised to discover that the blood libel was alive and well, at least in the Christian mind, in the 1920s, when it prevented one young man from ever entering a Jewish home.

The Jewish Museum itself, opened in 1984, is a major product of the problems I encountered as a would-be historian. It is a base from which local Jewish history, conceived in terms of the widest possible constituency, might be both saved and exhibited. Its current exhibition, put together by the museum's talented young curator, Alex Grime, and myself, is called 'Red Bank: a Seedbed of Modernity'. It draws on the museum's vast collection of photographs and artefacts to present a portrait of Jewish life in Red Bank, what was once an area of dire jerry-built housing sloping down from a sandstone bluff on Cheetham Hill Road to the polluted River Irk and the (literally) odious factories stretching along the archways of the Manchester–Liverpool railway, in which the first Jewish immigrants from the Russian Empire found a kind of sanctuary and created the *chevroth* which served as their first footholds into an unfamiliar and largely hostile city. The exhibition reflects the ethos of a museum which reaches beyond (but does not ignore) the Jewish great and good to portray the experiences of ordinary Jewish men and women. Needless to say, although this is implied rather than stated, it presents images of Jewish people which confound the kinds of distortion with which I was brought up.

Finally, for better or worse, I have shifted my research into a still wider context, not precisely that rightly stressed by Todd Endelman, but that of Manchester as an 'immigrant city': a city which, since the middle of the eighteenth century has attracted not only a continuous flow of newcomers from Ireland, Scotland, Wales and every part of England (almost everyone in Manchester has an immigrant origin), but, during the nineteenth century, fugitive blacks slaves, Indian Lascars, Germans, Greeks, Italians, the French, Americans, Moroccans and Syrians, and later (setting aside, but not forgetting, Jewish immigrants from Fascist Europe, Hungary, Egypt and north Africa) Pakistanis (who now far outnumber Jews, but whose historical paths many of them are now taking), Bangladeshis, Ugandan Asians, Vietnamese, Rwandans, Somalis, Bosnians, Poles, Ukrainians and many others.

The presence of all Manchester's immigrants are stamped clearly on the city, including on what remains (now not very much) of the old Jewish Quarter in Cheetham. A 'hat factory' (a posh title for a building manufacturing cloth caps) was founded in Julia Street by the Russian immigrant cap-maker Jacob Doniger in the 1890s, when he gave it the even posher name, the 'Clarence Hat Factory', was abandoned by the Donigers after the Second World War (when the fashion for cloth caps cam to an abrupt end) and converted at some time in the 1950s into the Pakistani Trade Centre. In the 1970s it was taken over by an Indian businessman from Uganda, refurbished with meticulous attention to detail, and became a wholesale warehouse for English fashion gear. Recently, as this businessman moved on to better things, it became a warehouse for foodstuffs supplying Manchester shops now dealing in Polish goods. It is a way, as Tony Kushner has it, of 'remembering refugees'.

There are things about the building which still symbolise significant changes in local Jewish history. Jacob Doniger was one of a new class of entrepreneurs of Eastern European origin (somewhat disparagingly described in the Yiddish press as the *alrightniks*) who in time inherited the dominant communal role played earlier by a merchant plutocracy. He was a patron of immigrant charities and the founder in 1884 of Manchester's first Zionist organisation. A notice still visible above a side-door of the factory, reading 'Entrance for Workpeople' is a small reminder of the gulf which separated Jewish industrialists from their Jewish workforces. The 'Clarence' of the title suggests not only a strategy for negotiating anti-Semitism, but one adapted by Pakistani entrepreneurs to negotiate racism, such as the firm just round the corner from the Clarence and named by its Pakistani owner 'Joe Bloggs Jeans'.

The context of a multi-national city offers its own insights and poses its own problems. How different is the history of the Jewish community from that of the colonies established in Manchester by the Germans, the Italians and the Irish? Is it possible to make useful comparisons? Did the relative speed of economic advance by the Jews of Eastern Europe depend upon a mediating, moneyed, and anglicised middle class which did not develop until much later in Manchester's Irish and which is still at an embryonic stage in Manchester's black communities? Why is it that some first generation German and German-Jewish merchant-immigrants of the early nineteenth century entered local politics and philanthropy without difficulty, while their Greek and Italian peers showed no such inclination? How did Jews relate to their fellow German immigrants in such societies as the Schiller Anstalt (of which Engels was a leading member) or the Society for the Relief of Really Deserving Destitute Foreigners? Did the links of class override anti-Semitism? At one stage that particular society had on its committee German Lutherans, Unitarians, Anglicans and Jews. Its 'honorary members' included the minister of the Manchester Lutheran Church, a German-Jewish nonconformist city missionary and the rabbi of the Reform Synagogue (Oh, to have been there). Only Frederick Engels refused a request to join, probably driven by his visceral suspicion of bourgeois philanthropy. The 'immigrant city' is a context which is all the time generating more questions worth trying to answer.

And maybe there is a hidden polemic in what I am now trying to write. Tony Kushner has written with erudite compassion of the place(s) of immigrants in British society. If Jewish history required a didactic structure to generate enlightenment, surely this is it: while not marginalising the 'Jewishness' of the Jewish historical legacy, it is possible to look back on the Jewish experience as part of a far wider flow of peoples; to relate the experience of prejudice experienced by Jews, and the difficulties faced even by refugees from Fascism in gaining entry to Britain, to the unacceptable problems facing today's immigrants, asylum seekers and 'failed asylum seekers'. A wider context is not only a matter for historians to better understand change in the Anglo-Jewish community; it is a means of taking that wider context seriously.

August 2010

APPENDIXES: RESOURCES

The Anglo-Jewish Community and Its Archives

KAREN ROBSON

2010 marks the twentieth anniversary of the arrival at the University of Southampton's Library of many of the collections gathered by the Anglo-Jewish Archives in its work over the preceding three decades to preserve the written heritage of Anglo-Jewry. This development marked both a culmination of previous endeavours to deal with what was termed the 'vanishing heritage' of Jewish archives and the commencement of new initiatives. In 1988, the British Library hosted a symposium to discuss the plight of Jewish archives, out of which a working party was formed which produced guidelines for the Anglo-Jewish community on the preservation of material and recommendations for depositing archives. As part of these recommendations, a framework was set up to deal with the preservation of archive material: UK archive offices and libraries agreed to become repositories for broad areas of Jewish manuscript material. London Metropolitan Archives became the repository for material of London based organisations, while the University of Southampton consented to collect material relating to Anglo-Jewry which had a national or international basis. The archives of local communities and organisations were to go to local authority record offices. Here, Manchester had acted as an ideal model, with material collected by the Manchester Studies Unit of Manchester Polytechnic (now Manchester Metropolitan University), deposited at local repositories, helping to develop the rich historiography of Britain's second largest Jewish community. As part of its remit the British Library would consider papers of Jewish individuals who had achieved prominence in British society. The Scottish Jewish Archives Centre, which was set up in 1987 as an initiative of the Jewish community itself, has been the major repository for archival material relating to the Jewish communities in Scotland. Sadly, the situation in

Wales was less satisfactory, although more recently attempts have been made to locate surviving material across the country.

In the two decades since 1990, the general situation with regard to archives of the Anglo-Jewish community cannot be separated from the developments of the designated repositories, in particular London Metropolitan Archives and the University of Southampton. London Metropolitan Archives has become the repository of archives of a range of London based Jewish organisations. Central to these are the collections of the Board of Deputies of British Jews, the United Synagogue and the Office of Chief Rabbi.[1] The material for the Board of Deputies dates from 1760 and relates to a wide array of subjects from immigration and anti-Semitism, to education, legal matters, shechita and trade. The collection also contains extensive information on the plight of Jewish communities across the globe. The United Synagogue archive, which includes material for the oldest Ashkenazi synagogues in London, represents London Metropolitan Archives' largest Jewish collection and it continues to grow, with a long series of marriage and burial registers for 1880–1994 added in 2009. Although there are smaller quantities of material for Nathan Marcus Adler and his son Herman Adler, it is the official papers of Joseph Herman Hertz, Sir Israel Brodie, Immanuel Jakobovits and Jonathan Sacks that form the bulk of the archive of the Office of Chief Rabbi. An associated collection is that of the London Beth Din,[2] which is the ecclesiastical authority on kashrut and shechita as well as dealing with such matters as determining Jewish status, conversions and divorces. London Metropolitan Archives holds significant collections for London based congregations, including for the Federation of Synagogues, the Western Synagogue, the Liberal Jewish Synagogue and the West London Synagogue.[3] Papers of two organisations founded in the nineteenth century, the Jews' Temporary Shelter and Food for the Jewish Poor, together with the Jewish Bread Meat and Coal Society, which began its work in 1779, provide examples of philanthropic work within the Jewish community in London.[4] The archive of the World Jewish Relief,[5] which was previously the Central British Fund for World Jewish Relief, provides an invaluable resource for Jewish refugees from Nazi Europe from 1933 onwards. Information on these collections and others at London Metropolitan Archives can be found through the on-line catalogue at: http://search.lma.gov.uk/opac_lma/index.htm.

It is no exaggeration to say the arrival of the collections of Anglo-

Jewish Archives at Southampton in 1990 transformed the scale and breadth of the University's holdings, adding some 5,000 boxes to the Library's Special Collections. The acquisition of Anglo-Jewish archival material has continued unabated in the last 20 years and the holdings have tripled in size, filling more than 2,500 metres of shelves.

The Library has more than 800 collections of manuscripts, mainly for the nineteenth and twentieth centuries, but with material dating back to the twelfth century, a deed granting land to 'Solomon the Jew'.[6] They include holdings for a wide range of individuals and national organisations as well as material relating to communities. Papers of individuals include those of Cecil Roth, of Selig Brodetsky, private papers of Chief Rabbi Joseph Herman Hertz and of Chief Rabbi Sir Israel Brodie, Neville and Harold Laski and their parents, members of the Henriques family, including Sir Basil Henriques, papers of the performer and writer David Kossoff, correspondence of Frederick Dudley Samuel, from the front line in World War I, sermons of Rabbi Abraham Cohen, papers of Sir Robert Waley Cohen and of William Frankel, correspondence between Mrs Joseph and her sister Lady Samuels and papers of Lady Swaythling. The collections also encompass material of lesser known individuals which provides a fascinating insight into many different facets of the Anglo-Jewish experience. The 45 volumes of the 'journal of a minor Anglo-Jewish communal official' kept by Samuel Rich over the period of 1904–49, for instance, are a eloquent commentary on developments in the Jewish community in London, at the Jews' Free School, where Rich taught, and on national and international events.[7] The experience of Jewish refugees in Great Britain in the 1930s is documented in, among others, papers of the Adler family from Vienna, who were befriended by Cecil and Joan Stott,[8] and papers of the Van der Zyl family, which includes material of Rabbi Werner Van der Zyl relating to his time at the Mooragh Internment Camp on the Isle of Man.[9]

The archives of organisations similarly encompass a vast spectrum of activities within the Jewish community, including philanthropy and social work, education, women's rights, religious practices and observances. The Jewish Board of Guardians, the London Board of Shechita, the Anglo-Jewish Association, the editorial correspondence of the *Jewish Chronicle* newspaper, the Union of Jewish Women, the World Union of Progressive Judaism and the Reform Synagogues of Great Britain, Jews' College, Youth Aliyah and the Jewish Lads' and Girls' Brigade, pressure groups such as Conscience and the '35s' or the Women's Campaign for Soviet Jewry are some of the organisations represented. The Library also holds extensive material for the Institute of Jewish Affairs and the British Section of the World Jewish Congress, the latter of which provides an invaluable source for the situation of Jewish communities in Nazi-occupied Europe through the 1930s and the wartime period.[10] Within the archives of Rabbi Solomon Schonfeld is a large section of material relating to the work of the Chief Rabbi's Religious Emergency Council and the rescue of members of the Jewish community in the 1930s and 1940s: this represents one of the most extant collections of such material for Jewish refugees that exists in Great Britain.[11]

This has led to the University of Southampton becoming one of the leading repositories of Jewish archives in Western Europe. As the basis of its collecting is much broader than that of other designated repositories, the scope of the archive collections at Southampton is far-ranging. They provide a rich and extensive source for the study of the Jewish community in the UK, as well as for many other communities of the diaspora. Information on the collections can be found at http://www.archives. southampton.ac.uk/guide/.

In parallel to its work as a repository for Jewish archives, the University of Southampton initiated, and has continued to conduct, a survey of Jewish archival material in the UK and the Republic of Ireland. This survey is both a means to bring together information about material on Anglo-Jewry held publicly and in private hands and of monitoring the situation and developments with regard to this material. As a first stage questionnaires were distributed to repositories, organisations and institutions in both Great Britain and Eire seeking information on their holdings. The survey questionnaire was designed so that it gathered information on whether repositories held material on a number of broadly defined categories and for four defined periods of time. The broadly defined categories of material were for synagogues and communities, on community, social and welfare organisations, on refugees or immigrants, on schools, educational or youth organisations, on business and of individuals or families. For all of these categories, repositories were asked to indicate whether material was pre-eighteenth century, eighteenth century, nineteenth century or twentieth century.

The survey work is on-going and incremental. It progresses the work in stages, focussing on different categories of material within these stages. Current work is focussed on identifying papers of individuals, while previous work has looked at those of communities, organisations and in 2004/5, with the support of the Hanadiv Trust, there was a specific project looking at papers of businesses and commercial organisations. At the heart of the survey work is a core master list of 8,000 prominent Anglo-Jewish individuals, 600 prominent organisations and 800 congregations and communities for which information on archival material is being compiled. Through the findings of the survey it is hoped to provide some insight into the evolving situation with regard to Jewish archives.

The results of the initial survey found that a much larger proportion of material that had found its way into repositories was for the twentieth century, nearly equalling that of the other three time periods put together.[12] While encouraging, this figure was also slightly misleading as it in part reflected the growing awareness of many local history collections, which were consciously acquiring material to represent the Jewish and other ethnic communities in their locality rather than material created by the Jewish communities themselves. Indeed, for congregations, businesses and educational organisations material tended to be concentrated in only a small number of places, usually of the larger Jewish communities, such as London, Liverpool or Manchester. What these initial survey results in fact showed was that only a fraction of the archive material relating to the individuals, organisations and communities represented in the master lists had found their way into archive repositories.

Over the last two decades a greater plurality has developed. Given the concentration of the Jewish community in particular geographic locations and of the collecting policy of repositories, such as the Scottish Jewish Archives Centre or the University of Southampton, certain repositories will always have a greater proportion of holdings. But there has been a growing amount of Jewish archival material deposited in archive repositories over a wide geographical area of Great Britain from Aberdeen to Truro, by way of Aberystwyth, Newcastle and the Isle of Man, as well as some for Ireland. In scope and time period it stretches as widely as the geographic coverage. It ranges from the charter of Robert de Quncy to the monks of Newbattle Abbey in which he leases to them the land of Prestongrange for 20 years in return for their having paid his debt of 80 pounds of silver to 'Abraham the Jew', 1171,[13] to papers of Aaron Rapaport Rollin relating to the National Union of Tailors and Garment Workers and disputes, 1934–50, at the Modern Records Centre, Warwick University Library.[14] Recently the Manx National

Heritage Library has acquired collections of personal papers of German Jewish refugees, such as for J. Alfred Brew and Michael Maynard, while the collection of papers for the journalist and poet Leslie Daiken at the National Library of Ireland contains material relating to Jewish publications.[15]

There has been a similar slowly developing trend of archives of synagogues and communities from a wider range of geographic locations (outside of London, Manchester, Liverpool or the Scottish Jewish Archives Centre at Glasgow) finding their way into archive repositories. The Exeter Hebrew Congregation papers can be found in the Devon Record Office, Tyne and Wear Archives Service holds material for Whitby Bay Hebrew Congregation, Sunderland Hebrew Congregation and Newcastle United Hebrew Congregation, Oxford Jewish Congregation material is lodged at Oxfordshire Record Office, Sir Moses Montefiore Memorial Synagogue, Grimsby, at North East Lincolnshire Archives, Chatham Memorial Synagogue at Medway Archives and Swansea Hebrew Congregation papers at the West Glamorgan Archives Service. The development of the Hull Archives Centre represents an initiative which will provide a focus and custodial care for material for that locality. Of course material remains with communities and work still needs to be done to further identify this and to explore ways to make it accessible and to ensure that it is preserved for posterity.

With regard to other categories of papers, superficially there seems to be a similar improvement in the situation. However, this is sometimes more the result of technological developments and the greater availability of information, such as on-line catalogues and finding aids. With the papers of individuals and families, for instance, though the survey is finding information on a greater number of people, somewhere in the region of 50 per cent,[16] this does not necessarily reflect a greater proportion of significant collections finding their way into archive repositories or being made available. For every very full survey entry, such as that for Sir Jacob Epstein, which describes material held by the Henry Moore Institute, Hull University, London Metropolitan Archives, Bolton Archives and Local Studies Service, the Royal Academy of Music, Whitechapel Art Gallery, the Scott Polar Research Institute, University of Cambridge, the Tate Gallery, Manchester University, Walsall Local History Centre, The National Archives, Leeds Museums and Galleries, the Jewish Museum, London, the British Library, the Parliamentary Archives as well as material held privately, there are many more modest entries. These, in contrast to the Epstein entry, describe small quantities of material, often items found in collections of others. These might include sequences of official government papers, such as those for the Home or Foreign Offices, or for educational establishments such as Gordonstoun school, university student records or for professional organisations such as those for the British Institute of Architects. For Elizabeth Esther Eppler, assistant director of the Institute of Jewish Affairs and secretary of the World Jewish Congress, for example, the material identified is an application for naturalisation held in Home Office papers at The National Archives,[17] while for Joel Cang, associate and foreign editor of the *Jewish Chronicle*, it is a Royal Institute of International Affairs tape recording of a meeting on Polish foreign policy and the German pact, 11 October 1943.[18]

Progress has been made in terms of collecting policy in the last two decades and it is to the credit of those involved in effecting this. But, as has been indicated, there is still much material for which proper provision has not been made, as well as work to be done to raise awareness of the importance of preserving the archival heritage and to engage the community with regard to this. The Religious Archives Survey undertaken by The National Archives, for which Southampton acted as an advisor on its steering committee, aimed not only to find out about archive material held by communities, but to raise awareness of preservation issues. The report of this survey was published at the end of 2010.[19] Issues of preservation become more complex and urgent in this new age of technology as we move away from the predominately paper based archival collections of the past.

The last two decades have seen a data revolution, as technological advancements, such as the expansion of the World Wide Web or the development of digitisation techniques, have moved us forward to an electronic age. This has transformed the way in which data can be accessed as well as the way in which records are created and the format of archives for the future. From the point of access to information, the ever increasing expansion of the electronic environment has been a great innovation. The development of collaborative cataloguing databases, websites and digitisation projects has allowed the greater dissemination of information about collections. Exploiting this new technology is one way of creating access to archive collections where recourse to the original items is a problem. The JewGen site, http://www.jewishgen.org, for instance, already acts as a host for information about archives of some local communities. While the quantities of information available on the World Wide Web sometimes create the false expectation that everything is, or should be, available there, an electronic presence is now a prerequisite. The Merseyside Jewish Community Archive website, http://www.mersey-gateway.org, is a good example of the way that the web has been used to promote the outcome of a cataloguing project to make the community's collections accessible.

The expansion of born-digital and digitised data adds a new dimension to the issue of preservation. Work might still need to be done to ensure that the archives of the past, predominately paper based collections, are preserved as part of the Anglo-Jewish heritage. Yet creating a framework for preserving the electronic archive of the future is of equal significance and becomes more pressing. Technology develops and moves on so quickly that obsolescent formats and unreadable data can become an issue within a short space of time. Issues of storage and migration of data can be complex. Preserving such electronic media will be one of the big challenges facing information specialists and the archivists for the future.

NOTES

1. London Metropolitan Archives: ACC/3121 Board of Deputies; ACC/2712 United Synagogue; and ACC/2805 Office of the Chief Rabbi.
2. LMA: ACC/3400.
3. LMA: ACC/2893 Federation of Synagogues; ACC/2911 Western Synagogue; ACC/3529 Liberal Jewish Synagogue; ACC/2886 West London Synagogue.
4. LMA: LMA/4184 Jews' Temporary Shelter; ACC/2942 Food for the Jewish Poor; ACC/2944 Jewish Bread Meat and Coal Society.
5. LMA: ACC/2793.
6. University of Southampton Library MS 28/1 Charter of Thurstan the huntsman granting 11 ½ acres of land in Heillesle (probably near Woodham Mortimer and Maldon, in Essex) to Solomon the Jew, early twelfth century.
7. USL: MS 168.
8. USL: MS 293.
9. USL: MS 297.
10. USL: MS 237–41.
11. USL: MS 183.
12. 45 per cent of respondents held twentieth century material, in contrast to 27 per cent for nineteenth century, 11 per cent for eighteenth century and 12 per cent for pre-eighteenth century.
13. National Archives of Scotland: GD40/1/6.
14. Modern Records Centre, Warwick University: MSS 240.
15. Manx National Heritage Library: MS 11799 papers of J. Alfred Brew and of Michael Maynard; National Library of Ireland: Acc 6784 papers of Leslie Daiken.
16. Survey results for names beginning with the letter A, the success rate is 50 per cent; for the letter E it is slightly lower at just over 46 per cent.
17. The National Archives: HO405/12632.
18. Royal Institute of International Affairs: RIAA/8/349.
19. Religious Archives Survey 2010 (The National Archives, November 2010).

Transforming the Jewish Museum: The Power of Narrative

RICKIE BURMAN

In March 2010 the Jewish Museum London reopened following a £10m transformation, creating a landmark museum celebrating Jewish life and cultural diversity. The launch of the new museum was greeted with acclaim in media ranging from *The Times*, *Independent* and *New York Times*, to the *Culture Show* and BBC TV News and Radio 4's flagship cultural programme, *Front Row*, and was also covered as far afield as India, Taiwan, Turkey and New Zealand. Such extensive media attention could not have been presumed for a museum about the Jewish community in the UK nor would it have been likely in any of its previous iterations. The reopening of the museum represented the culmination of a long process, which relates closely to changing perspectives in British Jewish history, as well as to new concerns regarding the societal role of museums.

Within a British context, the Jewish Museum has to face in two directions: it represents both a showcase presenting Jewish history and culture to the wider community, and a prism through which the Jewish community can examine its own roots and history. But in developing the museum we have sought to extend its contribution and to explore how it can play a more proactive role and fulfil a social purpose, for example by promoting community cohesion, by shifting perceptions and forging new relationships and connections – whether between past and present, between the Jewish experience and the mainstream or between the Jewish community and other minority groups.

As you enter the newly reopened Jewish Museum, you will be greeted not by a traditional array of objects from the Jewish community, but by five larger than life screens, which in the course of 20 minutes give you insights into the lives of ten extraordinarily diverse people who also happen to be British Jews. This display in our Welcome Gallery is only one of several aspects of the museum that challenges expectations of a conventional museum visit. On the floor above, the permanent displays conclude with the opportunity to investigate the Living Community through an interactive discovery table, while the adjacent Holocaust Gallery focuses on the narrative of a single individual, Leon Greenman OBE, an Englishman who survived Auschwitz. Between these points, the visitor will have many experiences, some more closely resembling conventional museum displays, but throughout, providing continuity to the displays, there is an emphasis on presenting the narrative of British Jewish history through an empathetic engagement with individuals and their stories.

Underlying the experience of the museum visit is the creative use of narrative. The challenge faced in these displays is to reconcile the parochialism of individual experience, as represented by these diverse portraits and in many subsequent stories, with a wider transcendent narrative, that of the history of the Jewish community as one of Britain's oldest minorities. The way in which the relationship between these two forms of narrative has evolved can be explored through a third narrative, the history of the Jewish Museum itself. The new Jewish Museum brings together the collections and activities of two complementary museums, the Jewish Museum and the former London Museum of Jewish Life. In 1995 the two museums amalgamated on an organisational basis, but it was only with the recent expansion that it was possible to achieve their physical integration. Both constituent museums were, to a considerable extent, products of their times, in terms of their aims, their approach to collecting and their presentation of Jewish life and history.[1]

The Jewish Museum was founded in 1932 in the Jewish communal headquarters at Woburn House in Bloomsbury. Its founders drew their inspiration and collections in part from the landmark Anglo-Jewish historical exhibition held in 1887 at the Royal Albert Hall on the occasion of Queen Victoria's Jubilee. This exhibition placed on public view for the first time in Britain extensive collections of Jewish ritual art and aimed to counteract prejudice by disseminating information about the Jewish community and its contribution to English life.

Although the museum was eventually established over 40 years later, the concerns of the founders had much in common with those of the organisers of the Anglo-Jewish exhibition. Its collecting policy aimed to illustrate Jewish religious practice and the history of the Jewish community in Britain, focusing on prints, portraits and ceremonial objects of historical interest and high artistic merit, and acquisitions were limited to items over 100 years old.

By the early 1990s, the museum's accommodation had become cramped and inadequate for its needs and plans to close Woburn House gave added urgency to the concern to relocate. The Museum Chairman, Raymond Burton, generously acquired two Grade II listed Victorian houses in Albert Street, Camden Town, then in use as an industrial workshop, to serve as the new premises for the museum. Following extensive building works, in 1995 the Jewish Museum opened in its new premises, which at last provided an attractive setting for its outstanding collection in an accessible and convenient location.

The London Museum of Jewish Life was founded in 1983 at the Manor House Centre for Judaism (later the Sternberg Centre for Judaism) in Finchley, north London. Initially entitled the Museum of the Jewish East End, it grew out of JEEP (the Jewish East End Project), launched under the auspices of the Association of Jewish Youth, which had several successful conferences and events to promote an interest in the history of the Jewish East End. The immediate concern of the museum was to preserve the disappearing heritage of the Jewish East End as the heartland of Jewish immigrant settlement in Britain, where a vibrant Eastern Europe Jewish culture had flourished prior to World War II. By the 1980s few Jewish residents or institutions remained in the East End, and it was recognised that there was a need to recover and preserve its history, since the collecting policy of the existing Jewish Museum did not encompass social history material or items less than 100 years old. Just as 50 years earlier the Jewish Museum had been founded in premises housing the United Synagogue, so the Museum of the Jewish East End was founded in a site housing the Reform Synagogue Movement, although in each case the museum was established as an independent charity, unaffiliated to any religious movement.

The new museum's development was influenced by the approach of the History Workshop movement, and in particular by the work pioneered by Bill Williams in the Manchester Studies Unit. Appointed as Museum Curator in 1984, I drew on my previous experience working with Bill Williams in researching Jewish history in Manchester and as Coordinator of the project to establish the Manchester Jewish Museum, which opened shortly before I took up this new post. In contrast to the existing Jewish Museum, the Museum of the Jewish East End thus adopted a proactive and democratic approach to recovering and preserving Jewish heritage in all its aspects, with an emphasis on oral history, outreach and the popularisation of Jewish history through talks, walking tours and regular Research Group sessions.

In 1988 the museum adopted the new title of the London Museum of Jewish Life in order to reflect its increasing scope in collecting and presenting material reflecting the diverse heritage of Jewish people in London, extending beyond the Jewish East End. The exhibitions created by the museum served as a stimulus to gather material and as a way to accord recognition to hitherto neglected aspects of British Jewish history. The 1980s exhibitions focused primarily on the East End. Our first exhibition *A Century of Migration*, looking at the changing history of Jewish settlement in the East End from 1885 to 1985, was followed by an exhibition marking the centenary of the Jews' Temporary Shelter, established to help Eastern European Jewish immigrants but in more recent years assisting new arrivals from areas as diverse as Romania, Aden and North Africa. In 1987 we mounted ground-breaking exhibitions on *Yiddish Theatre in London* and *East End Synagogues*. In each case, these exhibitions were stimulated by the urgent need to recover objects, photographs and testimonies to reflect the Jewish experience and drew on oral history interviews as a key part of the narrative.

In 1988 the museum created the first of many exhibitions relating to the experience of refugees from Nazism and Holocaust survivors: *Refugee from Nazism*, focusing on one woman's experience was to be followed by *The Last Goodbye* on the *Kindertransport*, *The Boys* on teenage survivors admitted to Britain after World War II, and *'Am I My Brother's Keeper?'* highlighting the stories of British rescuers and survivors now living in Britain, who were hidden or rescued. At the same time, we continued to reflect the heterogeneity of the community with *Living up West*, on Jewish life in London's West End, a detailed exhibition on the Jews of Aden, and *A Tapestry of Many Threads* reflecting the varied heritage of Sephardi and Eastern communities who have made Britain their home. Again, the collection and use of oral history, combined with the copying of photographs from a wide range of individuals, was central to the exhibitions, and the use of personal testimonies helped to create a direct, empathetic response.

As the scope of the museum developed, so too did its educational work. The museum pioneered an important programme of Holocaust education – one which continues to represent a major facet of its work. This involves working with a team of survivor speakers, who share their personal testimonies with young people within thought-provoking educational programmes. In 1995 the museum established a dedicated Holocaust Education Gallery focusing on the experiences of London-born Holocaust survivor, Leon Greenman. Living in the Netherlands at the time of the Nazi occupation, Leon had given his British passport and other papers for safekeeping to friends, who had destroyed them in fear for their own safety. This had tragic consequences: lacking papers to prove their status as British citizens, Leon was deported with his wife, Else, and two-year-old son, Barney, to Auschwitz. While Else and Barney were killed on arrival, Leon survived six concentration camps and, following liberation, devoted the rest of his life to speaking out against racism and prejudice. He spoke to thousands of school pupils within the context of the museum's Holocaust Education Gallery, which displayed some poignant personal items belonging to his family, retrieved after the war: Barney's sailor suit and patched-up shoes, and Else's wedding dress, dyed chocolate brown so that she could wear it on other occasions.

The amalgamation of the Jewish Museum and the London Museum of Jewish Life in 1995 forged one organisation, but due to space restrictions it continued to operate at two sites, the Jewish Museum – Camden Town and the Jewish Museum – Finchley, with complementary collections and activities, reflecting the historic division between the two former museums. Despite this separation, the museum was able to draw on the strengths of its two constituent partners, combining one of the world's finest collections of Jewish ceremonial art with a wide-ranging approach to Jewish social history, reflecting the diversity of Jewish roots and reaching out to varied audiences beyond the Jewish community. This inclusive approach was reflected in the mission statement of the new museum – to explore and preserve Jewish heritage, to celebrate diversity and to combat prejudice.

In the decade following amalgamation, the Jewish Museum gained increasing profile and recognition. In 1997 its Judaica collections were awarded Designated status by the Museums Libraries and Archives Council in recognition of their outstanding national importance. It developed as a leading independent museum in London, for example becoming a senior partner and major contributor to the Moving Here project, a consortium led by the

National Archives digitising materials reflecting migration to England. In educational terms too, the museum continued to develop, maintaining a continued emphasis on Holocaust and anti-racist education, while also developing Discovering Judaism programmes to promote understanding of Jewish religious life and traditions. Both programmes reached young people from varied faiths and backgrounds, with over 90 per cent of educational visits serving non-Jewish schools.

The museum's exhibition programme sought to achieve a synthesis of the approaches of both museums, aiming to integrate the display of art-historical and social history materials, and to bring together artefacts with the stories and life experiences of the individuals who used or created them. This integration was highlighted by exhibitions such as *By the Rivers of Babylon – The Story of the Jews of Iraq* and *Continental Britons – Jewish Refugees from Nazi Europe*, each drawing on testimonies and accompanied by a wide-ranging programme of events. Building on the success of these exhibitions, the museum became more explicit in developing and articulating its underlying social purpose, highlighting its relevance to contemporary issues and its resonance for the experience of other minority communities.

This approach was exemplified by our exhibition, *Closing the Door? Immigrants to Britain 1905–2005*, which marked the centenary of the Aliens Act, and looked at immigration over the last 100 years. The exhibition combined an account of immigration legislation and its impact on different immigrant groups with a consideration of the misconceptions and complaints endlessly recycled about different waves of migration, supported by film and personal testimonies from individuals who have come to Britain from different countries. It demonstrated that immigrants or refugees now valued for their positive contribution had in their own time encountered similar attitudes and accusations to new arrivals on the receiving end of negative media attention today. This exhibition was important in the development of a new relationship between personal narrative and the wider historical narrative. The stories it contained showed powerful analogous experiences between earlier Jewish migrants and more recent immigrants: the motivations for leaving one country for another, the challenges faced on the journey and on arrival, the common experience of racism and the difficulty of creating a new life in a new home.

The *Closing the Door?* exhibition became particularly topical as it coincided with the general election – and the memorable campaign slogan on immigration 'are you thinking what we're thinking?'. It provided a focus for more positive views of immigration and attracted attention in media such as the *Observer* and Radio 4's *Today* programme. Through the exhibition and associated events, such as panel discussions on the media and immigration and the role of refugees in the health service, we were able to bring in diverse audiences and to make connections with other minority groups. In our subsequent exhibition, *Identities*, we built further on these relationships, exploring the multi-faceted nature of identity in contemporary society, and holding creative workshops with groups such as the Filipino Centre and Congolese Action Group. Our following exhibition *Ghetto Warriors – Minority Boxers in Britain*, reflected not only on Jewish boxing champions such as Daniel Mendoza, Kid Berg and Kid Lewis, but also more recent heroes such as Lennox Lewis and Amir Khan, and enabled the museum to form new connections, for example with the local Irish Traveller movement.

In moving forward to the next stage of its development, the museum retained a commitment to this sense of relevance to contemporary social issues and to playing a continuing, active role in promoting community cohesion. Following the successful amalgamation of the two museums, it became increasingly evident that to realise fully the museum's potential as a cultural and educational resource it must be a priority to expand the museum and to bring together all its collections and activities within a single site. The first step on the long and challenging journey to realise this objective was achieved in 2002 with the purchase of a former piano factory building, adjoining the rear of the Jewish Museum's current premises in Camden Town, made possible by the outstanding generosity of two key museum supporters, Raymond Burton CBE and Kenneth Rubens OBE.

The next tasks were to start the process of planning the new museum and raising the funds to make it possible. We appointed as project architects Long & Kentish, an award-winning practice with a long history of developing museums and galleries including the British Library Centre for Conservation, Pallant House Gallery, Chichester (Museum of the Year 2007) and the National Maritime Museum in Falmouth. Exhibition designers, Event Communications, were also appointed at an early stage, enabling an integrated process between architectural and exhibition design. Following extensive work in planning the new museum, its business plan and audience development, interpretation and access strategies, in December 2005 the Jewish Museum Development Project was awarded a Heritage Lottery Fund Stage 1 grant award for £4.2m. This marked the starting point for further intensive work, allowing a period of 12 months for the submission of our Stage 2 application with detailed architectural and design plans and to raise the balance of project funding from other sources – the most challenging aspect of the project.

In spring 2007 the HLF grant was confirmed and in the following September both museum sites closed for preliminary works to take place. The museum offices moved to temporary accommodation and its collections were relocated to off-site storage. Building work took place on site through 2008 and 2009, in parallel with the process of exhibition production and installation, and in March 2010 the new museum opened, tripling the space of the previous Camden site and creating new exhibition galleries and improved facilities for education and visitor services. The new museum includes four permanent galleries (Welcome Gallery, *Judaism: A Living Faith*, *History: A British Story*, and Holocaust Gallery), a Changing Exhibitions Gallery, a multipurpose Auditorium, Education Space, café, shop, collections stores and research facilities. A medieval mikveh (ritual bath), excavated in the City of London in 2001, has been installed on the ground floor, while hands-on displays for children and families are integrated throughout the permanent displays.

Fundamental to the museum's development was a strategic visioning process, reviewing the role and mission of the museum and its target audiences, and consulting widely with different stakeholders and visitor groups, including those who were previous visitors or 'non-users', Jewish and not Jewish, individuals from other minority backgrounds, teachers and parents with young children. After defining our range of audiences, the museum's internal project team worked intensively with our exhibition designers, Event Communications, to define the key messages of the museum and each exhibition element, and, building on this, to develop the interpretation that underlies each display, the exhibition narrative, and selection of each object, image and interpretive media.

Through this process, we identified a set of key content and delivery principles to provide a conceptual framework both for the museum's permanent displays and for our future programming of changing exhibitions, education and events. These principles drew their inspiration from Jewish experience, history and culture and are reflected in the museum's collections: 'Identity and diversity' – exploring the ways in which people construct and maintain their identities in a multicultural, multi-faith society; 'Migration and diasporas' – examining the experiences of migration and settlement shared by many minority ethnic communities; 'Combating prejudice' – challenging all forms of prejudice, working to promote mutual respect and understanding. Underpinning all three themes is a further principle, fundamental to the museum's interpretation and its success in engaging visitors from a wide range of backgrounds: 'Peopling the story'. Viewing history through the prism of people allows visitors to gain a picture of the lived experience, it encourages empathy and builds connections between people on a human level, emphasising the commonalities of experience.

This distinctive approach finds its most explicit expression in the Welcome Gallery, the multi-media display that greets museum visitors on arrival. In this dramatic installation the narratives of ten different individuals are interwoven – a fourth generation smoked salmon producer; an Indian-born, marathon-running great-grandmother; a London taxi-driver; a Holocaust survivor who represented Britain as a weight-lifter in the Olympics; a sixth-former at the JFS school; an Orthodox rabbi involved in Muslim–Jewish dialogue; a Chinese convert to Judaism. These individuals communicate the key messages that, like Londoners in general, Jewish people come from diverse backgrounds and form part of Britain's ethnic and cultural diversity. They also demonstrate that Jewish people in Britain play an integral part in society, and illustrate the complex and multi-faceted nature of identities in Britain today, indicating that there are many different ways of being Jewish and expressing Jewish identity.

These same themes are further reflected and developed in the museum's other permanent galleries. In our gallery *Judaism: A Living Faith*, we aim not only to display the museum's outstanding Judaica collections, regarded among the finest in the world, but also to show Jewish people today practising Judaism as a living religion and to give a sense of Jewish ethics and values. Our interpretation is informed by the specific key messages we identified for the gallery: Judaism is a living world religion, a way of life with a rich heritage of religious traditions and festivals; the Torah is at the heart of Judaism, providing its core teachings; the home and synagogue are complementary settings for the practice of Judaism; beautiful items are used for worship as an expression of devotion to God; Jewish practices reflect the common thread of Judaism around the world and the diversity of backgrounds of Jewish people. An open Torah is displayed at the core of the gallery, reflecting the centrality of Torah to Jewish life; as you point an interactive *yad* (pointer) at the scroll, the Hebrew chanting of the Ten Commandments can be heard. Throughout the displays newly commissioned films show a range of contemporary families celebrating festivals and life cycle events such as a wedding and bar/bat-mitzvah, bringing an accessible, personal dimension to the practice of Judaism. A showcase illustrates Judaism around the world, with objects from areas as diverse as Europe, Afghanistan, North Africa and Yemen, while the diversity of religious viewpoints is conveyed in an 'Ask the Rabbi' touchscreen interactive, featuring rabbis from four different strands of Judaism. This display also highlights approaches to Jewish ethics, a theme further explored in a showcase entitled 'More than Charity', on the Jewish concept of *tsedakah*.

In our gallery, *History: A British Story* there is a strong emphasis on personal narrative, again using film and testimony, but also in communicating the stories behind the objects. We aim to show that Jewish people have come to Britain from across the world for different reasons and at different times; that the Jewish community is one of the oldest minorities in Britain; Jewish history is part of Britain and that the Jewish experience has resonance for other immigrant and refugee groups. The gallery opens with a map showing the different areas where Jewish people in Britain have come from, embedded with highly personal objects that they brought with them to their new country, for example a doll brought by a child refugee on the *Kindertransport*, nuts from a garden in Lithuania, and a bible which was the only object an anti-apartheid activist was allowed to take with him into solitary confinement in prison in South Africa. We personalise the early history of the community with a timeline looking at 'Medieval Lives', and the titling of the resettlement period highlights the wider resonance for the immigrant experience: 'A New Community', 'Putting down roots', 'Equal Rights'. Exploring the experience of Eastern European Jewish immigrants in the late nineteenth century, visitors can play the Great Migration board game which highlights the challenges faced by immigrants making the journey to a new country, while the interactive display 'The Same Old Story?' allows visitors to explore media attitudes to immigration over the past two centuries.

In the evocation of an East End street, you can meet the Jablonsky family and hear them talk about their journey to England, the difficulties of finding work and building a new life, the tensions as the next generation grows up with different values and new expectations. The tailoring workshop display highlights an occupation which has provided a livelihood for many immigrant groups; you can try the shears and lift up the pressing iron while characters from an enlarged photograph come to life to give different perspectives on work and conditions in the tailoring trade – the master tailor, hand-sewer and under-presser. There is a chance to enjoy immigrant culture with a Yiddish theatre karaoke presented by comedian David Schneider, whose grandparents were performers in London's Yiddish theatre, complemented by a display of costumes, posters and programmes from the museum's extensive collection.

In presenting the two world wars and the inter-war period, the Jewish experience is portrayed as part of the wider national experience ('For King and Country', 'A Step up the Ladder', 'The Home Front'). At the same time specifically Jewish dimensions are explored, for example with the development of Zionism and the rise of fascism. A range of interpretation media allow for varying levels and different kinds of engagement. You can open a drawer to view a pamphlet by Oswald Moseley and a propaganda gramophone recording from the British Union of Fascists, watch a film with rare testimonies of veterans who fought fascism at the Battle of Cable Street and in the Spanish Civil War, or use a touchscreen to explore documents, film and oral history relating to the Jewish experience in World War II. A window serves as a visual connecting point between the wartime experience and the adjacent Holocaust Gallery, the interface between Jewish servicemen in the British forces and the survivors of the concentration camps symbolised in a photograph of the marriage of a British army officer to a young survivor, her dress made from a parachute.

Just as throughout the displays in the other permanent galleries, there is an emphasis on individuals or families and their personal narratives, so in our Holocaust Gallery the focus is again on one individual, Leon Greenman, who was born in London's East End. Although his story should have followed the same trajectory as the other Jewish Eastenders whose history we follow in our History gallery, Leon was living with his family in Rotterdam at the time of the Nazi occupation of the Netherlands, with tragic consequences, as noted above. As in our previous Holocaust Education Gallery, the new gallery displays poignant personal items belonging to Leon and his family – his son's sailor suit and shoes, a hand-made wooden toy, Else's wedding dress and Leon's concentration camp uniform. However, in the new display the objects are shown alongside a film recorded with Leon before his death in 2006. Here, he handles the same items and explains their significance in the context of his experiences. Leon's narrative is complemented by a film showing the testimonies of four other survivors who settled in Britain after the war. Their stories highlight other aspects of the Holocaust, such as the experience of the ghetto, resistance and rescue. This emphasis on individual narrative has proved powerful in engaging the interest and empathy of visitors and the many young people who participate in our educational programmes.

Writing in *The Independent*, Jay Merrick comments: 'The decision to portray British Jewry's experience of the Holocaust in this way makes it personal and singularly touching, in a way that the overwhelmingly dreadful number, six million, cannot. The rigour of this focus on a single survivor pervades the overall exhibition strategy.'[2]

Following displays on rebuilding life after the war and the post-war migrations, the permanent displays conclude with the opportunity to investigate the 'Living Community' by tracing the significance and connections of disparate images – such as a Mars bar, a Tottenham *kippah* or a taxi-cab – which bubble to the surface of an interactive discovery table.

Now that the new museum is up and running, we are actively inviting visitor feedback, and the responses are very encouraging, suggesting the new displays are succeeding in engaging people from varied ages and backgrounds and communicating the messages we identified. However, the challenges continue. Looking ahead, alongside our key concern to raise funding to support and sustain the museum, we aim to continue to develop the museum as a vibrant space with a dynamic programme of exhibitions and events, underpinned by the content principles we have identified. We will seek to build on our previous work to create a museum that has relevance to social issues today, that serves not only as a place for education and entertainment, but as a forum for discussion and debate, and that brings together people from different backgrounds and experiences.

In the context of today's complex and cosmopolitan society, we hope that in presenting the experience of Jewish people in Britain in this way the Jewish Museum can play a positive role, not only in exhibiting cultural diversity, but, further, in building understanding and forging connections that at the same time both respect and transcend our diversity. Through a synthesis of narrative and interaction, the Jewish Museum provides a platform for people from all faiths and backgrounds to explore how new, more fluid forms of allegiances and interests may be embraced and combined with our own distinctive histories and identities. At the end of this story of the Jewish Museum we arrive at a greater appreciation of the role of stories, the personal narratives which help breathe life and meaning into our collections of Judaica and historical artefacts. It is the underlying humanism of narrative that creates the empathetic encounter between our visitors and these displays.

NOTES

1. More detailed accounts of the development of the two museums can be found in R.D. Barnett, *Catalogue of the Jewish Museum London* (London: Harvey Miller, 1974), and in R. Burman, 'The Jewish Museum, London: Introduction and History', in *Treasures of Jewish Heritage: The Jewish Museum London* (London: Scala Publishers, 2006).
2. Jay Merrick, 'History with Room to Breathe', *The Independent*, 16 March 2010.

Synagogues at Risk: Report Based on the Findings of a Survey Carried out by Jewish Heritage UK

SHARMAN KADISH

The Synagogues at Risk (SAR) Survey forms part of English Heritage's Heritage at Risk programme. It was commissioned by English Heritage in order to foster understanding of the specific needs of synagogues as a building type and to identify potential cases of 'Synagogues at Risk'. While recommendations were made on the basis of the survey, the decision on whether particular buildings are put on the Heritage at Risk Register rests solely with the relevant English Heritage regional team.

The SAR Survey has enabled the identification of synagogues that would most benefit from support in terms of grant aid and how to access it, as well as from professional advice regarding repairs and maintenance, security issues and development of tourism potential. The long term intention is to secure a sustainable future for historic synagogues not only as architectural heritage but also, wherever possible, as home to living congregations. To help address some of these issues, English Heritage has since offered Support Officer funding to Jewish Heritage UK.

Background

The primary functions of a synagogue are broader than the bald definition: 'The synagogue is the Jewish place of worship'. The word 'synagogue' derives from the Greek, meaning to assemble. The Hebrew term is *Bet Knesset*, literally 'house of assembly', denoting the three-fold function of the synagogue as house of prayer, study and assembly. The synagogue has always been a community building with a social function rather than a sacred shrine to which only an elite priestly cast has access. Synagogues may be susceptible to losing these primary uses through demographic decline or shift. Social changes may also adversely affect synagogue usage: changes in modes of worship, as a result of theology or fashion, or simply through the loosening of community affiliation, cultural ties and assimilation.

According to the 2001 Census, regarded as a conservative estimate,[1] the population of British Jewry[2] stands at 267,000. This figure represents less than half of one per cent of the total population of the UK. The Jewish community is thus a tiny minority. Its significance lies in its status as the oldest non-Christian faith minority in Britain. The Jewish community has almost halved in size from a reputed peak of 450,000 in the 1950s. In 1985 the Jewish population had dropped to about 330,000, and to 285,000 in 1995. This overall decline has been attributed to a number of factors, mainly a drop in the birth-rate, resulting in a rising age profile and an excess of deaths over births. Other significant factors are out-marriage, now believed to have risen to over 50 per cent, and emigration, mainly to Israel. Today, immigration of Jews[3] to Britain is negligible compared with the influx from eastern Europe (Russian Empire, Austrian Galicia, Romania) in the period 1881–1914 (100,000) and refugees from central Europe, (Germany, Austria, Czechoslovakia) in the 1930s (50,000–60,000 including 10,000 unaccompanied children).

In terms of distribution, the Jewish community is increasingly concentrated in a handful of urban and suburban areas in north-west London and north-west Manchester. This is resulting in the disappearance of smaller communities around the country, in both small towns and large cities, including Liverpool, Leeds, Birmingham and Glasgow. In contrast, Manchester's Jewish population, estimate 30,000–35,000, is showing a net increase. This is due to the localised expansion of the *Haredi* (strictly Orthodox) sector with a characteristically high birth rate. On present trends, the expansion of the *Haredi* sector will not result in net growth in the size of London Jewry. London historically has always been home to about two-thirds of British Jewry and remains so today. The Jewish population is estimated at about 179,500 in the Greater London area, including Hertfordshire, currently the focus for the growth of new communities affiliated to mainstream synagogue organisations.

It is now recognised that redundancy can pose a threat to the survival of the special interest of an historic building equal to that posed by the deterioration of its actual fabric, and that places of worship are particularly vulnerable in this regard. The battle against redundancy faced by historic synagogues is far more acute than that faced by urban churches because Orthodox Jewish law prohibits travelling on the Sabbath, so synagogues need to be situated within the Jewish neighbourhood and be accessible on foot.

Around the country, 20 synagogues built before the Second World War have closed since the start of the Survey of the Jewish Built Heritage in the UK & Ireland (SJBH) in 1996, and at least two post-war synagogues in London (Greenford, West Hackney). This represents one-fifth (21 per cent) of the number of then working pre-war synagogues included in the original Survey. Six synagogues have been demolished. In East London these are: the Wlodowa, Cheshire Street, E1 (1910, demolished c.2001), Great Garden Street Federation (Lewis Solomon 1896, gutted c.1997) and Clapton Federation Synagogue (Marcus K. Glass 1931–32) – the latter demolished in 2006 in the face of attempts to have it listed. In the Midlands, Stoke-on-Trent Synagogue, in Hanley (William Campbell 1922–23) was demolished c.2006 to make way for a new bus station, whilst Birmingham Progressive Synagogue, Sheepcote Street (Ernest Joseph 1938) was sold to developers who in exchange provided a small synagogue in a new residential complex a short distance away. Although a rare British example of an International Style synagogue, Birmingham Progressive was not listed. Jewish communities are disappearing from whole regions of England, the West Midlands (Wolverhampton, Coventry, Stoke and Birmingham), the North East (Sunderland, Middlesborough); as well as from less fashionable parts of London.

Whilst the SAR Survey was in progress, Bradford Synagogue (Reform) announced possible closure and Hackney Synagogue did close down just after completion of the survey (in July 2009).

Duration
Fieldwork for the SAR Survey was carried out over a period of four months between March and June 2009 and a report to English Heritage submitted in July 2009.

Personnel
The SAR Survey was carried out on behalf of English Heritage by Jewish Heritage UK. The fieldwork was carried out by Dr Sharman Kadish D.Phil., FRHist.S., FSA, Director, Jewish Heritage and Barbara Bowman RIBA, IHBC, Consultant Architect to Jewish Heritage. The itinerary of visits was organised by Hadar Sela, Jewish Heritage's Administrator. This report was compiled by Sharman Kadish.

Jewish Heritage was established in 2004 and became a registered charity in 2007 (No.1118174). Jewish Heritage is the first and only agency dedicated to caring for the historic buildings and sites of Britain's Jewish community, especially synagogues and Jewish cemeteries. It is an independent body that is aligned with no official bodies within the British Jewish community, whether religious or secular, and receives no funding from them. Its activities are underpinned by the Survey of the Jewish Built Heritage, fieldwork for which was mainly carried out between 1998 and 2001, supported by, amongst others, English Heritage and the HLF. For more information about Jewish Heritage visit http://www.jewish-heritage-uk.org.

Methodology

A basic one-page *Pro-Forma* and a list of sites was provided for SAR by English Heritage. The format was designed to standardise the information collected across all of the Places of Worship surveys commissioned for English Heritage's Heritage at Risk programme.

The SAR team devised two more detailed questionnaires on *Condition* and *Usage* for completion during site visits. In all cases, the *Condition* questionnaire was completed on site, usually by the Consultant Architect. Wherever possible, the *Usage* questionnaire was completed by a representative of the synagogue during the site visit. In some cases, it was completed as a follow-up, usually electronically, sometimes by post or telephone.

All buildings were photographed with an automatic focus 35 mm digital camera. Record photography included exterior shots, plus interior shots – where access was achieved and light levels permitted.

Scope

A total of 37 synagogues in England were originally included in the Survey but one (unlisted) declined to participate so there are 36 results in total. Another synagogue, Coventry, was only listed after the survey started so was not included. All English Regions were represented by at least one synagogue building. The sample represents 39 per cent of the total number (96) of in-use pre-1939 purpose-built synagogues in England included in the original Survey of the Jewish Built Heritage.

To qualify for inclusion in SAR a synagogue had to be currently in use for worship or, if closed, not yet converted to an alternative use. Three listed synagogues fell into the latter category: Sunderland,

Ryhope Road, which closed in March 2006, Liverpool, Greenbank Drive, which closed in January 2008, and Hackney Synagogue, which closed in July 2009 and was due to become a church.

Scope by Geographical Distribution

Of the 37 English synagogues included in the survey, 15 are located in Greater London. This preponderance might have been expected to be higher given that about two-thirds of the Jewish community resides in Greater London – a percentage that has remained constant throughout the modern history of Anglo-Jewry since the Resettlement under Cromwell in 1656. It may be deduced that the survival rate of historic synagogues has been lower in the capital than elsewhere in the country.

Three of the synagogues surveyed are located in Manchester, Anglo-Jewry's second city since the mid-nineteenth century, having by then overtaken Liverpool in terms of Jewish population. Liverpool is represented by two synagogues. Elsewhere, a single historic synagogue attests to the presence of a Jewish community in any given town or city.

Scope by Age and Protected Status

The SAR Survey included all of the listed synagogues in England. Three are listed at grade I. Until recently Bevis Marks Synagogue, London EC3, was the only grade I listed synagogue in the country. Bevis Marks, in the City of London, is Britain's oldest synagogue and has been in continuous use since 1701. In 2007 and 2008 two major Victorian synagogues dating from the 1870s – London's New West End, St Petersburgh Place, Bayswater and then its sister building Liverpool's Princes Road Synagogue – were awarded grade I status.

Eleven of the synagogues covered by the Survey are grade II* listed. These include the small group of surviving Georgian and Regency synagogues mainly in the West Country – Plymouth (1762–63), Exeter (1763–64) and Cheltenham (W.H. Knight 1837–39) – and Ramsgate (David Mocatta 1831–33). The rest are Victorian buildings: Birmingham's Singers Hill (H.R. Yeoville Thomason 1855–56), the earliest surviving example of the grand 'cathedral synagogue' type in the country. The building of monumental synagogues in public places is associated with the era of Jewish emancipation from the 1850s onwards. Important grade II* listed synagogues dating from the 1870s and 1880s are: in London, Hampstead (Delissa Joseph 1892), Brighton, Middle Street (Thomas Lainson 1874–75), Chatham (H.H. Collins 1865–70) and Bradford Reform, Bowland Street (Healey Bros. 1880–81), the last named upgraded whilst work on the SAR Survey was in progress. In fact, all of the grade II* Listed synagogues have been upgraded from grade II to grade II* since the 1990s.

A single twentieth century synagogue, Greenbank Drive, Liverpool (Ernest A. Shennan 1936–37) was upgraded to grade II* in 2008 thanks to the interest taken in this threatened building by the Twentieth Century Society.

Of the remaining grade II listed synagogues included, eight are in London, the most recent to be listed (December 2008) being Hackney (Delissa Joseph 1897, extended by Cecil Eprile 1936). The majority of the London synagogues are Victorian, except Sandys Row which was built as a Huguenot chapel in 1766 and remodelled as a synagogue in 1870. The early twentieth century in London is represented by the New Synagogue, Egerton Road, Stamford Hill, N16 (Joseph & Smithem 1915) and Golders Green (Lewis Solomon & Son 1921–22, extended by Messrs Joseph 1927). A single 1960s synagogue, Marble Arch (T.P. Bennett & Son 1960–61) is included.

All three Manchester synagogues included date from the early part of the twentieth century and are grade II listed. Of the remaining grade II listed synagogues surveyed, the following are purpose built Victorian buildings: Grimsby (B.S. Jacobs 1885–88) and Leicester (Arthur Wakerley 1897–98) whilst Reading (W.G. Lewton 1900–1901), Blackpool (R.B. Mather, 1914–16) and Sunderland (Marcus K. Glass 1928) date from the early twentieth century.

In addition to the listed synagogues, Jewish Heritage decided to include some other Victorian and early twentieth century synagogues that are not listed but that are of some significance on either architectural and/or social/historical grounds. The last remaining synagogues in the East End of London (in addition to Sandys Row): Congregation of Jacob (Lewis Solomon & Son 1920–21), Nelson Street (Lewis Solomon & Son 1922–23) and Fieldgate Street (William Whiddington 1899, rebuilt late 1950s) were visited during fieldwork.

Bristol Synagogue (H.H. Collins with S.C. Fripp 1870–71), currently unlisted, completed the West Country, the English region richest in synagogues and Jewish cemeteries dating from the Georgian and Regency periods. It was also intended to survey Bournemouth

Synagogue (Lawson & Reynolds 1910–11) which was under consideration for listing at the time of survey, but it was not possible to get access to the building.

Condition of the Building Fabric

The project brief laid down the parameters for the on-site survey of the condition of each synagogue in the following terms:

> The focus in assessing the condition of the building should be on grant eligible areas, namely roof coverings, drainage systems, high-level stonework and the basic structure of the building. Carrying out a full condition survey of the building is outside the scope of the project. Instead the fieldworker will be asked to sum up the overall condition of the building on the basis of a brief visual inspection and place it in one of the following categories:

Good = no obvious problems
Fair = one or two minor problems and general wear-and-tear
Poor = widespread problems; lack of basic maintenance
Very bad = serious problems which require urgent attention.

The findings of the condition assessments are summarised in Table 1. Twenty four (65 per cent) of the synagogues surveyed were deemed to be in 'Good' or 'Fair' condition. Almost one third (32 per cent), however, fell into the 'Poor' or 'Very bad' categories. One synagogue did not participate in SAR, representing another 3 per cent.

The condition of 32% of all the synagogues included in SAR is a matter for concern. Seven synagogues were undergoing, or were about to undergo, repair work at the time of our site visit. Scaffolding was in place either inside or outside the following buildings: Brighton, Ramsgate, Birmingham (Singers Hill), Liverpool (Princes Road), London (Hampstead) and London (Sandys Row), whilst at

TABLE 1
CONDITION OF THE BUILDING FABRIC

Condition	No of synagogues	% of survey
Good	3	8
Fair	21	57
Poor	9	24
Very bad	3	8
No return	1	3
Total sample	37	100

Manchester (Wilbraham Road) building work to convert the synagogue into a Jewish student centre was in abeyance.

Of the seven synagogues undergoing repairs at the time of our site visit, three were being renovated thanks to public funding under the Repair Grants for Places of Worship (RGPOW) Scheme, namely: London (Sandys Row), Brighton and Liverpool (Princes Road). Repairs to London (Hampstead), Ramsgate and Birmingham (Singers Hill) were being funded from private sources. Manchester (Wilbraham Road) was acquired by a Jewish-owned property company for redevelopment as a down-sized synagogue with a residential Jewish student-centre attached (See 'Case Studies' below).

Manchester (Higher Crumpsall) and London (New West End) have also received grants under RGPOW. There is every prospect that the condition of the New West End will be significantly improved as a result, whilst the problems faced by Higher Crumpsall – partially caused by poor construction and fabric – and partly as a result of other factors – remain to be solved fully (See 'Case Studies' below).

Whilst the SAR Survey was in progress, three out of the 12 synagogues that fell into the 'Poor' or 'Very bad' categories were up for sale or in the process of being sold out of the Jewish community. These were: London (Hackney), Liverpool (Greenbank) and Sunderland (Ryhope Road). Hackney has been sold to a Gospel church but the fate of the other two buildings has yet to be decided and they should therefore be considered to be 'At Risk'.

Turning to the other end of the scale: one out of the three – all London – synagogues found to be in 'Good' condition has been a beneficiary of RGPOW, namely Hampstead. Repairs at the other two, Bevis Marks and Congregation of Jacob (unlisted), have been paid for mainly from private resources.

Two synagogues in the 'Fair' category' have been recipients of public grant aid: Exeter Synagogue back in 1997 and the New Synagogue, Stamford Hill in 2005. As a result, the latter was removed from the Buildings at Risk Register, where it had been for over a decade.

Use

The vast majority (81 per cent) of the synagogues included in the SAR Survey hold religious services at least once a week in the main prayer hall. For our purposes, only services held in the actual prayer

TABLE 2
LEVEL OF USE FOR WORSHIP

Frequency of services	Number of synagogues	% of synagogues in survey
Full-time	3	8
Frequent (once a week)	27	73
Regular (once a month)	2	5
Occasional (six times a year)	1	3
Not in use	3	8
No return	1	3
Total sample	37	100

hall of the historic building were counted as 'usage' of the synagogue. Weekday or winter services held in a *Bet Midrash* or adjoining communal hall were generally excluded, unless the *Bet Midrash* is situated under the same roof as the historic synagogue.

This apparently healthy level of usage of historic synagogues masks underlying trends that may be cause for concern, revealed by a closer study of membership numbers and attendances at services. For example, two of the synagogues that claim to hold 'Frequent', i.e. weekly, services do not actually achieve a *Minyan*, i.e. the quorum of ten males over the age of 13 required to hold a full Orthodox service. Four (11 per cent) of the 37 synagogues in the Survey are affiliated with the Reform movement where women can count towards the *Minyan*.

Congregations were asked to give attendance figures for a normal *Shabbat* morning, and for the most important holiday, *Yom Kippur*, the Day of Atonement. Average figures are given in Table 3.

Whilst use of the building may be frequent, most commonly weekly, the number of users is, for the most part, quite small. Just over half (51 per cent) of synagogues attract weekly congregations of fewer than 50 people, men and women.

Eight congregations (21 per cent of the total) – are dipping below

TABLE 3
AVERAGE ATTENDANCE AT SERVICES

Number of people (M&F)	Number of synagogues	% of synagogues in survey
0–9	2	5
10–20	6	16
20–50	11	30
50–100	6	14
100–200	2	8
200–250	4	11
No return/closed	6	16
Total sample	37	100

TABLE 4
MEMBERSHIP SIZE

Number of households	Number of synagogues	% of synagogues
0–50	4	11
50–100	5	13
100–200	7	19
200–500	11	30
600–1000	3	8
1000+	1	3
Closed/no members	5	13
No return	1	3
Total sample	37	100

the viability level of 20 people (assuming that half of the congregation consists of men).

At the top end of the scale, no historic synagogue attracts more than 250 worshippers to an ordinary *Shabbat* morning service, although several big London synagogues can attract 600 or 700 worshippers on *Yom Kippur*. The best attended synagogues are all in London and have large memberships from a wide catchment area.

The returns on membership size for the historic synagogues included in the SAR Survey are shown in Table 4. Overall trends in terms of the growth and decline of membership of historic synagogues are shown in Table 5.

Synagogues are largely funded by revenue from membership fees. Synagogue membership fees are typically, but by no means always, divided into contributions for the upkeep of the congregation and for burial. The upkeep of the congregation generally includes payment of officials, such as the rabbi and the secretary, sometimes a *Hazan* and caretaker – as well as the running costs of maintenance and utility services to the building. Typically, it includes buildings insurance. Even in London, where umbrella organisations own most of the buildings, individual synagogues are responsible for their own

TABLE 5
TRENDS IN SYNAGOGUE MEMBERSHIP

	Growing	Static	Shrinking	Not applicable/no return	Total
London*	8	4	4	0	16
%	50	25	25	0	
Regions	2	4	10	5	21
%	9	19	48	24	
Totals	10	8	14	5	37
%	27	22	38	13	100

Note: * Including Elstree, Herts.

insurance arrangements. Many are insured with Ecclesiastical. Two provincial congregations with fewer than 50 members each complained about the burden of high premiums.

Independent congregations set membership fees at levels decided by their own management committees. London synagogues belonging to one of the umbrella synagogue organisations may find their fees set for them by the head office. Sometimes there is a sliding scale, whereby pensioners pay reduced fees. Fees in London, and especially in the more affluent neighbourhoods, tend to be higher than elsewhere. There is no single rate levy across synagogues, or even within particular synagogue bodies.

Underlying trends are also indicated by the statistics for overall growth and decline in synagogue membership, as summarised in Table 5. Overall, historic synagogues are losing members rather than gaining them. This trend is most marked in the regions, where nearly half are experiencing contraction.

All of the synagogues in London employ a rabbi or some other 'clergyman', at least on a part-time basis. Several of the large London congregations employ more than one minister, a *Hazan* or youth worker. In the East End, one rabbi is shared between the four Ashkenazi congregations. Twelve (57 per cent) of the provincial congregations do not have even a part-time minister and depend on competent laymen and periodic visits from the Minister to Small Communities, appointed by the United Synagogue. Only six (16 per cent) of synagogues have a Jewish university chaplain based locally who actually uses their buildings for student events.

Twenty-eight (76 per cent) of the synagogues lack a caretaker or other personnel (including the rabbi) living on site, despite the fact that many of the older ones were built with accommodation for staff. Nearly half of all provincial synagogues lack a resident caretaker, usually on the grounds of cost. In some cases ancillary accommodation has become dilapidated, particularly in the East End of London – even where the main prayer hall is in relatively good condition. Renovation and putting empty flats back into use would benefit congregations both as a potential source of revenue and by providing increased security. At the other end of the scale some large, affluent synagogues can afford a full-time 'maintenance officer'.

Summary Findings

The condition of one-third of synagogues in the survey (and 28 per cent of *listed* synagogues in the survey) is a cause for concern. Of the 12 synagogues in poor or very bad condition, six were undergoing work at the time of the survey, three of those with RGPOW grant.

English Heritage should consider putting Greenbank Drive Synagogue, Liverpool and Sunderland Synagogue on the Heritage at Risk Register on account of their condition and lack of use. The condition of the other synagogues in poor or very bad condition should be monitored on a regular basis.

Case Studies

1. *The New Synagogue, Stamford Hill, London, N16. Grade II*

Architectural Significance. Behind Ernest Joseph's Edwardian Baroque facade (1915), the interior is a partial replica on a smaller scale of the demolished New Synagogue in Great St Helen's, Bishopsgate, City of London and contains some of its original fittings, including the concave mahogany Ark, and candelabra.

The Challenge. The synagogue was on the English Heritage Buildings at Risk Register for over a decade (1996–2007). It was acquired in stages by a strictly Orthodox sect, the Bobover Hasidim, who come from a worship tradition very different to that of the United Synagogue, by which the synagogue had been built. Bobov today own the whole complex, comprising the New Synagogue itself, the 'Old' Bobov *Shul* and *Yeshivah* opposite (No.87 Egerton Road) and the Victoria Community Centre, now the *Talmud Torah* boys' school (No.90 Egerton Road) where a small United Synagogue *Minyan* still worships.

The Solution. The New Synagogue has been given a new lease of life. It is now used regularly for Friday night and *Shabbat* morning services. Services attract an average of 120–150 people. It now has a membership of 130 Bobover families and is growing. The Bobovers are taking increasing pride in their historic building, welcoming visitors, and would be amenable to participating in Heritage Open Days in the future.

The price paid for continuation in Jewish use was liturgical reordering. This involved the removal of the central *Bimah*, a pared

TABLE 6
ALL RESULTS

Total: 36*	Good	Fair	Poor	Very bad
Full time	1	1	0	0
Frequent	2	17	7	2
Regular	0	2	0	0
Occasional	0	1	0	0
Not in use	0	0	2	1

Note:* no visit was made to Bournemouth Synagogue.

Listed synagogues in use for worship

Total: 29	Good	Fair	Poor	Very bad
Full time	1	1	0	0
Frequent	1	17	6	1
Regular	0	1	0	0
Occasional	0	1	0	0
Not in use	0	0	0	0

London only (including Elstree)

Total: 16	Good	Fair	Poor	Very bad
Full time	1	0	0	0
Frequent	2	7	3	2
Regular	0	1	0	0
Occasional	0	0	0	0
Not in use	0	0	0	0

Outside London (excluding Elstree)

Total: 20	Good	Fair	Poor	Very bad
Full time	0	1	0	0
Frequent	0	10	4	0
Regular	0	1	0	0
Occasional	0	1	0	0
Not in use	0	0	2	1

down version of the 1838 original and its replacement by a small reproduction *Bimah* made in Israel. The four candelabra[4] from the corners of the original *Bimah* have been relocated on the Ark platform. Most of the pews, which dated from the 1915 rebuild, have been removed and replaced by simple trestle tables and chairs. A high *Mehitzah* gallery screen, a timber trellis, has been installed in the gallery to hide women worshippers from view according to Hasidic practice. The interior of the synagogue has been repainted magnolia and cream, thought to be closer to the original colour scheme than the pale blue decor dating probably from the 1960s. A new marble floor has been laid.

So far £1.5 million has been spent on renovations, including a small grant from the RGPOW Scheme for roof repairs. The Hasidim are raising funds for a lavish refurbishment of the interior including ancillary accommodation, renewal of the electrics and bespoke tables, chairs and chandeliers in order to turn the space into a synagogue *cum Bet Midrash*. Hidden lighting and air conditioning have already been installed. Repair of the 'Zion' window over the west gallery alone will cost £18,000. This window is claimed to be the earliest in the country to feature the emblem of the State of Israel after 1948. The architect of the renovation is Israel-based David Oestricher, who specialises in work for the *Haredi* community in Israel and internationally.

2. Sukkat Shalom Reform Synagogue, No. 1 Victory Road, Hermon Hill, E11. Grade II*

Architectural Significance. Housed in the Venetian Gothic former Merchant Seaman's Orphan Asylum designed by George Somers Clarke the elder in 1861–63, latterly part of Wanstead Hospital.

The Challenge. The redundant building was purchased by the new Jewish congregation in 1994, who restored and provided a home to the magnificent Ark and panelling rescued from the Synagogue within the Tottenham Jewish Home and Hospital (1913–15), with the support of the Heritage Lottery Fund. Ronald Wylde Associates were the architects. The building reopened as a synagogue in 2000.

The Solution. A successful conservation project that has rescued and reused one historic building using materials salvaged from another. Sukkat Shalom holds service at least once a week, has a membership of 315 families and is growing.

3. Greenbank Drive Synagogue, Sefton Park, Liverpool. Grade II*

Architectural significance. A rare art deco period synagogue designed in 1936–37 by Ernest Alfred Shennan, who was knighted for his work on the Mersey Tunnel. The tripartite brick-faced façade, by then traditional in synagogue design, was given an original twist through the use of tall vertical windows and countervailing curves in the quoins, arches and window surrounds. The light and airy interior makes extensive use of steel and reinforced concrete in the elegant curved cantilevered gallery and unusual arcaded clerestory girders.

The Challenge. Following closure early in 2008, this synagogue was upgraded to Grade II* thanks to the intervention of the Twentieth Century Society. The Liverpool Jewish Housing Association has been encouraged to look afresh at plans to convert Greenbank into a sheltered housing complex without destroying the integrity of the historic building.

The Solution. The likelihood now is that the housing scheme will be abandoned and the synagogue sold to a church organisation. If this can be done before the empty building falls prey to vandalism it should allow for retention of the building's special interest. In the meantime the building has been put on the Heritage at Risk register.

4. *Withington Congregation of Spanish & Portuguese Jews, West Didsbury, Manchester. Grade II*

Architectural Significance. In the 1930s the area around Palatine Road, Didsbury was nicknamed 'Palestine Road, Yidsbury' because of its visible Sephardi Jewish population. The Withington Synagogue was the last work of prominent Jewish architect Delissa Joseph in 1925–27. When Joseph died before completion, Joe Sunlight acted as ''supervising architect'. Occupying a 9,000 square foot site in Queenston Road, Withington Synagogue is notable for its monumental triple-height interior.

The Challenge. The building is now too large for the congregation's needs. The Jewish population of the immediate neighbourhood is diminishing. In 1996 the membership merged with the Oriental Jewish community that maintains its own synagogue (of 1924–25) nearby. The combined congregation, Sha'arei Hayim ('Gates of Life') also includes Sephardim who have moved out to Hale in Cheshire. In 2009 the total membership stood at about 600, the majority of whom no longer live in the immediate neighbourhood of the two 1920s synagogues. The regular *Shabbat* morning service at Withington draws about 130 people, a healthy number – but dwarfed by the size of the building. Regular weekday morning, afternoon and evening services, attracting 10 to 15 men, are held at in the *Bet Midrash* at Sha'are Tsedek.

After tentative moves to dispose of one or more of the buildings, the congregation has come to terms with the fact that, in the future, they will need to consolidate their remaining membership still living in the Didsbury area around the historic building on Queenston Road.[5] It is intended that all services will eventually be held there. Meanwhile, in 2008, proposals were drawn up to build a new synagogue in Hale, on the site of a former farm. The plans include a new-build synagogue for 200 with gallery, linked hall and ancillary space, plus residential conversion of an existing barn and farmhouse on the site.

This site is very close to the new Ashkenazi synagogue at Hale, and not far from the successor to Wilbraham Road (see below) at Bowden. Thus, in the early twenty-first century – in neighbourhoods of tertiary Jewish settlement (in Cheshire) the pattern of synagogue building in the inter-war period (in Fallowfield and Didsbury) – is being replicated. Demographic shift puts into question the long-term viability not only of Queenston Road but also of its un-built successor in Hale.

5. Former South Manchester Synagogue, Wilbraham Road, Fallowfield, M14. Grade II

Architectural Significance. One of the most significant early twentieth century synagogues in the country but threatened by closure in 2001. It was built just before the First World War, 1912–13, for the prosperous Ashkenazim who formed a breakaway from the Ashkenazi Great Synagogue in Cheetham Hill. The architect, like so many of his clients, was a self-made Russian-born immigrant Joe Sunlight (né Schimschlavitch 1889–1978), who went on to become a major developer in the City of Manchester.

Wilbraham Road was built in the style of a Turkish mosque with dome and minaret, in a bold, almost cubist treatment, clad in buff glazed terracotta. Sunlight professed to having used 'St Sophia of Constantinople' as his model, with a much scaled-down tower derived from Westminster Cathedral. In the estimation of *The British Architect* the whole gave 'a very satisfactory effect of an Eastern place of worship'.[6] 'Byzantine' synagogues were becoming fashionable on the continent in this period and the ambitious young architect also employed innovative German building technology in his only known religious commission; reinforced concrete for the 35 ft span of the dome – claimed to be the widest span yet built – and for the lattice girders carrying the gallery, thus dispensing with the need for column supports beneath – the earliest application of this technology in a fully realised manner to synagogue architecture in Britain.

The Challenge. In 2002 a new South Manchester Synagogue by Buttress Fuller Alsop Williams was opened in Bowden, Cheshire to where Ashkenazi communal life has shifted. The Grade II listed building in Wilbraham Road was rescued from redundancy by a Jewish property company who came up with the imaginative idea of converting the site into a residential Jewish student centre, it being conveniently situated close to the university campuses.

The scheme, by architects Provan & Makin (who have also worked on a number of church conversions), to downsize the worship space by one-half, has involved insertion of a floor at gallery level which significantly changes the character of the interior. As reconstructed, the downstairs remains in use as a synagogue. The existing pews have been retained, now divided lengthways in the American Conservative manner, by a metalwork screen *Mehitzah*. This serves to provide gender-separate seating, to compensate for the loss of the women's gallery. Such reordering was possible thanks to the Reformed layout of the original synagogue, with forward facing pews and the absence of a central *Bimah*. The architects have hived off the side aisles under the galleries, separating them from the main space by glass walls, to create, respectively, a meeting room and small *Bet Midrash*. In practice, the students tend to worship in the main space.

The ancillary Stern Hall was demolished in 2008 in preparation for the building of an accommodation block containing 65 single bedrooms. This part of the project is now on hold due to the recession. Despite this, the Manchester Jewish Student Centre project has already boosted usage of the building. During term time, morning services are held every day as well as regular Friday night and *Shabbat* morning services. Special events organised by the University Jewish Society and the Jewish Chaplain (Monday nights) bring in students: the monthly 'Friday Night Fever' attracts 200–250 for the *Shabbat* evening meal, currently catered from a makeshift kitchen on the ground floor. It remains to be seen whether an eventual 'enabling development' of 65 bed-sit units on the site of the Stern Hall will be viable. The present purpose-built (1980s) accommodation for Jewish students, Hillel House in Moss Side, M15, is currently experiencing difficulties filling places.

6. *Higher Crumpsall Synagogue, Bury Old Road, Manchester, M8. Grade II*

Architectural Significance. In classical style by local architects Pendleton & Dickinson, Higher Crumpsall Synagogue, built 1928–29, boasts a well-designed worship space with high quality fixtures and fittings and excellent Art Deco stained glass. The pair of windows over the Ark and behind the rear gallery is particularly notable, depicting a contemporary 'Vision of Jerusalem' and the rebuilt Temple of Solomon, rendering traditional symbolism in modernist style.

The Challenge. Despite grants in 2004 and 2006 totalling £281,000 under the EH/HLF Joint Scheme, this synagogue remains at risk. The building has been made water-tight, with renewal of the roof and repairs to the Ark wall. Serious problems, some damp, structural movement, corrosion of steel and reinforced concrete, remain. Phase 3 internal works will require not merely cosmetic decoration but will involve shoring up the ceilings which are becoming unsafe. Cracks have appeared and sections of plaster are loose or have fallen. Thus, the long-term future for this building has not yet been secured.

Although the synagogue is full to capacity on occasion, it is perceived by some within the Jewish community as too formal and old-fashioned. It is, however, situated barely five minutes walk away from one of the fastest-growing Jewish communities in Europe so there is potential for the utilisation of the synagogue both for continued worship and for additional multi-purpose activities. Unfortunately, the adjacent King David school, the largest Jewish school in Manchester, and the *Shul* are separated by the municipal boundary between the City of Manchester and Salford City Council. The future of the synagogue may well depend on reaching across that boundary.

7. *Sunderland Synagogue, Ryhope Road, Sunderland. Grade II.*

Architectural Significance. Built in 1928 and seen by Pevsner as 'vigorous and decorative', Sunderland was one of a series of synagogues designed in a distinctive cinematic art deco style by the under-appreciated Jewish architect, Marcus Kenneth Glass, who was based in Newcastle upon Tyne. The colourful façade features corner towers, red and yellow *ablaq* striped brickwork, arcaded porch with Byzantine basket capitals, mosaic and abstract stained glass.

The Challenge. This synagogue was listed in 1999 and even then faced redundancy as the once-vibrant Jewish community in the town dwindled. It now stands empty and neglected; the schoolhouse next door has been damaged by arson. In 2006 its sister building, the Clapton Federation Synagogue, Lea Bridge Road, London (1931–32), Glass's only London synagogue, was demolished in the face of attempts made locally to get it listed.

The Solution. During the SAR Survey Sunderland was put on the market and, thanks to publicity in the local media, excited some interest. Possible uses mooted are: a Buddhist temple, a restaurant or even a boxing-ring.

ACKNOWLEDGEMENTS

Document reproduced by kind permission of English Heritage which owns the report. The editors would like to thank Nick Chapple of English Heritage for his help in this matter.

NOTES

1. David J. Graham and Stanley Waterman, 'Underenumeration of the Jewish Population in the 2001 Census', *Population, Space and Place*, 11.2 (2005), 89–102. The 2001 Census for the first time included the optional questions: 'What is your religion?' and 'What is your ethnic group?' The compilation of Jewish population statistics is fraught with methodological and definitional problems. Perhaps as much as one-third of Jews in Britain are not members of a synagogue.
2. David Graham and Daniel Vulkan, *Britain's Jewish Community Statistics 2006* (London: Board of Deputies of British Jews, 2007). Compare with research from twenty years earlier: Stanley Waterman and Barry Kosmin, *British Jewry in the Eighties: A Statistical and Geographical Study* (London: Board of Deputies of British Jews, 1986).
3. Mainly from South Africa, Argentina and Israel. Israel received almost one million new immigrants from the former Soviet Union after 1989; very few came to Britain.
4. One of these is reproduction, having been stolen *ca.* 1997 when the building was redundant.
5. Since the time of writing, Sha'are Tsedek has closed down and was due for demolition in January 2011.
6. *British Architect*, 20 February 1914, pp.157–8.

APPENDIX 1
LIST OF SYNAGOGUES IN THE SURVEY

Region	Name	Listing grade	In use as synagogue
East Midlands	Leicester Synagogue	II	Yes
East Midlands	Nottingham Synagogue	II	Yes
East of England	Liberal Synagogue, Elstree	II	Yes
London	Golders Green Synagogue	II	Yes
London	Hampstead Synagogue	II*	Yes
London	Bevis Marks Synagogue	I	Yes
London	Marble Arch Synagogue	II	Yes
London	West London Synagogue	II	Yes
London	New West End Synagogue	I	Yes
London	Lauderdale Road Synagogue	II	Yes
London	New London Synagogue	II	Yes
London	New Synagogue, Stamford Hill	II	Yes
London	Hackney Synagogue	II	No
London	Sukkat Shalom Synagogue	II*	Yes
London	Sandys Row Synagogue	II	Yes
London	Fieldgate Street Synagogue	Unlisted	Yes
London	Nelson Street Synagogue	Unlisted	Yes
London	Congregation of Jacob	Unlisted	Yes
North East	Sunderland Synagogue	II	No
North West	Withington Synagogue,	II	Yes
North West	South Manchester Synagogue	II	Partly
North West	Higher Crumpsall Synagogue	II	Yes
North West	Blackpool Synagogue	II	Yes
North West	Princes Road Synagogue, Liverpool	I	Yes
North West	Greenbank Synagogue, Liverpool	II	No
South East	Reading Synagogue	II	Yes
South East	Middle Street Synagogue, Brighton	II*	Yes
South East	Chatham Memorial Synagogue	II*	Yes
South East	Montefiore Synagogue, Ramsgate	II*	Yes
South West	Bristol Synagogue	Unlisted	Yes
South West	Plymouth Synagogue	II*	Yes
South West	Bournemouth Synagogue	Unlisted	Yes
South West	Exeter Synagogue	II*	Yes
South West	Cheltenham Synagogue	II*	Yes
West Midlands	Singers Hill Synagogue, Birmingham	II*	Yes
Yorkshire	Grimsby Synagogue	II	Yes
Yorkshire	Bradford Synagogue (Reform)	II*	Yes

APPENDIX 2
LIST OF GRANTS OFFERED TO SYNAGOGUES UNDER THE REPAIR GRANTS FOR PLACES OF WORSHIP (RGPOW) SCHEME

Year of Stage 1 offer	Name of synagogue	Value of grant offer (£)
2003	Brighton Middle Street	342,000
2003	Plymouth	26,000
2004	Manchester Higher Crumpsall	145,000
2005	London New Synagogue	62,000
2006	Manchester Higher Crumpsall	151,000
2007	Liverpool Princes Road	112,000
2008	London New West End	106,000
2009	London Sandys Row	254,000
2009	Liverpool Princes Road	71,000
Total		1,269,000

APPENDIX 3
UK JEWISH POPULATION

2001	Census Deputies	Board of 1995	UK faiths		
Greater London	149,790	182,700	Christian	71.6%	42,079,000
Surrounding areas	18,990	13,650	Muslim	2.7%	1,591,000
Rest of Home Counties	10,760	8,300	Hindu	1.0%	559,000
Greater Manchester	21,730	26,000	Sikh	0.6%	336,000
Leeds	8,270	10,000	*Jewish*	*0.5%*	*267,000*
Glasgow	4,330	5,600	Buddhist	0.3%	152,000
Brighton and Hove	3,360	5,300	Other	0.3%	179,000
Southend	2,720	3,400			
Liverpool	2,700	3,800	No religion 15.5%		
Birmingham	2,340	4,000	No answer	7.3%	
Bournemouth	2,110	3,000			
Gateshead	1,560	1,100			
Newcastle	960	1,100			
Cardiff	940	1,500			
Edinburgh	760	900			
Southport	700	1,100	*Boroughs with highest*		
Hull	670	1,100	*concentration of Jews*		
Nottingham	630	1,000			
Luton	530	1,300	Barnet	14.8%	46,690
Rest of Britain	33,160	8,350	Hertsmere	11.3%	10,710
			Harrow	6.3%	13,110
UK total	*267,000*	*285,000*	Redbridge	6.2%	14,800
			Camden	5.6%	11,150
England	258,000		Hackney	5.3%	10,730
Scotland	6,600		Bury	5.0%	8,920
Wales	2,200				

Source: Figures reproduced from *Jewish Chronicle*, 21 February 2003.

Abstracts

Anglo-Jewish Historiography and the Jewish Historiographical Mainstream
by Todd Endelman

This chapter examines how the writing of Anglo-Jewish history became detached from the writing of modern Jewish history more generally. It suggests that the price of this isolation has been the loss of a pan-Jewish, transnational perspective with the potential, ironically, to shed light on events and trends in Anglo-Jewish history and to explain what is uniquely 'English' or 'British' about them. It also argues that this detachment has impoverished mainstream Jewish historiography by depriving it of the contributions and insights that are the hallmark of Anglo-Jewish history writing – a tradition of social history and a well-developed sense of the way local environments and social formations and customs shape historical outcomes.

Between Integration and Separation: Jews and Military Service in World War I Britain
by Anne Lloyd

Wartime military service severely challenged the Jewish community in Britain, comprised at *fin de siècle* of a small anglicised component and a much larger immigrant sector, in which ethnicity remained central to its identity and *modus vivendi*. Recent research has focused on the conscription of Russian Jews, with little attention given to the reluctance of many 'new' British Jews to volunteer, or to the impact of military duty on young Jewish men. These perspectives are explored through the activities of the principal Anglo-Jewish committees associated with military service. Confronted with the complexities of identity, their independent enlistment campaigns and liaison role at the War Office exposed the dichotomy of integration and separation in a diverse community. Their responses to these dilemmas adversely affected the traditional relationship between the communal leadership and the state, and resulted in the resentment of many Jewish soldiers.

Jews, Britons, Empire: And How Things Might be Very Different
by Mark Levene

Offering a broad overview, this contribution seeks to consider why the radical tradition of Judaic-informed dissent has not only remained marginal in the Anglo-Jewish experience but why few researchers, if any, have sought to investigate further. It takes as its premise the urgency for the mobilisation of the radical tradition in this time of acute environmental crisis. However, its historical method is to attempt to apply Albert Hirschman's famous 1970 'Exit, Voice and Loyalty' thesis, about subaltern strategies in the face of dominant power, to the Anglo-Jewish community. Its findings are that successive, even competing Anglo-Jewish elite formations have subordinated ' voice' to 'loyalty' with 'exit' effectively 'loyalty' under a different heading. The conclusion is that if we wish to explore genuine Jewish dissent ('voice') we must investigate beyond normative communal confines while equally seeking to understand why conformity within the community has become hegemonic over time.

Dilemmas of Jewish Difference:
Reflections on Contemporary Research into Jewish Origins and Types from an Anglo-Jewish Historical Perspective
by Gavin Schaffer

This chapter interrogates scientific theories concerning Jewish origins and racial difference, setting contemporary research on these contentious subjects in the context of Anglo-Jewish scholarship from the inter-war period. In particular, it explores academic discussion and debate about how to respond to Nazism, focusing on conflict between two senior British scholars of Jews, Charles Singer (1876–1960) and Redcliffe Salaman (1874–1955), who argued about the extent and implications of Jewish/non-Jewish racial difference. These inter-war debates then provide the context for an analysis of the proliferation of contemporary research into Jewish origins and difference. Ultimately, it contends that research of this nature, like its historical antecedents, remains inextricably tied to ideological considerations, and that personal beliefs continue to render the study of the Jewish past and present as contentious as it was in the inter-war period.

How Post-war Britain Reflected on the Nazi Persecution and Mass Murder of Europe's Jews: A Reassessment of Early Responses
by David Cesarani

During the 1990s historians began paying attention to how societies in the post-war era reflected on the destruction of Europe's Jews between 1933 and 1945 and soon a consensus evolved that there had been a brief burst of media coverage and outrage related to the liberation of the concentration camps and war crimes trials in 1945–46 which soon faded. However, from 1999 a number of historians looking at the USA and other countries went beyond the identification of a post-war 'silence'. They argued that it was broken by a deliberate effort of Jewish organisations, mainly in America, for the purpose of creating sympathy for Israel and the Jews more generally. This contribution re-assesses recent trends in the scholarship concerning post-war responses in Britain to the Jewish catastrophe of 1933–45. It argues that we are mistaken if we look in the past for representations of what we recognise today as 'the Holocaust' or if we treat the apparent marginalisation of the Jewish experience as a sign of malevolence or indifference. It concludes by suggesting that if during the 1950s there was a dropping off of publications about the Nazi persecution and mass murder of the Jews, this may have been because the market was satiated.

'The Wandering Jew has no Nation':1 Jewishness and Race Relations Law
by Didi Herman

This essay considers judicial discourse on Jews and Jewishness in UK race relations law. Beginning with an account of how 'the Jew' appeared in legislative debates, the essay goes on to explore the confusions, paradoxes, and underlying normativities revealed in both legislative and judicial narratives of Jews and Jewishness. The essay concludes with a discussion of the first two decisions in the Jews' Free School case.

Childcare Dilemmas: Religious Discourse and Services among Jewish and Christian 'Orphanages'
by Susan L. Tananbaum

This chapter explores the goals of Jewish and Christian sponsored orphanages in late nineteenth and early twentieth century England and identifies ways that religious institutions served the needy, constructed their self-identify, and that of their 'inmates'. Christian charities, especially evangelical institutions such as Barnardo's and the National Children's Homes (NCH), focused not only on the rescue of children, but their salvation. Policy at Norwood, the Jewish orphanage, reflected a combination of Jewish charitable tradition, alongside a self-consciousness about reputation and anxiety over anti-Semitism, and anti-alienism. In response, Norwood developed an extensive programme designed to raise respectable, anglicised Jews who would remain members of Britain's Jewish community.

Counter-Institutionalism in Anglo-Jewry: The Norwood Rebellion
by Lawrencew Cohen

This study researches the history of an institution making extensive use of oral history based on the recollection of scholars' (i.e. students') accounts from the Jewish orphanage, Norwood. Their version reveals a culture of counter-institutionalism that was exceptionally expressed in the Norwood Rebellion. The rebellion was one act of defiance. As an ongoing protest against the regimentation, it was organised as opposition to the discipline and in particular corporal punishment endemic at Norwood. The importance of oral history as a source is examined in the last section. The counter-cultural research provides an addition to the institutional assessment for judging whether Norwood was 'good enough' for the children.

British Jewish Literature and Culture: An Introduction
by Nadia Valman

This chapter traces the historiographical evolution of studies in and of British Jewish literature and culture, and identifies new directions currently animating this field of research. It describes the development of a body of work exploring the complex ambivalence of Semitic representations and challenges more regressive tendencies that regard representations of Jews exclusively as evidence of an enduring and hostile anti-Semitic tradition in Britain culture.

Blurring the Boundaries of Difference: *Dracula*, the Empire, and 'the Jew'
by Hannah Ewence

Bram Stoker's *Dracula* (1897) has evolved into a fantastical staple of the gothic horror genre for the modern age, yet the metaphorical implications of the tale still remain illusive and, consequently, contested. Stoker himself chose to perpetuate this illusiveness, admitting that 'every book of the kind must contain some lesson' yet intriguingly insisted that he 'prefer that readers should find it out for themselves'. Exploiting that 'free licence' this chapter explores Count Dracula as an articulation of the Jewish immigrant 'other' – an interpretation which draws upon the broader national context and anxious socio-cultural climate in which the novel was produced. However, when read in this way, it is suggested that, remarkably, *Dracula* appears to disrupt rather than validate the typically rigid and polarised positions which mark out, define and quantify difference. Instead the novel celebrates the blurring of boundaries between the British-Self and the Semitic-Other – a conclusion given credence by Bram Stoker's own marginalised racial and sexual identity.

Wandering Lonely Jews in the English Countryside
by Tony Kushner

This study analyses the experiences of and responses to Jewish child survivors of the Holocaust who came to Britain to recuperate months after the end of the Second World War. It does so through the literary-cultural trope of the 'Wandering Jew', a figure which, from the eighteenth century onwards and especially through Romanticism, was represented in an increasingly ambivalent manner. The focus is on Windermere and the Lake District where the largest number of the children were initially settled. Through the exploration of place identity and Englishness, it analyses how far the experiences of these children have become part of local narratives of the past.

Assimilated, Integrated, Other: An Introduction to Jews and British Television, 1946–55
by James Jordan

Through the use of production files, correspondence and press cuttings held at the BBC's Written Archives Centre, this chapter provides an overview to the variety of Jews and Jewish life seen on British television from 1946 to 1955, including examples of television's first engagement with the Nazi persecution of the Jews of Europe. In so doing it demonstrates not only the diversity of representations, and thereby the multiple Jewish identities on display in post-war Britain, but also the richness of television and the BBC's archives for scholars of British Jewish studies.

Displaced, Dysfunctional and Divided: British-Jewish Writing Today
by Ruth Gilbert

In fiction, memoirs and journalism, writers are addressing increasingly challenging questions about what it means to be both British and Jewish in the twenty-first century. This chapter explores the ways in which these questions are debated within a range of contemporary Jewish literature. The chapter concludes that contemporary British-Jewish writers highlight the desire to identify the particularity of their difference, whilst acknowledging that that difference is neither fixed nor final, but always open to change, re-signification and re-interpretation.

Negotiating Jewish Identity through the Display of Art
by Kathrin Pieren

Research on museums has proved useful in understanding the social dynamics of groups and societies and their use of material culture for the construction and reaffirmation of cultural identities. A comparison between two exhibitions of Jewish art and history taking place in London at the turn of the twentieth century reveals a gradual shift in the museological representation of Jewish identity from a focus on religion towards ethnicity. The inclusion of visitor perceptions and of unintentional and contradictory meanings of the exhibits, however, illustrates that these representations were not necessarily the outcome of a clear strategy and were socially contested.

From Bola d'Amour to the Ultimate Cheesecake: 150 Years of Anglo-Jewish Cookery Writing
by Jane Gerson

The Jewish Manual, published in Britain in 1846, is regarded as the first Anglo-Jewish cookery book. It has established its author Judith Montefiore, wife of British philanthropist Moses Montefiore, as a seminal cookery writer defining Jewish food in Britain. Yet the recipes contained in the cookery book no longer correspond to the construction of 'Jewish' food in modern Britain. The chapter surveys three groundbreaking Jewish cookery writers – Judith Montefiore, Florence Greenberg and Evelyn Rose – offering a close textual reading of their work to determine the historical and cultural processes which inform our ideas about the identity of Anglo-Jewish food.

From *Mon Pays*, the *Shtetl* and the *Desh* to London's East End:[1] A Rationale for Comparative Migrant Studies
by Anne Kershen

Based on research carried out in the East End of London over a number of years, this chapter sets out to present an agument in favour of comparative migrant studies. As the traditional first point of settlement for migrants, the East End is a rich resource of immigrant history and contemporary ethnic activity, for over a century providing a fertile laboratory for those wishing to study the migrant experience. All too often the studies have been mono-focal, concentrating solely on one of the three main groups that settled in the area from the seventeenth century onwards: Huguenots, Eastern European Jews and Bangladeshis. This chapter demonstrates the issues arising from the migrant presence, particularly the impact of the outsider on housing and jobs, are not just a manifestation of the late twentieth and early twenty-first centuries, but a recurrent theme, articulated in the late seventeenth and early eighteenth centuries following the influx of French Calvinists, in the late nineteenth century in reaction to the arrival of Eastern European Jews and, in the latter decades of the twentieth century, as the Bangladeshi presence became permanent rather than transitory.

Notes on Contributors

Rickie Burman is the director of the recently refurbished Jewish Museum, London. She has also researched and published widely in the field of British Jewish history as part of the Manchester Studies Unit with a particular interest in the experiences of Jewish women from Eastern Europe in Britain.

David Cesarani is research professor in History at Royal Holloway, University of London. His books include *Major Farran's Hat: Murder, Scandal, and Britain's War against Jewish Terrorism, 1945–1948* (2010) and *Eichmann. His Life and Crimes* (2004).

Lawrence Cohen completed his PhD at Southampton University. Previously he undertook a Masters on the theme of the Jewish Orphanage at Norwood which was extended for his PhD thesis 'A Study in Institutionalism – The Jewish Children's Orphanage 1876–1961', an occupational redirection from his previous employment experience as an accountant.

Todd Endelman is William Haber Professor of Modern Jewish History at the University of Michigan. A specialist in Anglo-Jewish history and the social history of modern European Jewry, he is currently writing a history of conversion and radical assimilation in Europe and America from the Enlightenment to the present. His most recent book is *Broadening Jewish History: Towards a Social History of Ordinary Jews* (Littman Library of Jewish Civilization).

Hannah Ewence has completed her PhD, which was funded by the Arts and Humanities Research Council and affiliated with the Department of History and the Parkes Institute for the Study of Jewish/Non-Jewish Relations at the University of Southampton. Her PhD thesis explores cultural representations of Jewish immigrants in Britain in the nineteenth and early twentieth centuries across time, space and genre, and reflects her broader research interests in Jewish history and culture.

Jane Gerson is currently a part-time lecturer in the Department of History at the University of Southampton with specialisms in food history, migration and East European Jewish culture. In 2008 she was awarded her doctorate 'Eating into Jewishness: Food and Jewish Identities in Britain 1955–2005'. Prior to that she had a career in arts development focusing on film and media.

Ruth Gilbert is senior lecturer in English at the University of Winchester. Publications include books on early modern literature and culture. She has published articles on contemporary British-Jewish writing and is currently working on a book-length study *Writing Jewish: Contemporary British-Jewish Literature* (1990–the present), to be published by Palgrave.

Didi Herman is Professor of Law at the University of Kent and the author of *An Unfortunate Coincidence: Jews, Jewishness and English Law* (Oxford University Press, 2011), as well as numerous other works in the area of law and social change.

James Jordan is the Ian Karten Research Fellow within the Department of English and the Parkes Institute for the Study of Jewish/Non-Jewish Relations at the University of Southampton and is currently engaged in a research project which explores the impact and representation of Jews on and in British television in the twentieth century.

Sharman Kadish is Director of Jewish Heritage UK. Her books include *Jewish Heritage in England* (English Heritage, 2006); *Jewish Heritage in Gibraltar* (Spire Books, 2007) and her *The Synagogues of Britain and Ireland – An Architectural and Social History* was published in 2011.

Anne Kershen is Barnet Shine Senior Research Fellow at Queen Mary University of London: she founded the Centre for the Study of Migration in 1995 and was its Director until 2009, at which time she became Deputy Director. She has published widely on immigrants and immigration, with particular focus on arrival and settlement in London.

Tony Kushner is Marcus Sieff Professor of Jewish/non-Jewish relations, Parkes Institute and History Department, University of Southampton. His most recent book is *Anglo-Jewry since 1066: Place, Locality and Memory* (Manchester University Press, 2009).

Mark Levene is a member of the Parkes Institute at the University of Southampton, a scholar of genocide, and a grass-roots environmental and peace activist. See Crisis Forum, http://www.crisis-forum.org.uk.

Anne Lloyd has recently completed a PhD thesis at the University of Southampton on the Jewish community and military service in World War I Britain.

Kathrin Pieren has completed her PhD at the Institute of Historical Research (University of London) about the construction of Jewish identities in exhibitions of Jewish art and history in London between the late nineteenth and the mid twentieth centuries. She holds an MA in Museum Studies from Newcastle University and a 'Lizentiat' in Italian language and literature (major); sociology, and politics (minor) from the University of Bern (CH).

Karen Robson is the senior archivist in the Special Collections archive at the University of Southampton, which holds a substantial and growing collection relating to Anglo-Jewry and on the relations between the Jews and other peoples.

Gavin Schaffer is senior lecturer in race and ethnicity in the Department of History at the University of Birmingham. He is currently completing a monograph on race relations and the media, looking in detail at the BBC's attempts to deal with racial issues on television and radio in the 1960s and 1970s.

Susan Tananbaum is Associate Professor of History at Bowdoin College. Her research focuses on the acculturation of women and children in London's Jewish immigrant community and religiously-sponsored care of Jewish and Christian orphans in Britain. She has been the recipient of grants from the NEH, the Littauer Foundation, Radcliffe and Bowdoin Colleges, and was a Visiting Scholar at the Kaplan Centre at the University of Cape Town, South Africa during autumn semester, 2008.

Nadia Valman is Senior Lecturer in the Department of English at Queen Mary, University of London. Her publications include *The Jewess in Nineteenth-Century British Literary Culture* (2007) and the co-edited volume *'The Jew' in Late-Victorian and Edwardian Culture: Between the East End and East Africa* (2009).

Bill Williams' monograph *The Making of Manchester Jewry 1740–1875* (1976) led the way for contemporary research in the field of modern British Jewish studies and marked the beginning of a long research career on the history and heritage of that community. The Bill Williams Jewish Studies Library opened in 2006, bringing together a significant collection of works on Anglo-Jewish history.

Index